Making the World a Better Place

Pittsburgh Series in Composition, Literacy, and Culture

David Bartholomae and Jean Ferguson Carr, Editors

Making the World a Better Place

African American Women Advocates, Activists, and Leaders, 1773–1900

Jacqueline Jones Royster

University of Pittsburgh Press

Published by the University of Pittsburgh Press, Pittsburgh, Pa., 15260

Manufactured in the United States of America
Printed on acid-free paper
10 9 8 7 6 5 4 3 2 1

Cataloging-in-Publication data is available from the Library of Congress

ISBN 13: 978-0-8229-6706-4
ISBN 10: 0-8229-6706-5

Cover photo: Bob Linsdell, *Boston Women's Memorial, Commonwealth Ave, Boston*. Photograph. 30 September 2013. Licensed under CC BY 3.0.
Cover design: Melissa Dias-Mandoly

To the researchers and scholars across many academic disciplines who have made the documentation and interpretations presented in this volume possible, but most of all, to the African American women across the generations who have been relentless in doing whatever they could do and needed to do to sustain hope, to provide care for others and for themselves, and to push a reluctant nation toward freedom, justice, equality, empowerment, and peace.

Contents

Preface and Acknowledgments

This book had three beginnings. The first was with regard to what I consider an organic next step from my last book, *Traces of a Stream: Literacy and Social Change among African American Women* (2000). My core commitment as a researcher and scholar has been to render more visible and to engender more appreciation for the lives and work of African American women, to clarify and contextualize the inventive ways in which, as sociopolitical actors in various arenas of activity, they have claimed literacy and rhetorical action as an asset.

The second beginning was in 2010 when I took an administrative position at the Georgia Institute of Technology. I discovered that my office was just one block away from the spot where the leaders of Atlanta surrendered the city to General William Tecumseh Sherman during the American Civil War. The building itself had been constructed on the site of a Union fort, and the window in my office looked out on the spot where the Ponder House had once stood (now the site of the Georgia Tech recreation center). This house was the site of the first bombing strike in the battle of

Atlanta. I had never been so viscerally aware, rather than just intellectually aware, of the geography of war in my home state. With this increased sensitivity to my own physical context, I realized that, as an archival researcher who had been focusing for two decades on the nineteenth century, I had paid very little attention to the materiality of the Civil War. It was for me a curious realization.

The third beginning came soon after, in 2011, with the robust celebration in Atlanta of the sesquicentennial of the Civil War and a parallel celebration of the seventy-fifth anniversary of the publication of Margaret Mitchell's *Gone with the Wind* (1936). To be noted, the City of Atlanta has defined itself quite iconically as the city that quickly rose, like a phoenix from the ashes, after Sherman burned it to the ground. This memorialization positioned the whole city as a monumental commemoration to southern ingenuity and survival. Even further, however, with the celebrations in 2011, I also became more aware that the public imagination related to women at war during this time period was still linked rather nostalgically to the imaging of Scarlett O'Hara, Melanie Wilkes, maybe Belle Watling, Mammie, and Prissy in the novel and the movie *Gone With the Wind*.

With this moment of self-realization, I smiled to myself at the extent to which almost all those narratives were tied to quite surface interpretations of the realities of the era, especially by recent historical publications (from a stunningly long and deep body of academic and public scholarship). I would like to mention just a few points concerning the limitations of presumptions that were still alive and well in the public imagination. Atlanta was burned by both the Confederacy and the Union. The characters of Scarlett O'Hara and Belle Watling as business women (a feature not particularly foregrounded in the film) only scratched the surface of the range of work that southern white women (and African American women as well) performed during the war, on both the home front and the battlefront. The characterization of Mammie and Prissy as slaves did not even begin to capture either the conditions of life, work, and survival for enslaved women or the nature of their resistance; neither did these characterizations capture the fact that not all African American women during this era were enslaved. Even beyond such shortcomings in the public imagination, the presumptions that still seemed quite vibrant about women at war demonstrated very little consciousness of the long list of memoirs, biographies, autobiographies, and letters that were written by and about women during this time period and that offered a far richer view and interpretation of the era.

My realizations, though, were not simply about criticizing flaws in others. My concern was about my own blind spots, even as I considered myself an astute researcher and scholar of this century. I smiled, quite ironically, at how very little I had done to incorporate the Civil War as an iconic national moment in any material way into my own work or to render it as a dynamic factor, rather than a deeply symbolic event, in the lives of the African American women whom I studied. Essentially, in my focus on African American women, I had positioned the war as, essentially, an un-interrogated prop in keeping with the notion "and then there was a war."

With this more conscious awareness of the Civil War as a specific part of the environmental and metaphorical context for my own work, my questions were basic. So, what were the women really doing? How was this war more substantially part and parcel of the fabric of their lives before, during, and after the four-year event? This combination of beginnings set me on a path that focused and enriched my original desire to elaborate on the lives and practices of African American women advocates, activists, and leaders in their relentless quest for freedom, justice, equality, and empowerment, and in their profound commitment to making the world a better place.

In seeking to address such questions as a researcher and scholar in rhetorical studies, I was particularly interested in seeing more through the eyes of the women themselves—across race, class, status, and region. Their memoirs, biographies, autobiographies, and letters were especially instructive as women across a range of identities and sociopolitical locations were able to speak for themselves. I found the real lives of these women far more interesting than the fiction. I also found, though, that my passion and interest in bringing forth visibility and appreciation for African American women's lives and work remained most compelling.

Over the course now of almost ten years of research and writing, I have many people to acknowledge for helping me get this work done, starting with the Georgia Institute of Technology for the research funding that permitted me to build a library of interdisciplinary resources to expand my understanding of the historical era. I am grateful to Seymour Goodman, professor in the Nunn School of International Affairs, for coteaching with me an undergraduate course on Georgia and the Civil War, which helped me give more focused attention to the project. I thank Joanna Gabriel, the executive assistant in the Ivan Allen College of Liberal Arts at Georgia Tech during my administrative leadership, for providing a full range of administrative support and personal encouragement for this work. I am grateful to Steve Hodges, the director of information technology, for his patience and generosity in helping me identify the technological resources that kept the project going. My thanks go to Gregory Abrams, finance administrator in the Ivan Allen College Finance Office, for his efficiency in supporting book purchases, travel, and conference participation in support of my research and scholarship. I am grateful to two graduate students—Michael Vogel in the School of Literature, Media, and Communication and Emily Kim in the Nunn School of International Affairs and later the School of Public Policy—for their invaluable technological expertise in helping me build databases and develop visualizations based on the data. I thank various colleagues across the nation who invited me occasionally to share my findings and to get feedback from people who were actually interested in the subject. Key among this group is Gesa E. Kirsch, a cowriter with me on several related projects, whose work on white professional women in the nineteenth century complemented my own. As always, I am pleased to acknowledge that everything I do is possible because of my family and the unconditional affirmation and encouragement they provide for me personally, as well as their steadfast support of my professional work. Thank you, Pat, Rebecca, Giles, Kate, Elleanor, and Jackson, for being the light of my life.

Making the World a Better Place

Overview

In public discourses about American life and culture, the contributions of African American women have not yet been fully acknowledged, accredited, or valued, especially in terms of their participation in sociopolitical advocacy and action, their expertise and innovation, or their leadership. Although their stories are being increasingly documented in various arenas, these women's lives and achievements are still typically unknown to the general public. With precious few exceptions they are not incorporated into public lore concerning heroes, legends, and leaders. They are also not regularly included in the core curricula of schools as preparation for an educated citizenry.

One noticeable exception is that their accomplishments have been gaining some vibrancy recently in limited ways. For example, during women's history month or African American history month, there are now highlights in social media of high-achieving individual women in various work arenas. Barbie dolls have been created in celebration of women such as Maya Angelou, Ella Fitzgerald, Michelle Obama, Rosa Parks, Ida B. Wells, and more. In colleges and universities, there is now an extended range of specially focused elective courses, and occasionally, at all educational levels, there are opportunities for extracurricular and often extra credit community engagement assignments. Occasionally also, there is the spectacle and surprise of popular media films such as *Harriet* (about Harriet Tubman), or *Hidden Figures* (about three African American women at NASA who were pioneers in science and technology), or *The United States vs Billie Holiday* (about the iconic jazz singer), or the Netflix series *Self Made: Inspired by the Life of Madame C. J. Walker* (the remarkable entrepreneur who was the first African American woman to become a millionaire), or the CNN documentary on Rosa Parks (the civil rights activist who was more than just a tired woman who sat down on a Montgomery bus).

Although this increase in visibility is certainly noteworthy, the stories of African American women quite often do not garner the spotlight or even legibility in the narratives that are regarded as officially meaningful to the society as a whole or consequential in national enterprises. These accounts are positioned as marginal to the center of the American story, part of the backdrop against which other accounts deemed more significant in national schema are told. Or, when there is a spotlighting of their work, the women are regularly presented, whether in curricula or popular culture, as exceptional or extraordinary examples rather than as part of well-grounded and laudable patterns of expertise and achievement that should be more explicitly appreciated. My intention in this volume is to participate in shifting this paradigm.

A significant lever for change has been the effort of an array of researchers both academic and public to document the lives and work of African American women over time. The persistent flow of scholarship produced by these researchers over the last half century or more is indeed noteworthy and crosses multiple disciplines, especially in the arts, humanities, and social sciences. From this diverse body of work, we now have more documentation of the many roads taken by African American women toward advocacy, activism, and leadership, and a clearer explication of the contexts and conditions surrounding their contributions and achievements. Included in this oeuvre is African American women's participation in civic discourses and sociopolitical activities with focus on the levels of their engagement in the actual development of their communities and in the building of our new world nation.

Within this scholarly effort, my desire to shift conceptual paradigms suggests a presumption. The efforts of African American women to participate in managing their own lives and in working with others to build and sustain the nation have been in motion from the beginning of their presence in North America—from 1619 (the year currently identified as the original moment of their migration to North America, involuntary though this process may have been for most) through the current era. The scholarly challenge in operationalizing this presumption is to have enough imagination and fortitude to search for evidence from wherever it may be located and to extend the scope of analysis and interpretation to account for these data, whether quantitative or qualitative, with respect and regard.

A frequently used analytical approach with this type of research and scholarship has been based on a feminist rhetorical framework, as is the case in this volume. With specific attention to explorations of sociopolitical engagement, I am using a multi-lensed theoretical and analytical viewpoint to examine the writing, rhetorical performances, and operational patterns of women in context. As is typical with this approach, I focus particularly on intersections of gender, race, culture, class, power, and place, exploring the women's uses of language in various communities, work arenas, societal events, and social movements. My central priorities have been to bring a more fully rendered sociohistorical texture to the rhetorical actions of individuals and cohorts in social, public, and institutional space; to take into account their standpoints as a particular set of stakeholders within community-building and nation-building processes; and to make clearer the impacts and consequences of their actions.

Within this general schema, what feminist rhetorical studies also does (which is not centralized in this volume) is to cast more direct attention not simply toward the analysis and interpretation of gender, race, and power (included here as key factors) but also toward sexuality and power (which is not specifically included). In this latter case, feminist rhetorical studies tends to interrogate questions such as (1) the importance of understanding woman-centered friendships and women's loving relationships with other women as part and parcel of women's identity, voice, and agency; (2) the formation, development, and deployment of societal attitudes, norms, and practices related to sexuality; and (3) the ways in which women's sexual choices, behavior, and relationships are often used in social, public, and institutional space to constrain, control, compromise, punish, and marginalize their agency, their authority, and their participation in circles of power and possibility.

Overwhelmingly in the nineteenth century, such concerns were not front and center in women's rhetorical actions and agenda in public but were cloaked in invisibility and silence. Although such concerns were present and relevant for all women during this era, for African American women the obfuscations and silences were even more complex. Everything was exacerbated by several critical challenges, mainly the need to establish themselves as "human," as "ladies," and as worthy of respect, without regard for their race and no matter their class, status, condition, or sexual identity. Unlike their elite white sisters, African American women were not put on pedestals to be adored. In contrast, the sexual and physical abuses they suffered were not considered of critical concern at all in the society generally. Moreover, their sexual desires were deemed wanton, inappropriate, and subject to exploitation by others. In other words, the ways and means of sexuality in women's lives, especially from African American women's own perspectives, were just not put forth front and center by them in public discourses—except to be steadfast about their perceptions of themselves as worthy women, as ladies.

Instead of bringing the specific views of their sexuality into the public sphere, these realities were set aside, ignored, and hidden, and they remained so until the late twentieth century with the rise of Black women's studies as a field of inquiry and the rise of writers such as Audre Lorde who boldly claimed all of herself as an African American woman doing the work she chose to do. In "The Transformation of Silence into Language and Action," she states: "I have come to believe over and over again that what is most important to me must be spoken, made verbal and shared, even at the risk of having it bruised or misunderstood. That the speaking profits me, beyond any other effect. I am standing here as a Black lesbian poet, and the meaning of all that waits upon the fact that I am still alive, and might not have been" (Audre Lorde 1984, 40).

In resonance with Lorde's point of view, I assert that the rhetorical legacies of African American women as sociopolitical actors need to be "spoken, made verbal and shared." The pathways for accomplishing this task are complex, however, with multidimensionalities that matter. In facing this complexity, consider Alice Walker's images of African American women's expressiveness in the essay

"In Search of Our Mothers' Gardens" (1983) with her articulation of an innovative array of expressive outlets that these women have found for themselves historically, including their flower gardens. Incorporating Walker's viewpoint in this analysis, I realize that one volume really cannot adequately address all dimensions of African American women's expressiveness that matter. That being so, I focus most directly on one, arguably key, expressive vista—their use of written language in public arenas. My imperative is to listen to what they actually say in order to gain a clearer line of sight from which to interrogate who these women were, what they did, and what the legacies of their lives and work have been.

A signal opportunity in understanding the scope of this study is to underscore the value of extending a special invitation to others to join in the ongoing scholarly effort. In my view, collective action, as this cohort of African American women asserted by their activities, will go farther in making a meaningful difference in knowledge-making and understanding than singular and solitary efforts. The imperative is to add depth, breadth, variety, and texture to the scholarly landscape. The presumption is that moving collectively to fill in gaps in knowledge-making and in the presentation and representation of scholarship—given the various approaches that we might identify and use—has a twofold capacity to push us along the way to a more robust understanding. On one hand, we create sharper lenses through which to appreciate, understand, and respect these women's lives and work. On the other hand, we generate greater capacity for determining the extent to which their work has participated in the specific priority of advancing the causes of freedom, justice, equality, and empowerment. By such collective commitments the ultimate benefits for our contemporary world become more evident. We gain clarity about the essentially untapped wellspring of African American women's experiences, expertise, and wisdom in negotiating the ongoing challenges of living and working in a nation that struggles still to honor our bedrock proclamations of freedom, truth, justice, equality, and the pursuit of happiness—for all.

Simply put, then, I have designed this book not to be all-inclusive of everything that constitutes the fullness of African American women's lives for all times. A single volume just cannot do so. Instead, my design is to take a closer look at a key piece—the women's rhetorical prowess in specific contexts. The focus and scope of my analysis centers primarily on using the words of African

American women themselves to track the ways and means of their work as sociopolitical beings in public space over what we call in rhetorical studies the long nineteenth century from the founding of the United States of America in 1776 to the turn of the century in 1900. From this perspective, I have identified three chronological anchor points: (1) the founding of the nation, which I symbolize by acknowledging Phillis Wheatley as an African American woman who fashioned space from which she raised her voice and vision in the cause of freedom even as an enslaved woman; (2) the American Civil War, which marked a monumental shift in horizons for African Americans, including African American women, and for the nation; and (3) the rise of the Black Clubwomen's Movement, as evidence of an evolving intensification of efforts over the full course of the century by African American women leaders to be values added in community development and nation building agenda.

With these three chronological anchor points established, I direct special effort toward respecting the ways in which the women saw themselves as actors and talked about their own lives and work. I have taken care to resist the tendency to cast twenty-first-century conceptual frameworks backward in filtering the women's actions through our contemporary priorities rather than the opposite view of using their words, experiences, and expertise to inform our contemporary thinking. Much to my advantage, this cohort actually did articulate their own visions and raised their own voices from the birth of the nation across the next century. My fundamental task, then, has been to listen, to honor what they articulated for themselves, and then to look forward from their visions and voices in evolutionary ways. It has also been to respect their lives and their work more forthrightly and to incorporate their insights, actions, and legacies more dynamically into our ongoing analytical and interpretive frameworks.

In my examinations of the space between the founding of the nation and the turn of the nineteenth century, my imperative has been to look for root systems; for continuities of concern, patterns of practice, echoes, and resonances over time; for insights and legacies. A basic point of leverage has been to recognize dynamic linkages among issues of race, gender, power, authority, place, and space. With this focus, I acknowledge the problems and challenges that the women experienced as they were fighting for respect and regard as "humans," as "ladies," and most boldly, as agents of change. Certainly, I also acknowledge that there is still much more to discover, document, and understand about the fullness of their lives than I am showcasing in this book. Most certainly, just as the patterns of their rhetorical prowess deserve critical attention, so too do other dimensions of their lives (for example, their sexuality, their expertise with art and design, and more) as we continue to draw forward a more richly rendered view of who these women actually were and what they were able to accomplish.

That said, with a specific focus on African American women as task-oriented rhetorical actors in time and place, it becomes clearer that the nineteenth century is a compelling point of interest for tracking and interrogating their patterns and performances. In point of fact, the founding of the nation left much about our national values and identity unresolved, as evidenced most explicitly by the constitutional declaration of a commitment to freedom, justice, equality, and the pursuit of happiness for all while being still a very active slaveholding nation. These discontinuities were loose ends, and they foreshadowed the coming of the American Civil War. This war constituted a critical moment for ongoing national decision-making directed toward clarifying the kind of nation that we were determined to be. As such, the war constituted also fertile ground for African American women's sociopolitical work in helping to make the nation into the place that they wanted and needed to exist.

Identifying the three anchor points (the founding of the nation, the American Civil War, and the rise of the Black Clubwomen's Movement) makes more apparent the viewpoint that for African American women the whole century was metaphorically a "black box" (in fact, a series of them). This metaphor symbolizes the complexities of the gaps between what we know on the surface about African American women and what we do not substantively know about them as fully rendered human beings. The questions are basic. Since African American women were neither mushrooms that simply grew in the dark nor blank slates on which the world was writing, what were the women actually thinking, saying, and doing? What were their interests and concerns? How were they managing to live and survive amid disempowering circumstances or to engage in actions that were not dictated or controlled by power elites? What were the conditions and circumstances that either enabled or hindered their actions? What difference did their thoughts and actions make in the course of human events? How do we shift perspectives so that we enable more visibility (to see them), audibility (to hear them), and intelligibility (to understand them)? How do we analyze and interpret their lives, work, and achievements with an eye toward creating a respectful and rightful place for them in our narratives of nation, in our national celebrations of heroes, legends, and leaders?

The use of intersectional perspectives of race, class, gender, and culture as well as interrogations of identity, agency, authority, power, sociopolitical hierarchies, systems of entitlement, and so forth have fostered two quite fundamental conclusions. One is that, although African American women were fully present in many communities across the nation during the nineteenth century, their presence was ignored. They were systematically cast in shadow by discriminatory practices related to race, gender, and class, and by the images that had emerged and dominated in the American environment related to their being Black, women, low status politically, and mainly slaves. The women were positioned within this framework as chattel, ignorant, passive, and inconsequential. A second more affirming conclusion, however, is irrefutable. These women were indeed present. From the growing archival evidence, in fact, we can see that they actually had deep stakes in fomenting transformative change, as women of a downtrodden race who were relegated, not by their own choice but via the will and practices of others, to living and working in an overtly inhospitable world.

To be emphasized, therefore, is the point that it is not a stretch to imagine that sociopolitical action mattered to African American women, and likewise, that the outcomes of the Civil War, as a critical national event, mattered specifically in terms of their ongoing desires and claims for freedom, justice, equality, and empowerment. A closer examination of the whole cloth of their advocacy and action over time offers compelling evidence of the multiple ways they found, even during these early decades of the nation, to do their parts, large and small, in the grander enterprise of building a nation where the values on which the nation claimed to stand (truth, freedom, justice, equality, empowerment) would prevail for all, including themselves. In support of these assessments, I have divided the book into three parts to get a better hold of this complex landscape: Visibility, Audibility, Intelligibility. Each part constitutes a lens through which to analyze and interpret the lives and work of this cohort of women.

Starting with Part I, "Visibility," I acknowledge historically popularized characterizations of African American women as pawns rather than as players in American life and culture. They have been positioned traditionally as passive participants in the American ecosystem who were only modestly significant, if at all, in the making and shaping of the nation. Basically, they are deemed to be present historically, perhaps, but they are not deemed to be significant as full-bodied corporeal subjects of interest. This view of them came to be institutionalized from 1619 and their first steps on the North American Continent into subsequent decades as policies and practices affirmed this positioning and set expectations and operational frameworks. By 1776 and the Declaration of Independence, African American women were typically designated in the social order as chattel rather than as human beings and as unworthy of acknowledgment and consideration in human enterprises. The analytical imperative, therefore, with visibility as the lens of interrogation is to resist this categorization. The task is to look for evidence wherever it may reside of their corporeality and, in this case, to be deliberate in foregrounding recent archival research that is becoming available about their lives and living during these early years of the nation.

In Chapter 1, "A Pentadic View of African American Women during the American Civil War," I use Kenneth Burke's pentad as a heuristic in drawing forth a compendium of evidence. My effort is to examine critically the contexts and activities of these early generations of women through an interrogation of scene, act, agent, agency, and purpose. As Burke stated in *A Grammar of Motives*:

> What is involved, when we say what people are doing and why they are doing it? . . . We shall use five terms as generating principle of our investigation. They are: Act, Scene, Agent, Agency, Purpose. In a rounded statement about motives, you must have some word that names the *act* (names what took place, in thought or deed), and another that names the *scene* (the background of the act, the situation in which it occurred); also, you must indicate what person or kind of person (*agent*) performed the act, what means or instruments he used (*agency*), and the *purpose*. Men may violently disagree about the purposes behind a given act, or about the character of the person who did it, or how he did it, or in what kind of situation he acted; or they may even insist upon totally different words to name the act itself. But be that as it may, any complete statement about motives will offer some kind of answers to these five questions: what was done (act), when or where it was done

> (scene), who did it (agent), how he did it (agency), and why (purpose). (1969a, xv)

Burke first published this statement in 1945, offering to rhetorical (and other) analyses an intuitive framework, a pentad, designed to gather together a fuller, more detailed understanding of human action. The advantage in using the pentad here is that, as a heuristic, it generates multidimensional data by which we can gain an evidence-based clarity about the American ecosystem before and during the American Civil War. Centered in the materiality of human motivation, this approach permits the identification of a broad array of details that can be configured and reconfigured fluidly. From this enriched and well-grounded analytical landscape, we can draw interpretations with enhanced potential to bring visibility, audibility, and intelligibility both to specific parts of the design (for example, African American women as agents of transformative change) and to the whole (for example, rendering a fuller accounting of the American Civil War as a complex multi-stakeholder event in the history of the nation).

This multifaceted analysis permits us to "tack in" and "tack out" in understanding and interpreting action, motivation, and consequence in context. This approach is in keeping with a concept used by anthropologist Clifford Geertz in *The Interpretation of Cultures* (1973). He offered this sailing metaphor of tacking in and out as a tool for obtaining more vibrant interpretations of various cultures. I chose the pentadic analysis to enrich the analytical landscape and the Geertz metaphor of looking and looking again from different perspectives to enrich the quality of the interpretations drawn from this landscape. The effort in the interpretive process is both to tack in to generate a more coherent, fully rendered, multidimensional view of African American women as actors at this specific point in US history and to tack out to demonstrate that, for this group, the Civil War and the nineteenth century as its more ample context provide a particularly instructive window for enriching our view of the longer trajectories of African American women's sociopolitical participation in community-building and nation-building agendas over time.

In essence, the circumstances and conditions of the women's lives during this era formed the landscape for their hopes, desires, and interests. In turn, this landscape constituted an inspirational infrastructure for the ways in which the women engaged in identity and ethos formation—that is, in the formation of their views of their speaking and writing selves and in the formation of their sense of agency and authority for action. This operation landscape constituted, thereby, the context within which they built expressive practices and traditions and in which they were able to perceive opportune occasions for sociopolitical action. Fundamentally, then, for this group, the decades between 1776 (the founding of the nation) and 1896 (the launching of the National Association of Colored Women) offered a prime—though extended—occasion that they used well to prepare themselves to emerge nationally by 1900 as advocates, activists, and leaders capable of enabling what they perceived to be much needed transformative social change.

In Chapter 2, "Negotiating Ways Forward," I look at the era of reconstruction, that is, at processes for the reunification of the nation after the Civil War. This era continued to be a time of complexity with multiple stakeholders. I take up a regional point of view to examine many uncertainties that surrounded African American women in this context to draw attention to the reality that their negotiating of ways forward was mired in complexity. Emphasis, however, is on the notion that, even in this imperfect and uncharted world, African American women had great expectations that the nation was moving toward positive change for their race. They took very seriously their opportunities to forward progress and change and, perhaps even more seriously, their personal obligations to respond to their opportunities well. In their commitments to action despite ongoing oppressions and persistent acts of disregard and discrimination they claimed space for their strengths and abilities, tried to shoulder their part of the load, worked conscientiously and faithfully to make whatever differences they were able to make, and held fast to their hopes and dreams.

In viewing this first part of the analysis more holistically, my intention is to clarify that, even though power elites may not have noticed or understood a rationality for paying attention to African American women, there is, nevertheless, an escalating body of evidence that African American women were indeed actively and thoughtfully engaged in sociopolitical work. In Part I, the imperative is to bring greater visibility to their ways of working—by their own lights, in keeping with their own living conditions and opportunities, and by means of the resources for action that were available to them. Thus in Chapter 2, I concentrate on sharing some of the ways in which the women were implementing their visions. The purpose for presenting these examples is to show how the women were creating space for themselves to survive and to prosper in doing whatever they could to help both their communities and themselves. This approach to argumentation by examples is designed to illustrate specific ways in which the nineteenth century became, in effect, a cauldron in which African American women were using their hearts, minds, fortitude, and backbones to do what they thought needed to be done. By these strategies, I posit that they were evolving as sociopolitical actors, building up their experiences, and creating a remarkable cache of wisdom.

The central touchstone in this section is an acknowledgment of Phillis Wheatley (1753–1784) as an enslaved woman who stepped out with distinction as the first African American woman to publish poetry. I emphasize, however, that she was also among the first African American women to use her public presence as a published author to build a network of relationships with power elites, nationally and abroad. In the years leading up to the Revolutionary War and the formation of the nation, Wheatley engaged in regular communication with members of her network, from Samuel Occom (Native American pastor and missionary) to George Washington (the leader of the rebellion and future president of the United States). In these conversations, she shared her views, advocating for the idea that all humans are the handiwork of God regardless of their abilities, and by extension, indicating her interests in human rights, the recognition of human potential, and of course, underscoring the ways in which Christian belief supported the ending of slavery. While Phillis Wheatley wrote herself into the founding of the nation, the general status of African American women in the United States at that time was based on their categorization as chattel. What becomes evident, therefore, is that, whether enslaved, freed, or freeborn, their lives in the larger society were defined and shaped by their oppressed status and downtrodden condition, such that any self-determined actions were acts of defiance, which ultimately became a primary source for the stereotyping of African American women, regularly, as "sassy" women who defied their place in the social hierarchies of their day.

In noting the sassiness stereotype for African American women's behavior, it is within the scope of a good imagination to see that their unauthorized and unrecognized work was unorthodox by mainstream standards and expectations, and thereby unintelligible. The proposition here, though, is that quite likely their habits of care were culturally informed and that these identity and ethos formation processes did not begin on North American shores in 1619. More likely, the first women and girls of African descent in the Americas brought with them values, principles, and habits of action from their African communities to their new homes. The presumption is that they were able to pass these frameworks on from generation to generation, as I articulated, for example, in *Traces of a Stream* (Royster 2000, 77–107).

The bottom line in this assessment is that African Americans—enslaved, freed, and freeborn—were present in the colonial world. A reasonable expectation, therefore, is that in the 1770s, as word about the revolution as a war of independence spread throughout colonial territories, African Americans, including the women, could see for themselves that the Americans' fighting for independence was a phenomenon in motion. Being human beings with functioning brains and powers of observation and critique (rather than being animalistic and inferior), with the possibility of the colonists winning the war, they understood what was happening and they were encouraged by these points of view to imagine better horizons for themselves. It is not hard to imagine, therefore, that they saw the founding of the nation as a democracy for all to be a beacon of hope and great expectations.

A point to be highlighted in rethinking this time period with African American women in mind is that the long-standing strengths of these women as women who worked outside of the domestic sphere of their own homes and families can be documented archivally throughout these early years. By all accounts, their abilities to work and to get things done (for example, as house servants, field workers, seamstresses, and so forth) became part of their sense of sociocultural identity. By mid-nineteenth century, after more than 150 years of devastating conditions, African American women certainly knew, as Sojourner Truth proclaimed in her "Ain't I a Woman" speech (1851), that she could do the job of any man and that she could survive horrors (beatings, rapes, hard work of various kinds, family being stripped away, and more). They also knew, as Truth suggested, that their efforts to survive contributed in meaningful ways to their claims to truth, justice, equality, and empowerment for the race.[1] From this perspective, we can conclude that over the decades since 1619 the behavior and actions of these early generations of African American women informed an ever-evolving sense, not so much of identity and voice in simplistic terms, but a "New World" sense of agency, vision, and personally defined authority within the larger American democratic experiment.

The core assertion in Chapter 2, thereby, is that, historically, African American women have been engaging in sociopolitical work over the course of their presence on the North American continent in that they have brought their talents and sensibilities to bear in doing their parts to survive amid devastating conditions. While they infamously were called upon to do whatever they managed to do surreptitiously, their ability to speak out publicly about their visions and observations depended on their status, resources, and often their geographical locations For example, the women who were living in the North away from slave plantations were able to participate more regularly in the Black abolitionist movement (as in the case of Sojourner Truth, Harriet Tubman, Sarah Mapps Douglass, Josephine St. Pierre Ruffin, and others). Even so, when these women spoke out, typically they were heard by specialized audiences (African American audiences, audiences filled by other abolitionist or abolitionist leaning groups) rather than being taken seriously by white elites in the traditional arenas of power—where, by both race and gender, African American women were not even permitted to participate or to be officially recognized but where terms of engagement for what constituted value and the story of American excellence were largely determined.

Despite persistent barriers and constraints, however, another key point to highlight is that, still, during these years African American women were speaking and writing. Increasing numbers of African American women were developing their literate abilities and engaging in an escalating level of rhetorical events that enhanced their levels of rhetorical expertise. With these tools and talents, they were negotiating their ways forward, ramping up their capacities to speak for themselves via multiple genres of expression and demonstrating that they were quite able, as well, to use these growing strengths to pose, analyze, and solve problems in support of progress and change. Two such women in the North who were openly exercising their talents and abilities during and after the Civil War were Maritcha Rémond Lyons and her friend and colleague Victoria Earle Matthews. Lyons was a freeborn African American woman from New York who became an educational administrator. Matthews was born enslaved in Fort Valley, Georgia, but moved with her family to New York after the ending of slavery and built a remarkable career in community development and journalism.

In the South before the Civil War, opportunities were certainly not open for African American women, regardless of whether they were enslaved, freed, or freeborn, but some of them found ways, nevertheless, to fashion inventive opportunities for themselves, as I highlight in Chapter 1 via the showcasing of Aspasia Cruvellier Mirault in Savannah, Georgia, and Mariah Lilly Hunt in Hancock County, Georgia. Drawing attention to the ways of working for women who were living and working in the South rather than just the North underscores how, during these early years of the nation before, during, and after the Civil War, new generations of women were rising—continuing to demonstrate capacities to find or make their way to survival and prosperity and, as the decades proceeded, to become themselves or to support other women who would go on to become high-performing leaders in their community. Throughout these years African American women exemplified patterns of leadership and action that were steadily coalescing over the nineteenth century as evidence of their escalating strengths as sociopolitical advocates, activists, and leaders.

Not to be underestimated, by the middle of the nineteenth century, the Civil War did, in fact, legally end slavery, offering the nation a signature opportunity to recalibrate its commitments to truth, freedom, justice, equality, and empowerment—even though the nation did not adequately live up to its potential for change. For African American women, however, the moment of emancipation via the Thirteenth, Fourteenth, and Fifteenth Amendments became a catalyst for bolder dreams and more robust action. They could see that this situation was an excellent opportunity to make more room for themselves in the inhospitable world they inhabited. By law they were free to participate in public spaces. They courageously shared their insights, spoke for themselves, and were innovative in addressing the problems that plagued both their communities and themselves.

The opportunities African American women encountered after the war permitted them to broaden their geographical scope without permission, to increase the number of women with the privilege to participate more freely in sociopolitical action and public venues, and to extend the range of available means and mechanisms for action. In effect, the war functioned as a point of coalescence for more strategic utilizations of their evolving habits and their sensibilities of themselves as socially responsible political actors in a changing world. From this perspective, as devastating and violent as it was, the Civil War was also a breath of fresh air for this group of people who, after more than two hundred years of intensely oppressive conditions, really needed a good cleansing breath. The war functioned as a dramatic kairotic opportunity to breathe more deeply and to exercise their hopes and dreams of a better world in addressing and advancing their own priorities, needs, and desires.

The questions in analyzing and interpreting these assertions and the bodies of evidence of engagement that support them are really basic ones. What was the range of African American women's work before, during, and after the Civil War? What were their responsibilities, challenges, and concerns? To what extent did their work demonstrate sociopolitical awareness? What were the values added as these women were inventive in taking advantage of opportunities of various kinds, including their acquisition of literacy and their growing expertise in using this New World tool as writers, speakers, and strategic thinkers and problem solvers? How did their patterns of work over this time period evolve amid their negotiations of possibilities for going forward into more coherent strategies for sociopolitical action in their multilayered quest for truth, freedom, justice, equality, and empowerment?

In exploring the answers to such questions, I track the escalating presence of African American women in various civic discourses through their work and their rhetorical performances from the founding of the nation, through the Civil War, and through the turn of the twentieth century. The Civil War in particular constituted a moment of opportunity for transformative change for the women in leveraging a more robust capacity to engage in important sociopolitical work. With this trajectory as context, the inquiry goals for this project inevitably became: (1) to subvert the neutralizing frameworks imposed on African American women's lives and achievements by their historically designated status as chattel and to see them more clearly as consequential beings; (2) to listen as the women speak for themselves about their own visions and experiences and to use data analytics and various tools of visualization capable of yielding more generative and dynamic perspectives of the nature and scope of the women's work; (3) to counter ungrounded presumptions about their lack of value and consequence via different theoretical frameworks and interpretive sight lines that cast light on the breadth and depth of their labor and, more pointedly, on the aspects of this labor that are definable explicitly within the contours of ambitious sociopolitical work; and (4) to recalibrate the paradigms for analysis and interpretation so that we can be more respectful of their actual lives, contributions, and achievements in recognizing the extent to which they deserve to have their stories of excellence told in our narratives of nation.

My core assertion here is that, by the end of the nineteenth century, these women had found ways to broaden the circles of their rhetorical and sociopolitical engagement. When we pay attention to their efforts, they were doing so with noticeable impact with regard to their increased participation in activities related to social justice and social reform. I draw attention to the archival evidence of their participation in various enterprises, their sociopolitical awareness, their rhetorical prowess, and their astute strategic planning in taking advantage of opportunities to address various problems and issues in their communities. Of particular note is that, through their acquisition of literacy as a new operational tool and their increasing opportunities over the century to exercise their growing multimodal expertise as speakers and writers, these women were able to build a remarkable record of their lives and work.

This base of information offers contemporary researchers and scholars a useful springboard for rethinking interpretive frameworks—for sense-making, knowledge-making, history-telling, and storytelling processes. From the perspective of feminist rhetorical studies, we have a signal opportunity to engage in more robust examinations of the ways in which African American women over this time period managed to operationalize and sustain a sense of self and agency; to craft a dynamic vision of democratic values and civic, social, and ethical responsibility; and to enhance operational habits and patterns for advocacy, action, and leadership—despite the fact that their range of motion was significantly constrained, still, by the mores of their day. My view of this opportunity is that a compelling way to operationalize it is to use three specific lenses for interrogation identified in this study: visibility, audibility, and intelligibility.

With the Civil War as the standpoint, the imperative is to look backward from 1865—that is, before, during, and at the ending of the Civil War—in order to gain a clearer understanding of African American women as women constantly under siege rather than simply at war in a national military conflict. What we know is that

African American women were relentlessly under attack in an inhospitable society. Their constant task was to demonstrate that, although incessantly maligned and besieged, they were steadfast and courageous in maintaining focus and working to advance progress and change with an indomitable spirit very much intact. When we look forward from the Civil War toward the end of the nineteenth century, the imperative is to formulate more richly rendered views of the evolution of their actions. The task is to bring forward evidence to clarify and confirm the patterns, practices, and legacies of the work they set in motion over the fullness of this time period.

In Part II, "Audibility," my concern is with countering the marginalizing of the visions and voices of African American women. The effort, therefore, is to acknowledge that these women have had things to say all along and that, as rightful citizens of the nation, we should treat their visions and voices with more respect and regard than heretofore. What have they been saying? Why? How? Does their thinking and problem solving deserve more attention, especially since the issues and problems that have drawn their attention continue in our own time to be societal challenges? To address such questions, I cast more direct attention on a range of ways in which African American women did speak for themselves across the nineteenth century. I focus on the need to amplify these voices and to enrich our understanding of the range of their interests and commitments over the century. My approach is to identify fifteen short texts or excerpts from longer texts written by African American women whose work confirms they were game changers both within and often well beyond their own communities. I cluster the exemplars into Chapter 3, "Before the Civil War," Chapter 4, "During the Civil War," Chapter 5, "After the Civil War," and Chapter 6, "At the Turn of the Century."

With this set of texts I proclaim the women's presence, as declared through their own writing and through the proactivity of their visions, voices, and concerns. Given the genres they chose, which included poetry, essays and speeches, journalism, autobiography, and professional analyses, these texts offer provocative opportunities to consider the processes and patterns by which the women performed their work in facing challenges and fomenting positive change. Their words stand today as witness to their deliberate uses of language as advocates, activists, and leaders and serve as artifacts of their visions and desires for social justice and transformative social change. In essence, African American women spoke up for their ideas and demonstrated that they were inspired to work, even as they were surrounded by inhospitable conditions. At this point, the multiple genre evidence of their textual record confirms their focus on and commitments to making meaningful differences in their own lives and in the lives of others.

The first text is an essay written by Maria Miller Stewart, "Religion And The Pure Principles Of Morality, The Sure Foundation On Which We Must Build." It was published on October 8, 1831, by William Lloyd Garrison and Isaac Knapp in *The Liberator*. Stewart is considered to be the first woman and the first African American woman to speak on political issues in public, before mixed audiences of men and women. I draw the other texts from various public arenas in which African American women were writing over the remainder of the century. My imperative is to demonstrate the fluidity of their choices within the typical generic practices of their day and to document their habits of using whatever means were available to carry out their desires and address their concerns. Part II ends with a focus on the implications of these exemplary texts in illustrating African American women's habits of leadership and action.

In Part III, "Intelligibility," I focus attention on the need to use the enhanced visibility and audibility presented in Parts I and II to shift paradigms for interpretation. The presumption is that, although historically it may have been policy and practice to ignore the viability, impact, and consequence of African American women, evidence suggests that continuing to do so is not productive for our nation or the world. My focus, then, is on developing tools and frameworks that permit us to see this landscape more fully and to determine the extent to which there may actually be value to add for community development and national building agenda. The proposition is that, as evidenced by the cohort of women that I showcase in this book, African American women have generated swirls of impact and consequence. Perhaps more importantly, the valuing of these legacies matters in the ongoing human enterprise of making a better world for us all.

In this section, I take the information from Part I and Part II and use it as leverage for resetting conceptual frameworks and for interrogating the impacts and consequence of African American women's sociopolitical labor. The intention is to shift the paradigm for interpretation—that is, to construct an ideological framework within which these women's sociopolitical labor gains intelligibility, both individually and collectively. I direct specific attention to the

1890s as the era of post-Reconstruction, the rise of the Black Clubwomen's Movement, and the formative years of the National Association of Colored Women (NACW, renamed the National Association of Colored Women's Clubs in 1904). NACW was established at the turn of the nineteenth century and continues to function in the twenty-first century as a nationwide organization with a robust agenda for social action.

The decade of the 1890s serves as the third in a triad of markers indicating the trajectories of African American women as sociopolitical actors across the nineteenth century—with the founding of the nation and the American Civil War constituting the other two critical moments. During this third time period, the resurgence of southern elite leadership and Jim Crowism as common practice underscores that, despite ongoing oppressions, the decade was a time of intense activity for this cohort of leaders. They were able to maximize habits of action that had been evolving over decades, and with their ongoing commitments to the bedrock values of the nation they were able to set in motion an array of legacies to get things done. Over the decades since then, their work has demonstrated strength: in offering tools for enabling and sustaining change, in supporting various sociopolitical agenda, and in being a model capable of replication in other instances as well—such as the Black sorority movement (as the numbers of college-educated African American women increased), the modern Civil Rights Movement (as the need for social justice and social change escalated in the twentieth century, and the negotiation of participation in various professional communities (as African Americans entered all sorts of professions).

With a focus in Part III on using the first two sections to develop a more generative model for analysis and interpretation, this section begins with Chapter 7, "Recasting Frameworks for Engagement and Regard." I explore the landscape for African American women's sociopolitical work that had formed by the 1890s. More explicitly, I look at the roles that literacy and rhetorical prowess played in the hands of women who had gained knowledge and experience as speakers, writers, organizers, and community leaders in various professional arenas, and who had also formed strong linkages with the African American periodical press. In this chapter I cast a brighter light on mechanisms and strategies that the women used to sharpen their visions, amplify their voices, expand their audiences, and build collaborative relationships with others.

One critical factor at the time was that, through these experiences, they became increasingly and painfully aware of the need not simply to participate and join with others to do their parts but to be more aggressive in setting their own national agenda for their own agency, action, and leadership—if they were going to create the impacts and consequences in the world that they wanted to create.

In Chapter 8, "Shifting Interpretive Paradigms," I take on the challenge of dismantling myths that continue to cloud the public engagement and sociopolitical impact of African American women. I pull together the information presented in the preceding chapters to show the rise of the NACW as a crystalizing moment. I direct specific attention to the process of institution building and the role played by Josephine St. Pierre Ruffin, her network of colleagues and collaborators, and her newspaper *Woman's Era* in facilitating a collective and coherent national agenda for African American women's activism and leadership. My intention in Chapter 8 is not to rehearse facts about NACW that are already in evidence, given the steady scholarship that has been produced and published by historians, particularly African American scholars, over the last forty years (see Wesley 1984, Salem 1990, White 1999, Cash 2001, Tuuri 2018, and others). This cohort of researchers and scholars have been compelling in documenting the Black Clubwomen's Movement as robust and substantive. In complement to this scholarship, the focus here is on the strategies that Ruffin used to build community and to create an institutional infrastructure for action.

In Chapter 8, therefore, I focus more specifically on *Woman's Era*, as a manageable data set of published work. Using mapping and other analytical tools associated with digital humanities, I sort through the three years of issues of this journal (1894–1897). The intention is to articulate the strategic framework used by Ruffin in organizing and developing the journal; to look closely at the mission, concerns, and the network of contributors; to place the journal's "Call to Confer" within the context of African American women's culturally informed habits of sociopolitical work; and ultimately, to account for the ideological choice of founding NACW as an innovative and coherent mechanism for social change—with the motto "Lifting As We Climb."

In the concluding section, "Last Words," I focus on envisioning the last mile of a worthy quest. A core imperative for this final section is to reemphasize the notion that the long-standing labor of African American women with sociopolitical intentions has been persistent, innovative, and strategic. Across the nineteenth century, cohorts of these women have been active and outspoken as advocates, activists, and leaders in the persistent quest of African American citizens for human and civil rights. Evidence abounds that they took advantage of whatever resources were available to advance truth, freedom, justice, equality, and empowerment and to create a more hospitable place for their own lives and work.

In claiming a rightful place for the strengths and capacities of African American women leaders, I accept the reality that, historically, they have been categorized overwhelmingly as women: (1) who engage in physical labor—in keeping with the metaphor made famous by Zora Neale Hurston that African American women are "the mules of the earth"; and (2) who are capable of carrying a heavy load in silence. In this volume I proclaim, however, that despite the elements of this metaphor that may have some merit, African American women's work has evidenced more than mere physical labor. We should not ignore or set aside the evidence of their intellectualism, their sociopolitical imperatives and intentions, including their awareness of the world around them, their understanding of the limitations imposed upon their choices, their inventiveness in the face of inhospitable circumstances and conditions, and their negotiating of pathways to survival and prosperity using a range of strategies.

The ultimate assertion, though, is that, fundamentally, whether enslaved, freed, or freeborn, African American women were called upon throughout the nineteenth century, by their conditions and circumstances within a culture deeply invested in the institution of slavery and its resilient effects, to hold fast to their own sense of possibility and potential. In keeping with their cultural frameworks, the central priority has been for them to be socially responsible in taking care of themselves and others, in whatever ways they could—because they knew that they could do so and, therefore, should do so. With this role as a vital mandate, the core proposition is this: African American women's experiences kept demonstrating a basic truth. They were quite viscerally aware of the oppressions that surrounded them, and they understood that changes in their horizons would not be presented to them on a silver platter. It was, therefore, no stretch for them to see that any improvements, far more often than not, would depend on their own ingenuity—in finding or making their own paths; in using their own visions, inventiveness, and hard work to do what was needed; and in supporting others who might carry on for the future. This awareness is poignantly illustrated, in fact, by the jazz singer Billie Holiday in the popular song "God Bless the Child That's Got His Own." African American women have not simply found ways to act; they have also had to create them, and they have shared with younger people the necessity of understanding this maxim. For the generation of women leaders who launched NACW at the end of the nineteenth century, this organization became a beacon of light as a prime example of a distinctive process for what it can mean to make your own way.

As we imagine the last mile of this worthwhile journey, it becomes much clearer that many African American women (more, in fact, than many people might imagine) were sociopolitical actors, variously defined. The social, political, and ethical dimensions of their lives and work need to be envisioned, acknowledged as worthy, and incorporated into the official narratives of excellence for the nation. My goal is to confirm that their work in support of the progress and survival of themselves and their communities, as illustrated across the nineteenth century, was not just reactive, random, or mindless. Before the Civil War, specific women managed to achieve noteworthy accomplishments, with the use of whatever resources and support were available to them. With the coming of the Civil War, more means emerged. After the Civil War, by the laws of the land, there were cracks in the armor of their oppressors that permitted an envisioning of transformative change, and the women rose gallantly to new occasions—with literacy, learning, rhetorical prowess, and a broader set of work experiences in their hands. By the end of the century, African American women were far better positioned to profit from their collective energy and to function more coherently and strategically in fomenting the changes that they felt would make a better nation and world. More important than their ambitious goals, however, is the evidence that, by thought, word, and deed, they saw their work as normal and necessary investments in themselves, in others, and in the future of the nation.

A final point in this last chapter is that the benefits of taking the work of African American women more seriously—and as consequential for the narratives of nation—are manifold. At the crux of these benefits is the notion that the legacies of African American women's work have continued over the decades to leverage possibilities for making the world a better place. Although the ecosystems in which this work has continued to occur have ebbed and flowed from generation to generation in terms of providing nurturing and supportive environments or not, what has been constant is the women's dedication to offering their labor to support sociopolitical interests. A closer view of this work confirms that these nineteenth-century women were warrior women on a grand quest for truth, freedom, justice, equality, empowerment, and peace; they were resilient and relentless in getting good work done, with a sense of obligation to pass their legacies of thought and action forward for future generations.

Bringing a critical vision to this landscape, the most consequential assertion I make in this volume is that African American women are worthy exemplars of what it means to work for change—deliberately and intentionally in time, place, and space. Both individually and collectively they have exhibited ethically responsible decision-making, culturally respectful action, and a multivariant sense of purpose, well-grounded both tacitly and overtly in their lived experiences and intricately entwined with their long-standing patterns of socially responsible engagement. Historically, these factors have shaped and deployed a distinctive and richly endowed intellectual history that remains in motion still.

Based on this assertion, the imperative for research and scholarship is to shift analytical and interpretive paradigms. In shifting our own ways of working, a primary task is to be more generative in using frameworks and methodologies that interrogate this history more carefully and caringly and that have a greater capacity to cast deliberate attention toward understanding the patterns of this work and its intellectual underpinnings in terms of both theory and practice. By doing so, we gain a better hold of the nature, ways, means, and impact of a fuller vista of sociopolitical work, and we are better positioned to recognize, acknowledge, and appreciate a group of women who perfected over time a compelling operational model. Central to operationalizing this type of approach is recognizing the necessity of seeing these women, not simply as hardworking women (as indeed they have been) but, rather, as advocates, activists, and leaders with a purpose who have performed with consequence in their worlds. They have been (and continue to be) assets in the places and spaces where they work. Our opportunity, then, is to look for where they are doing this work; to interrogate kaleidoscopically what, how, and why they are doing what they are doing; to listen to their words and advice; and to presume that their work might likely have values at the local level but also far beyond. In the twenty-first century we have, as we have periodically had in the past, a sterling opportunity to broaden the scope of our expectations as we keep the arc of our national history (and the stories that we tell) bending toward freedom, justice, and equality—for all.

Part I

Visibility

Chapter 1

A Pentadic View of African American Women during the American Civil War

The analytical design for this book is multidimensional in keeping with current practices in feminist rhetorical research and scholarship. At the core of the design is Kenneth Burke's pentad, which has five points of focus: scene, act, agent, agency, and purpose. Using a pentadic methodology, my goal is to create an evidence-informed convergence of quantitative and qualitative information that is capable of enriching the scope and texture of this analysis. My intention is to cast a brighter light on nineteenth-century African American women, both individually and in various cohort groups, who engaged in work that embodied their sociopolitical interests and concerns. The imperative is to interrogate the ways and means of that work in order to bring more visibility to the presence of these women in various action arenas and to create a stronger springboard for incorporating their insights and actions with more vibrancy into our narratives of nation.

To be boldly underscored with this approach is that, while Burke's pentad is multifocal, there are even more analytical lenses that, if one chooses, might be added to this particular performance-oriented set. Recognizing that there are many inquiry models and analytical opportunities highlights, in effect, how unlikely it is that any singular project can possibly give adequate attention to everything that matters in assessing the relevance and consequence of African American women's presence and thus provide the end all and be all for their actions and achievements across the nineteenth century. It seems wiser not to presume a possibility of being all inclusive in one volume, but instead to be more intentional about articulating what it means to take a manageable step toward an ambitious and complex goal. In keeping with such an intention, the goals here are to excavate the rhetorical landscape of African American women's lives during the long nineteenth century, as a key knowledge-making step; to make manifest a more fully rendered view of these women's work in this time and space; and to highlight the general contexts of their lives and living in order to provide leverage for constructing a clearer, more productive point of view of the value of their insights and achievements. With these goals, I recognize that enriching the knowledge-making landscape in under-interrogated areas such as this one calls for a cross-disciplinary approach with the analysis informed by several areas of research and scholarship. I recognize, as well, the importance of remembering the crucial point that where we stand in our interrogations matters, particularly if the ultimate goal also includes being respectful of the women's rights to tell their own stories, rather than having them filtered through the experiences and perspectives of others.

Given this cautionary tale and the complexities of the task, I focus explicitly on the ways and means of African American women's work specifically as advocates, activists, and leaders in making and sustaining their communities and the nation. I leverage this performance-oriented interrogation with the use of the pentadic framework of scene, act, agent, agency, and purpose. In contrast to this design, we might well give more attention to other dimensions of their lives—for example, to their spirituality as an empowering force; their sexuality as a defining factor that is both diverse and fluid; or to the ways and means of their friendships, comradery, and collective action. My focus here, however, is on the women's sociopolitical work, on the scope of their actions, and also on the merging of operational, cognitive, and affective factors related to those actions in the face of the ordinary and extraordinary challenges that surrounded them. All of these details are important and deserve specific, serious, and ongoing critical attention as we build a better base of knowledge and a deeper understanding.

In seeking to be sharply focused in this project and to draw forth just one, albeit one compelling, set of multidimensional data, my use of a pentadic framework centralizes the imperative of bringing visibility, audibility, and intelligibility to the import of African American women's rhetorical prowess during this era in carrying out the work that they chose to do. Positioning pentadic data within the context of the interdisciplinary research on the nineteenth century that is now abundant, we are well positioned to underscore a fundamental challenge. Historically in the United States, default terms of engagement, credibility, and value in work arenas have been established by white, male, Eurocentric elites with the social, political, and economic power to do so. The operational systems they fashioned have cast in shadow the lives and work of anyone who does not align with their traits, practices, and expectations.

By this schema, African American women constitute distant and extreme examples of misalignment. In a basic comparison to elite white males, they are neither white by race nor male by gender; neither Eurocentric by culture nor elite by sociopolitical status. The effect of these binary and hierarchical assessments has been to create inhospitable conditions and an unaccommodating framework through which to perceive and to interpret the presence, impact, and value of African American women as actors. By default, the women become invisible, inaudible, immaterial, and unintelligible, setting in motion patterns for this group to be treated with either low or no regard and with no rationality for being granted either hospitality or respect. Their identity in the operational system is not visible. They are not entitled to participate. They have no designated agency or authority to act or to have their actions acknowledged, appreciated, or accredited. By these measures, they have no meaningful presence.

In seeking to recover and reinscribe African American women's presence with greater vibrancy, analyses such as this one face the basic challenge of overcoming the manifold barriers of discrimination and disregard that engulf this group. To mediate the task of recalibrating the unnoticed and unacknowledged, a pentadic analytic design can draw into focus elements and details of these women's lives and work that collectively enable the disrupting, and perhaps dismantling, of such defaulted barriers. With clearer evidence of the contours of African American women's presence and experiences in context, we can articulate a different view of the women and their work, and ultimately a different view of the benefits of constructing more diverse and more fully rendered narratives of the nation and its citizens, with these women meaningfully and rightfully included.

In interrogating the roles of African American women as actors, the long nineteenth century provides an instructive window of opportunity, with the American Civil War serving as a critical mid-century anchor point. Using Burke's pentad, I draw forth at this anchor point various contextual details that surrounded these women and their fellow stakeholders. These data help to bring this era more vibrantly to life. They help also to bring corporeality to the women, enhancing our capacity to see them in more full-bodied terms as actors and agents who engaged within this context with sensibilities, intentions, and purpose. This richer data set permits us to see, first, who these women actually were, where they were primarily located during this century, and what they managed to do. The analytical objective is to reset the narrative to the women's point of view and to fashion a more diversely rendered story with their experiences in mind. With a more full-bodied rendering of the women over the century, it is easier to see and understand that by the end of the century and the rise of the Black Clubwomen's Movement (a second anchor point in this analysis), their work was not at all serendipitous. It was inevitably and intricately linked to the long and winding quest by African Americans for freedom, justice, and equality, with African American women being no exception as warriors in this worthy cause.

Scene and Act

Consider the American Civil War as a specific setting and a particular moment in time. An instructive step in drawing forth elements of the scene to inform an understanding of how the war functioned for stakeholders is to establish at least a general sense of its ecosystem, the environment in which this act of war was conducted. Factors that come into view include an acknowledgment of its impact on governance for a house divided; the geographical boundaries of the conflict in broad scope; the technological and medical innovations that became basic resources during the fighting; and the ways in which literacy created a specific set of communication and memorialization processes. Significant also is an understanding of how this combination of scenic factors, with their range of social, political, economic, cultural, and ethical implications, contributed to the formation of kairotic occasions for the participation of African American women in sociopolitical action.

A House Divided

On June 16, 1858, in a speech at the Republican state convention in Springfield, Illinois, after he had been chosen as the Republican candidate for the US Senate to run against the Democrat Stephen A. Douglas, Abraham Lincoln made the now famous statement:

> A house divided against itself cannot stand.
> I believe this government cannot endure, permanently, half slave and half free.
> I do not expect the Union to be dissolved—I do not expect the house to fall—but I do expect it will cease to be divided.
> It will become all one thing or all the other.
> Either the opponents of slavery will arrest the further spread of it, and place it where the public mind shall rest in the belief that it is in the course of ultimate extinction; or its advocates will push it forward, till it shall become alike lawful in all the States, old as well as new—North as well as South. (Lincoln 1991, 25)

Even though Lincoln lost the Senate race, his statement proved to be prophetic. Less than two years later, he was president of the United States and the nation was indeed divided, with eleven of its thirty-six states in secession (there were twenty Union states, five border states, and eleven Confederate states). The war between the United States of America and the Confederate States of America had begun. This war remains the bloodiest the nation has ever experienced, and it stands both symbolically and materially as a transformative event in establishing a path for how the nation, as one nation, would go forward.

By 1865, despite the devastation and horrific effects of war, there was, in fact, just one nation that emerged—with slavery defined, in the end, as an illegal institution and with the question of the full rights of citizenship and participatory governance a more open question than ever before. Noticeably, the open question was not just about the presence and participation of people of African descent but also symbolically about others who did not fit so neatly under the umbrella of white, male, Eurocentric, Christian, elite,

American-born, and so on. Going forward the nation would have much work to do, still, work that has proven over the decades to be filled persistently with challenge and struggle. In a situation that has been rife with both progress and disappointments of various kinds, African American women have been caught across the decades in an ever-present web of challenge and struggle. Within this complex ecosystem, however, they have managed to exhibit by thought, word, and deed the desire to participate actively as nation-builders in this difficult work.

Geographical Divides

After losing the Senate race, Lincoln followed with a victory against Senator Douglas in the presidential election of 1860. South Carolina seceded from the United States on December 20, 1860, before he could take office on March 4, 1861. This state was joined in quick order by Mississippi, Florida, Alabama, Georgia, Louisiana, and Texas. The group of seven formed the Confederate States of America (the Confederacy) on February 4, 1861, and created a Confederate constitution on March 11, 1861, in Montgomery, Alabama. Montgomery was identified as the Confederate capital until May 29, 1861, at which point the capital site was shifted to Richmond, Virginia. Jefferson Davis (from Kentucky), who had been serving as a senator from Mississippi to the US Congress, was elected president of the new nation. Alexander Stephens (from Georgia), who had been serving in the US House of Representatives from his state, was named vice president. The United States refused to recognize the secession or the sovereign status of the Confederacy as a new nation, as is typically the case in the beginning of secession movements with other nations as well.

On April 12, 1861, in South Carolina (the first territory to be claimed by the new nation), the Confederacy fired on Fort Sumter, a major US military installation off the coast of Charleston. The United States declared the seven states that constituted the Confederacy to be in rebellion, and President Lincoln called for a volunteer army to restore territory and order. With this call, four additional states (Virginia, Arkansas, Tennessee, and North Carolina) joined the Confederacy, making a total of eleven states in secession, all slaveholding. In addition, although there was no formal secession in two more states (Missouri and Kentucky) or in the newly acquired territory of Arizona, there were significant numbers of Confederate allies in each of these areas.

By this general process, the geographical scenes were set for war. In being present across these locations—in the Union, the Confederacy, and the border states—African American women had opportunities to gain a sense of how they were connected or not connected to the issues that were occurring around them. In keeping with the variability of their living conditions and circumstances, they had opportunities to find ways to engage or not engage as agents of change. Certainly, as the war dragged on, they also had opportunities to see their circumstances broaden and diversify as they discovered mechanisms for the survival of their families and themselves, as well as for participating in activities in support of social advocacy, activism, and leadership, thus laying foundations for their work for decades to come.

Technological and Medical Innovations

In 1861 the American Civil War was in motion, with armies gathering in both the North and the South. A crucial element for this war was also the emergence of several technological innovations as defining assets of its material context. Worthy of note is that, ultimately, this war was categorized as the first modern technological war. Charles D. Ross states: "The American Civil War was a war of transition . . . the war became a laboratory for applying adolescent technologies to military situations" (2000, viii–ix). The nature of war going forward would be forever changed. According to Shane Mountjoy (2009) technological innovations included:

changes in weaponry (rifles, shells, canons, land mines, torpedoes, hand grenades, machine guns, revolving turrets, etc.);
ships powered by steam engine instead of sails (for example, ironclads and submarines);
a new aeronautics corps for scouting and other intelligence-gathering missions using balloons;
nationwide railway systems for the movement of troops, supplies, food (for troops and animals), and medicine;
the use of the telegraph in developing instant communications;
the use of cryptography in the transmittal of coded information;
the use of photography in mapmaking, spying, scouting terrain, and documenting the images of war; and
the use and development of medical resources and technologies (for example, the widespread use of anesthesia and other pharmaceuticals in treatment, innovations in reconstructive surgery, etc.).

A striking example of how such transitions reset the watermarks for the operational landscape of war is at the convergence of war, technology, and medical practices. In this war, there were not only changes in medical resources (e.g., the use of anesthesia and other pharmaceutical innovations, including quinine, opium, and morphine) and technological innovations (such as improvements in reconstructive surgery and the replacement of lost limbs) but other innovations as well, as documented by Mountjoy (2009). These innovations included the renovation of naval ships for use as hospital ships (a role they continue to fill in current times) and new systems for care, which included the development of triage protocols to enhance survival and the return to fighting, and more cost-effective embalming processes, which made it possible for more of the dead to be shipped home for burial.

In turn, this point of coalescing assets occasioned specific human-centered impacts and consequences. Consider the high volume of deaths and injuries. Most dramatically, with innovations in weaponry, the casualty numbers were overwhelming, including, not only battle deaths and wounds but also sickness and death from diseases such as dysentery and malaria. Estimates of the loss of life among the military confirm that the Civil War was the deadliest of all conflicts in which the United States has been involved. According to James McPherson, documented casualties include 620,000 soldiers, 320,000 from Union forces and 260,000 from the Confederacy. These numbers indicate losses greater than all the nation's other wars combined through the Vietnam War (McPherson 2003, 854). McPherson confirms also that war-related civilian losses are unknown, but conservative estimates for the Confederacy, as the larger theater of the conflict, indicate as many as 50,000 casualties, thus pushing the casualties to at least 670,000 (619n53), with some estimates going significantly higher.

Within such overwhelming losses, a noticeable shift was away from the practice of soldiers taking care of their fallen comrades with the help of a small core of medical personnel. What became more evident was the need for trained medical services to be more systematically available in order to address the staggering need. Another shift was the recognition that, beyond the injuries themselves, conditions for adequate and sanitary care were in dire need of improvement. There were various consequences of these differences. Doctors came to be designated as noncombatants (Mountjoy 2009, 100–102) and, thereby, were not subject to capture as prisoners of war. Women emerged as leaders in advocating for sanitation and hygiene. Ultimately, leadership by women in caring for warriors was instrumental in making a place in nursing care for the professional training of women as health-care providers.

In the South and the border states especially, the sounds and silences of war were persistent. Whether inside or outside the theaters of actual fighting, the boundaries between battlefield and home ground were frequently blurred with impacts for both combatants and civilians. Generally, women, across all identity categories, could not easily escape these realities. As Mark M. Smith points out:

> Southerners on the home front, then, did not always have to see the war to know that it was happening or interpret its meaning. Plainly, sounds of the sick, the injured, and the dying—all intimately tied to the blasts of cannon—scared Southern civilians. Many of them heard these noises and came to resent the nervousness that booms and blasts caused them, not simply because such noises were the harbingers of physical pain but also because they disrupted social and aural registers. Union and Confederate forces alike generated new sounds and noises, and both came in for criticism from civilians upset with the disruption of their customary keynotes. . . . Military sounds threatened the function of civil ones and, in the process, tapped into Southerners' deepest fears. How were urban Confederates supposed to distinguish between sounds of martial war and sounds of civil war? How were they to know when bells signaled military invasion or servile insurrection? Bells, rattles, and miscellaneous aural cues had been used in the Old South to alert whites to slave insurrection. Now those cues were muddled and confused. (2002, 17)

Smith cites correspondence to the *Charleston Mercury* on June 28, 1864: "As late as 1864, Charlestonians complained still of the 'strange commingling of sounds,' namely, 'the soft, sweet tones of the church bells inviting the people to the house of prayer, and the boom of cannon and crash of shells summoning the unfortunate soldier to the dark abodes of eternity. The one was the gentle messenger of peace and life, the other the dread summoner of suffering and death!'" (18). In the South, there was also the reality that bells—made from much needed metal—were being totally silenced as they were being transformed into ammunition.

In addition to these examples of technological consequence,

one reality was that technology enabled the war to live beyond the fields of battle themselves—and to do so not simply in the minds of the people but in symbolic representations in word and image. With regard to images, the Civil War was the first war to be documented through photography, with a cohort of photographers, such as Mathew Brady and his group of over twenty other photographers, showing war from a closer and more human-centered level than ever before. As Mountjoy asserts: "Photographers captured images of virtually every aspect of the war. These included images of battlefields, hospitals, encampments, the men of military units, their officers, and escaped and freed slaves. In many respects, these photographs recorded the day-to-day monotony of life at war. Taken together, the photographs make up an impressive and compelling record of the war" (2009, 107). As sociocultural artifacts, these battlefront and home-front images become vivid metaphors that encode a national trauma, the meaning of which we are still sorting through in our contemporary world.

Basically, the ubiquitous nature of technological and medical innovations underscored how difficult it was for stakeholders, including African American women, not to be touched in some way by the material realities of the war. In this regard, a fundamental question concerns the ways in which the existence of war, as devastating as it might be, might affect visions of possibility among the downtrodden. There is no doubt that African Americans thought about what might happen if the Union Army won the war and that they came to the central conclusion that Union victory might mean brighter horizons for their people, starting with the presumption of freedom for the enslaved from bondage. Whatever their sense of self and agency, documentary evidence of their wartime activities confirms that African Americans, including African American women, were encouraged by the potential of Union victory to imagine themselves living in a better world and participating in this world in whatever ways possible to remake a better nation going forward.

Literacy as an Innovative Tool

In addition to photographs, another asset for memorializing the war was literacy. This medium of expression was also enhanced by technology even though traditionally it may not have been immediately identified in this light. To illustrate this point, during the nineteenth century, there were noticeable advancements in communication technologies that we now take for granted, such as the telegraph, a technology that was developed and refined during the 1830s and 1840s. Essentially though, acts of literacy of various kinds benefited greatly from basic touchstone technologies rather than higher profile ones. Consider, for example, the manufacture of pencils, pens, paper, and ink, and innovations in printing processes. During this era, these core assets combined with the broader availability of schooling and literacy for a larger number of people than in preceding eras. In addition, a livelier public and counter-public sphere emerged, as evidenced by escalating numbers of newspapers, pamphlets, magazines, and books that were produced across diverse communities. This set of resources offered connectivity and engagement for more people than ever before—including women.

As chronicled by historians of rhetoric (e.g., Johnson 1991; Graff 1991; Royster 2000; Logan 2008), in the nineteenth century literacy knowledge and practices blossomed. Reading and writing increased in value over the century as an essential personal, social, political, and cultural tool. By mid-century, there was an escalating sense that the United States was becoming, in fact, a literate society with a range of literate practices—that is, various uses of reading and writing, in full sway. One such practice already in evidence was letter writing. Another was personal writing—that is, the keeping of journals and diaries, and the writing of personal essays and memoirs, by a variety of citizens from different social strata. With the advent of war and the presence on the battlefront and the home front of larger numbers of people with reading and writing skills, these practices escalated. As Lauren Cook Burgess notes:

> Civil War armies were the most literate in history to that time. More than 90 percent of the white Union soldiers and more than 80 percent of Confederate soldiers could read and write. Many of these three million soldiers were away from home for the first time during their military service. With strong ties to family and community, they stayed in touch by writing home and receiving letters in return—hundreds of millions of letters during the four years of the war. . . . They are the best source for understanding the real war as experienced by the men who fought it. (1994, xi)

Moreover, the impact of literacy was facilitated by a postal service (that functioned more predictably for the Union than for the Confederacy but which functioned for both nevertheless) that became the resource by which these readers and writers were able to create a documentary legacy. Directly or by proxy, men and women across different socioeconomic classes and social identities—including free and enslaved men and women—wrote letters, kept journals and diaries, and occasionally (especially after the war) wrote memoirs. Such texts now constitute a substantial documentary record of the daily thoughts, lives, and experiences of a broader range of citizens than ever before. This body of texts has become a vital resource from which we can now draw a more fully rendered and more inclusive documentary history of the Civil War, generally, and of the participation of women in particular since they too, whether on the battlefront or the home front, were engaged actively in literate practices.

In effect, during the Civil War, literacy functioned quite dramatically as a tool for individuals not only to claim their own agency and authority to write down their lives but also to acknowledge their own human value and presence in the world. In their own words, Union and Confederate stakeholders, including the women within these groups, chronicled how they perceived, were affected by, and were involved in the war (see the list of texts in the appendix). Men and women wrote their own stories, and as part of this operational landscape, so did African American women.

Basic Implications

Bringing together factors related to scene and act during the Civil War as a specific moment in time underscores the point that this war was indeed a horrific undertaking that led to thousands of people being killed and untold numbers wounded. The impacts and consequences were manifold. This war was defined by innovative technological and medical advancements that enhanced not only its devastating effects but also the level of public awareness about its ways and means. As a literate war it permitted a range of ground-level personal perspectives to be shared well beyond those who witnessed the battlefields directly, viewpoints that memorialized the experience of war for generations to come. The conflict also marked a moment when African American men were able to join military units as official warriors rather than as servants and laborers, a change that provided yet another symbol for the African American community, including African American women, of their rights as citizens. In other words, for African Americans as a specific stakeholder group, the Civil War became a point of leverage for transformative change, inspired by a passion for their possibilities in freedom, possibilities that they were quite literally fighting to reify.

Agents

A Broader Range of Stakeholders

From the perspective of the general public imagination, when we think about the intersections of events, people, and places during the Civil War, despite full and ample documentation indicating otherwise, an apocryphal view has been that the white men of the nation—elite and poor—were at war, brother against brother, and white women were keeping the home fires burning in both the North and the South.[1] Such presumptions, despite truths to the contrary, die hard. Similarly, the defaulted view of African Americans generally in the public imagination has been that both men and women, with precious few exceptions, were mostly enslaved in the South. The presumption has been that during the war this group lived passively in their plantation homes struggling alongside their plantation mistresses to hold everything together, exhibiting in their ongoing work considerable loyalty to their slave–owning families. Or, if they were not on the plantations, they were dislocated and on the move, roaming the cities and countryside, as it were, sometimes following behind Union troops but, in either case, living mainly as pawns or instruments in a larger tale rather than deliberately and actively involved in the sociopolitical agenda of war and nation building. With regard to other ethnic groups, they just do not factor at all into the popular story, as a "black" and "white" story. However, all these presumptions fly in the face of service records and scholarly documentation of the actual activities of stakeholders, as confirmed by the interdisciplinary research and scholarship that has recovered more inclusive information.[2]

African American men, as a prime example in this study, served in both the Union army and the Union navy, with an estimated 179,000 serving in the army and 19,000 serving in the navy. The documentation of participation in the National Archives shows that in addition to the general classification of soldiers and sailors their military roles included carpenters, chaplains, cooks, guards, laborers, nurses, scouts, spies, steamboat pilots, surgeons, and teamsters, with an estimated eighty commissioned officers. This accounting does not include the involuntary service of enslaved African Americans in noncombat roles in the Confederate army.[3]

Other men, considered in our contemporary society to be from minority groups, also served during the war, for example Hispanic Americans and Native Americans, who have experienced very little presence at all in the popular national imaginary.

The US Department of the Interior and the National Park Service document that people of Spanish heritage were well established in North America long before the Civil War (National Park Service 2011b). After its founding as a nation, the United States carved away at the huge landownership in North America that had been acquired by Spain since the landing of Columbus in the New World. There remained, however, populations of Hispanic heritage throughout the Southeast and the Southwest and in urban centers in the North as well, such as Philadelphia, New York, and Boston. By 1861 and the beginning of the Civil War, these groups were also engaged in the war from the first battle to the last in both the Union and the Confederacy in the same ways that others of varying European heritage were. Examples include Captain Luis Emilio (Twenty-Third Massachusetts Volunteer Infantry), who was selected as one of the officers to lead the African American Fifty-Fourth Massachusetts Regiment; Captain Michael Usina (Eighth Georgia Volunteer Infantry), who was wounded at Manassas and subsequently joined the Confederate navy; Admiral David Farragut (raised in Tennessee), who was most celebrated for his capture of Mobile Bay; Commander Ambrosio Gonzales (South Carolina), who earned commendation from the Confederacy for the bombardment of Fort Sumter; Lieutenant Colonel J. Francisco Chaves (New Mexico), who led the First New Mexico Volunteers with Colonel Kit Carson; Lieutenant Colonel Manuel Chávez (New Mexico), who played key roles in the Union win at the battle of Glorieta; and Colonel Santos Benavides (Texas) who, with his brothers Refugio and Cristobal, served the Confederacy with distinction.

Likewise, among Native American groups, historical relationships before and after the formation of the United States directed and shaped the complexities of their participation.[4] In the main, Native American communities both east and west were surrounded by the Confederacy, and, as groups living in southern territories, they were often slave-owning themselves. Native groups living in the West and Midwest were often already involved in long-standing conflicts with the United States, as in the case of the Apache, Navajo, and Sioux. In the Southeast, the Cherokee had already been pushed off their homelands in Georgia, Alabama, and Tennessee and subjected from 1838 to 1839 to the Trail of Tears (the horrifying walk from the Southeast to Indian Territory, now the state of Oklahoma). With these distinctive examples of oppression and domination, other Native American groups were also concerned about their rights to their lands being likewise compromised. As William Loren Katz states about Native American groups living in the western states:

> The Civil War pitted brother against brother, and nowhere more painfully than among the Five Civilized Nations. "Mixed bloods," committed to slavery clashed with "full bloods" and their black allies who just wanted to be left in peace.
>
> The Indian Territory in 1861 was surrounded by the Confederacy and flooded with agents and sympathizers. Then Confederate officials and troops arrived to control matters and U.S. power was nowhere in sight. By the time Fort Sumter surrendered that April, Chickasaws and Choctaws had signed treaties with the Confederacy. Cherokees, Creeks, and Seminoles were told by Confederate officials "there ain't no more U.S.—ain't any more Treaty—all be dead." By August the leaders of these nations had caved in and allied their members to the new Confederacy.
>
> Red and Black Indians favoring neutrality or the Union (including most black members) grouped around a wealthy Creek Chief, Opothle Yahola. He secretly wrote to President Lincoln asking for the protection promised, saying "now the wolf has come. Men who are strangers tread our soil. Our children are frightened & mothers cannot sleep for fear." Getting this letter to the Union forces proved almost impossible. Getting Union help in 1861 was impossible.
>
> Opothle Yahola and his followers hoped to live out the war in peace. They moved away from the pro-Confederate Indians and camped out on the Indian Territory's southwestern frontier—men, women, and children with stores of food, livestock, and wagons of possessions. Half of the Seminole Nation joined them, as well as blacks from all Five Nations and Kickapoos, Shawnees, Delawares, and Comanches. (Katz 1986, 141–42)

Ultimately, there was indeed fighting between the Opothele Yahola "peace" group and the Confederate forces, which culminated on December 26, 1861, with the peace forces horribly defeated (Wagner 2011, 46). The Union army did eventually step in to provide supplies to what was left of the camps, and loyalties to neutrality and the Union continued. In January 1862, William Dole, US commissioner of Indian affairs, asked Native American agents to "'engage forthwith all the vigorous and able-bodied Indians in their respective agencies.' The request resulted in the assembly of the 1st and 2nd Indian Home Guard that included Delaware, Creek, Seminole, Kickapoo, Seneca, Osage, Shawnee, Choctaw and Chickasaw" ("We Are All Americans"). Across all territories, estimates suggest that more than twenty thousand Native Americans served in the Union and Confederate armies. The Union troops included members of the Catawba, Cherokee, Chickasaw, Choctaw, Creek, Delaware, Huron, Iroquois, Kickapoo, Lumbee, Odawa, Ojibwe (Chippewa), Osage, Pamunkey, Pequot, Potawatomi, Powhatan, Seminole, Seneca, and Shawnee. Those fighting with the Confederacy were mostly from the southeastern tribes and included the Catawba, Cherokee, Choctaw, Creek, and Seminole.

The most famous Native American unit in the Union Army in the East was Company K of the First Michigan Sharpshooters who participated in several battles ("We Are All Americans"). Notable, also, was General Ely S. Parker of the Seneca who wrote the articles of surrender that General Robert E. Lee signed at Appomattox Court House. Trained as a lawyer, Parker served as General Ulysses S. Grant's military secretary. With regard to the Confederacy, a leader from the Cherokee Nation was Stand Watie (Cunningham 1998), also a lawyer. He led his group to the Confederacy. He was the only Native American in either the Union or the Confederacy to reach the status of brigadier general.

In other words, with the growing amount of interdisciplinary research and scholarship, we can see the stakeholders in this war extend well beyond the previous presumption that the war was the story of and about only white men. We have substantial documentation of a broader range of people who actually participated in and were affected by the conflict. We have a signal opportunity to go beyond the mythos of this war as white brother against white brother and to debunk popularized notions. Quite importantly, we are much better positioned to replace limited views of who participants and stakeholders were with facts that are themselves quite interesting and inspirational.

Debunking the Mythos of Women at War

In the case of women at war, interdisciplinary research and scholarship are also vibrant in building documentary evidence for what diverse groups of women were doing during this time period. From the perspective of the public imagination, however, the most enduring presumptions about women in the Civil War come rather persistently and mythologically through acts of literacy—from two works of fiction in particular. The writers were women who were professional writers. Their narratives were drawn from historical accounts of women's lives during this era in the North and in the South, and both novels have come forward in time with frame-setting power within the popular imagination of the nation.

Stories from the Union

The first account is by Louisa May Alcott, who lived and wrote during the Civil War. Born on November 29, 1832, in Germantown, Pennsylvania, Alcott was the second of four daughters of Amos Bronson Alcott and Abigail May Alcott. Her father was a well-known progressive educator, philosopher, and leader in the Transcendentalist Movement. The transcendentalist group was a collective of writers and thinkers in the Northeast in the early nineteenth century who believed in the power of intuition, the innate possibilities of human beings, the need for individuals to be self-reliant and to engage in critical deliberation, and the importance of the natural world. Her mother was a social activist dedicated to women's rights, temperance, and abolition. Although Bronson Alcott struggled to support the family financially, their circle of friends—which included elites such as Ralph Waldo Emerson, Henry David Thoreau, Nathaniel Hawthorne, and Margaret Fuller—offered his daughter a distinctive cauldron for intellectual development.

Louisa May Alcott ultimately became a social and political activist in her own right. She began publishing her writing as a teenager and over the years used the earnings from her publications as well as earnings from teaching, journal editing, and domestic service to supplement the family income. Among her thirty fiction publications, the best known is her novel *Little Women*. It was a coming of age narrative based on her own experiences during the Civil War. The story was set in Concord, Massachusetts, and drew from the experiences of her family's life at home in the North without their father, who was off fighting in the war. Alcott's narrative showcased the commitment of women and girls to keep the home fires burning in the midst of challenge.

Against the backdrop of the Civil War, she presented the struggles of the family with poverty, their social responsibility in supporting those poorer than themselves, the vulnerability of the community to devastating disease, and the efforts of women to gather resources of various kinds to support the men at war, including the need of Mrs. March, the mother in the story, to travel (like so many women during the war) to a distant hospital to care for her wounded husband—supported in part by a loan from a more affluent family member and by Jo's (the central character's) sacrifice in selling her hair to help out with expenses. These images of the impact of the war at home resonated with audiences in 1868 and 1869 when the novel was published in two parts. The novel attained immediate popularity and has continued to be widely read over the decades, with a secure place in the American literary canon and a distinctive place in film history. In its broadly based popularity, this account of Union girls and women during war has functioned compellingly to set the framework for the loyalty, steadfast support, and self-reliance of women at home in the North during times of personal and national challenge.

Little Women has come to be known in popular culture more as a "coming of age" novel than as a "Civil War" novel. However, among Alcott's works is a more explicitly Civil War volume actually published during the war years, *Hospital Sketches* (1863).[5] It is a volume that received acclaim during its own time because of Alcott's depiction of life at a hospital during the Civil War. It is a fictionalized account based on Alcott's six weeks as a nurse from December 13, 1861, to January 24, 1862, when she volunteered to serve as an army nurse in Washington, DC, and was accepted at the Union Hotel Hospital in Georgetown.

Over the course of her career, Alcott had a steady stream of publishing successes. *Hospital Sketches* was no different. It was well received by contemporary audiences. Alcott provided what was recognized as an authentic look at the day-to-day experiences of women across the North and the Midwest who were devoting themselves to the care of war wounded under harsh conditions for the wounded and for themselves. Alcott herself contracted typhoid pneumonia, a deadly disease, and was sent home within six weeks of volunteering. In this volume, Alcott used the eyes of her heroine, Nurse Tribulation Periwinkle, to bring the horrors of war closer to noncombatants at home and to subsequent readers over the generations.

Hospital Sketches has not been as appreciated by the reading audience as overwhelmingly as *Little Women*. During its own era, while Nurse Periwinkle's viewpoint did capture authentic experiences of women as nurses in wartime, these experiences were located in the public domain (deemed at the time more appropriate for men's work) rather than the private domain (which was more familiar as appropriate for women). Away from home and away from the protection of male relatives, Nurse Periwinkle's story actually violated propriety. In contrast, *Little Women* chronicles life at home mostly under supervision and surveillance. It underscored respectability, loyalty, and service to one's family and community in what was deemed a more appropriate domain for women's presence. In effect, the reception of both Nurse Periwinkle and Jo March suggests that these characters were encapsulated by the expectations of their day for women's place and women's possibilities.

In essence, one might say that *Little Women* was, and continues to be, a pacesetter in American culture, defining what it means for socially acceptable girls to come to maturity during challenging times. One might also conclude that in this novel Alcott was able to stretch the imagination of her readers, albeit in a fictionalized way, about the boundaries of women's possibilities. She took advantage of her and her family's lived experiences and equally excellent advantage of her growing success as a popular woman writer. Functioning in this way within the realm of general knowledge and expectations, she was able to deepen the view of women's lives and work at home by adding in Jo's experiences as a young girl with deep desires (as in her own case) to be a paid writer.[6]

By contrast, in *Hospital Sketches*, the story of Nurse Periwinkle gained visibility during Alcott's own time period by lifting a veil on war experience. This narrative, however, functioned outside the circle of compelling (and perhaps appropriate) stories about women's lives and women's place in society. Women did not normally work in fields of war. Their place was at home. Nurse Periwinkle was off on her own, away from home, away from male oversight and protection. One might reasonably conclude that, unlike *Little Women*, *Hospital Sketches* functioned in newer territory for women's place and possibilities rather than familiar territory. In light of these gendered circumstances, *Little Women* became iconic over the generations, but after a relatively short time, *Hospital Sketches* lost presence and visibility.

Stories from the Confederacy

The second writer who created an iconic image of women during the Civil War is Margaret Mitchell, author of *Gone with the Wind* (first published in 1936). It is almost redundant to say that *Gone with the Wind* is a love story of epic scale, as well as a dramatic tale of survival. Unlike Alcott, who positioned the war as the backdrop for her Massachusetts-based story of *Little Women*, Mitchell set her story in the war-torn landscape of the South, where the war was far more explicitly a part of the narrative rather than a backdrop.

Mitchell was born in Atlanta, Georgia, on November 8, 1900. The daughter of Eugene Muse Mitchell, an attorney, and Mary Isabel Stephens Mitchell, a suffragist, she grew up in a wealthy and politically prominent family. Influenced by both her father and her mother, Mitchell was a talented writer and an adventurous young woman surrounded by the expectations of her elite class standing. By the age of twenty-five she was well launched on a journalism career, although this move was not sanctioned by her more traditional family. She worked as a feature writer for the *Atlanta Journal* and happily settled in a second marriage after being divorced from her first husband. After a car accident in 1926 that resulted in her leaving her job, she began to fill her time by writing a novel.[7] Throughout her childhood, she had had innumerable opportunities to hear stories from family and friends about the antebellum South, life during the miseries of the Civil War, and the impact of loss and transformative change on southern cultural sensibilities. Mitchell chose to write about this era. In what would be a ten-year commitment, she succeeded in crafting the most compelling fictional account of the Civil War ever to be written.

During the year that her book was published (1936), Mitchell received the National Book Award for Most Distinguished Novel. In 1937 she was awarded the Pulitzer Prize for Fiction. In 1939 the book was made into a blockbuster movie by Selznick Studios. The movie opened to tremendous fanfare in downtown Atlanta at a theater that was not freely open to African Americans, and the movie received several Academy Award honors. Across the decades since their publication, both the book and the movie have endured with distinction as a popular novel and a top tier classic film. Even though Mitchell's novel was published seven decades after the actual events, it has assumed its own iconic value (enhanced, of course, by the movie version) as a story of the South—seen through the eyes of the white southern elite. The novel is focused on the life and actions of Scarlett O'Hara, a southern belle living in the Atlanta area at the dawning of the Civil War, on events that occur afterward, and on Scarlett's experiences through Reconstruction. Mitchell captures the spirit of the antebellum era as it transitions dramatically into war, loss, and survival, and she does so through the eyes of a fascinating woman with quite amazing ingenuity and "gumption."

Over the generations, as novel, movie, and mega enterprise, Mitchell's narrative has achieved great power and acclaim, not only financially but also in capturing the imagination of audiences around the world—again through the eyes and experiences of women (Scarlett O'Hara and her sisters, along with Melanie Wilkes, Belle Whatling, Mammy, Prissy, and others). The novel stands unparalleled in symbolic power, as the defaulted definition of southern life during the Civil War, with its crumbling façade, its devastations—in terms of the sorrowfully increasing material wants and needs, as well as its unfathomable breakdowns in "social order." As the southern author Pat Conroy states in the preface of the Pocket Books edition:

> I was raised in a house without books, but the ones displayed and laid out flat for the inspection of visitors were the Bible and *Gone with the Wind*, in no particular order of importance. . . . Few white Southerners, even today, can read this book without conjuring up a complex, tortured dreamscape of the South handed down by generations of relatives who grew up with the taste of defeat, like the bluing of gunmetal, still in their mouths. What Margaret Mitchell caught so perfectly was the sense of irredeemable loss and a backwater Camelot corrupted by the mannerless intrusions of insensate invaders. . . . To Southerners like my mother, *Gone with the Wind* was not just a book, it was an answer, a clenched fist raised to the North, an anthem of defiance. If you could not defeat the Yankees on the battlefield, then by God, one of your women could rise from the ashes of humiliation to write more powerfully than the enemy and all the historians and novelists who sang the praises of the Union. (Mitchell 2008, v–vi)

Both of these narratives, *Little Women* and *Gone with the Wind*, presented iconic views of women at war that are both compelling and inspirational. They were not designed, however, to offer a full spectrum of who women actors during this era really were historically, or what they were doing, and why. Such popularized stories constitute an important lens for understanding how pivotal this era has been in the evolution of the nation. They underscore also some key roles played by women in keeping the home fires burning, both north and south. However, the documentation of the actual activities of a broader range of women enhances exponentially the effort to build better knowledge and understanding of the impacts and consequences of historical women's activities in the making and remaking of a nation.

Recovering Historical Women's Experiences

With the attack on Fort Sumter and calls to arms from both the Union and the Confederacy, men across both nations rushed to volunteer to fight, leaving the women to run farms, households, and businesses on their own in order to keep their families going. At the same time the women, individually and through their local societies, rushed with equal enthusiasm to support their troops and equip them with the supplies they needed such as food, clothing, and medical supplies. Just as passionate and as patriotic as their men, many of the more adventurous women also found an array of ways to join their men on the battlefront. In *Women in the United States Military*, Judith Bellafaire states: "Although most women who left home to involve themselves in the Civil War worked as nurses, smaller numbers dressed themselves as men and volunteered for duty with the Union and Confederate Armies. . . . Women also involved themselves in war by serving as volunteer and official spies" (2011, 20).[8]

There are stories to be told about these gender-bending activities that promise to add depth and texture to women's narratives of engagement. Even at a general level, recent scholarship is confirming striking examples of clusters of women who supported their causes. With considerable dedication, ingenuity, and courage, women found multiple ways to demonstrate their national loyalties. On the home front, with so many able-bodied men going off to war, women in southern and border towns and cities where most of the fighting was occurring took on the responsibility of forming home guard units. They trained in military tactics and the use of weapons and prepared themselves to fight, if necessary, for their families, homes, and communities. Of particular notice in both the North and the South, some women also disguised themselves as men and boys—with married women sometimes choosing disguises mainly to be able to follow their husbands into war zones—but sometimes not just to follow. In significant numbers, married, widowed, and single women actually joined the military to fight as soldiers alongside their male comrades. This pattern has now become normalized in our contemporary times, with significant numbers of women choosing to work in the military as leaders and defenders of the nation and dedicating themselves also to stabilizing fairness and equity as they rise in military ranks.[9]

During the Civil War, women took on other types of work beyond being soldiers. On one hand, women across race and class used the novelty of their presence in war zones to operate as spies, as documented by Ellen Forbes (1998) and Richard H. Hall (2006). For both white and African American women, gender expectations of the time were an asset. Elite white women were presumed to be too genteel and focused on home and family to be involved in war or the deceptions of spying. In the case of African American women, their ability to succeed as spies was strengthened by social presumptions about their intellectual inferiority and by the work that was deemed appropriate for their station in life as domestics (for example, as cooks, housekeepers, and laundresses), which permitted them open and unique access to circles of knowledge and power.

Mainstream Exemplars from the North and the South

One story of a successful African American woman spy was Mary Elizabeth Bowser, who in 1861 was living as a free woman but who had grown up a slave in the Van Lew household in Virginia. Bowser was freed at the age of eighteen and was subsequently educated in Philadelphia. When the war started she went undercover as "simple-minded" Ellen Bond, a spy in a cohort of northern spies managed by the daughter in her former slave household, the Richmond heiress Elizabeth Van Lew. Notably, Van Lew's work casts light on the diversity of opinions that remained throughout the South about what and how the nation should be. Even though the dominant view supported secession, opinions actually varied, including in key southern cities such as Richmond, in Van Lew's case, or Atlanta, as confirmed by Thomas G. Dyer in *Secret Yankees* (1999). Van Lew placed Bowser in the home of Jefferson Davis, president of the Confederacy, where Bowser gained the trust of President Davis as a house servant and was able, therefore, to overhear all sorts of privileged information, which she then conveyed to Lew. This level of valuable military intelligence helped the Union to secure the fall of Richmond.

A second case is Mary Louveste, who was enslaved to one

of the engineers working at the Gosport Naval Yard in Norfolk to convert the captured USS *Merrimac* into a Confederate ironclad. At considerable risk, Louveste took some of the plans from her slave master. She got them across the Potomac to Gideon Welles, secretary of the Union navy, and provided invaluable technological information to the Union in their developing of naval countermeasures.[10]

Among women who were more adventurous, there was also a rush to volunteer for other noncombat roles as well. One role that they frequently chose was as teachers to educate newly freed African Americans along the Port Royal Sound off the coasts of Georgia and South Carolina. Their students included freed African American women, children, men who were civilians, and also freed men who volunteered in increasing numbers for military service and who, like their civilian counterparts, wanted to learn to read and write. Critical interrogations of these battlefront roles and responsibilities offer a clearer, more fully rendered accounting of the ways in which women, including African American women, lived and worked during the Civil War.

Even with these amplifications, however, nursing still stands out as the dominant story. Women rushed, both north and south, to equip their troops for war. They also rushed, with courage but typically no professional training or preparation, to volunteer as nurses, especially for their own family members. As might be expected, with the profound and more visible impacts of both fighting the enemy and fighting diseases, providing nursing care was an especially strong incentive for women since this type of work was already viewed as gender appropriate, particularly as it related to the care of family members. Not surprisingly, women's service as health-care providers, especially for their own family members, was deemed politically and morally appropriate. What had not been previously deemed appropriate was their providing such services as supervisors of care with decision-making authority or as women acting independently (without the protection and supervision of male family members) in theaters of war. With the Civil War's fragile boundaries between the battlefront and the home front, however, these expectations for both nations were stretched beyond traditional limits.

Women, in fact, were passionate about supporting the troops and ministering to the wounded. As Drew Gilpin Faust states in her chronicles of southern women's involvement:

> In professional armies, nurses were almost invariably detailed or disabled soldiers, males, of course, who fit neatly within the structures of military hierarchy and routine.
>
> Manpower shortages, escalating casualty rates, and patriotic ambitions, however, overrode custom and pushed southern women toward work with the sick and wounded, a movement encouraged by the innovative and much admired role Florence Nightingale had played in Britain's Crimean War of 1853–56. A woman of unchallenged respectability and high social standing, Nightingale had through her selfless actions and her widely read *Notes on Nursing*, first published in the United States in 1860, established a conceptual legitimation for females nursing. The notion that woman's moral and emotional attributes uniquely fitted her for hospital work gained strength and currency, and women North and South found in Nightingale a model for female heroism. (Faust 2004, 92)

In the South, white exemplars included Catherine Gibbon of North Carolina and Julia Tutwiler, Kate Cumming, and Phoebe Yates Levy Pember of South Carolina, all of whom found ways, despite social pressure and family opposition, to put their talents to good use in ministering to the Confederate troops, as documented by Mary Elizabeth Massey (1994) and Drew Gilpin Faust (2004). Among Union women were activists such as Mary Ann Ball Bickerdyke, Dorothea Dix, Clara Barton, and Elizabeth Blackwell (Giesberg 2000, 2009; Royster 2003) who found ways to use their talents in support of Union troops. Without military sanction, for example, Bickerdyke (a widow and an expert in herbal medicines who was born in Ohio but lived in Illinois) became noted for walking the battlefields alone with a lantern in search of anyone alive who might have been missed. Ultimately, she built a distinctive reputation for excellence, and General William T. Sherman asked her to serve with his troops as they marched through Georgia in 1864.

Like Bickerdyke, Clara Barton also worked independently. At the beginning of the Civil War, she was one of very few women working for the federal government, in the US Patent Office in Washington, DC. She saw the critical needs of Union troops who were beginning to crowd the capital city. She began appealing to the public and collecting food, clothing, and medical supplies to help them. She was successful also in obtaining government and army passes to bring volunteer services and supplies to the battlefront. She became known as the "Angel of the Battlefield." These practices and her subsequent experiences with the global Red Cross network laid the groundwork for her to become a founder of the American Association of the Red Cross in 1881.

Another example of volunteerism is Dorothea Dix, who by the Civil War had already emerged as a passionate and outspoken advocate for health reform for indigents who suffered with mental illness. As Judith Ann Giesberg reports in *Civil War Sisterhood* (2000), on the day that the Confederates fired on Fort Sumter, Dix had already arrived in Washington from Massachusetts. She went straight to the White House to offer her services, and on June 10, 1861, she was appointed superintendent of women nurses. She established the rules and protocols for the participation of women as nurses in the Union army. She served in this position for four years—but not without encountering persistent challenges to her authority as a woman in a man's domain and as an assertive volunteer without professional medical training (Giesberg 2000, 18).

In addition to all of the nursing volunteerism that grew out of the commitment of individual women, however, there was the collective commitment of northern white women who created the US Sanitary Commission, an organization without a counterpart in the South. Organizational leaders included the activists Mary Ashton Livermore (Chicago), Louisa Lee Schuyler (New York), and Abigail Williams May (Boston). A key figure was Elizabeth Blackwell, who was born in England but grew up in Cincinnati, Ohio, where she demonstrated a determination to become a medical doctor (Royster 2003, 82). In 1849, against great odds, she received a degree from the Geneva Medical College in New York, the first woman in the United States to achieve this accomplishment. She had additional training from Saint Bartholomew's Hospital in London and at La Maternité in Paris, and by the Civil War she had established a medical practice in New York City.

Seeing the wave of women's spontaneous benevolence, Blackwell recognized the potential to organize this volunteerism into a collective force, and with gender consciousness she recognized how important it was for such efforts to have the endorsement of influential men.[11] On April 25, 1861, in New York, she called an informal meeting of prominent women who were leaders in various sorts of community-based urban reform work in order to discuss the formation of the Woman's Central Association of Relief (WCAR), to provide a mechanism for creating a more systematic means to increase the numbers of much needed trained nurses. Blackwell invited interested women from this group to a second meeting four days later at Cooper Union, an educational institution in New York for the advancement of science and arts. This meeting was led by Reverend Henry Whitney Bellows, a Unitarian clergyman. Dr. Valentine Mott, a physician, was elected president of the WCAR and Bellows was elected vice president. Working with Dorothea Dix, Bellows established the concept of a US Sanitary Commission (USSC), and Blackwell and Dix worked together to train nurses for hospitals in the Washington area.

The USSC was authorized by Secretary of War Edwin M. Stanton and approved by President Lincoln on June 9, 1861, in order to promote clean and healthy conditions among the wounded Union troops. The USSC raised money and collected food, clothing, and medical supplies. They outfitted hospital ships, established a hospital directory of the sick and wounded, established convalescent lodging and care for discharged soldiers, and after the war assisted veterans with getting various types of benefits. Bellows served as president, and other influential men stepped forward to support the new organization, including the journalist and landscape designer Frederick Law Olmsted, who served as executive secretary; the lawyer and diarist George Templeton Strong, who served as treasurer; and physicians Elisha Harris and Samuel Gridley Howe. Giesberg states:

> Historians estimate that some 7,000 soldiers aid societies in towns and villages throughout the North and West supported the United States Sanitary Commission during the Civil War. Twelve major regional branches administered this vast network of local organizations or affiliates, and the branches were run by women with a variety of backgrounds and skills. . . . Though the branches were technically expected to defer to the commission's all-male executive board, branches maintained independent command structures and agendas and in practice the reverse was often the case—the executive board often deferred to the branches in matters of day-to-day operations. (2000, 5)

This highly effective and efficient organization was significant in the Union's success in winning the war. After the war, members helped to rehabilitate the veterans and assisted families with their ongoing needs before the organization disbanded with a distinctive record of service.

The Historical Presence of African American Women

Consider another view from the North. While activism was occurring among white women and men, a comparable spirit of action was happening among northern African American women and men. One difference, however, was the interconnections for the support and services that African Americans were needing to provide, not only to the troops at war, especially the African American troops, but also to African American refugees who were escaping from the South. To be sure, one consequence of war between the Union and the Confederacy was the creation of "contraband," the human "property" that was acquired by the Union as a consequence of battle. These "contraband"—the men, women, and children who were no longer controlled by their former enslavers—sought refuge in various ways but significantly by migrating to what they considered to be safer places, including the Union capital, Washington, DC, and other cities in Union states. The living conditions they found in these places, however, were horrible, making the first order of business for northern African American women who lived in refugee sites to be garnering resources to help the newcomers.

Included also in this web of support was the co-related activism that remained critical for the ongoing agitation of these northern African American women for justice and equity in their own communities. One illustration is the battle to secure access to streetcars in Philadelphia. As chronicled by Giesberg (2009, 92–118), before the Civil War Philadelphia was already a very active site for abolitionism and civil rights, a commitment that continued during the Civil War and afterward in the face of ongoing injustice and racist violence. African American women were active participants in this work and took leadership roles in the continuous struggles for social and political change.

Consider the circumstances surrounding the organization in April 1863 of the Ladies' Sanitary Association of The African Episcopal Church of Saint Thomas as an auxiliary to the USSC. This group was prepared to provide support for the injured US Colored Troops (USCT), but they needed access to public rather than private transportation (i.e., to the city's streetcars) in order to carry out their relief efforts.[12] The injured soldiers were housed some distance from African American neighborhoods—in places such as Camp William Penn, which was more than thirteen miles north of the city. The women needed, therefore, safe and systematic access to transportation. With Jim Crow policies firmly in place and the arbitrary likelihood of ejection from the streetcars ever present, these women had to be deliberate and strategic about their movements across the city in order to perform appropriate care and accomplish the organizational goals they were determined, despite racist oppression, to accomplish. In effect, however, they were subjected to injustices throughout the war.

Social justice was slow in coming, and changes in law and practice, locally and nationally, were not accomplished until after the war when lawsuits had worked their way through the legal system in cities such as San Francisco, New York, Washington, DC, and Cincinnati. In Philadelphia, women took their cases of abuse to the courts from 1865 to 1867. As Giesberg reports: "On March 22, 1867, Pennsylvania governor John Geary signed a law outlawing segregation on streetcars and railroads. The law allowed judges to either fine or imprison (or both) conductors who denied service to black riders or those who employed subterfuge in order to avoid serving black riders on an equal basis with whites. Reflecting the humiliating experiences of black riders during the war, the law explicitly stated that *any* service given or withheld on account of race was prohibited, including compelling riders to sit in special seats or seating them apart from other riders" (2009, 13). During the Civil War, however, these laws were not in place. Even so, stories of action by urban African American communities in the North are abundant, and nowhere more so than in the stories of support that African Americans in Philadelphia provided to the steadily flowing stream of refugees who were coming into the city over the course of the war.

Certainly, some free African American women, both north and south, participated in white women's relief organizations and worked through these more mainstream organizations to provide support. In terms of initiatives for the explicit support African Americans, over the four war years, local organizations joined together to form large umbrella groups such as the US Commission for the Relief of the National Freedman in 1863 and the American Freedmen's Aid Union in 1865. On March 3, 1865, the Bureau of Refugees, Freedmen, and Abandoned Lands (the Freedmen's Bureau) was established by the US Congress (Forbes 1998, 68); it was a federally funded group that provided critical support such as food, clothing, housing, and education. African American women participated in an array of these efforts, and they also formed their own organizations. As Ella Forbes reports in *African American Women during the Civil War*: "Free women used the networking and organizing skills they had gained in other activities [anti-slavery, social reform, educational reform, etc.] to provide assistance to their needy people. The ladies founded new organizations and expanded the missions of old ones to raise money and produce goods for medical supplies, schoolbooks, clothing and food for refugees. In true womanly fashion, they formed sewing circles, conducted fairs, gave bake sales, and wrote and sold personal narratives to provide material support" (Forbes 1998, 66).

One example of organizational leadership is Elizabeth Keckley, who is better known currently as the personal dressmaker for and friend and confidante of First Lady Mary Todd Lincoln. Keckley knew how to use her network and influence well, however. She helped to arrange a meeting between Sojourner Truth and President Lincoln and to facilitate the relocation of Maria Stewart (the first known African American political activist and writer) from Boston to Washington, DC (Forbes 1998, 68). Beyond using her political influence, however, Keckley was also a founder of the Contraband Relief Association in August 1862, the name of which was later changed to a much less negative title, the Ladies' Freedmen and Soldiers' Relief Association.

The Ladies' Freedmen and Soldiers' Relief Association was one of a long list of organizations in free African American communities across both the North and the South. Other organizations included the Colored Ladies' Relief Association and the Fugitive Aid Society of Boston, which combined to form a branch of Keckley's organization; the Union Relief Association in Washington, DC; the Union Relief Association of the Union Bethel African Methodist Episcopal Church in Washington, DC; the Colored Ladies Freedmen's Aid Society of Chicago; the Colored Ladies Freedmen and Soldiers Aid Society of Elmira, New York; the Colored Ladies' Sanitary Commission of Boston; the Freedmen's Aid Society of Worcester, Massachusetts. There were groups of women in cities across the South (in Memphis, Natchez, Richmond, Beaufort, and many others), and even a group in London, England, where Ellen Craft (who had escaped slavery in 1848) raised money to support freed African Americans; she joined the Ladies' Auxiliary of the British and Foreign Freedmen's Aid Society. Simply stated, while constraints on the possibilities and actions of African American women in the South were extreme, African American women who lived in the North and had less constraint in their lives saw both need and opportunity during the war and responded with action.

In contrast, consider also a view of African American women's work in the South. Within an environment infused by the extreme conditions and constraints of the institution of chattel slavery, African Americans inevitably lived precariously, whether they were free or in bondage. To be underscored, there were free African Americans in the South, not just in the North. While the state of North Carolina led the numbers with more than thirty thousand (Franklin 1995), free persons were also present in other southern states as well. When African Americans did have free status, they sometimes functioned under the protection of white allies, supporting themselves with their skills and labor. Consider, for example, the account of free women in Georgia as documented by Adele Logan Alexander in *Ambiguous Lives* (1991). Alexander's research, anchored in her own family history, established the existence of 365 registered free people of color in just eight counties in Middle Georgia.[13] This number is part of a larger story of the African American population of this state by 1850, as documented by Wilma King in *The Essence of Liberty: Free Black Women during the Slave Era*: 1,403 Black and 1,528 Mulatto, for a total of 2,931 free African Americans; 359,013 Black and 22,669 Mulatto, for a total of 381,682 enslaved African Americans (King 2006, 17). These numbers confirm that free African Americans constituted about 8 percent of the total number of African Americans in Georgia, while across the nation there was a total free and freeborn population of 434,495 (18).

In Alexander's account, she confirms that the women in her family lived as the spouses of affluent plantation owners, which was the case for some of the other free African American women in Middle Georgia as well. She also clarified the point that many of the other free families in the area lived in clusters, with the women working their farms and sometimes laboring as laundresses, seamstresses, spinners and weavers, and house servants. In either case, the more typical situation was that tens of thousands of African Americans (a total of 3,204,313) living in the South were not free (King 2006, 18). They were enslaved, had little or no mobility, and no authority to act with any social, political, or economic agency. They lived and worked at the will of the whites who held them in bondage within a society that devalued their existence as human beings and certainly did not acknowledge their rights of citizenship.

Before, during, and after the Civil War, regardless of status, African American women were always under threat. They were called upon to be inventive in fighting, as they were able, to take care of themselves and their families and to advocate for and with others for survival. Focusing on the wartime, however, as asserted by Emily West in *Enslaved Women in America: From Colonial Times to Emancipation* (2015): "The fight between Blue and Gray [North and South] was, for black women, often overshadowed by more immediate concerns about their everyday survival, protecting children, and staving off poverty, hunger, and ill health. But the war also increased women's gendered and racial oppression in the form of physical and sexual assaults by soldiers and by the economic hardships it caused" (West 2014, 81).

African American women had the lowest priority for any type of concern—after white soldiers, white men generally, white women, African American men, and then, at the end of the line, African American women. As confirmed by West (2014) and King (2006), during the war, their work responsibilities escalated, often exponentially. White men went off to war, which African American women actually welcomed in that it reduced their vulnerability—for a time at least—to sexual assault. These women were called upon both to take care of their regular tasks and also to take up the slack of the absent men. African American men were often required by slaveowners to follow them into war, with the result that African American women suffered the consequences. They were left with no help in taking care of the plantation households and families. On farms and plantations, they cooked, cleaned, polished, washed, tended the needs of white women, planted, hoed, weeded, plowed, lifted equipment, harvested crops, mended fences, and performed other backbreaking tasks. Increasingly, as well, physical abuses continued to exist by both white men and white women who retaliated against them. Abuses included their heightened vulnerability to being evicted from the plantations or having their cabins (i.e., their homes) demolished, and as King states: "When plantation families, who were becoming the refugees of war themselves, left African American women behind, the women had to contend with abuse by soldiers, both Confederate and Union, who perceived them to be sexually available" (2006, 176).

In other words, African American women suffered from the reduced economic capacity of their plantation families; from shortages of food, clothing, and housing; from overwork and from increasing vulnerabilities to illness. They remained persistently under siege and outrageously oppressed under increasingly debilitating conditions. Those who remained in rural areas on plantations had little capacity to engage, as northern African American women were doing, in robust sociopolitical activities in support of freedom or social justice. They were instead engaged in other types of robust activities, often working with each other to the extent possible, in support of their own survival and that of family and neighbors. What they gleaned from these experiences, however, is the knowledge of their ability to work hard and to accomplish tasks not typically deemed the work of women. Their awareness of this type of self-reliance and strength as women was indicated—earlier in the century, in 1851—in a speech by Sojourner Truth at the Women's Rights Convention in Akron, Ohio: *Ain't I a Woman.*

The women who left the plantations to find loved ones from whom they had been separated earlier or who followed their husbands and family members to the Union forces, often ended up in "contraband" camps (King 2006, 176–81). Conditions there were also challenging—with food shortages, overcrowding, disease (smallpox, yellow fever, cholera, dysentery, malnutrition), and sexual abuse, based particularly on the presumption that African American women were prostitutes and immoral. Despite the pervasiveness of the debilitating conditions, these women actually had more mobility, especially if the camps were in border areas (closer to the North and farther from the institution of slavery). They had more opportunities to work in jobs that were available to support the troops—as cooks, laundresses, domestic servants, nurses, and to some extent spies and soldiers. A basic conclusion to draw forward is that all of the women, regardless of circumstance—free or enslaved, in the North or the South—wanted to be part of a better world, with opportunities to care for themselves and their families in peace and prosperity. Although their individual circumstances might be complicated by multiple factors, they understood that the war was important and that it held great promise for helping to bring about a brighter day. In 1865, when the Union forces were victorious, African American women were jubilant, even as they realized that this victory did not automatically change their own lives.

A Note about Native American Women

Carolyn Ross Johnston, in *Cherokee Women in Crisis: Trail of Tears, Civil War, and Allotment, 1838–1907* (2003), confirms that

Native Americans of various groups were drawn into the Civil War by both the Union and the Confederacy. The reasons for their involvement were multilayered, including the historic political relationships of their nations to the United States in struggles to retain their own sovereignty, lands, and cultural identities; their operational practices, for example, the slaveholding practices of affluent members of the southern tribes; and their socioeconomic needs (for example, the scarcity of resources that resulted when treaties with the United States were not fulfilled). Within this context, Native American women were also affected by the Civil War and experienced it in a range of ways that were similar to their white women counterparts in the North, South, and West, depending on the geographical locations of the particular Native American communities.

Stating that the lives, circumstances, and achievements of Native American women during the Civil War are under-researched is quite an understatement. From a general perspective, however, Johnston's account of the experiences of Cherokee women offers an instructive example (2003). According to Johnston, for the Cherokee people, whether living in the South or in lands designated by treaty to be "Indian Territory," many husbands, sons, and brothers fighting in the war were lost, wounded, or disabled. Family properties were burned and destroyed, leaving many of the women homeless and living as refugees. They needed to fend for themselves and their families: "They had to expand their roles as wives and mothers to encompass what were considered male responsibilities in a Euro-American framework of values. Cherokee women had to raise crops; haul wood and supplies; care for the sick; bury the dead; spin, weave, and sew if they were to have any clothes; and endure the psychological terror of robberies, violence, and the destruction of their homes and property" (Johnston 2003, 104). Cherokee women, and other Native American women as well, found ways to endure and to survive during this era, with stories of their work and achievements yet to be documented and incorporated into the official narratives of the nation.

Agency

With the focus in this volume on African American women, an interrogation of agency—the means, methods, tools, and opportunities for action—necessarily shifts attention to the options that were available to this group in particular, as a group that is often presumed during this era to have little or no agency at all. The presumption of little or no agency, however, in the face of a broader view of what constitutes action under deep distress, is ungrounded given the realities of the women's actual lives and work. The task of recovering and reinscribing the ways and means of their agency, therefore, calls for a disruption of defaulted beliefs and expectations. Instructively, enhancing our capacity to see African American women as individuals and groups with the power to act can not be persuasively framed simply in the general terms of Euro-American expectations. Instead, the task calls for serious and direct interrogations of their status, conditions, and circumstances as members of a downtrodden race in a highly gendered and deeply entrenched slaveholding society. More importantly, the task also calls for serious and direct interrogations of the ways, means, and consequences of what they were actually doing and trying to do.

To be sure, the trauma of living in a slaveholding society, whether the women were living in Union territory or Confederate, provided this group with more stimuli than anyone would ever really need to spark their imaginations, their visions of possibility, and their dreams and desires for a brighter day for themselves and others like them. In a fundamental way, the women's sensibilities were vibrantly animated by the materiality of their existence. In contrast, however, to the expectations of despair under such circumstances and the presumptions of little or no agency, the women persistently demonstrated that they wanted to be free, that they wanted to live in a fair and just society with all rights of citizenship, that they wanted access to opportunities to take care of themselves and their families without fear and without oppression, and that they were willing to work hard and innovatively to see their dreams come true. It seems inevitable that their lives endowed their sensibilities about what the world was and was not for them and what they would prefer it to be instead.

Acknowledging that African American women had their own points of view about survival and prosperity despite the precarious conditions that surrounded them leaves open the expectation that they would develop other perspectives as well. For example, they might be more inspired to find and create opportunities to do whatever they could to support their sense of autonomy and to enable freedom, justice, equality, empowerment, and peace for themselves and their people. The question, then, for building knowledge and understanding of African American women's sense of agency within this context remains the question of what they found and created as tools and resources to do what they felt that they needed to do.

Available Means for African American Women's Action

On one hand, the materiality of African American women's lives was fertile ground for their formation of ethos and agency—that is, for the formation of their ways of thinking, being, and doing as human beings in the world. On the other hand, despite having various levels of drama in their lives capable of inspiring visions and desires, the complex challenges for actually exercising their inspirations were, of course, magnified by the gendered expectations of the nineteenth century and by the rampant systems of racial discrimination in the slaveholding culture in which they existed. Essentially, their capacity to engage in self-directed action was intricately entwined with barriers and constraints. If indeed African American women chose to act with sociopolitical awareness in their own interests and in the interest of their communities, rather than just in compliance with the expectations of others, their mandate was to do so strategically and innovatively.

Two examples for exercising their own agency in the South are instructive. Both women were free African Americans, who might be presumed to have more options than their enslaved sisters but who needed, nevertheless, to be inventive in using their resources strategically to live as they wished to live and get things done for their families. Consider the life of Aspasia Cruvellier Mirault, a free African American woman who lived in Savannah, Georgia, as chronicled by Janice L. Sumler-Edmond in *The Secret Trust of Aspasia Cruvellier Mirault: The Life and Trials of a Free Woman of Color in Antebellum Georgia* (2008). Mirault was born in Santo Domingo in 1800. When she was an infant, she immigrated to Savannah with her family—her mother, Hagar, and three siblings, Frances, Peter, and Justine. The family, like many emigrés from the French Caribbean during this time period, chose to leave the tribulations and turmoil of the Haitian Revolution (1791–1804) and migrate to what they hoped would be a more stable United States. In Savannah, the Cruvelliers joined a community of free people of color that, by 1810, numbered 578 and included a number of closely knit families from their home area of Santo Domingo (Sumler-Edmond 2008, 8).

Mirault's family established a tailoring shop, operated by her older brother Frances, where, as a young woman, she worked as a seamstress along with her sister Justine. The shop was likely destroyed by a devastating fire in Savannah in 1820. However, with an entrepreneurial spirit, Mirault and her sister saw opportunity and started a baking business. By the mid1820s, Mirault had married Samuel Mirault, another free African American, and she had become the mother of two children, Louisa and Letitia. In 1831 her husband died, intensifying her responsibility to provide for her children. By this point Mirault, who had become an accomplished pastry chef and had opened her own bakery, worked hard to assure her family's survival. Over the next decade, she built a successful bake shop, a confectionary that specialized in ice cream products. During this time period Mirault formed a liaison with John Oliver, who was married to another free African American woman, Rosella. She gave birth to three more children, Joseph, Robert, and James (who died), and her liaison with Oliver continued until he died in 1835. As with the death of Samuel Mirault her responsibilities to assure the survival of her enlarged family continued, as did her success in building her family's economic security.

In 1842, in support of her desire to secure a financial legacy for her children, Mirault entered into a "secret" trust with a white carpenter, originally from Massachusetts, named George Cally. Establishing a trust as a mechanism for building wealth and status was not unusual. By Georgia law, free African Americans needed a white guardian or agent in order to transact legal and economic matters and because of an 1818 Georgia law that free African Americans could not purchase land in Savannah. Mirault, however, wanted land for a better home for her children and her business. She circumvented the law, thereby, and arranged for Cally to purchase land on her behalf, which he would manage in trust for her family. Sadly, over the decades this decision did not have the desired result for the future generations of her family. During her lifetime, however, this purchase leveraged her family's success. By the 1840s Mirault was a landowner with a sizable home, an entrepreneur with a successful business, a slaveowner (which was not unusual among more affluent free African Americans), and an active member of the Catholic Church. Thus, she exhibited important metrics for high socioeconomic status during her day, even though other elements of her personal life—namely, being Black and female—defied traditional boundaries.

Mirault died in 1857, before the Civil War, but she left a substantial legacy for her four children, who carried on her businesses and continued their active engagement with the African American communities in Savannah until the Civil War. During the war, her son Robert Oliver volunteered as a musician in the Confederate army. He survived the war and returned to Savannah to continue working as a brick mason.[14] In the decades following the Civil War, Cally betrayed the family and their landownership. He claimed the family's land as his own and sold it. Despite their intense efforts to regain their legal rights, the Mirault family lost their case in the Georgia Supreme Court. The success of the family members themselves continued, however. They were a civic-minded family who engaged energetically in the activities of their church and various community organizations. They were able to educate their children and send them to college when the opportunity to do so became available.

In other words, Mirault was "determined to fashion her own destiny" (Sumler-Edmond 2008, 2). She leveraged the means that were available to her and set a foundation for success, even though it was complicated ultimately by racial discrimination. Despite these complications, her dreams for her family did come true. She was successful in providing a good launch point for the future generations. The resources she accumulated helped them to survive and prosper through the Civil War and beyond, and her legacies helped to ground them as people who understood their rights and fought valiantly for them, though unsuccessfully, in the legal courts of Georgia.

The second example is Mariah Lilly Hunt (1833–1895). She was a free African American woman who was born and lived in Hancock County, Georgia. She grew up in comfort in the plantation home of Nathan Sayre with her mother, Susan (also a free woman of color), who lived surreptitiously as Sayre's spouse. Hunt was educated—able to read, write, and play the piano, and well versed in social graces. As a young woman, like her mother, she formed a long-lasting, though ambiguous, spousal relationship with Henry Alexander Hunt, the youngest son of another affluent white plantation family and lived for many decades as his spouse.

The African American Hunts were part of the network of 365 African Americans officially registered as free in Middle Georgia (Alexander 1991). During the Civil War Hunt's white spouse, Henry, enlisted in the Confederate army, and she and her mother contributed blankets and rugs to the Confederacy's military needs.

After the war Hunt concentrated on preparing all of her eight children for their new horizons, successfully educating all of them, including her daughter Adella. Born during the Civil War, Adella was a high achiever. She graduated from the normal school at Atlanta University (established as the first university in Georgia for African Americans and also the first institution of higher education in the City of Atlanta). She went on to a distinguished career as educator, advocate for women's education and woman's suffrage, writer, and leader in the Black Clubwomen's Movement.[15] Such stories of free African American women in the South are repeated in other geographical locations as well. Their ethos and agency were significantly linked to their own survival and prosperity, to the survival and prosperity of their families, and to the work they were determined to perform in support of sustaining their communities.

For African American women living in border states (i.e., closer than their southern counterparts to free territories), there were more opportunities to be mobile and visible in public space. In effect, their greater mobility meant that these women had more available mechanisms for self-determination and self-direction. Consider, as examples, the work of Mary Elizabeth Bowser and Mary Louveste, both of whom functioned during the war with substantial agency as Union spies. In similar manner, for women living in the North (e.g., the renowned writer Frances Ellen Watkins Harper in Philadelphia and the highly regarded community activist Josephine St. Pierre Ruffin in Boston), not only were there more tools for agency and self-direction, there was also company, groups of other African Americans who, by the Civil War, had already built a rich history of activism and leadership.

Many northern women who had access to activist groups engaged enthusiastically in several sorts of activities that confirmed their commitment, not just to work and service, but to a serious sociopolitical agenda. Before the war, the agenda included, for example, abolitionist activities as well as activities to secure educational opportunities for their children. During the Civil War, their collective action involved providing much needed supplies to African American soldiers and medical care for the sick and wounded as well. Both during and after the war, their agenda continued to be robust, providing much needed resources to African American refugees from the South, even as they continued to fight against ever present racial discrimination and injustice within their northern communities.

In working over the decades to improve their horizons, women across all of these geographical locations were both consciously aware of their own needs for personal autonomy and specifically attuned to the pressing needs of their communities. The southern women were clear about the critical nature of their constraints and limitations. Likewise, the women in border states and northern states were clear that they too faced social, political, and economic barriers, but these latter groups were also painfully aware that their sisters in the Deep South functioned under far more extreme conditions. Thus, with the advent of the Civil War, African American women saw this dramatic event as a particularly opportune moment for them to do whatever they could to leverage transformative change.

A Context for Women's Awareness

In both the Union and the Confederacy, military leaders had expected fighting the Civil War to be short-lived. They were wrong. The war raged on for four years, with devastating effects that became increasingly evident year after year. In both the North and the South, scenes of war were consistently in view. Most dramatically, people were constantly on the move. There was a constant flow of huge numbers of injured and dead. With improvements in weaponry, hospitals were filled with the wounded—and with improvements in embalming, which made the return of some of the fallen more possible, trains were filled with the dead. In addition to plantation families being pushed out of their homes and dislocated, African Americans were also migrating, following behind the Union army, escaping the horrors of the war at home, looking for family members who had been previously sold away.

Geographically, an important reminder, though, is that most of the theaters of war were in the South. Many people across the Confederacy who were not warriors were experiencing the conflict, up close and personal, but other civilians who were not as geographically close to the fighting were constantly aware as well. There were letters from people in conflict zones offering insights into and observations of what was happening. These communications brought the experiences of war home even when the fighting was farther away. In multiple ways, therefore, a combination of factors filled the environment with awareness and provided visceral evidence for overwhelming numbers of the population, including African Americans, that the divided nation was at war and that the war was devastating.

In the actual theaters of war, homes were destroyed not only in battle but also by confiscation, and not only for white Americans who lived on plantations but for African Americans as well. An interesting example of this point was the home and lands of Elizabeth Proctor Thomas. As documented by the National Park Service, the American Battlefield Trust, and the *Afro American* newspaper, Thomas was a freeborn African American woman whose family had settled before the war in a community of free African Americans known then as Vinegar Hill in northwest Washington, DC. Her family's farm (eighty-eight acres) was located at the highest elevation point near the Seventh Street Turnpike (now Georgia Avenue). This road was a major entryway into the capital city and constituted a prime location for its defense. In September 1861, Union forces took possession of this family's land, despite Thomas's protests. They destroyed her two-story home, barn, orchard, and garden, and built a fort, first named Fort Massachusetts and later renamed Fort Stevens in honor of General Isaac I. Stevens (a Washington politician and a career US army officer)—as she watched in tears with her baby in arms. During the war Thomas lived nearby on her family's remaining land and worked for the fort, cooking, cleaning, doing laundry, and helping with the ammunition. She kept her own shotgun by her side at the ready to participate actively in the defense of the president, who was a frequent visitor to the fort, and in defense of her country, if necessary.[16]

The message underlying all these accounts is that the Civil War was devastating for everyone, and everyone, including African American women, needed to find ways to use all their talents and resources to sustain themselves. The complex realities of daily life under the conditions of war provided leverage for action. With the separation of men from families, women needed to step up to fill new roles. With specific focus on the South, for example, southern white women and the African American women whom they enslaved were called upon to carry on the management of farms and plantations (as chronicled in the memoirs and autobiographies cited in the appendix). Similarly, urban southern white women and any women and men whom they enslaved were called upon to step up to run businesses of various kinds. Women's roles included teaching and home health care, and in some instances, the white women were also able to perform other types of work, as well, such as being writers and journalists. An example of a northern white woman using her expertise as a writer during the Civil War era was

Louisa May Alcott. An example of a southern white woman was Mary Clarke, a poet and essay writer from North Carolina, who was successful before, during, and after the war.[17]

Among African American women from the North, a distinctive example of journalistic work was Mary Shadd Cary. She was a freeborn African American woman who grew up in Pennsylvania, but with the passing of the 1850 Fugitive Slave Law, she migrated to Canada. Before the war she was successful in founding and operating her own newspaper in Ontario, but when the war started she returned home to engage directly in support of the Union cause. In the decades after the war Cary lived in Washington, DC, and went on to accrue a distinctive list of accomplishments.

In contrast to these types of actions amid war, the more general story for southern women was often very different. The southern home front suffered a substantial degree of scarcity. Cities became crowded with growing populations and suffered staggering shortages. As documented in *A Changing Wind: Commerce and Conflict in Civil War Atlanta* by Wendy Hamand Venet, many women in the South (including African American women) were not able to stay at home but often needed to flee their homes in the face of battle. They became refugees, migrating to cities across the South in search of safety and opportunities for work. Issues were manifold. Union blockades and the destruction of other transportation systems such as bridges and railroads significantly disrupted the flow of supplies. Both armies consumed remarkable amounts of food, clothing, and other resources, including medical supplies, which meant that prices for food, clothing, and housing were very high. In addition, with the escalating density of urban populations, many diseases such as smallpox, pneumonia, dysentery, scarlet fever, and typhoid fever were raging. Under these conditions life was difficult for women. Jobs were scarce. White women sometimes found work as theatrical performers, servants in households, workers in munitions factories, spinners and weavers who made cloth for clothing, and seamstresses (paid and volunteer) who made uniforms and knitted socks for the military, and more.

Before the war, across the United States women's horizons, with specific emphasis on white women's opportunities for autonomy, were defined by male-centered and male-controlled power dynamics and the social norms and practices that were institutionalized during this era to support these dynamics. This ideological framework dictated that women were expected to function primarily within the domestic sphere of home and family rather than in public or institutional arenas. The war disrupted these expectations. Necessity became the mother of invention, with incentives for action for women across sociocultural identities being informed typically by the changing and deteriorating circumstances of a society at war. By necessity, white women, typically without regular male oversight, were called upon to take advantage of whatever opportunities were available to survive. Numbers of them found inventive ways to do what they believed needed to be done in broader spheres of work than they had ever experienced before.

In contrast, the case for African American women was different, not in kind but often in intensity. Their positioning (whether enslaved, freed, or freeborn) was exacerbated by the laws, policies, and practices of a slaveholding nation that considered people of African descent to be chattel and inferior. In rather dramatic terms, their opportunities for work were complicated not just by their gender and class under the conditions of war but also by their race. This distinction in their operational landscape had been set in motion well before the Civil War by their sociopolitical status, by systemic limitations on their choices for work (or the lack thereof), by their geographical locations, and by the hierarchies of eligibility among those in need, with African American women occupying the lowest realms of regard. Without a doubt, African American women were viscerally aware of these constraints in their environments. However, with the coming of war, their lives within this configuration of complexities shifted, with constraints still present but re-forming to function not simply to limit their possibilities for agency and action but to serve as a cauldron in which the women were called upon to sharpen their focus and direct their energies more intentionally toward both survival and their never-ending quest for freedom, equality, social justice, empowerment, and human rights. Over subsequent decades, this quest continued to evolve—in freedom—as African American women were able to develop a coherent sociopolitical agenda by the end of the century.

Purpose

A cautionary tale in this analysis is the need to keep a weather eye on the ecosystem of the war as a complex occasion for identity formation for the nation itself, and not just a moment of hope and great expectations for African Americans. Imperatives for decision-making and action were intricately entwined, not simple. Certainly, African Americans saw the war as an occasion to hope for a better world and to fight for freedom and full citizenship under the laws of the land, but core questions are: What was really at stake for the nation and all of its stakeholders? Who were the stakeholders? What sort of pathways forward were being negotiated in war? Given this conceptual framing, the cautionary tale is the need to think carefully and closely about the deeply seated ideological concerns at the very heart of this iconic conflict. Questions include: What is "the nation"—by identity and by ethos? What are its values and principles? How will it live up to those values and principles? How should governance work? Who has rights, entitlements, and authorities? How should cultural beliefs, values, rights, principles, and practices be defined and deployed? How should "opportunity" be envisioned and for whom? How should the nation function with regard to a sometimes competing array of social, political, economic, and cultural priorities? How will peace and prosperity function in a nation defined by both its wide ranging diversity and its democratic values?

From our contemporary perspective, such points of inquiry help us to understand more robustly the multiple pathways that ultimately brought the regions—the North and the South—to war and that continue even in the twenty-first century to be a source of discord and conflict. Even before the nineteenth century and the broad array of stakeholders emerging in the new nation, citizens from all sectors were entwined within this intricately cast web of long-standing values, beliefs, and concerns. This complicated construct of interests became a prime driver of passions and loyalties and, ultimately, instrumental in fashioning and exercising a sense of nationhood and national identity—for both the Union and the Confederacy.[18]

In broad scope, a continuum of differences during this era included regional economic priorities (in the North, South, West, and Midwest); a range of policies and practices for defining "property," controlling economic participation and growth, and building wealth and financial power. It included differences in political perspectives linked at that time to the Republican Party as the political party of the North and the Democratic Party as the political party of the South. Existing also were differences between rural development with its agricultural base and urban development with its manufacturing base; the self-determination of state and regional independence versus the strengthening of national authority and federal accountabilities; geographical expansion and the forming of new states and territories as either slaveholding or non-slaveholding, anchored by questions regarding whether the nation would operate based on one economic model or the other.

As 1860 dawned, economic, social, political, and cultural preferences, though certainly intricate and dynamic, clustered regionally. In the Northeast, economic growth was increasingly linked to urban development and manufacturing with supply chains connected to the raw materials of the South. The economy of the South, where cotton was king, was heavily rural, agricultural, and dependent on the involuntary labor of slaves, with economic prosperity linked to manufacturing assets that were in the North and in Europe (for example, with Great Britain as a manufacturing center). In the Midwest, with its steady increases in European migration, economic systems were based increasingly on a combination of family farms, transportation hubs, and commerce. Similar to the Northeast, the Midwest was linked also to the development of urban industries. Territories in the Far West held the economic bargaining power of their large deposits of gold, silver, and other precious metals, offering opportunities for building wealth through natural resources. This region's transportation pathways to the Far East offered also excellent potential for a more global reach and quite specific opportunities to establish a bold sense of coherence and security for the nation.

At upper echelons of national identity and authority, the most comprehensive mandates for power and control were imperial, with emphasis on forwarding a sense of "manifest destiny." By this priority, the United States could be positioned as the rightful and righteous world leader in moving the future of civilization westward. Advocates of this view perceived that the nation held in its hands signal opportunities for a coherence of power—geographically, economically, and politically, in fulfillment of the mandate to dominate all within its scope and to occupy North America totally from sea to shining sea. A few decades after the Civil War the patriotic hymn "America, the Beautiful," written by Katherine Lee Bates after an inspiring cross-country trip in 1893 celebrated this nationalistic view.

In the early decades of the nineteenth century, however, there was a significant wrinkle in this plan. A considerable amount of the interior regions of North America was actually already occupied by France, Spain, and most especially, by Native Americans who had huge stakes in how the various national annexation projects (slaveholding and not) were impacting their lands and their own opportunities for sovereignty and self-determination. All of these factors affected the making and shaping of national identity and informed various processes related to the dividing of the nation by war, and ultimately to its remaking as well.

One Nation or Two

Because of the limitations of space, this explanation of the ideological frameworks for the Union and the Confederacy is necessarily very general and not intended to be comprehensive. My intention instead is to suggest mainly a basic pattern for interrogating the war as a decision-making moment for both nations. Going to war for both the Union and Confederacy was a moment for nation building, for clarifying the existing governance model (the Union) or establishing the Confederacy as a new nation. The differences in conceptual framework marked a difference going forward in national identity, and in the ways of being and doing as a governmental entity.

What stands out—for both the Union and the Confederacy, in terms of the conceptual design for each nation—is that both nations connect in mirror image of each other, as illustrated by a textual analysis of their founding documents. Consider the Declaration of Independence of the American Colonies from Great Britain as the springboard for comparison. The idea is that each nation used the same basic framework to shape its imperatives for identity as an "independent" state. The Declaration states:

> When in the Course of human events, it becomes necessary for one people to dissolve the political bands which have connected them with another, and to assume among the powers of the earth, the separate and equal station to which the Laws of Nature and of Nature's God entitle them, a decent respect to the opinions of mankind requires that they should declare the causes which impel them to the separation. . . . We, therefore, the Representatives of the United States of America, in General Congress, Assembled,

> appealing to the Supreme Judge of the world for the rectitude of our intentions, do, in the Name, and by Authority of the good People of these Colonies, solemnly publish and declare, That these United Colonies are, and of Right ought to be Free and Independent States . . . and that as Free and Independent States, they have full Power to levy War, conclude Peace, contract Alliances, establish Commerce, and to do all other Acts and Things which Independent States may of right do. And for the support of this Declaration, with a firm reliance on the protection of divine Providence, we mutually pledge to each other our Lives, our Fortunes and our sacred Honor.

Similarly, in declaring the right to self-determination for the former American Colonies, the preamble of the US Constitution states: "We the People of the United States, in Order to form a more perfect Union, establish Justice, insure domestic Tranquility, provide for the common defence, promote the general Welfare, and secure the Blessings of Liberty to ourselves and our Posterity, do ordain and establish this Constitution for the United States of America."

There is no specific explanation of who "We the people of the United States" are and who they are not. In comparison, the preamble for the Constitution of the Confederate States of America states: "We, the people of the Confederate States, each State acting in its sovereign and independent character, in order to form a permanent federal government, establish justice, insure domestic tranquility, and secure the blessings of liberty to ourselves and our posterity invoking the favor and guidance of Almighty God do ordain and establish this Constitution for the Confederate States of America." In this case as well, there is no specific explanation of who "We, the people of the Confederate States" are and who they are not.

Based on a textual analysis of the corpus of the three founding documents—the Declaration of Independence, the Constitution of the United States, and the Constitution of the Confederate States—we can see that structurally the documents cluster around some basic terms such as state/states, confederate, constitution, president, citizen (see figure 1.1). What stands out are the similarities rather than the differences. There are echoes from one document to the other, illustrating a common conceptual frame for their em-

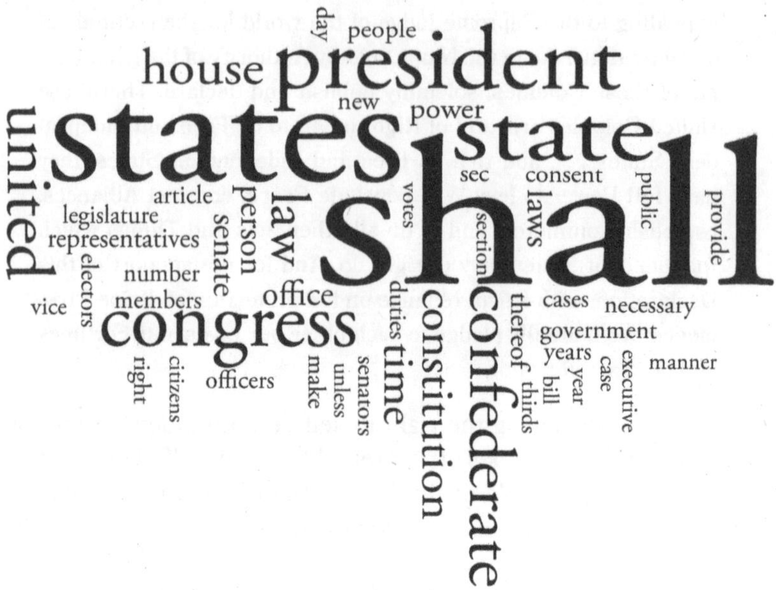

Figure 1.1: The shared pattern of frequent terms for three governance documents: Declaration of Independence, the Constitution of the United States, and the Constitution of the Confederate States.

bedded presumptions about independence, autonomy, and power, and with regard to the policy and governance statements about managing participation in the nations. From this type of textual analysis, we can draw a twofold conclusion. If the constitutions were overlaid with each other, the similarities would be striking, and metaphorically, the differences between the documents could be interpreted, not so much as differences in *song* but differences in *ideological verse*.

These comparisons are well demonstrated by the language related to slavery that is used by both the Union and the Confederacy. Consider the crafting of the US Constitution. When it was ratified on June 21, 1788, and became effective on March 4, 1789, the new nation was indeed a slaveholding nation. Despite the fact that several states had chosen to abolish slavery before the First Constitutional Convention in 1787 (among them, Vermont, New Hampshire, Rhode Island, Massachusetts, Connecticut), national leaders needed to negotiate the ideological and operational differences between the slaveholding areas and the non-slaveholding areas, and to manage, thereby, a consensus in the crafting of this document in order to strike a specifically mediated rhetorical stance (see table 1.1). This stance was a use of language in the US Constitution that did not mention the words *slave* or *slavery*, while still encoding what in practice were fugitive slave laws (see, for example, Article 4, Section 2, Clause 3). Their rhetorical framing included also a statement that extended any consideration of abolishing slavery to 1808 (see, for example, a reference to this date in Article V).

The crafters of this document wrote about "citizens" and "citizenship" as unspecified categories. However, they drew forward another term, "person," to cover a spectrum of personal identities, including African Americans. They used this term as an unmodified nominal form to indicate a general category, presumably for all whites regardless of race and ethnicity. They also used it as a noun with modification: adding "free Persons," which would have included sizable numbers of free African Americans who lived both in the North and the South; and "other Persons," which, by default, referred to enslaved African Americans. With regard to Native Americans, the document positioned this constituency as unconnected and separate from the nation.

Within this rhetorical framework, the positioning of African Americans as "free Persons," "other Persons," and also "persons in service," functioned in juxtaposition to the unmodified "Persons," which served as the default term for "white persons." The rhetorical effect is that African Americans, free or enslaved, were not categorized as "property," even though they were also not included in the category "citizen," which was an unspecified term. To reemphasize the point, the US Constitution, as a governance document, did not reference "slavery" directly. Instead, the crafters used the term "Persons" to negotiate these contentious sociopolitical relationships and the value constructs that surrounded them—that is, the national bedrock values of "freedom," "justice," and "equality for all" that were articulated in the two founding documents. Thus, the crafters of the US Constitution sidestepped the misalignments of slavery with national values and sidestepped as well the ideological differences between the territories with slaves and the territories without them, with an acknowledgment in this analysis that, when the Constitution was ratified, the establishment of the status of territories without slaves had only been recently accomplished.

Table 1.1. Constitutional Language Related to the Existence of Slaves and Slavery: Union States of America and Confederate States of America

The Constitution of the United States of America	**The Constitution of the Confederate States of America**
Article I, Section 2	Article I, Section 2
Clause 2 **No Person** shall be a Representative who shall not have attained to the Age of twenty five Years, and been seven Years a Citizen of the United States, and who shall not, when elected, be an inhabitant of that State in which he shall be chosen.	
Clause 3 Representatives and direct Taxes shall be apportioned among the several States which may be included within this Union, according to their respective Numbers, which shall be determined by adding to the whole Number of **free Persons,** including **those bound to Service for a Term of Years**, and excluding **Indians** not taxed, **three fifths of all other Persons.**	Clause 3 Representatives and direct taxes shall be apportioned among the several States, which may be included within this Confederacy, according to their respective numbers, which shall be determined by adding to the whole number of free persons, including those bound to service for a term of years, and excluding Indians not taxed, **three-fifths of all slaves** . . .
Article I, Section 3, Clause 3	
No Person shall be a Senator who shall not have attained to the Age of thirty Years, and been nine Years a Citizen of the United States, and who shall not, when elected, be an inhabitant of that State for which he shall be chosen.	
Clause 6 The Senate shall have the sole Poer to try all Impeachments. When sitting for that Purpose, they shall be on Oath or Affirmation. When the President of the United States is tried, the Chief Justice shall preside: And **no person** shall be convicted without the Concurrence of two thirds of the Members present.	

Article I, Section 6	
Clause 2 No Senator or Representative shall, during the Time for which he was elected, be appointed to any civil Office under the Authority of the United States, which shall have been created, or the Emoluments whereof shall have been increased during such time; and **no Person** holding any Office under the United States, shall be a Member of either House during his Continuance in Office.	
Article I, Section 7	
Clause 2 Every Bill which shall have passed the House of Representatives and the Senate, shall, before it become a Law, be presented to the President of the United States . . . But in all such Cases the Votes of both Houses shall be determined by yeas and Nays, and the Names of the **Persons** voting for and against the Bill shall be entered on the Journal of each House respectively . . .	
Article I, Section 9	**Article I, Section 9**
Clause 1 The Migration or Importation of such **Persons as any of the States** now existing shall think proper to admit, **shall not be prohibited by the Congress prior to the Year one thousand eight hundred and eight**, but a Tax or duty may be imposed on such importation, not exceeding ten dollars for each **Person**.	Clause 1 The importation of **negroes** of the **African race** from any foreign country other than the **slaveholding States or Territories** of the United States of America, is hereby forbidden; and Congress is required to pass such laws as shall effectually prevent the same.
	Clause 2 Congress shall also have power to prohibit the introduction of **slaves** from any State not a member of, or Territory not belonging to, this Confederacy.
Clause 4 No Capitation, or other direct, Tax shall be laid, unless in Proportion to the Census or enumeration herein before directed to be taken.	Clause 4 No bill of attainder, ex post facto law, or law denying or impairing **the right of property in negro slaves** shall be passed.

[See Article I, Section 2, Clause 3 For an indication of how **"three-fifths of all other Persons**—or the enslaved persons—will be factored into representation and, in this case, taxation.]	
Clause 8 No Title of Nobility shall be granted by the United States: And **no Person** holding any Office of Profit or Trust under them, shall, without the Consent of the Congress, accept of any present, Emolument, Office, or Title, of any kind whatever from any King, Prince, or foreign State.	
Article II, Section 1	
Clause 2 Each State shall appoint . . . a Number of Electors . . . but no Senator or Representative, or **Person** holding an Office of Trust . . . Clause 3 The Electors shall meet in their respective States, and vote by Ballot for two **Persons**, of whom one at least shall not be an inhabitant of the same State with themselves . . . The President of the Senate shall, in the Presence of the Senate and House of Representatives, open all the Certificates, and the Votes shll then be counted. The **Person** having the great Number of Votes shall be the President . . . and if no **Person** have a Majority, then . . . after the Choice of the President, the **Person** having the greatest Number of Votes of the Electors shall be the Vice President.	
Clause 5 **No Person** except a natural born Citizen, or a Citizen of the United States, at the time of the Adoption of this Constitution, shall be eligible to the Office of President . . .	

Article III, Section 3	
Clause 1 Treason against the United States, shall consist . . . **No Person** shall be convicted of Treason unless on the Testimony of two Witnesses . . .	
Article IV, Section 2	
Clause 2 **A Person** charged in any State with Treason, Felony, or other Crime, who shall flee from Justice, and be found in another State, shall on Demand of the executive Authority of the State from which he fled, be delivered up, to be removed to the State having Jurisdiction of the Crime. [Note that running away as a slave, essentially absconding with a slaveowner's property,'was a crime.]	
Clause 3 **No Person held to Service or Labour** in one State, under the Laws thereof, escaping into another, shall, in Consequency of any Law or Regulation therein, be discharged from such Service or Labour, but shall be delibered up on Claim of the Party to whom such Service or Labour may be due. [An articulation of a "fugitive slave law"]	
Article IV, Section.2	Article 1V, Section.2
	Clause 1 The citizens of each State shall be entitled to all the privileges and immunities of citizens in the several States; and shall have the right of transit and sojourn in any State of this Confederacy, with **their slaves and other property**, and **the right of property in said slaves** shall not be thereby impaired.

Clause 3 No **Person** held to Service or Labour in one State, under the Laws thereof, escaping into another, shall, in Consequence of any Law or Regulation therein, be discharged from such Service or Labour, but shall be delivered up on Claim of the Party to whom such Service or Labour may be due.	Clause 3 No **slave** or other person held to service or labor in any State or Territory of the Confederate States, under the laws thereof, escaping or lawfully carried into another, shall in consequence of any law or regulation therein, be discharged from such service or labor; but shall be delivered up on claim of the party to whom such slave belongs, or to whom such service or labor may be due.
Article V	Article V
. . . no **Amendment which may be made prior to the Year One thousand eight hundred and eight** shall in any Manner affect the first and fourth Clauses of the Ninth Section of the first Article; and that no State, without its Consent, shall be deprived of its equal Suffrage in the Senate. [Note that the year 1808 was agreed on as the date before which there would be no consideration of abolishing slavery.]	. . . **amendments to the Constitution** . . . But no State shall, without its consent, be deprived of its equal representation in the Senate.
	Article IV, Section.3
	Clause 3 The Confederate States may acquire new territory; and Congress shall have power to legislate and provide governments for the inhabitants of all territory belonging to the Confederate States, lying without the limits of the several States; and may permit them, at such times, and in such manner as it may by law provide, to form States to be admitted into the Confederacy. In all such territory **the institution of negro slavery**, as it now exists in the Confederate States, shall be recognized and protected by Congress and by the Territorial government; and the inhabitants of the several Confederate States and Territories shall have the right to take to such Territory any **slaves lawfully held** by them in any of the States or Territories of the Confederate States.

Note: The bolding of terms is mine.

In contrast, the Constitution of the Confederate States of America, created on March 11, 1861, and ratified on March 29, 1861, used explicit language. At six points in the CSA Constitution, the drafters of the document put rhetorical stakes in the ground for actually institutionalizing slavery within their nation. They referred directly to "slaveholding states or territories." They stated explicitly "the importation of Negroes of the African race," using language typically associated with the importation of "goods" rather than using terms associated with the migration of people. They proclaimed "the right of property in negro slaves," and they proclaimed the authority of their Congress to establish new states and to recognize and protect "the institution of negro slavery" in such areas, in keeping with the operations of slavery in the existing Confederate States (compare examples of the language differences in table 1.1).[19] The contrasts between the two constitutions are basic. Both articulate similar presumptions about "independence" and "self-determination," and they both present similar frameworks for governance policies and practices. However, in the CSA document, the language is forthright in support of a national identity as a "slaveholding" nation, and forthright, as well, with regard to the authority and power of the owners of "negro property" (i.e., the slaveholders) and the rights of this group to control and protect their property. My point in offering these details is that the CSA Constitution defined African Americans explicitly as chattel—that is, as property. With this specificity, the CSA Constitution cemented the identity, entitlements, and authority of the southern power elites, and it secured thereby their slave-based economic system and their wealth, as well as their social order and their independence from accountability to others (in this case, any sense of accountability to the non-slaveholding states of the United States), all accomplished in the language of the document with "slavery" and "negro slaves" serving as operational levers.

In other words, both the Union and the Confederacy staked their claims to national identity, agency, and authority within a framing of independence and self-determination. While not forthright in its phrasing, the US Constitution established conceptual room for the USA to see itself as a nation with a commitment to freedom, justice, and equality—for all, and without a direct identity as a slaveholding nation—even though it indeed was a slaveholding nation. Far more explicit in its phrasing, the Confederate Constitution resolved the ambiguity. The drafters of this document declared the Confederacy to be, without question, a slaveholding nation, with the CSA Constitution serving as the springboard for secession from the Union and providing a clear indication that this group of states was willing no longer to be positioned otherwise. They defined and normalized the CSA's identity as a slaveholding nation. For seventy-three years, from 1788 to 1861, these two ideological desires had existed under one flag. In 1861 the newly formed Confederate States of America seceded, planting its own flag. The United States of America declared this act to be an act of war. The two nations fought, and African American women were called upon to figure out how to survive and how to leverage the opportunity of war to forward their quest for freedom and autonomy.

Rationales for War

As confirmed by the proclamations of the abolitionist movement, slavery was recognized as a heinous practice, an ethically questionable way of life, and an important reason for the nation to engage in war to protect its bedrock democratic values. The story of slavery as a long-standing societal institution, however, is a complicated one. In clarifying, therefore, the actual rationales of the Civil War within the nineteenth century as a complex ecosystem is not simple. A key example is that being pro-Union did not automatically mean being antislavery. To repeat, rationales for war were complex, with various factors functioning more at a convergence of interests and concerns. The waging of war did not pivot in this regard solely on humanitarian values or human rights—that is, on a belief or nonbelief in the normalcy of slavery—or on a critical questioning of the subjugation, oppression, and total domination of people of African descent by people of European descent. There were, instead, many economic and political intricacies and convolutions that informed the decision-making processes.

To use President Lincoln's image, "dividing the house" into the United States and the Confederate States was intricately intertwined with pivotal questions that needed to be addressed with purpose and intention as "national" action: What is the nation? What should the nation be, and which region gets to decide? What are the economic bases for prosperity? Should the nation's economy be anchored by rural or urban infrastructures and lifestyles? What is a workable balance between local and federal authority? And, indeed, what is the place in North America for the supremacy of "whiteness"? Amid the values espoused by the Declaration of Independence (truth, freedom, justice, equality, the pursuit of happiness—for all), can or should it be acceptable as policy and practice to normalize the notion of "owning human property" or to have an economic system anchored in involuntary unpaid labor? What might cause the nation to divide into parts and go to war with each other? Such negotiations raged in the nineteenth century—and continue to do so into the twenty-first century—as the nation and all of its citizens continue to ask: Who are we or should we be as a nation? What will we fight for and why will we fight? What do we gain by the model of governance that we embrace? What do we lose?

Implications

Through this pentadic approach in considering the scene, act, agent, agency, and purpose of the Civil War, we generate multilayered views of various data about the nineteenth century and about the Civil War within this time frame as an iconic national moment. As these data converge to create a more fully rendered view, it becomes easier to see the ways in which this century mattered greatly for African American women. This type of multidimensional analysis helps us to understand the fullness of this landscape as a vital and vibrant ecosystem, embedded quite certainly with ideological, sociohistorical, and ethical values and encrusted as well with a configuration of economic, political, and cultural imperatives. African American women—whether free, freed, or enslaved—lived within this ecosystem. Ultimately, then, a core objective in this analysis is to understand more fully the nature of this context. It was a dynamic kairotic space in which African American women's sociopolitical activities emerged, gained greater definition, and built a clearer momentum for strategic action. By the end of the century, these women had propelled themselves forward to another iconic moment where they created a coherent sociopolitical agenda and launched transformative legacies for leadership and action—as women in freedom.

Chapter 2

Negotiating Ways Forward

For both the Union and the Confederacy, the war was devastating, such that the arguments for sustaining a commitment for the war effort ebbed and flowed across a range of rationales. Over time, economic imperatives and political imperatives as logical proofs waned as means of persuasion for sustaining commitments of the people to fight. The question was whether these rationales were enough of a reason to put so many lives on the line. Rising more compellingly and inspirationally were ethical and pathetic proofs. For example, ethical imperatives in the Union were anchored in commonplace arguments that positioned rationales for war to be against slavery as cruel, immoral, and inhumane, and to be for freedom and justice for all as the bedrock values of the nation. The social imperatives in the Confederacy were anchored in commonplace arguments for a way of life and a social order. For the Confederacy, war was necessary to preserve the political power of the elite and to preserve the social order of a southern aristocracy in a system whose success required involuntary labor—without the pressures of abolitionism. The way forward, from this perspective, was as a slaveholding nation with authority vested in the rights to state control and with the hierarchies of rural and agricultural system intact—without accountability for the institution of slavery in making the approach work. With social imperatives, appeals to pathos, to emotions, ran high.

Ultimately, ethical and pathetic proofs in both regions "won" the day, with slavery functioning for both nations, Union and Confederacy, as a code by which the definition and purpose of "nation" was determined. Slavery functioned for both regions as a symbolic operational lever, encoding variously the conceptual designs for each nation and setting the parameters by which national practices within the designated system of law and policy would function. From the perspective of the Confederacy, the ways and means of nation were secured and enacted with the institutionalized practice of slavery normalized and positioned as a positive factor. In other words, in this system, slavery was part and parcel of economic and sociopolitical hierarchies. The inhumanity of human beings acting viciously against other human beings did not leverage decision-making. Within the social order Africans were deemed to be chattel, nonhuman, inferior, undeserving, and inconsequential. In contrast, from the perspective of the Union, the ways and means of nation were secured and enacted by principles (freedom, justice, equality) that presumed people of African descent to be human beings and slavery to be inhumane and unethical, a viewpoint that left slavery as a concept essentially with little specific presence in national law and policy.

With the horrors of the Civil War coming officially to an end in 1865 and victory going to the United States of America instead of the Confederate States of America, the challenge after this war was not the separation of states as it had been in the case of the Revolutionary War but, instead, the reunification of a fractured nation in need of consensus around bedrock national values and around a sustainable operational identity. The most fundamental question was: How could the severed nations be knitted back together? Satisfactory answers for such a complex question cannot be adequately presented in the space available in this volume, but it remains critically important, nevertheless, to raise the question—especially since, by all accounts, the challenge of knitting together a divided nation remains palpable even in our contemporary era. The thorniness of this task is still evident across various arenas of engagement, but most forthrightly in political arenas, where such questions remain in motion: Who are "we"? What do we believe in as a collective, as a nation? What do we do? What do we not do? What does it mean to govern in a diversity-filled nation?

The Era of Reconstruction and Post-Reconstruction

After the Civil War, the Union and the Confederacy needed to undergo a reunification process. The critical task was to turn a nation that had been divided into two warring nations back into one again. The ideological differences, which had been shaped and defined significantly via the institution of slavery, needed to be resolved, presumably once and for all. The nature of the resolution was controlled by those who won the war—that is, the United States of America, not the Confederate States of America. In victory, however, with slavery declared illegal and with the infrastructures of accountability brought out of the shadows and systemically enforced, the Union needed to go well beyond a general proclamation of principles to make reconstructing processes work well.

For Unionist stakeholders as the victors of the conflict, war had been necessary in order to preserve the existing Union. The clear, present, and quite inescapable imperative of Reconstruction was twofold, tied to both economic imperatives and social imperatives. With regard to economic imperatives, the decision-making task was to recalibrate the system. Political leaders chose industrial capitalism, the shift to a paid labor market system from a free labor market system, and toward urban models of development—with all that technological innovation might permit. As a dramatic operational change, an interrogation of this system offers a particularly instructive opportunity for understanding reunification processes as multidimensional (see Levy 2021; Hahn 2021). Directing focused attention on the ways and means of production and wealth building as an analytical lens casts light on the ways in which power elites demonstrated two desires that would propel the nation forward for generations to come. Internally, the effort was to expand the geographical boundaries of the nation. Externally, the effort was to centralize the priority to make a place for the still new nation among centuries older nations on the world's stage rather than on a provincial stage. This identity—as a geographically humongous nation well positioned to be in the lead globally—set new watermarks going forward for who we are as a nation. In this latter case, the scope of the ways forward included, not only the North and South as original territories, but by the second half of the nineteenth century also western expansion and territorial expansions beyond the continental shores (to Puerto Rico, the US Virgin Islands, American Samoa, Guam, Hawaii, Alaska, etc.). Significantly, the nation-building process was both ideological and territorial: continuing to develop the United States as an ambitious experiment in democracy; continuing to move the nation forward in making "a more perfect union"; and simultaneously, moving the nation to be more aggressive in making a place for itself on the global stage.

Economic imperatives constituted a complex challenge, but some of the thorniest challenges were connected to social imperatives with their specific focus on the need to decide on an ethical and workable stance concerning slavery. The pivot point among the full slate of rationales both for war and for reunifying the nation was the task of resolving the dilemma of having one region that defined specific human beings as chattel and another that, with a subtle sidestepping of the issue, had not written them directly into the narratives of nation. After the war, a continuation of disparate perspectives—as inherently counter perspectives within the scope of a reunited nation—was still not sustainable. The two models were incoherent, inevitably in conflict, and unmanageable. To sustain ourselves by law and policy and in peace, the nation needed to choose, and the right to choose went to the victors, the North.

In bringing credibility to the task, the Union had ostensibly already made its choice before the Revolutionary War—in principle—when several of the states had chosen to divest from the business of enslaving people. With the advent of Civil War, therefore, the United States had been positioned to accept its constitutional commitment to freedom, justice, equality, and the pursuit of happiness (or, in contemporary vocabulary, empowerment). After the war, victory meant that the nation was positioned, likewise, to accept a national identity as a non-slaveholding nation. Within this framework, the task of fashioning a successful Reconstruction process was not simply the declaring of slavery to be against the law of the land. Social imperatives required instead a resetting of not only economic priorities but also sociocultural practices, law, and policy, as well as the upholding of accountabilities capable of assuring freedom, justice, equality, and empowerment for all. The nation needed to be intentional in establishing a new and more coherent infrastructure and a more ethically congruent system of management.

In order to facilitate change, political leaders needed to vest more authority and accountability in federal decision-making—that is, in controlling regional discontinuities and sentiments across all territories. Two illustrations that offer evidence that political elites understood these responsibilities were led by the Radical Republicans, a group of northern political elites. On a local level, a key decision was the federal occupation of the South by the Union military immediately after the war to manage governance and safety. From a federal perspective, another decision was to clarify the term *citizen* and the rights of citizenship through three constitutional amendments. The Thirteenth Amendment abolished slavery on December 6, 1865. The Fourteenth Amendment assured equal protection under the law on July 28, 1868. The Fifteenth Amendment assured protections for the rights of citizenship (for example, the right to vote) on February 3, 1870. By these amendments, the enslavement of human beings was explicitly deemed illegal, and citizenship in the United States was defined with full rights, regardless of race, class, previous condition, or national origin.

The impact of these two decisions on the implementation and sustainability of democratic values, however, was sobering. Essentially, the momentum for accountability in monitoring progress and change lasted officially only until 1877. Under the governance of new national leadership that included former Confederates, laws, policies, and practices began to drift back to old watermarks for agency, power, and authority, and away from democracy for all. The effect was that from 1878 forward the nation entered the post-Reconstruction period. Over subsequent decades, the systemic oppression of African Americans, other peoples of color, and a range of citizens marginalized by other factors (for example, gender, class, place of origin, and condition) became entrenched, with discriminatory policies and practices being increasingly normalized and calcified.

Within this postwar post-Reconstruction ecosystem, the argumentative viewpoint for the presence and participation of African American women is informed by the nature, ways, and means of nation building (or, in this case, nation rebuilding). A basic conclusion is that, with both nation-building and reunification processes functioning within a multi-stakeholder environment, African American women were engulfed, perhaps inevitably, within the power dynamics of this era. Negotiations for ways forward were occurring largely beyond the scope and potential of their authority and without their interests, concerns, and welfare deliberately in mind. The crucial implication for them was that they had little or no choice but to figure out strategically how to intervene in, disrupt, and influence these processes if they were going to have a chance of bringing about the changes that would make a meaningful difference to their communities and to themselves.

With agency, power, and authority for law, policy, and social practice being in hands other than their own, African American women continued to exercise their problem-posing and problem-solving talents in support of their communities and themselves. By 1878 it became clear to most, if not all across the African American community, that, just as political elites had sidestepped action during the original framing of the Constitution, they were sidestepping action in Reconstruction as well. They had taken a good first step with clarifying citizenship and establishing management oversight, but the energy to follow through with stabilizing this infrastructure for all was waning. The effort at the federal level to actually set in place laws, policies, and practices that were capable of mediating the full, fair, and equitably applied implementation of bedrock national values (freedom, justice, equality, and the pursuit of happiness for all) across all regions of the nation was left incomplete. Although Reconstruction did indeed reknit the North and the South into one nation under the flag of the United States, the balancing of economic, social, and political imperatives was not viscerally entwined with systems of accountability in monitoring and assuring freedom, justice, equality, and empowerment for all. Essentially, Reconstruction occurred within a politically shifting kaleidoscope of national interests that brought traditional elite power brokers—North and South—back to power and authority as these relationships pretty much were before the Civil War. This process of recalibrating power relationships left African Americans (and others who were marginalized by one definition or another) in an ongoing struggle for justice.

Basically, even though the Confederacy lost the Civil War, the era of Reconstruction did not prevent southern elites from regaining their status, power, and control. They regained all with a key change. While they had agreed to reunify under one flag, they still held onto their ideological positions. The incongruity of ideological differences with the nation's bedrock democratic values called for southern political elites to shift their symbolic language. They did. In political terms, Reconstruction processes were reencoded by southern elites to be the protection of states' rights as the governing principle and, thereby, as an enabling force for action and inaction.

Southern elites created a new infrastructure, the Jim Crow system, described by Douglas A. Blackmon (2009) as "slavery by another name." Jim Crowism rose quickly as an operational force. These policies and practices institutionalized discrimination and became a successful mechanism for preserving the deeply ingrained social order of slavery. White supremacy remained very much intact as the way of southern life from post-Reconstruction going forward, keeping African Americans within the inhospitable framework of being free but not free, equal but not equal, with access to justice—but then not. The conclusion to be drawn is that, although the Confederate States lost the proverbial battle, confederates won the political war with the essence of their ideologies, beliefs, and practices prevailing (largely without northern ideological intervention) until the mid-twentieth century and the rise of the modern Civil Rights Movement.

In effect, economic, social, and political imperatives were all fully in motion in the last four decades of the nineteenth century and in strong competition for attention. On one hand, the imperative of Reconstruction was to reduce friction between the North and the South over competing social and cultural values and practices and to find a way forward to recalibrate the economic system. On the other, the imperative was to push beyond the new constitutional amendments to establish an infrastructure that was capable of supporting all citizens, regardless of race, gender, class, and creed, and strengthening the nation's identity across all regions as a nation with bedrock democratic values. By 1878 and the post-Reconstruction era, southern elites had indeed regained their strengths with regard to agency, authority, and power. The reality of the decades following the war was that, with southern power brokers reestablished, the nation had—and continues to have—a difficult time living up to its declared values for all (including its African American citizens) and sustaining its bedrock ideological commitments.[1] This postwar context constituted an ongoing challenge for African American women.

A Sight Line for African American Women

At the end of the Civil War, for African Americans, the Union victory provided a sterling occasion for transformative change in their status and in their opportunities as human beings, not chattel, to exercise their rights as American citizens. For more than two centuries before the war African Americans had held in their hearts—against all odds—hopes and dreams about a better world. Moreover, they had worked actively (free, freed, and enslaved, North and South) whenever possible to live, learn, and forward their activist causes so that they would be ready for this better world. With the coming of war, they perceived by logos, ethos, and pathos that a new day was finally possible, and many of them—including many African American women—were impassioned to step up to the cause of freedom, equality, justice, and empowerment for all, translating these causes more boldly than ever before into the causes of human and civil rights.[2]

The outcome of the translation process was that African Americans found it necessary to continue to fight—no matter what—as made evident by the move from the era of slavery to the era of Jim Crowism and the systemic practices of white supremacy and discrimination. For this racial group, the war had been both real and symbolic. For them, the symbolic war did not end in 1865 with the Union victory but could be perceived as an apparently never-ending struggle for social change and social justice. African Americans came to see the ending of the war as an occasion for taking advantage of new opportunities for action as full-fledged citizens, even in the face of ongoing danger. They perceived their sociopolitical goals in a free and just nation to be rightful and true. They were consciously aware of the necessity of fighting for their rights at all costs, as well as the necessity in this relentless fight of setting and sustaining agenda and strategies that are instrumental in rebuilding a nation that really needed to live up to its bedrock principles—for all citizens, including themselves.

African American women actively counted themselves as high stakeholders in these efforts, as demonstrated by their words and actions. As was the case for their male counterparts, the Civil War had been generative in adding even more inspiration to their existing desire to engage in robust sociopolitical action in support of transformative change. Consider two distinctive points.

One point is that the war years shifted the available means for the participation of African American women. By its proximity to the spaces and places occupied by women, the Civil War persistently offered occasions for women to engage in ordinary and extraordinary actions, often stretching the boundaries of sociocultural expectations. To be emphasized, the social hierarchies of the day dictated (with white women as the metric) that women should not be directly involved in public actions at all, and certainly not as warriors. Neither literally nor metaphorically were they envisioned as people who normally occupied spaces outside of the home, or away from the protection, supervision, and control of males, or independently in any public spaces where "respectable" women were not expected to function either as leaders or as service providers. This war, however, kept breaching traditional boundaries for many reasons: the intoxicating closeness of battlefields that were in front yards and back yards, across rivers, down roads, and over hills, especially for women in southern and border states; the scale of the war's human devastation, with the stunning level of casualties; and also the rising trajectory of women's activism (e.g., in abolitionism, human rights, women's rights, woman's suffrage, educational advocacy, and professional development for women); and so forth. All of these factors made way for more people than ever before, even women, to take on roles to support and sustain the war effort. Before, during, and after the war, habits of thought and action shifted the paradigms for what women had the desire, the capacity, the will, and (given the critical needs of war) a newly expanded experience and authority to do in terms of leadership and service. To be noted, however, is that while the framework for understanding this point may have been articulated with white women in mind, there was also an expansion of horizons for African American women as well.

A second point is that, during the nineteenth century, the imperialist interests of the United States in expanding its geographical boundaries, as well as several increases in the availability of infrastructure resources for transportation and communication, became particularly dynamic. On one hand, in exercising their desires for the growth and dominance of the United States on the world stage, power elites needed better transportation and communication systems in order to manage their aggressive national-building agenda. Even though at mid-century the Civil War was indeed an iconic internal moment, we simply cannot set aside the fact that, in the first half of the nineteenth century, the United States had been engaging in a tremendous imperialist effort to expand its geographical holdings. These initiatives included, for example, the Louisiana Purchase, the annexation of Florida and Texas, the War of 1812 (which affirmed US rights, in resistance to Great Britain, to pursue territorial expansion), the creation of the Oregon Treaty (also a resolution for competition between the United States and Great Britain), and the Gadsden Purchase, which brought in New Mexico and Arizona. These initiatives were not simple acquisitions but, rather, occasions of bloody conflicts over territory and power. Conflicts with Native Americans offer striking examples. In the South alone, US invasions of territory took away land and sovereignty from southeastern tribes, as evidenced by two wars with the Seminoles, multiple battles with the Creeks, the Trail of Tears, the infamous forced walk of the Cherokee to the West, and more.

By 1861, with the ever-broadening scope of imperialist growth, the sense of what constituted the nation had expanded well beyond notions of North and South to a sense of a power and control that would reach ultimately from sea to shining sea. Infrastructure advancements to support this expansion included the invention of steamboats and the establishing of transportation waterways; the invention of steam-driven trains and the establishing of railway lines, such as the Baltimore and Ohio; the emergence of streetcars as public transportation in northern cities; the invention of the telegraph, the laying of telegraph lines, and the establishing of a more efficient communications net; the creation of a larger network of roads; and the creation of a relatively inexpensive national postal system.

With such an array of technological advancements, the potential benefits for various stakeholders were inevitably perceived to be ubiquitous for one and all—that is, viewed as having advantages that were available for any and all who pursued them. In the case of African American women, while the systems were not designed to be an asset for women or African Americans (and certainly not African American women), still, the potential was known by each cohort to be there. With specific regard for women who were able to use these technologies, the various new resources helped to enhance their range of vision and experience and, most particularly, to enable a wider range of independent movement. Women traveled more easily and comfortably—with or without male escorts. They sustained more vibrant communication networks, both personally and via public information tools such as newspapers. They broadened their horizons, literally and metaphorically, with the capacity to meet and interact with a broader range of people. Most provocatively, they were better positioned to use their new access to space and information to imagine themselves and their work in different ways, not just in the home but in social, institutional, and public space as well.

Benefits emerged for all, whether Union or Confederate, white or African American, women or men. Essentially, all Americans regardless of race, gender, class, previous condition, or creed were entering a modern world with ideological, political, and social baggage but also with upgraded technologies that were capable of supporting not only growth but new layers of social access and sociopolitical agency. African American women were no exception.

Creating Space in Narratives of Nation

The five anchor points of Burke's pentad constitute a heuristic for interrogating the locations of multiple stakeholders within the larger scope of the American Civil War. This heuristic enables us to generate a more robust data set from which to determine the nature, ways, and means of African American women's presence and participation in the nation and within which to understand the fullness of this century as a dynamic ecosystem for their progress and development as advocates, activists, and leaders. With an expanded data base, researchers and scholars are better positioned to conduct closer, more thoroughly rendered, and more insightfully determined analyses and interpretations in support of the assertion that across the nineteenth century African American women were, in fact, on a trajectory for making space for themselves as full-fledged citizens in our narratives of nation. With this methodological approach, the imperative is to develop an enhanced framework for making the sociopolitical actions of African American women more visible and audible and to draw forth inferences and implications that permit us to think critically about both the circumstances and the conditions for the women's operational success, as well as for the evolution, impacts, and consequences of their civic engagements.

With this type of analytical and interpretive outlook for this time period, we have a robust mechanism for seeing how African American women managed and negotiated their lives. The fundamental assertion is that the women certainly engaged in activities for survival, as they are occasionally recognized as doing, but from a different point of view their activities suggest as well that they also had eyes on ways that their activities might support and enable sociopolitical change. They listened to the discourses swirling around them and spoke their truths in whatever ways they could. They read—or had read to them (in keeping with Shirley Wilson Logan's analysis in *Liberating Language* [2008])—various written documents that were available and informative in clarifying their causes and opportunities for strategic actions. They dreamed the worlds that they wished for, adapted to the conditions facing them, and took advantage of whatever opportunities for action that were evident. They refined and developed innovative strategies for taking care of themselves, their families, and their communities amid persistently hostile environments. They created collaborative relationships for sanity, for survival, for collective action, and for organized sociopolitical reform. They made their own room to do what they needed to do for themselves, their communities, and their nation.

In effect, then, I use the Civil War as a key point in the mid-nineteenth century in order to look both backward and forward in understanding the nature, ways, and means of African American women's sociopolitical trajectories. I also use the Black Clubwomen's Movement at the turn of the nineteenth century as a complementary point for marking progress and change. The intention of using this kaleidoscopic methodology is to help us bring visibility and audibility to the women and their work and to leverage our ability to offer a more substantive and respectful account of their participation, contributions, and accomplishments, not simply as hardworking women but also as citizens of the nation.

To summarize the basic facts that I have drawn forth from the pentadic analysis, after four hard-fought years of Civil War, the Confederacy (smaller, with fewer resources, and home to more theaters of battle) lost the war. They did not gain sovereignty or national dominance. The United States of America won and brokered an agreement from the Confederacy to reunite the nation. Two nations remained as one under the authority and control of the United States of America. Slavery as a legal institution was ended. From 1865 to 1877, during the Reconstruction era and the resetting of the ways and means of nationhood, the sense of purpose to "make a more perfect union" was in motion, at least temporarily, until the turn in 1878 toward the post-Reconstruction era, a resurgence of white supremacy in the South, and the rise of the Jim Crow era.[3] The sense of purpose for nation building was exemplified by attention to a "federal" system for operations; an emphasis, within the economic system, on industrial capitalism and paid labor; and a level of commitment in governance to freedom, justice, equality, and empowerment—despite the fact that, from the perspective of African American women, this commitment was thoroughly inadequate to get the job actually done and done well.

Fundamentally, the attention to governance was marked by the amendments to the Constitution. In the eyes of the millions of freed slaves, the significant numbers of African Americans who were already freed before the Civil War, and those who were born free, these amendments were designed to clarify the definition of the term *citizen*, to provide equal protection for all under the law, and for African Americans in particular, to protect the voting rights and prospects of former slaves. US soldiers were deployed to the South as an occupying force to assure safety and compliance with law and policy, although the deployment lasted only a relatively short time.

These shifts in the identity of the United States to a non-slaveholding nation committed to honoring democratic principles and values—and committed specifically to honoring the full rights of all of its citizens—mattered to African Americans. Even with such transformative changes, however, imperatives for African Americans, including African American women, remained essentially the same. A critical need continued to be for another layer of federal laws, policies, and practices. The ongoing imperative for African American activism was to normalize specific ways in which the nation would hold itself persistently accountable to its bedrock values as an actual, rather than mainly a proclaimed, operational reality—that is, in establishing systems and protocols capable of assuring freedom, justice, equality, and empowerment for all of the citizens of the nation and not just for some. Both before and after the Civil War, the struggle for security, dignity, prosperity, and peace continued.

With the war over and challenges continuing, the central questions remain fundamental. How did women emerge into the reconstructed nation? What did the war change for African American women? As Mary Elizabeth Massey suggests:

> Had every woman and girl of the 1860s described the ways in which she was affected by the Civil War, no two accounts would have been alike. Some might have said they were scarcely aware that a conflict raged, most would have noted varying degrees of stress, and many would have reported direct involvement in the

> horrors of war. Rich and poor, young and old, white and colored, slave and free, Confederate and Unionist were all caught in the turbulence. . . . The Civil War compelled women to become more active, self-reliant, and resourceful, and this ultimately contributed to their economic, social, and intellectual advancement . . . it is obvious that even today its effects are still in evidence; but such is the case in social revolutions, and the Civil War was in part a social revolution. (1994, xxi–xxii)[4]

Given current efforts to rethink women's variously rendered participation in the Civil War, Massey's assessment suggests a pattern. During the Civil War a substantial number of African American women found inventive ways to intensify their engagements in social, public, and institutional space—regardless of sociohistorical expectations.

After the Civil War this cohort took their experiences and habits of thought and action into their postwar lives. They created legacies of advocacy, activism, and leadership that were enriched and informed by the range of experiences they managed to garner, particularly in light of the opening of more educational opportunities for them in becoming women in the professions (Aptheker 1982; Royster 2000). These factors strengthened their capacity to participate in social, institutional, and public arenas, as their engagement with various social causes continued—for example, with regard to human and civil rights, woman's suffrage, temperance, worker's rights, the military, and so on (e.g., see Bellafaire 2011). A closer and more caring interrogation of this work brings vitality to the rising tide of their experiences and expertise as sociopolitical actors.

As Massey claims, from this perspective the Civil War was indeed the beginning of a gendered revolution, one that is still playing out today, as women continue to take on identities that are beyond the previous societal norms—for example, as military women in combat zones, as corporate executives, as governmental leaders, policymakers, scientists, technology experts, academic leaders, public intellectuals, and so on. This ongoing activism pushes forward the battle for justice and equality, with women across many identities seeking to dismantle traditionally gendered hierarchies. Such persistent work over the decades has underscored not just the benefits of inclusion but the shared responsibilities of all for assuring a better world. Within this framework of continuity, a pentadic perspective helps us to gain a clearer sense of the long view of transformative change with attention in this case on the trajectories of women's participation across social identities (race, class, culture, gender, sexuality, etc.), as well as across generations and geographical locations.

In general terms, that literacy and professional development were important in achieving these trajectories almost goes without saying, but it needs to be stated nevertheless. The level of literacy in the United States during the nineteenth century became critical for individuals and communities across the nation. We have examples of the insights and experiences of African American women as they themselves have expressed them. A primary focus in this volume, therefore, is on exploring, through an examination of the women's own words, the extent to which this group over the decades used their literacy and rhetorical prowess to gain both visibility and audibility in civic participation and sociopolitical action.

From the narratives they left behind as archival evidence of their presence, experiences, and achievements we can draw a basic conclusion that African American women lived and learned with purpose. Given the swirls of inhospitality that surrounded them, a primary purpose was survival. They wanted to create better conditions for themselves and others, but in full scope, ultimately, they also wanted to make the world a better place. They found ways to exercise vision and strength through strategic use of their culturally infused, experientially informed ways of seeing, being, and doing. When we identify the Civil War as a specific standpoint, we can ascertain that over the generations African American women have functioned as torchbearers for transformative action. Their legacies of advocacy, activism, and leadership are filled with inspiration for others who would carry forward the never-ending quest for freedom, social justice, equality, human rights, empowerment, and peace. In essence, for most of the nineteenth century, these women dreamed a world that they were prohibited from creating, but they managed, nevertheless, to pass their dreams along to subsequent generations. They spoke for themselves to whoever was listening. With the distinct continuities of their lived experiences as an under-considered marginalized group, their words have echoed across the decades and now constitute legacies of thought and action that have continued into the twentieth century and now into the twenty-first.

A Cauldron for Sociopolitical Growth and Development

Notably, it is not news to assert that African American women are members historically of a socially constrained gender and a downtrodden race. This statement has become a commonplace. For centuries these women were enslaved in overwhelming numbers and thus neither economically privileged within the American sociocultural context nor granted any recognition of their own agency, authority, power, or entitlement—to anything. Although both race and gender oppressions are now easily fathomable as distinctive phenomena, what remains newsworthy is the complication for African American women (and other women of color) of having both race and gender identities operating at once within a shadowy interstitial space. Essentially these women fall through the cracks of legibility, as has been well articulated in contemporary feminist analyses by several thinkers and writers.

One striking example is the seminal volume *All the Women Are White, All the Blacks Are Men, But Some of Us Are Brave: Black Women's Studies*, edited by Akasha (Gloria T.) Hull, Patricia Bell Scott, and Barbara Smith and published in 1982. This volume raised for closer scrutiny the notion that African American women have been historically rendered invisible, inaudible, and unintelligible. In pulling together an array of scholarship from multiple perspectives, the editors cast a brighter light on the material and symbolic realities of the ways in which African American women have been relegated to living and working in dark shadows. The editors' imperative was to point out the critical need to debunk myths about this group, to document with more care and consideration their actual work and accomplishments, and to invent Black women's studies and establish it as a legitimate field of study.

A few years later, in 1990, in a volume edited by Joanne M. Braxton and Andrée Nicola McLaughlin, *Wild Women in the Whirlwind: Afra-American Culture and the Contemporary Literary Renaissance*, these imperatives were raised again with particular attention directed to the unintelligibility of the women's presence. In the foreword Audre Lorde states: "It's not that we haven't always been here, since there was a here. It is that the letters of our names have been scrambled when they were not totally erased, and our fingerprints upon the handles of history have been called the random brushings of birds" (Braxton and McLaughlin 1990, xi). Lorde underscores in sociohistorical terms that the challenge of recovering the presence, lives, conditions, and accomplishments of African American women is no small or simple task. With the compelling metaphors of scrambled and erased names and "the random brushings of birds," she clarifies that the task of recovery and reinscription is in fact daunting. Specifically in the face of acute sociocultural disbelief, the task is to document with precision what has been deliberately and systemically hidden.

Challenges in researching African American women as sociopolitical beings have been manifold, starting with the need to acknowledge persuasively the very existence of the evidence of presence and performance, despite a persistent expectation that there is no such thing. At this point, a basic opportunity is to value the evidence that is coming forward and to recognize the fact that there may be more, even though there are provocative misalignments within systems of credibility (related, for example, to race, gender, sexuality, and also class and status) about who is worthy of regard and who is not. Perhaps most importantly, given the growing knowledge base, we have opportunities to bring to bear more generative frameworks for interpreting evidence and incorporating insights respectfully into national narratives even when there is, still quite often, no prior or particular inclination to be either inclusive, fair, or respectful.

A moment to mark as we take advantage of contemporary opportunities is the timing of the publication of these two volumes as examples—1982 and 1990, coming in these two cases almost ten years apart. We should not miss the point that, in recognizing such rudimentary details, we gain a clearer sense of the difficulties of disrupting old habits and practices. The good news nowadays is that the tedious but invigorating work of recovering and reinscribing an intellectual ancestry and a history of practices continues to go forward with escalating vibrancy in the twenty-first century. With growing enthusiasm about the discoveries that are coming forward, we have opportunities to create a scholarly landscape that is far richer than many researchers and scholars could have ever imagined.

In particular, there has been an upward trend in dismantling the misperception that African American women have not contributed substantially to the nation. The presumption, thereby, is that in our narratives of nation this group would have little or no claim to either ordinary achievements or extraordinary excellence, and certainly not to any recognition for long-term patterns of impact. In this regard, specific dismantling processes have centered on escalating efforts to interrogate and disrupt the misperception that African American women were not actively engaged in civic enterprises during the nineteenth century. With the rising mound of research, we now know such presumptions to be, quite simply, untrue. Even so, much work is yet to be done. There remains a need for more productively rendered interrogations of the women and their work over time. From this perspective, casting attention in this volume to the long nineteenth century—from the founding of the nation through the Civil War to the turn of the nineteenth century—becomes a prescient window for reconsidering potential and possibilities and for gaining a deeper, more respectful point of view.

A Light Shines in the Darkness

The first generations of African American women living under the flag of a reunited United States of America found leverage and power in their abilities to use their rhetorical knowledge to speak and write—using literacy, learning, and professional expertise as tools for engaging in sociopolitical leadership and action. With each generation, their strategic understanding of their own status and the implications of that status was evident in their ways with words. They were willing to speak up and out. They chose whatever genres were available to express themselves, and they were willing to work hard to get important work done.

African American women speaking up and out did not begin, however, after the Civil War. Exemplars of literate and rhetorical expertise arose early in the history of the nation, even before 1776 in fact, as indicated by the writings of Phillis Wheatley (c.1753–1784). Encouraged to learn and to write by the family who owned her, Wheatley had things to say even as a young girl (see figure 2.1). The genre that was available to her was poetry. With the quality of her poems, she took the nation by surprise, not just because she was a woman who could write within the expressive traditions of her day but because she was enslaved and thereby not expected to be capable of artistic expression or of demonstrating the wealth of knowledge and learning she had acquired. Wheatley was not distracted by these presumptions, however, and used her writing to light the way not only for an appreciation of her imagination and creativity as a writer but also for encouraging a higher regard for African American people.

Figure 2.1: Phillis Wheatley

Born in West Africa, Wheatley was captured and enslaved as a young girl and sold in Boston to John Wheatley, whose family members were progressive enough to educate her well beyond the norms of the day and to support her talents as a creative writer. With their advocacy Wheatley achieved considerable success. She became the best-known African American of her day, although she garnered more recognition for her poetic talents in Europe than in the United States. Indeed, her first book of poetry was published in London, not in the United States. The excellence of her reputation as a writer also leveraged her ability to be in conversation and correspondence with leaders of the day—for example, George Washington, John Hancock, Benjamin Franklin, Dr. Benjamin Rush (signer of the Declaration of Independence from Philadelphia), the Reverend Samson Occom (a member of the Mohegan Nation and the first Native American to publish writing in English), the lord mayor of London, the countess of Huntingdon, and more.

Notably, Wheatley was among the very first women in the American colonies to publish a book of poetry—in 1773, which established her as the first African American and the first African American woman to do so. Louis Henry Gates Jr. credits Wheatley as the "progenitor" of Black literary traditions (Gates 1988), pointing out the progenitor status of other African American women writers, as well—namely, Ann Plato (c. 1820–unknown), who was the first to publish a book of essays (1841); Harriet E. Adams Wilson (1825–1900), who was the first to publish a novel (1859), *Our Nig: Sketches from the Life of a Free Black*; and Jarena Lee (1783–1864), who was the first to publish an autobiography (1849) (Gates 1988, vii–xxii). Each of these writers demonstrated that they were keenly aware of the materiality of their own lives and that they had things to say.

In Wheatley's case, she was acknowledged for her expertise as a writer of imaginative literature. What was more in question was her subject matter, given the view that she focused on classic themes without engaging actively or directly with the institution of slavery. With regard to the goals of this analysis, however, there are two points to keep in mind. One is that, despite her living under more progressive conditions than most, Wheatley was a slave until 1774, after her travels to London and after the publication of her book there. An inference to be drawn here with regard to her not engaging actively or directly with slavery is that she did not directly bite the hands that nourished her—the family who owned and supported her. Without question, though, she lived the experiences of a human being who was not free, who did not have authority or control over her own life, and who in her new country (the American colonies) did not automatically enjoy the acceptance of a talented person capable of writing fine poetry. These observations lead to the second point. In order to function as a writer, Wheatley needed advocates who were white and elite. Even with advocates, however, she was still called upon to defend her "genius" as a writer before eighteen "august gentlemen" (Gates 1988, vii–ix), who agreed to attest to the fact that she had herself actually written what she had written.

With regard to Wheatley centralizing the institution of slavery in her poetry, even though she did not choose that priority, there were other ways that her writing offered windows into her sociopolitical concerns. For example, in the poem "To the University of Cambridge in New England," Wheatley acknowledged American excellence, indicating that her enslavement provided opportunities for her to learn ("brought me in safety from those dark abodes")—that is, from darkness into light. Simultaneously, though, she declared that those who were being educated at this university should exercise the grace and mercy of the Son of God and turn away deliberately from evils:

> Improve your privileges while they stay,
> Ye pupils, and each hour redeem, that bears
> Or good or bad report of you to heav'n.
> Let sin, that baneful evil to the foul,
> By you be shunn'd nor once remit your guard;
> Suppress the deadly serpent in its egg.
> Ye blooming plants of human race divine,
> An *Ethiop* tells you 'tis your greatest foe;
> In transient sweetness turns to endless pain,
> And in immense perdition sinks the foul. (Wheatley 1988, 16)

We might reasonably surmise that Wheatley considered the absence of freedom and educational opportunity to be evils against humanity, a category that Wheatley might well conclude would define also people of African descent.

Given her precarious status as a pioneering writer, however, Wheatley was able to make space for herself more astutely in other poems by proclaiming her patriotism in the tributes she wrote for George Washington, the support she articulated for the rise of the nation in freedom, and the compassion she demonstrated concerning the death of various others. In contrast to the more subtle and indirect allusions in her published work is her personal correspondence with the Reverend Samuel Occom. In a letter dated February 11, 1774, responding to a letter from Occom, Wheatley writes:

> Reverend and Honoured Sir,
>
> I have this Day received your obliging kind Epistle, and am greatly satisfied in your Reasons respecting the Negroes, and think highly reasonable what you offer in Vindication of their natural Rights: Those that invade them cannot be insensible that the divine Light is chasing away the thick Darkness which broods over the Land of

> Africa, and the Chaos which has reigned so long, is converting into beautiful Order, and reveals more and more clearly, the glorious Dispensation of civil and religious Liberty, which are so inseparably united, that there is little or no Enjoyment of one without the other: Otherwise, perhaps, the Israelites had been less solicitous for their Freedom from Egyptian Slavery; I do not say they would have been contented without it, by no Means, for in every human Breast, God has implanted a Principle, which we call Love of Freedom; it is impatient of Oppression, and pants for Deliverance, and by the Leave of our Modern Egyptians I will assert, that the same Principle lives in us. God grants Deliverance in his own way and Time, and get him honor upon all those whose Avarice impels them to countenance and help forward the Calamities of their Fellow Creatures. This I desire not for their Hurt, but to convince them of the strange Absurdity of their Conduct whose Words and Actions are so diametrically opposite. How well the Cry for Liberty, and the reverse Disposition for the Exercise of oppressive Power over others agree,—I humbly think it does not require the Penetration of a Philosopher to determine. (Wheatley 1988, 176–77)

Although the framing for this message is ideologically Christian and can be interrogated in those terms, it is evident that Wheatley is asserting her belief that the "Love of Freedom" is a principle implanted by God in the human heart, that those who defy this principle and "forward the Calamities of their Fellow Creatures" are subject to the judgment of God, and that this disconnect between principle and action in the nation is obvious. Wheatley did not champion this view aggressively in her writing, but she spoke of it in this correspondence to the Reverend Occom as a hospitable listener.

To illuminate the general circumstances of Wheatley's life as an eighteenth-century African American woman, a summary of a few key details offers insight about her achievements in context. Wheatley's volume of poetry was published in September 1773, while she was enslaved, albeit with the advocacy and sponsorship of the Wheatleys as a progressive slaveholding family in New England. At the end of that year, after the publication of her book, her immediate owner, Susanna Wheatley (who had been given the fragile young Phillis as a gift by her husband, John) granted Wheatley her freedom. Of note is that this manumission occurred before 1787 when Massachusetts had joined several other northeastern states in abolishing slavery before the signing of the US Constitution.

From spring 1774 to 1778 Wheatley's closest advocates and sponsors died (John and Susanna Wheatley and their daughter Mary).

In the years that followed, Wheatley was a freed woman of color living in Boston, but her horizons became dramatically constrained. During this time period opportunities for African Americans ranged from slim to none. A basic reality for Wheatley was that, although she kept writing and published a poem here and there, publishers were not inclined to be supportive of her talents. In the inhospitable context of eighteenth-century America as a slaveholding nation, she did not have mentors to guide her, and she no longer benefited from the advocacy of white allies or their support of her talents and abilities. Wheatley did not thrive. She died at thirty-one years of age, alone and in abject poverty—with her spouse in jail and her small child having died.

The point here is not to rehearse that Wheatley was a highly respected poet, nationally and internationally, or even to recognize her as an inventive progenitor of African American literary traditions. It is to proclaim, instead, that a case can also be made for her being a pioneering torchbearer for sociopolitical thought and action among African American women. She was a dedicated supporter of freedom, justice, equality, and the pursuit of happiness as the bedrock values that would define the new nation. She demonstrated a capacity to speak out, and she managed to be heard both internationally and nationally even though her direct participation in such nation-building discourses was constrained by her enslaved status. In contrast to an active engagement with sociopolitical concerns, Wheatley was positioned to perform more as a "museum piece," as a magnificent exception in her race and gender in being the first African American woman poet to be published. She was not positioned to function aggressively as a sociopolitical thinker and actor. In acknowledging her efforts to use her talents well and to be true to herself in doing what she was able to do amid the conditions and circumstances of her life, the imperative is not to ignore the resonances in her work and relationships as a limited and modest display of a sociopolitical agenda. Rather, the imperative is to embrace these resonances as part and parcel of the strong foundation that future generations of African American women would continue to fortify with particular vigor as their operational horizons expanded going forward into the nineteenth century.

To be sure, the specific point to embrace is that Wheatley did put an invaluable stake in the ground for the building of sociopolitical strength among African American women. By her very presence, the quality of her work as a poet, and her remarkable ability to network with leaders both nationally and internationally, she was a compelling torchbearer. She contributed quite meaningfully to the novel idea in the eighteenth century that African American women were human, not chattel; that they were robustly endowed with human talents and abilities; intellectually capable, ethically connected, and hardworking. The touchstone is that, in the light cast by Wheatley's accomplishments in the late eighteenth century, despite the oppressive conditions of her life, African American women and men were better positioned to demonstrate and to declare that they were worthy of respect and regard by all as full-fledged citizens of the new nation.

Souls of Iron

A fundamental proposition in the recovery and reinscription of African American women's sociopolitical leadership and action is reflected in a quotation from Maritcha Rémond Lyons (1848–1929). As documented by Tonya Bolden in *Maritcha: A Nineteenth-Century American Girl* (2005), Lyons was born free and raised in New York City in a well-connected, well-respected, politically active family (see figure 2.2).[5] They ran a boardinghouse for African American seamen and later an ice cream shop and catering business. Before the Civil War they were actively engaged in the Underground Railroad. This combination of entrepreneurial spirit, community consciousness, and social activism enwrapped Lyons, providing an environment for her that was filled with high-achieving people whom she admired, including her parents, and with a level of social awareness and responsibility that defined and shaped her ways of thinking, doing, and believing. Lyons stated her imperative: "To do the best for myself with the view of making the best of myself" (Bolden, back cover), and she did.

Lyons began her education at Colored School No. 3 in Manhattan, but when it was time for her to go to the next level, there was no high school in all of New York City for African American students, so her family chose to sue the state of Rhode Island for her admission to Providence High School. This process required that Lyons be interrogated by the state legislature of Rhode Island. She did testify, and she was successful in gaining admission to the school. Her case was part of a series of events that led to Rhode Is-

Figure 2.2: Marchita Lyons

land passing a law guaranteeing that no child would be denied admission to a public school in the state. The law took effect on May 15, 1866, and in 1869 Lyons became the first African American to graduate from the school. In her memoir, she reflected on her experiences as she attended the school: "By this time I had become one of the foremost of the leaders [but] the iron had entered my soul. I never forgot that I had to sue for a privilege which any but a colored girl could have without asking. Most of the classmates were more or less friendly. If any girl tried to put 'on airs' I simply found a way to inform her of my class record. As I never had less than the highest marks, to flaunt my superiority in scholarship was never hard" (Sterling 1984, 189). Like other African American women, Lyons was called upon to make space for herself and her talents and to declare them worthy, not just by her own judgment but by the criteria of the systems that surrounded her. She went on from a moment of challenge as a young girl to build a long and successful career as an educator in Brooklyn. By the end of her career, she was the assistant principal of an integrated school, Public School No. 83.

Figure 2.3: Victoria Earle Matthews

Beyond her professional activities, Lyons followed the pattern taken on by her parents as social activists and community leaders. She built a reputation as a highly regarded leader who was engaged in many activities designed to strengthen the community. She was particularly well known for her collaborations with a journalist, Victoria Earle Matthews (1861–1907), who was herself a respected writer, journalist, and community activist (see figure 2.3). Together, in 1892, they cofounded the Women's Loyal Union of New York and Brooklyn. Together, they cosponsored a testimonial for Ida B. Wells (1862–1931) in New York's Lyric Hall on October 5, 1892, where Wells presented her first public address. On February 11, 1897, they cofounded the White Rose Mission, a home for African American women and girls who were migrating to New York from the South and the West Indies.

A point to underscore regarding Lyons's statement that the "the iron had entered" her soul (Sterling 1984, 189) is that the patterns of oppression in African American women's lives and work have been in motion for several centuries, even as their records of achievement have continued to blossom. If, as suggested here, we can pay more attention to the blossoming, then the nineteenth century can be envisioned as a cauldron in which these women gained strength, capacity, and confidence as sociopolitical actors able to flourish, despite constraints, and to do so in increasing numbers in the presence of ever-broadening audiences. Essentially, from the formation of the nation in 1776 through the growing political tensions over models of governance and definitions of citizenship, through the division of the nation into two nations, Union and Confederate, through the early decades of reunification after the Civil War under the flag of the United States, and to the patterns of women's participation that evolved by the turn of the twentieth century, African American women were very much aware of the sociopolitical implications of their times. Many of them found opportunities to engage forthrightly within the vibrancy of the sociopolitical environments that surrounded them—for example, as abolitionists, not passive nonperformers. With their activities so clearly and inevitably rooted in the contexts in which they lived, they performed as engaged citizens and they evolved. They also spoke and wrote for public audiences, leaving behind a record from which, in the twenty-first century, we might hear and know them better if we take the time to listen.

Living and Working in Dark Shadows

Looking from the perspective of elite white women, we can see that during the nineteenth century women stretched the boundaries of the private sphere, the domain that was articulated for them during this era as the arena of their societal authority and responsibility—the home. Over the course of the nineteenth century, however, they were able to move more toward action in the public sphere. These changes were occasioned by specific events and conditions (the abolitionist movement, the Civil War, the woman suffrage movement, and so on), various technological innovations (such as transportation and communication technologies), the novelty of their experiences outside the home (such as the various new roles as head of household and service providers for their national causes during the Civil War), and expanding opportunities for education and training.

The Civil War was a prime stimulus for transformative change. With the men at war, women had to step up and out in order to meet their needs for survival, as they also sought to sustain some degree of normalcy for their families and communities. These types of activities had not been within the scope of their authority before. Most obviously, white women needed to run farms, keep businesses afloat, provide food, clothing, and shelter for their families, educate and protect their children, and more—as heads of households and also as soldiers, spies, nurses, doctors, and so on in actual theaters of war. Their very lives and the future of their nation (whether Union or Confederate) depended on their figuring out how to do what needed done.

African American women were in a similar situation, whether they were helping white women or trying to take care of their own needs. In contrast to their white women counterparts, however, their status was outside the social hierarchies on not one but two counts (both gender and race). Even further, they had not been granted the privilege of having any kind of a "domain." In American ideological frameworks, despite being called upon to be laborers of various sorts, African American women had no officialized site of agency and authority within the social order. They were positioned, instead, as not having sociopolitical substance, or any human presence at all, and not having any rights to be respected or regarded. From their own perspectives, however, they saw themselves as worthy and respectable women who deserved consideration and deserved the rights of citizenship just like everybody else. In their own words they declared that they held in their hearts and minds the notion that they were able and ready to stand up and speak up for themselves and to accept the social responsibility of doing their parts in helping to make the world a better place—for all.

The evidence of their experiences suggests that African American women were accustomed to finding pathways to success as individuals who by their living conditions had to be inventive in meeting needs and taking on opportunities that might arise—for example, as heads or partners in their households, teachers, entrepreneurs, health-care providers, and more. They did not have to wonder about their strengths and capacities. They could see by their survival in persistently trying times that they could do what needed to be done. Metaphorically, they were warrior women, always ready to fight for right, goodness, and survival. Their words and the evidence of their work suggest that they felt their contributions were necessary to take themselves and others into the future, even when that future was a life and living that they could only imagine. With these types of visions of the past, present, and future, they indicated that they felt obliged to take advantage of opportunities and to use their talents well rather than succumb to doubt or despair or inaction.

In essence, African American women authorized themselves to take advantage of whatever opportunities crossed their paths—as agents of survival and change, as community builders and nation builders, and as people who had something to say and to contribute that made a difference to community sustainability and to their own survival. They claimed agency as women who deserved the right to pursue happiness and the right to do whatever they could to affirm themselves and their desires as human beings and citizens of the nation. This operational framework is exhibited in compelling ways by the communities of practice that they passed along from generation to generation. This framework is exhibited also through the productivity of those with the literate and rhetorical expertise to speak and write their own lives. By these means, the generations of nineteenth-century women—before, during, and after the Civil War—functioned as traces of a stream (see Royster 2000), albeit with sobering obstructions, in declaring themselves to be present, aware, capable, and consequential.

Literacy, Learning, and Action

A point worth repeating is that the Civil War was a specific moment of coalescing circumstances for women in general. In the case of white women, the war enabled a broader range of motion for them to function across personal, social, institutional, and public arenas. It became more normal to see them literally out of place by the mores of the day—outside of the home and operating with some independence away from the oversight of men. In the case of African American women, their expanded level of independence was even more basic—being seen away from the oversight and surveillance of everybody. In both instances, white and African American, women's opportunities for a broader set of activities animated their lives and their obligations. Their work as women at war generated new ways of thinking about their own capacities and thereby their sense of agency, identity, and authority.

An especially critical lever for their shifting sensibilities was already in motion—the quest for educational opportunities. Before, during, and after the war, literacy and learning were on the rise in both the North and the South, ultimately including escalating opportunities over the century for public education, presumably for all. Over the course of the century there were also more opportunities for women to go to college—as indicated by the history of Oberlin College. It was the first institution in the United States to permit the enrollment of women (in 1833), including African American women—without their suing. Such opportunities and experiences laid firmer ground for a rising trajectory for African American women's work and their operational patterns, as well as for their readiness to pursue activist agendas as well-educated professional women.

The African American community as a whole recognized the vital importance of literacy and education in the accomplishment of ambitious sociopolitical goals (see Royster 2000, 176–206). Over the centuries this group demonstrated a steadfast commitment to learning and the advancement of reading and writing skills. When opportunities for higher education opened up in the 1830s, they demonstrated both a steadfast commitment to supporting as many people going to college and university as possible and also an urgency to take advantage of these new opportunities, again with the inclusion of African American women. One of the first women of African descent to be enrolled at Oberlin was an African woman, Sarah Margru Kinson, who was captured in Africa as a child and brought to the United States on the *Amistad*, made famous by the insurrection that occurred on it and that occasioned a high profile legal case about the rights of the Africans to be released and returned to their homes in Africa. Another enrollee was Lucy Stanton (1831–1910) who became the first African American woman to graduate from the Ladies' Course in 1850. Between 1834 and 1860, before the abolition of slavery, there was a total of seventeen African American women who completed this course of study.

By 1865, with the Civil War raging, Oberlin had admitted 152 women who can be identified as African American (Lawson 1984). Among this group, in 1862 Mary Jane Patterson (1840–1894) was the first African American woman to receive a bachelor's degree, not only from Oberlin but the first from any accredited American college. The most powerful opportunity for education for African Americans came with the founding of a substantial cluster of colleges that were designated for African Americans, with the earliest ones being:

Cheyney University—1837 (first known as the African Institute, then as the Institute for Colored Youth, in 1913 as Cheyney College, and in 1983 as Cheyney University of Pennsylvania)

Lincoln University of Pennsylvania—1854 (first known as the Ashmun Institute)

Wilberforce University—1856

LeMoyne Normal and Commercial School—1862

Atlanta University—1865 (now known as Clark Atlanta University)

Lincoln University of Missouri and Fisk University—1866

Morehouse College—1867 (first known as the Augusta Institute and later Atlanta Baptist Seminary)

Saint Augustine Normal School and Collegiate Institute—1867 (changed to Saint Augustine College in 1927 and Saint Augustine's University in 2012)

Clark College—1869 (now Clark Atlanta University)

Bennett College—1873 (founded as a coeducational institution that transitioned into a college for women in 1926)

Spelman College—1881 (the first college for African American women)[6]

One point to be added to this list, which is drawn primarily from the website of the *Journal of Blacks in Higher Education*, is that the first African American woman to be appointed a college instructor was Sarah Jane Woodson Early (1825–1907). She graduated from Oberlin College in 1856. After teaching in African American community schools in Xenia, Ohio, in 1858 she received a teaching appointment at Wilberforce University where she taught until 1862, when the university closed for a year during the Civil War. She was rehired in 1866 as a professor, serving as preceptress in English and Latin and as lady principal and matron until 1868, when she married Reverend Jordan Winston Early, moved to North Carolina, and continued to teach there.

This accomplishment by Sarah Woodson Early was not the only such appointment. A second exemplar was Fanny Jackson Coppin (1837–1913). In 1864, while still a student at Oberlin, she was selected to teach a course (see chapter 5) that was very well received. After graduation she was invited to teach at the Institute for Colored Youth (later renamed Cheyney College). She was successful as a teacher, as an administrator in charge of the women students, and as part of the leadership team that established an industrial education unit for the institute, which, along with the academic unit, proved very successful in preparing African American students for their new world.

Data suggest that, by the end of the century, with the founding of higher education institutions both private and public that were dedicated to the education of African American students, the pipeline of graduates was flowing liberally—with increased numbers also coming from students who were graduating from white universities as well. With regard to African American women graduates, the situation was the same. The numbers of women entering the professions was on the rise. A few data points, focused only on health-care professions, begin to tell this part of the story.

Sarah Mapps Douglass (1806–1882) was the first to complete a medical course at an American university in 1858.

Sarah Parker Rémond (1826–1894) was the first to receive a medical degree from an international medical school—from Santa Maria Nuova Hospital in Florence, Italy, in 1871. Rémond remained in Italy and died there.

Rebecca Lee Crumpler (1831–1895) was the first to receive a medical degree from an American institution, the New England Female Medical College, in 1864. She was also the first to practice medicine in the United States.

Halle Tanner Dillon (1864–1901) was the first woman physician (African American or white) to practice in Alabama.

Verina Morton-Jones (1865–1943), was the first woman physician to be licensed in Mississippi.

Matilda Arabella Evans (1872–1935) was the first woman physician to be licensed in South Carolina.

Sara Garland Boyd Jones (1866–1905) was the first woman physician to be licensed in Virginia.

Susan Smith McKinney Steward (1847–1918) was the third African American woman to receive a medical degree in the United States. She graduated as class valedictorian from the New York Medical College for women in 1870. The first African American woman to practice medicine in New York City, she specialized in obstetrics and gynecology but actually served both women and men, and both African Americans and whites.

Mary Eliza Mahoney (1845–1926) was the first to receive a diploma in nursing, from the New England Hospital for Women and Children in Boston in 1879.

Ida Gray Nelson Rollins (1867–1953) was the first to receive a degree in dentistry—from the University of Michigan in 1890.

Matilda Lloyd, Margaret A. Miller, Bella B. Coleman were the first to receive degrees in pharmacy—from Meharry Medical College in 1894.

The success of African American women in other professions was also striking, for example in law and teaching, with success gaining momentum in the twentieth century. Sadie Tanner Mossell Alexander (1898–1989), for example, became one of the first three women to receive a PhD—in her case from the University of Pennsylvania in 1921, becoming the first African American in the United States to receive a PhD in economics. She was also the first woman to receive a law degree from the University of Pennsylvania and the first African American woman to practice law in the state of Pennsylvania.

The conclusion with this litany of achievements is specific. With literacy and higher education as part of their operational tool kit, African American women saw themselves as having capacity—as active contributors and agents of change, as community builders and nation builders, as women with all of the rights of citizenship. They actively engaged in ambitious pursuits of various kinds, all of which connected meaningfully to a master agenda for sociopolitical action in making the world a better place—as Maritcha Lyons had stated, "by making themselves better." At this dynamic intersection of talents and abilities, as well as educational preparation, they demonstrated that they were not just willing to lead but much better prepared to do so. In being conscious of the importance of legacy and sustainability, they were also well prepared, by the examples of their lives and leadership, to push their knowledge and experiences forward in both deed and word. As the century proceeded, there was a steady increase in opportunities for African American women to serve as torchbearers and pathfinders, and with an eye toward the generations of women who would follow them, they told their stories and wrote their narratives.

Making Their Own Way

The latter part of the nineteenth century constitutes an instructive opportunity for seeing and measuring the impact of a novel level of trendsetting achievements among women in general that would foretell the changing professional world for women in the twentieth century and beyond. One striking example that has reverberated throughout the decades is Ohio-born Victoria Claflin Woodhull (1838–1927). With her sister, Tennessee Claflin (1844–1923), Woodhull was the first woman to establish a brokerage firm on

Wall Street—Woodhull, Claflin, and Company. Her business was successful, but even as a white woman, she was still considered to be out of order as a woman in public arenas typically occupied by men. Notably, though, she was a pacesetter in other ways as well, establishing herself as a community leader who advocated for woman suffrage, labor relations, and issues related to personal and social freedom.

In 1872 Woodhull became the first woman to run for president of the United States—even though at the time, women had not yet secured the right to vote nationwide. She was nominated by the Equal Rights Party, who also nominated Frederick Douglass as her vice-presidential running mate. This statement by the party was, of course, a bold one, but not surprisingly, Woodhull lost, whereupon she moved to England and died there (Royster 2003). The point to be highlighted is that Woodhull's actions in the nineteenth century cast light on pathways that women had not followed before in business and in politics, offering evidence that, although these pathways were uncharted, the potential for success was actually there. As reflected in recent decades, perhaps slowly but certainly surely, other women have taken up these gauntlets. Since 1872, we have witnessed a substantial line of women both white and African American who, with varying success, became presidential candidates—for example, Belva Lockwood (1884), Margaret Chase Smith (1964), Charlene Alexander Mitchell (1968), Shirley Chisholm (1972), Hillary Rodham Clinton (2008, 2016), Jill Stein (2012, 2016), Elizabeth Warren (2016, 2020), Kamala Harris (2020), Amy Klobuchar (2020), and others.

For nineteenth-century African American women, doors were beginning to open across all sorts of professional arenas. Although their horizons continued to be constrained in various ways, by the turn of the century they were more determined than ever to walk through any open or crackable door. They were enthusiastic and inventive about finding ways to participate in their operational circles as advocates, activists, and leaders of survival, progress, and change. They took advantage of available opportunities, expanding their experiences as women who perform work that matters. They honed their expertise as master strategists, and they used all available means, among them rhetoric and writing, to get work done that they deemed necessary. With pen and voice, they sharpened their visions and focused their actions. By the end of the century, they were no longer willing to be ignored or to wait to be recognized and anointed as deserving of appreciation and honor. Instead, speaking for themselves, they formed their own national agenda for collective action. Ultimately, the Black Clubwomen's Movement was born.

The question of outcomes for this sociopolitical work and the robust set of experiences and expertise that created it raises another set of questions: As women at work who had evolved over the decades in the Americas, what were their patterns of thought and action? What legacies did they set in motion in terms of intellectual vision, agency, and action? How did their lives and experiences—from Wheatley's first publication in 1773 through the end of the Civil War in 1865 and Reconstruction in 1877—light pathways to ongoing sociopolitical action? How did they move forward from the broadly rendered setbacks of post-Reconstruction to the organized national agenda that they formulated in the 1890s in their launching of the Black Clubwomen's Movement? How did they find or make their ways forward?

The Shifting Ground for Agency and Authority

The long nineteenth century, from the founding of the nation to 1900, was a vibrant time for transformative change within the United States. For African Americans, it was an era in which new opportunities emerged. In 1776 there was the centralizing of national bedrock values: freedom, justice, equality, and the pursuit of happiness. This national choice incentivized the rise of abolitionism in animating with renewed energy the quest of African Americans for freedom, justice, and the rights of citizenship. Ultimately, with the ending of institutionalized slavery after the Civil War and the underscoring of the need to pursue a more perfect nation, among African American women and men there were clearer expectations for human and civil rights and for greater prosperity. In essence, the founding of the nation marked a kairotic occasion for this downtrodden group to prepare themselves to be fully present in nation-building processes with their own agency, identity, and authority. In fact, both African American women and men were crystal clear about a critically important protocol. Seeing the need for expertise and skills, they were passionate about the urgency of pursuing education and professional development. They heartily embraced the need to take advantage of a growing range of opportunities to enhance their literate abilities, to develop their rhetorical prowess, and to build their knowledge and expertise in a broad range of work arenas.

The consequence of understanding the need for this protocol is evidenced in the steadily growing numbers of African Americans, across age levels and including African American women, who went to school—legally. Going to school for some of them included also going to college and university and building their capacities to work in professional arenas—as doctors and nurses, lawyers, teachers and school administrators, scientists, business owners, community organizers, journalists, and more. To emphasize the trajectories for African American women within this shifting context, we are well advised to remember that in overwhelming numbers this cohort already had two hundred years of experience as workers at the will of others. With expanding opportunities, though, they were better able to focus on translating their long-standing experiences into well-grounded visions of possibility and into their own definitions of self in society as they gained even more experience in exercising their own agency and authority and operationalizing their own agendas.

A specific innovation grew out of strategies that women of African descent have been recognized as utilizing since 1619 and before—that is, the culturally informed practices of getting their work done by sharing knowledge and workload. They are noted for being astute at working together collaboratively. In the context of nation building, these practices were transformed dynamically into organizational structures of various kinds that were designed to support community development and social reform. The evolution of these practices in the context of the United States is documented by Martha S. Jones (2007), who chronicles the ways in which African American women built organizations within existing community institutions such as churches, political organizations, mutual aid societies, schools, and so on. Elizabeth McHenry (2002) also adds insightful observations in this area. Her research expands the record of African American reading practices in literary clubs and associations and connects these traditions to civic participation, the African American press, and the commitments of African American women, in particular, to literary activities.

A general example is the various ministries and auxiliary groups in churches that were designed to provide support for the needs of the church community, from assistance with food, clothing, and shelter to assistance with job opportunities, health needs, and burials, to opportunities to engage with the Bible and religious teachings, to opportunities to encourage civic participation. Another example is literary associations, such as the lyceum that journalist Ida B. Wells found when she moved to Memphis, Tennessee. The lyceum to which she belonged was composed mainly of teachers. It offered them access to many expressive activities such as recitations, essays, debates, musical performances, and a newspaper, the *Evening Star*. The paper contained news items, literary pieces, commentary on local programming, and reports of community pleasantries. Each issue was prepared by the editor and read aloud to the group. Wells became one of the editors of the lyceum's newspaper and later of another paper, *The Living Way*, which was a religious weekly associated with the Baptist Church. This latter example highlights a particularly strong mechanism by which African American women enhanced the assets they brought to opportunities for advocacy, activism, and leadership. As they increased their literate and rhetorical abilities, they also took advantage of opportunities to perform various roles related to the periodical press—as journalists, as contributing writers, operations managers, editors, and owners.[7]

The evidence of visibility and impact, given the oppressive conditions that surrounded the women throughout this era, is clear enough to support the assertion that the network of African American women working with the African American periodical press was robust (see figure 2.4).[8] An examination of their activities confirms that they were energized by both their own personal desires as writers and their ideological commitments as women who cared about and for their communities. Figure 2.4 maps the geographical scope of the African American periodical press as a national enterprise. With emphasis on women's participation, it represents a preliminary snapshot of this group's efforts to use their literate abilities through their social and professional networks and, thereby, their efforts to be civically engaged. The open circles indicate the general distribution of the periodicals. The lighter circles indicate the sites where African American women were participating. The darker circles indicate the sites where the periodicals were woman-owned and operated. As this graphic shows, African American women were part of a vibrant public discourse and from the vantage point of civic participation can be seen as "traces of a stream."[9] This map of the periodical press from 1827–1900 confirms that in order to make African American women's presence

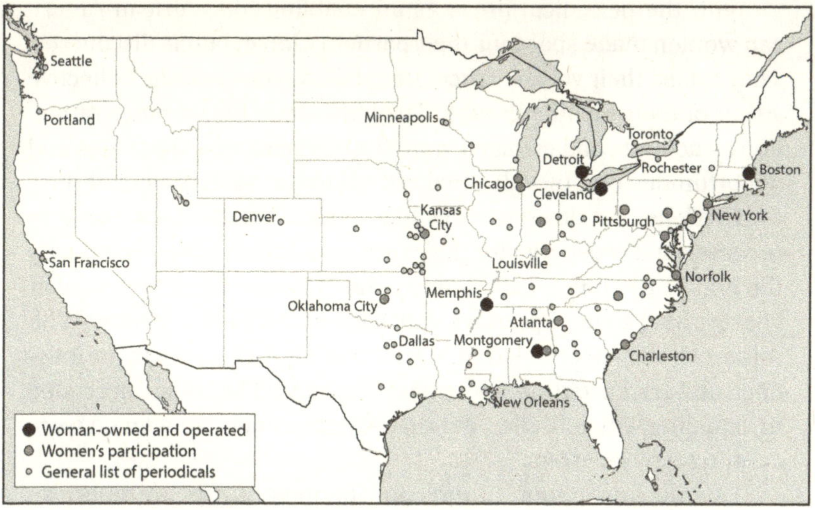

Figure 2.4: Sites for African American Periodicals, 1827–1900, with Women's Major Contributions Identified

and impact in civic discourses visible, we can ask some fundamental question: Where were the women located? What sorts of roles did they fill for the publications at which they were associated? We might also ask another layer of questions: What were the cultural expectations for their participation? What were their habits of action? What were the outcomes and consequences of their contributions and leadership?

As documented in a preliminary way by the database from which this map was created, there were at least sixty-five women from 1853 to 1900 who were functioning as active writers for the periodical press (see figure 2.5). With a focus on their work as women journalists immediately before, during, and after the Civil War, the documentary effort is to confirm the range and intensity of their participation. The circles on the map indicate by size a clustering of women in a particular site who can be identified as actively engaged in journalistic activities. In viewing this visualization, we can see more clearly that the group of women represented on the map constituted a national network of women professionals and community leaders. Over the decades from 1827–1900, they used the periodical press as a means to fulfil their expressive desires and to engage collaboratively with their compatriots in sociopolitical action.

With the periodical press as an enabling tool, African American women made space for their participation in public discourses. They raised their voices, articulated their visions and the collective vision of their identity groups. They broadened their range of motion as activists and engaged various audiences with the issues and opportunities that they deemed critical to the achievement of their own visions and desires, as well as critical for the forwarding of progress and prosperity for their race as a downtrodden people. By the end of the nineteenth century these journalists were regularly exercising their expressive expertise in the public sphere. With this work they succeeded in strengthening their capacity to influence and lead progress and positive change. They also succeeded in signaling with a bright light that African American women were creating new horizons.

This documentation of the contributions of African American women to the African American periodical press functions at the convergence of opportunities to exercise more agency and authority, opportunities for education (including higher education), significant work experiences, and a habit of collective action. This convergence of factors leveraged the ability of this group of women as visionary strategists to launch the Black Clubwomen's Movement, to articulate an ambitious national sociopolitical agenda, to implement it, and to get this work stabilized quickly—in less than two years. The multilayered proposition in this analysis is that, across the nineteenth century, African American women were very much aware of their material realities, their expanding opportunities, their strengths, talents, and abilities, and the persistent array of needs that surrounded them. They were focused on and conscientious about taking advantage of opportunities and about using their available means to get things done.

Most provocatively, these women leaders understood that over the decades they were able to build an infrastructure for their new organization on the existing foundation of their social networks. In this case, documenting their work as journalists confirms that their existing relationships to and knowledge of each other as journalists constituted an invaluable resource. Beyond this core professional network, however, the women also were linked to multiple other enabling networks that were similarly available to them, including their church memberships; their relationships with those who had attended their same colleges; their roles and connections as educators; the social and professional connections among their

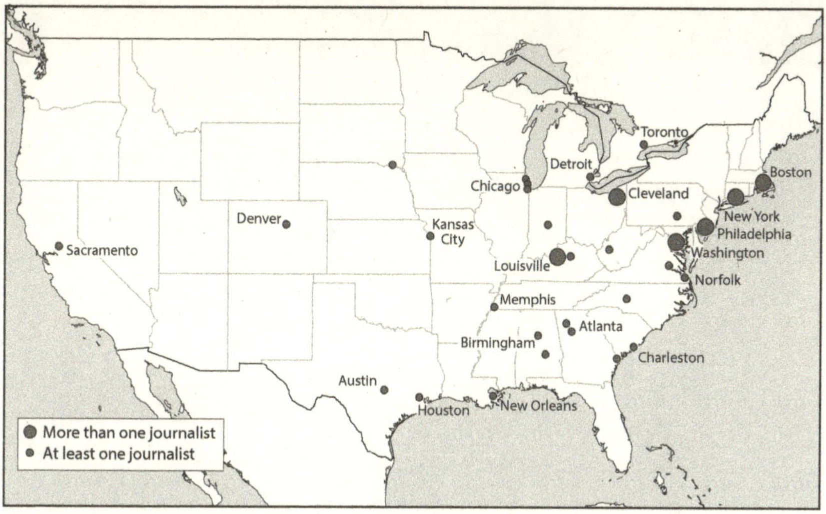

Figure 2.5: A Network of African American Women Journalists, 1853–1900

husbands, fathers, and brothers; their geographical connections; their cross-connections to other organizations; and so on. By all measures, this group fashioned strategies and practices to develop and organize NACW as a coherent sociopolitical initiative that was capable of enhancing their agency and authority to lead and support transformative change. Their actions demonstrated that, even with a provocative range of diverse ideas and interests and with their aspirations for visibility and impact on a national rather than a local scale, they had actually prepared themselves well. They were prepared and ready to do whatever they needed to do to articulate and implement a very ambitious agenda. Their goal was to improve their own horizons as they worked conscientiously to make the world a better place for all. In 1896, they chose their pathway forward, and they made it work.

Part II

Audibility

Chapter 3

Before the Civil War

Despite the persistent challenges that African American women faced over the nineteenth century, the good news is that they managed, quite noticeably, to increase the frequency and volume of their voices in institutional and public spaces. By whatever means were available to them, they found ways to speak for themselves with eloquence and rhetorical prowess. The nineteenth century defines, therefore, an era of development and expansion of the women's rhetorical expertise and experience, with the result that their civic participation blossomed. They were able to exhibit their sociopolitical visions and to display their expertise in strategic planning and problem-solving. Over the decades, they raised their voices forthrightly, with a clearer expectation that they might be able to generate persuasive effects in helping to bring about the positive changes in their world that they wanted to see. This last point becomes instructive for achieving the goals of this analysis.

A growing mound of evidence confirms that during this era African American women regularly exercised their rhetorical abilities, both speaking and writing in social, institutional, and public spaces. These data offer a compelling tool, thereby, for tracking the contours, continuities, evolution, and consequences of these performances as sociopolitical work. The tracking process deployed in this analysis begins with the showcasing of women who were writing before the Civil War and then proceeds in clusters in subsequent chapters to three additional chronological milestones: during the Civil War, after the Civil War, and at the turn of the century. With emphasis on the fact that this set of exemplars wrote for public audiences, the imperative with each writer is to provide a sampling of what they had to say in their own words.

Using a chronological lens, each cluster benefits from our examination in Part I of the nineteenth century as a specific time-bound context in which we can then cast light on each woman showcased as an exemplar of sociopolitical behavior in their particular environment. The imperative is to gather more fully rendered data in order to see the ways in which these women conveyed their expertise as thinkers and actors within their various networks; created space for themselves as speakers and writers amid whatever challenges and barriers they faced; were able to work strategically for progress and change, taking advantage of available opportunities; and embodied in terms of identity, agency, and authority the categories advocate, activist, and leader. This first cluster, before the Civil War, sets a pattern for examining the next three clusters with the effort to draw forward inferences from the women's performances to leverage a more generative interpretive framework.

The clusters of texts in Part II are not intended to be viewed as comprehensive in capturing the totality of African American women's sociopolitical leadership and action across the century, or as a full array of individual women's rhetorical performances, or even as a complete assessment of their prowess as rhetors. Instead, the clusters highlight this particular set of speakers and writers as exemplars of excellence in rhetorical behavior during their day and as significant in understanding the strong foundation on which the stories of African American women's rhetorical prowess stands. The individual selections are presented as exemplary of the ways in which the women have used the genres that were available to them for expressiveness in such a vibrant, though still constrained, rhetorical context. Core to this analysis, however, the clusters offer an opportunity, ultimately, for seeing the operational patterns of African American women's lives and work over time, not just superficially as women who wrote but, more explicitly, as sociopolitical actors who functioned strategically with an agenda.

We might consider Part II, as a whole, to be a case study in which the imperative is to examine the women's rhetorical behavior over time as deliberate action. We can interrogate ethos formation, voice, and imperatives; topics, genres, and texts; and audience. We can look more closely at their visions of possibility and self-reported desires. We can draw from this configuration of factors evidence of the ways in which they enacted their commitments to social justice and social change, and we can notice also whatever they shared with others as inspiration for the ongoing work.

Before the Civil War, there was a very narrow sociocultural expectation for African American women having any sort of public rhetorical presence in keeping with the mores and practices of the time period. They participated nevertheless. A critical point to note, however, is that this study does not centralize African American women's speaking presence as much as it does their writing presence, especially before the war. Although there were women who spoke in public during the early days of the century (for example, the abolitionists and northern educators), their actual words are more difficult to document, as indicated by the existence of different versions of the famous Sojourner Truth speech, "Ain't I a Woman." Instead, the analysis here is anchored more explicitly by their writing presence, the texts of various kinds that they left behind, whether originally spoken or written. This choice underscores how much remains to be done in capturing the truths of African American women's lives and achievements more fully as well as in documenting the scope of their productivity as expressive beings with purpose.

In this analysis I take note, as well, of the expressive genres the women chose for themselves or that were available to them in keeping with the writing and publishing practices of their day. In examining these choices in generic terms, we can see that they obviously had precious few officialized occasions to choose sermons, with no record at this point of their being able to utilize this form during the early years of the nation. However, like Phillis Wheatley, they did write poetry. Also, in response to the rising imperatives of abolitionism and the need for compelling eyewitness accounts to forward this cause, they wrote narratives. To be underscored here, I do not refer to the narratives in this volume by the formulaic ways in which former slaves were called upon to recount their lives in slavery. While I recognize that the imperative in these texts to support freedom and justice are certainly evident, I do not classify the narratives as "slave" narratives, a categorization based on the sociopolitical status of the writers. Instead, I see the importance of classifying them in keeping with their form and purpose as memoirs and autobiographies, an idea based on the fact that the writers chose a genre with purpose, one that permitted them to write their own lives.

In addition, the first generation of African American women writers also wrote essays and speeches. Like the memoirs and autobiographies, these texts, by rhetorical imperative, functioned within the context of abolitionism and community building. Further, with regard to their more private writing, like other women of their day, they kept diaries and wrote letters. In this chapter (and in subsequent chapters), I present the writers selected, thereby, not simply with a sense of chronology but with a specific sense of their generic choices also in mind, as texts written with intention and purpose. The imperative is to ground the analysis in the materiality of the ways in which the women's writings reflect their opportunities to engage in public arenas in the context of various constraints.

In this way, the texts themselves become instructive in two specific ways. Quite fundamentally, they are artifacts of the women's efforts to express themselves, an impressive achievement for their day and time. They had things to say and they managed to say them. Simultaneously, however, the texts are also the embodiment of the women's sociopolitical visions, desires, and imperatives, such that their texts offer rhetorical evidence—not simply of their desires to express themselves but their decisions to share their thoughts in public and to proclaim agency in the presentation of a speaking self. An essential point to be drawn forward is a fundamental one. By means of their rhetorical decision making, these women conveyed their commitments, regardless of genre, to their worthiness as women, to their rights to speak, and to their capacities to participate in discourses that mattered to them, but most especially they demonstrated their ability to help in making the world a better place.

Maria W. Stewart

Maria Miller Stewart (1803–1879), born free in Hartford, Connecticut, was an abolitionist and women's rights activist.[1] She is recognized as the first African American woman to write political essays and speeches and the first woman to speak publicly on political subjects. Orphaned at five years old, Stewart began working at this young age as an indentured servant and then as a domestic servant. In 1826 she married a financially successful shipping agent and became more secure financially and socially within the small circle of Boston's very politically engaged African American community, which included the revolutionary abolitionist David Walker, author of *An Appeal to the Colored Citizens of the World* (1830; see D. Walker 1993). In 1829, Stewart's husband died suddenly, which left her vulnerable to the oppressions that surrounded African Americans during this era. She was defrauded of her inheritance by his white business partners. However, instead of keeping quiet about the discriminatory practices she experienced, she became an outspoken advocate for justice. She took advantage of social connections in the community and the ways in which this group was connected to the white abolitionist community, and she was successful in getting her first essay (included below) published in *The Liberator* by William Lloyd Garrison and Isaac Knapp on October 8, 1831.[2] It was addressed to "the people of color." Over the next three years as a public speaker before both male and female audiences, she gained a reputation for being outspoken, fiery in the jeremiad tradition, revolutionary, and out of order with regard to her thinking and operating outside of the gendered and racialized social mores of her day.

In this first essay, Stewart uses the essay form but crosses generic boundaries as well to include in her essay a prayer and a poem. Through these generic choices, she established a matrix of concerns that have resonated from her day forward. Embedding her ideas in Christian beliefs and teachings and in her own lived experiences, she emphasized the importance of living by moral values and principles, working for good, embracing self-definition and self-help. She emphasized the necessity that every person commit to doing their best to distinguish themselves, advancing a community-wide commitment to the education and mentorship of youth, creating legacies capable of living beyond our own lives, and helping to guide current and future generation. She emphasized the rationality of being dedicated to truth, freedom, justice, and equality, being determined to act on moral values and principles, and on what we know to be true. She highlights also the impact of gender on agency and action, and especially the differential experiences and treatment of women of African descent.

Stewart's groundwork constitutes a springboard for understanding the conceptual evolution in subsequent decades of two key analytical points: the double jeopardy of race and gender; and the even broader configuration of sociopolitical impacts that have now gained visibility as intersectionality—which takes into account not only race and gender but also class, sexuality, culture, ideology, and so forth. One might say, in fact, that for Stewart, the essay form facilitated a process of distillation that allowed her to articulate, for her immediate audience and for generations beyond, a compelling rhetorical agenda designed to bring visibility, audibility, and intelligibility to the sociopolitical position of the subject, to the materiality of experience, to context and condition, and to the politics of agency and credibility.

Maria W. Stewart

Excerpts from "Religion and the Pure Principles of Morality, the Sure Foundation on Which We Must Build," *Maria W. Stewart: America's First Black Woman Political Writer*, ed. Marilyn Richardson (Bloomington: Indiana University Press, 1987), 28–42.

> For sale at this office, a tract addressed to the people of color, by Mrs. Maria W. Steward [*sic*], a respectable colored lady of this city. Its title is, 'Religion And The Pure Principles of Morality, The Sure Foundation On Which We Must Build.' The production is most praiseworthy, and confers great credit on the talents and piety of its author. We hope she will have many patrons. Extracts of the paper hereafter. Price 6 cents.
>
> *The Liberator*, 8 October 1831

Religion And The Pure Principles of Morality,
The Sure Foundation On Which We Must Build

Production From The Pen Of Mrs. Maria W. Steward [*sic*],
Widow Of The Late James W. Steward, Of Boston

Introduction

Feeling a deep solemnity of soul, in view of our wretched and degraded situation, and sensible of the gross ignorance that prevails among us, I have thought proper thus publicly to express my sentiments before you. I hope my friends will not scrutinize these pages with too severe an eye, as I have not calculated to display either elegance or taste in their composition, but have merely written the meditations of my heart as far as my imagination led; and have presented them before you in order to arouse you to exertion, and to enforce upon your minds the great necessity of turning your attention to knowledge and improvement.

I was born in Hartford, Connecticut, in 1803; was left orphan at five years of age; was bound out in a clergyman's family; had the seeds of piety and virtue early sown in my mind, but was deprived of the advantages of education, though my soul thirsted for knowledge. Left them at fifteen years of age; attended Sabbath schools until I was twenty; in 1826 was married to James W. Stewart; was left a widow in 1829; was, as I humbly hope and trust, brought to the knowledge of the truth, as it is in Jesus, in 1830; in 1831 made a public profession [of] my faith in Christ.

From the moment I experienced the change, I felt a strong desire, with the help and assistance of God, to devote the remainder of my days to piety and virtue, and now possess that spirit of independence that, were I called upon, I would willingly sacrifice my life for the cause of God and my brethren.

All the nations of the earth are crying out for liberty and equality. Away, away with tyranny and oppression! And shall Afric's sons be silent any longer? Far be it from me to recommend to you either to kill, burn, or destroy. But I would strongly recommend to you to improve your talents; let not one lie buried in the earth. Show forth your powers of mind. Prove to the world that

> Though black your skins as shades of night,
> Your hearts are pure, your souls are white.

This is the land of freedom. The press is at liberty. Every man has a right to express his opinion. Many think, because your skins are tinged with a sable hue, that you are an inferior race of beings; but God does not consider you as such. He hath formed and fashioned you in his own glorious image, and hath bestowed upon you reason and strong powers of intellect. He hath made you to have dominion over the beasts of the field, the fowls of the air, and the fish of the sea [Genesis 1:26]. He hath crowned you with glory and honor; hath made you but a little lower than the angels [Psalms 8:5]; and according to the Constitution of these United States, he hath made all men free and equal. Then why should one worm say to another, "Keep you down there, while I sit up yonder; for I am better than thou?" It is not the color of the skin that makes the man, but it is the principles formed within the soul.

Many will suffer for pleading the cause of the oppressed Africa, and I shall glory in being one of her martyrs; for I am firmly persuaded, that the God in whom I trust is able to protect me from the rage and malice of mine enemies, and from them that will rise up against me; and if there is no other way for me to escape, he is able to take me to himself, as he did the most noble, fearless, and undaunted David Walker.

Never Will Virtue, Knowledge, And True Politeness Begin To Flow, Till The Pure Principles of Religion and Morality Are Put Into Force.

My Respected Friends,

I feel almost unable to address you; almost incompetent to perform the task; and at times I have felt ready to exclaim, O that my head were waters, and mine eyes a fountain of tears, that I might weep day and night [Jeremiah 9:1], for the transgression of the daughters of my people. Truly, my heart's desire and prayer is, that Ethiopia might stretch forth her hands unto God. But we have a great work to do. Never, no, never will the chains of slavery and ignorance burst, till we become united as one, and cultivate among ourselves the pure principles of piety, morality and virtue. I am sensible of my ignorance; but such knowledge as God has given to me, I impart to you. I am sensible of former prejudices; but it is high time for prejudices and animosities to cease from among us. I am sensible of exposing myself to calumny and reproach; but shall I, for fear of feeble man who shall die, hold my peace? Shall I for fear of scoffs and frowns, refrain my tongue? Ah, not I speak as one that must give an account at the awful bar of God; I speak as a dying mortal to dying mortals. O, ye daughters of Africa, awake! Awake! Arise! No longer sleep nor slumber, but distinguish yourselves. Show forth to the world that ye are endowed with noble and exalted faculties. O, ye daughters of Africa! What have ye done to immortalize your names beyond the grave? What examples have ye set before the rising generation? What foundation have ye laid for generations yet unborn? Where are our union and love? And where is our sympathy, that weeps at another's woe, and hides the faults we see? And our daughters, where are they? Blushing in innocence and virtue? And our sons, do they bid fair to become crowns of glory to our hoary heads [Proverbs 16:31]? Where is the parent who is conscious of having faithfully discharged his duty, and at the last awful day of account, shall be able to say, here, Lord, is thy poor, unworthy servant, and the children thou hast given me? And where are the children that will arise and call them blessed? Alas, O God! Forgive me if I speak amiss; the minds of our tender babes are tainted as soon as they are born' they go astray, as it were, from the womb. Where is the maiden who will blush at vulgarity? And where is the youth who has written upon his manly brow a thirst for knowledge; whose ambitious mind soars above trifles, and longs for the time to come, when he shall redress the wrongs of his father and plead the cause of his brethren? Did the daughters of our land possess a delicacy of manners, combined with gentleness and dignity; did their pure minds hold vice in abhorrence and contempt, did they frown when their ears were polluted with its vile accents, would not their influence become powerful? Would not our brethren fall in love with their virtues? Their souls would become fired with a holy zeal for freedom's cause. They would become ambitious to distinguish themselves. They would become proud to display their talents. Able advocates would arise in our defence. Knowledge would begin to flow, and the chains of slavery and ignorance would melt like wax before the flames. I am but a feeble instrument. I am but as one particle of the small dust of the earth. You may frown or smile. After I am dead, perhaps before, God will surely rise up those who will more powerfully and eloquently plead the cause of virtue and the pure principles of morality than I am able to do. O virtue! How sacred is thy name! How pure are thy principles! Who can find a virtuous woman? For her price is far above rubies [Proverbs 31:10]. Blessed is the man who shall call her his wife; yea, happy is the child who shall call her mother. O woman, woman, would thou only strive to excel in merit and virtue; would thou only store thy mind with useful knowledge, great would be thine influence. Do you say you are too far advanced in life now to begin? You are not too far advanced to instil [*sic*] these principles into the minds of your tender infants. Let them by no means be neglected. Discharge your duty faithfully, in every point of view: leave the event with God. So shall your skirts become clear of their blood [Jeremiah 2:34].

When I consider how little improvement has been made the last eight years; the apparent cold and indifferent state of the children of God; how few have been hopefully brought to the knowledge of the truth as it is in Jesus; that our young men and maidens are fainting and drooping, as it were, by the way side, for the want of knowledge; when I see how few care to distinguish themselves either in religious or moral improvement, and when I see the greater part of our community following the vain bubbles of life with so much eagerness, which will only prove to them like the serpent's sting upon the bed of death, I really think we are in as wretched and miserable a state as was the house of Israel in the days of Jeremiah.

I suppose many of my friends will say, "Religion is all your theme," I hope my conduct will ever prove me to be what I profess, a true follower of Christ; and it is the religion of Jesus alone what will constitute your happiness here, and support you in a dying hour. O then, do not trifle with God and your own souls any longer. Do not presume to offer him the very dregs of your lives; but now, whilst you are blooming in health and vigor, consecrate the remnant of your days to him. Do you wish to become useful in your day and generation? Do you wish to promote the welfare and happiness of your friends, as far as your circle extends? Have you one desire to become truly great? O then become truly pious and God will endow you with wisdom and knowledge from on high.

Come, turn to God, who did thee make
And at his presence fear and quake;
Remember him now in thy youth,
And let thy soul take hold of truth.
The devil and his ways defy,
Believe him not, he doth but lie,
His ways seem sweet: but youth, beware!
He for thy soul hath laid a snare.

Religion is pure; it is ever new; it is beautiful; it is all that is worth living for; it is worth dying for. O, could I but see the church built up in the most holy faith; could I but see men spiritually minded, walking in the fear of God, not given to filthy lucre, not holding religion in one hand and the world in the other, but diligent in business, fervent in spirit, serving the Lord, standing upon the walls of Zion, crying to passers by, "Ho, every one that thirsteth, come ye to the waters, and he that hath no money; yea, come and buy wine and milk without money and without price [Isiah 55:1]." Turn ye, turn ye, for why will ye die [Ezekiel 33:11]? Could I but see mothers in Israel, chaste, keepers at home, not busy bodies, meddlers in other men's matters, whose adorning is of the inward man, possessing a meek and quiet spirit, whose sons were like olive-plants, and whose daughters were as polished corner-stones; co[u]ld I but see young men and maidens turning their feet from impious ways, rather choosing to suffer affliction with the people of God than to enjoy the pleasures of sin for a season; could I but see the rising youth blushing in artless innocence, then co[u]ld I say, now, Lord, let thine unworthy handmaiden depart in peace, for I have seen the desire of mine eyes, and am satisfied."

Prayer

O, Lord God, the watchmen of Zion have cried peace, peace, when there was no peace [Jeremiah 6:14]; they have been, as it were, blind leaders of the blind [Matthew 15:14]. Wherefore hast thou so long withheld from us the divine influences of thy Holy Spirit? Wherefore has thou hardened our hearts and blinded our eyes? It is because we have honored thee with our lips, but our hearts were far from thee. We have polluted thy Sabbaths, and even our most holy things have been solemn mockery to thee. We have regarded iniquity in our hearts, therefore thou wilt not hear. Return again unto us. O Lord God, we beseech thee, and pardon this the iniquity of thy servants. Cause thy face to shine upon us, and we shall be saved. O visit us with thy salvation. Raise up sons and daughters unto Abraham, and grant that there might come a mighty shaking of dry bones among us, and a great ingathering of souls. Quicken thy professing children. Grant that the young may be constrained to believe that there is a reality in religion, and a beauty in the fear of the Lord. Have mercy on the benighted sons and daughters of Africa. Grant that we may soon become so distinguished for our moral and religious improvements, that the nations of the earth may take knowledge of us, and grant that our cries may come up before thy throne like holy incense. Grant that every daughter of Africa may consecrate her sons to thee from birth. And do thou, Lord, bestow upon them wise and understanding hearts. Clothe us with humility of soul, and give us a becoming dignity of manners: may we imitate the character of the meek and lowly Jesus; and do thou grant that Ethiopia may soon stretch forth her hands unto thee. And now, Lord, be pleased to grant that Satan's kingdom may be destroyed; that the kingdom of our Lord Jesus Christ may be built up; that all nations and kindreds and tongues and people might be brought to the knowledge of the truth, as it is in Jesus, and we at last meet around thy throne, and join in celebrating thy praises.

I have been taking a survey of the American people in my own mind, and I see them thriving in arts and sciences, and in polite literature. Their highest aim is to excel in political, moral and religious improvement. They early consecrate their children to God, and their youth indeed are blushing in artless innocence. They wipe the tears from the orphan's eyes, and they cause the widow's heart to sing for joy [Job 29:13]! And their poorest ones, who have the least wish to excel, they promote! And those that have but one talent they encourage. But how very few are there among them that bestow one thought upon the benighted sons and daughters of Africa, who have enriched the soils of America with their tears and blood: few to promote their cause, none to encourage their talents. Under these circumstances, do not let our hearts be any longer discouraged; it is no use to murmur or to repine; but let us promote ourselves and improve our own talents. And I am rejoiced to reflect that there are many able and talented ones among us, whose names might be recorded on the bright annals of fame. But "I can't," is a great barrier in the way. I hope it will soon be removed, and "I will," resume its place.

Righteousness exalteth a nation, but sin is a reproach to any people [Proverbs 14:34]. Why is it, my friends, that our minds have been blinded by ignorance, to the present moment? 'Tis on account of sin. Why is it that our church is involved in so much difficulty?" It is on account of sin. Why is it that God has cut down, upon our right hand and upon our left, the most learned and intelligent of our men? O, shall I say, it is on account of sin! Why is it that thick darkness is mantled upon every brow, and we, as it were, look sadly upon one another? It is on account of sin. O, then, let us bow before the Lord our God, with all our hearts, and humble our very souls in the dust before him; sprinkling, as it were, ashes upon our heads, and awake to righteousness and sin not. The arm of the Lord is not shortened, that it cannot save; neither is his ear heavy, that it cannot hear; but it is your iniquities that have separated you from me, saith the Lord. Return, O ye backsliding children [Jeremiah 3:22], and I will return unto you, and ye shall be my people, and I will be your God.

O, ye mothers, what a responsibility rests on you! You have souls committed to your charge, and God will require a strict account of you. It is you that must create in the minds of your little girls and boys a thirst for knowledge, the love of virtue, the abhorrence of vice, and the cultivation of a pure heart. The seeds thus sown will grow with their growing years; and the love of virtue thus early formed in the soul will protect their inexperienced feet from many dangers. O, do not say you cannot make any thing of your children; but say, with the help and assistance of God, we will try. Do not indulge them in their little stubborn ways; for a child left to himself bringeth his mother to shame. Spare not for their crying; thou shalt beat them with a rod, and they shall not die [Proverbs 23:13], and thou shalt save their souls from hell. When you correct them, do it in the fear of God, and for their own good. They will not thank you for your false and foolish indulgence; they will rise up, as it were, and curse you in this world and, in the world to come, condemn you. It is no use to say you can't do this, or you can't do that; you will not tell your Maker so, when you meet him at the great day of account. And you must be careful that you set an example worthy of following, for you they will imitate. There are many instances, even among us now, where parents have discharged their duty faithfully, and their children now reflect honor upon their gray hairs.

Perhaps you will say that many parents have set pure examples at home, and they have not followed them. True, our expectations are often blasted; but let not this dishearten you. If they have faithfully discharged their duty, even after they are dead their works may live; their prodigal children may return to God and become heirs of salvation; if not, their children cannot rise and condemn them at the awful bar of God.

Perhaps you will say that you cannot send them to high schools and academies. You can have them taught in the first rudiments of useful knowledge, and then you can have private teachers who will instruct them in the higher branches; and their intelligence will become greater than ours, and their children will attain to higher advantages, and their children still higher; and then, though we are dead, our works shall live: though we are mouldering, our names shall not be forgotten.

Finally, my heart's desire and prayer to God is that there might come a thorough reformation among us. Our minds have too long grovelled in ignorance and sin. Come, let us incline our ears to wisdom, and apply our hearts to understanding; promote her, and she will exalt thee; she shall bring thee honor when thou dost embrace her. An ornament of grace shall she be to thy head, and a crown of glory shall she deliver to thee. Take fast hold of instruction; let her not go; keep her, for she is thy life [Proverbs 4:13]. Come, let us turn unto the Lord our God, with all our heart and soul, and put away every unclean and unholy thing from among us, and walk before the Lord our God, with a perfect heart, all the days of our lives: then we shall be a people with whom God shall delight to dwell; yea, we shall be that happy people whose God is the Lord.

I am of a strong opinion that the day on which we unite, heart and soul, and turn our attention to knowledge and improvement, that day the hissing and reproach among the nations of the earth against us will cease. And even those who now point at us with the finger of scorn, will aid and befriend us. It is of no use for us to sit with our hands folded, hanging our heads like bulrushes, lamenting our wretched condition; but let us make a mighty effort, and arise; and if no one will promote or respect us, let us promote and respect ourselves.

The American ladies have the honor conferred on them, that by prudence and economy in their domestic concerns, and their unwearied attention in forming the minds and manners of their children, they laid the foundation of their becoming what they now are. The good women of Wethersfield, Conn., toiled in the blazing sun, year after year, weeding onions, then sold the seed and procured enough money to erect them a house of worship; and shall we not imitate their examples, as far as they are worthy of imitation? Why cannot we do something to distinguish ourselves, and contribute some of our hard earnings that would reflect honor upon our memories, and cause our children to arise and call us blessed? Shall it any longer be said of the daughters of Africa, they have no ambition, they have no force? By no means. Let every female heart become united and let us raise a fund ourselves; and at the end of one year and a half, we might be able to lay the corner stone for the building of a High School, that the higher branches of knowledge might be enjoyed by us; and God would raise us up, and enough to aid us in our laudable designs. Let each one strive to excel in good housewifery, knowing that prudence and economy are the road to wealth. Let us not say we know this, or we know that, and practice nothing; but let us practice what we do know.

How long shall the fair daughters of Africa be compelled to bury their minds and talents beneath a load of iron pots and kettles? Until union, knowledge and love begin to flow among us. How long shall a mean set of men flatter us with their smiles, and enrich themselves with our hard earnings; their wives' fingers sparkling with rings, and they themselves laughing at our folly? Until we begin to promote and patronize each other. Shall we be a by-word among the nations any longer? Shall they laugh us to scorn forever? Do you ask, what can we do? Unite and build a store of your own, if you cannot procure a license. Fill one side with dry goods, and the other with groceries. Do you ask where is the money? We have spent more than enough for nonsense, to do what building we should want. We have never had an opportunity of displaying our talents; therefore the world thinks we know nothing. And we have been possessed by far too mean and cowardly a disposition, though I highly disapprove of an insolent or impertinent one. Do you ask the disposition I would have you possess? Possess the spirit of independence. The Americans do, and why should not you? Possess the spirit of men, bold and enterprising, fearless and undaunted. Sue for your rights and privileges. Know the reason that you cannot attain them. Weary them with your importunities. You can but die if you make the attempt; and we shall certainly die if you do not. The Americans have practised nothing but head-work these 200 years, and we have done their drudgery. And is it not high time for [us] to imitate their examples, and practice head-work too, and keep what we have got, and get what we can? We need never to think that anybody is going to feel interested for us, if we do not feel interested for ourselves. That day we, as a people, hearken unto the voice of the Lord, our God, and walk in his ways and ordinances, and become distinguished for our ease, elegance and grace, combined with other virtues, that day the Lord will raise us up, and enough aid and befriend us, and we shall begin to flourish.

Did every gentleman in America realize, as one, that they had got to become bondmen, and their wives, their sons, and their daughters, servants forever, to Great Britain, their very joints would become loosened, and tremblingly would smite one against another; their countenance would be filled with horror, every nerve and muscle would be forced into action, their souls would recoil at the very thought, their hearts would die within them, and death would be far more preferable. Then why have not Afric's sons the right to feel the same? Are not their wives, their sons, and their daughters, as dear to them as those of the white man's? Certainly God has not deprived them of the divine influences of his Holy Spirit, which is the greatest of all blessings, if they ask him. Then why should man longer deprive his fellow-man of equal rights and privileges? Oh, America, America, foul and indelible is thy stain! Dark and dismal is the cloud that hangs over thee, for thy cruel wrongs and injuries to the fallen sons of Africa. The blood of her murdered ones cries to heaven for vengeance against thee. Thou art almost become drunken with the blood of her slain; thou has enriched thyself through her toils and labors; and now thou refuseth to make even a small return. And thou hast caused the daughters of Africa to commit whoredoms and fornications, but upon thee be their curse.

O, ye great and mighty men of America, ye rich and powerful ones, many of you will call for the rocks and mountains to fall upon you, and to hide you from the wrath of the Lamb [Revelation 6:16], and from him that sitteth upon the throne; whilst many of the sable-skinned Africans you now despise will shine in the kingdom of heaven as the stars forever and ever. Charity begins at home, and those that provide not for their own are worse than infidels. We know that you are raising contributions to aid the gallant Poles; we know that you have befriended Greece and Ireland, and you have rejoiced with France, for her heroic deeds of valor. You have acknowledged all the nations of the earth, except Hayti; and you may publish, as far as the East is from the West, that you have two millions of negroes, who aspire no higher than to bow at your feet, and to court your smiles. You may kill, tyrannize, and oppress as much as you choose, until our cry shall come up before the throne of God; for I am firmly persuaded, that we will not suffer you to quell the proud, fearless and undaunted spirits of the Africans forever; for in his own time, he is able to plead our cause against you with swords and staves, as against a thief [Matthew 26:55]; but we will tell you that our souls are fired with the same love of liberty and independence with which your souls are fired. We will tell you that too much of your blood flows in our veins, too much of your color in our skins, for us not to possess your spirits. We will tell you that it is our gold that clothes you in fine linen and purple, and causes you to fare sumptuously every day [Luke 16:19]; and it is the blood of our fathers, and the tears of our brethren that have enriched your soils. AND WE CLAIM OUR RIGHTS. We will tell you that we are not afraid of them that kill the body, and after that can do no more, but we will tell you whom we do fear. We fear Him who is able, after He hath killed, to destroy both soul and body in hell forever. Then, my brethren, sheath your swords, and calm your angry passions. Stand still and know that the Lord he is God. Vengeance is his, and he will repay. It is a long lane that has no turn. America has risen to her meridian. When you begin to thrive, she will begin to fall. God hath raised you up a Walker and a Garrison. Though Walker sleeps, yet he lives, and his name shall be had in everlasting remembrance. I, even I, who am but a child, inexperienced to many of you, am a living witness to testify unto you this day, that I have seen the wicked in great power, spreading himself like a green bay tree, and lo, he passed away; yea, I diligently sought him, but he could not be found [Psalms 37:35]; and it is God alone that has inspired my heart to feel for Afric's woes. Then fret not yourselves because of evil doers. Fret not yourselves because of the men who bring wicked devices to pass; for they shall be cut down as the grass, and wither as the green herb. Trust in the Lord, and do good; so shalt thou dwell in the land, and verily thou shalt be fed. Encourage the noble-hearted Garrison. Prove to the world that you are neither ourang-outangs [orangutans], or a species of mere animals, but that you possess the same powers of intellect as the proud-boasting American.

I am sensible, my brethren and friends, that many of you have been deprived of advantages, kept in utter ignorance, and that your minds are now darkened; and if any one of you have attempted to aspire after high and noble enterprises, you have met with so much opposition that your souls have become discouraged. For this very cause, a few of us have ventured to expose our lives in your behalf, to plead your cause against the great; and it will be of no use, unless you feel for yourselves and then your little ones, and exhibit the spirits of men. Oh then, turn your attention to knowledge and improvement; for knowledge is power. And God is able to fill you with wisdom and understanding, and to dispel your fears. Arm yourselves with the weapons of prayer. Put your trust in the living God. Persevere strictly in the paths of virtue. Let nothing be lacking on your part; and in God's own time, and his time is certainly the best, he will surely deliver you with a [mighty] hand and with an outstretched arm.

I have never taken one step, my friends, with a design to raise myself in your esteem, or to gain applause. But what I have done, has been done with an eye single to the glory of God, and to promote the good of souls. I have neither kindred nor friends. I stand alone in your midst, exposed to the fiery darts of the devil, and to the assaults of wicked men. But though all the powers of earth and hell were to combine against me, though all nature should sink into decay, still I would trust in the Lord, and joy in the God of my salvation. For I am full persuaded that he will bring me off conqueror, yea, more than conqueror, through him who hath loved me and given himself for me.

Boston, October 1831

Hymn

God is a spirit, just and wise;
He knows our inmost minds:
In vain to heaven we raise our cries,
And leave our souls behind

Nothing but truth before his throne
With honor can appear:
The painted hypocrites are known
By the disguise they wear.

Their lifted eyes salute the skies,
Their bended knees the ground;
But God abhors the sacrifice
Where not the heart is found.

Lord, search my heart, and try my reins,
And make my soul sincere;
So shall I stand before thy throne,
And find acceptance there.[3]

Figure 3.1: Jarena Lee

Jarena Lee

Jarena Lee (1783–1864) was the first African American woman to have her autobiography published in the United States. It was printed first in 1836 as *The Life and Religious Calling of Jarena Lee, A Coloured Lady, Giving an Account of Her Call to Preach the Gospel* and in an extended version in 1849 as *Religious Experience and Journal of Mrs. Jarena Lee, Giving an Account of Her Call to Preach the Gospel* (this volume is the source for the excerpt below). Lee was born free in Cape May, New Jersey. She began working as a live-in servant at the age of seven years. She moved to Philadelphia as a teenager and continued to work as a domestic servant. After moving to Philadelphia, she began attending Bethel African Methodist Episcopal (AME) Church where she was deeply inspired by Richard Allen who had founded the church in 1794.

During the early years of her religious fervor, she felt called to preach but was not allowed to do so because of gender restrictions, so she participated instead via more traditional roles for women in the church, such as leading prayer meetings. In 1811 she married Reverend Joseph Lee, supporting him as pastor of a church outside of Philadelphia. However, she was widowed after seven years and returned to her home church, Bethel. At an opportune moment in a Sunday service, she stepped up boldly to finish a sermon of a minister who was faltering. After this performance, Reverend Allen was impressed and in 1819 authorized her to preach. She was the first woman in the AME church to be granted this privilege. As confirmed in her autobiography, Lee delivered sermons at Bethel and traveled widely, as well, in support of her desire to spread the gospel.

In addition to her religious work Lee was also active as an abolitionist, attending meetings, speaking, and networking with other abolitionist activists and leaders. In 1853 she was invited to speak at the American Anti-Slavery Society's convention in Philadelphia, a prestigious body that included William Lloyd Garrison, Lucretia Mott, and Sojourner Truth. During this meeting, she joined other African American women abolitionists in declaring her support of the convention's anticolonization resolution, an action that suggests her belief that African Americans had the right to freedom, justice, equality, and the pursuit of happiness in the United States rather than being required to leave it for a better life.

In the final decades of her life, Lee's presence as a public speaker waned as did her resources. She died in 1864 in poverty, having struggled to survive. What stands, however, is her own account of her life and work as a pioneering religious leader. This leadership as a preacher and an advocate for abolitionism offers evidence from well before the Civil War of her desire not just to express her spiritual commitments, which was clearly the case, but also to share her sociopolitical work with others of faith and beyond. Through her writings, Lee established a place for herself in a deeply gendered institutional arena, not just a private one. As part of the documentary record for African American women, this account continues to raise questions, both then and now, about negotiating constructions of agency, authority, and sociopolitical consequence in light of a matrix of issues related generally to identity, place, and space, but, as in Lee's case, quite materially to boundaries imposed not only by race, class, and gender but specifically during this time period by marriage, financial crises created by widowhood, the challenges of working under the cover of widowhood, and the exclusionary practices of professional arenas.

Jarena Lee

Excerpts from *Religious Experience and Journal of Mrs. Jarena Lee: Giving an Account of Her Call to Preach the Gospel* (1849), introduction by Sue E. Houchins, The Schomburg Library of Nineteenth-Century Black Women Writers (New York: Oxford University Press, 1988).

My Call to Preach the Gospel

Between four and five years after my sanctification, on a certain time, an impressive silence fell upon me, and I stood as if some one was about to speak to me, yet I had no such thought in my heart.—But to my utter surprise there seemed to sound a voice which I thought I distinctly heard, and most certainly understand, which said to me, "Go preach the Gospel!" I immediately replied aloud, "No one will believe me." Again I listened, and again the same voice seemed to say—"Preach the Gospel; I will put words in your mouth, and will turn your enemies to become your friends."

At first I supposed that Satan had spoken to me, for I had read that he could transform himself into an angel of light for the purpose of deception. Immediately I went into a secret place, and called upon the Lord to know if he had called me to preach, and whether I was deceived or not; when there appeared to my view the form and figure of a pulpit, with a Bible lying thereon, the back of which was presented to me as plainly as if it had been a literal fact.

In consequence of this, my mind became so exercised, that during the night following, I took a text and preached in my sleep. I thought there stood before me a great multitude, while I expounded to them the things of religion. So violent were my exertions and so loud were my exclamations, that I awoke from the sound of my own voice, which also awoke the family of the house where I resided. Two days after I went to see the preacher in charge of the African Society, who was the Rev. Richard Allen, the same before named in these pages, to tell him that I felt it my duty to preach the gospel. But as I drew near the street in which his house was, which was in the city of Philadelphia, my courage began to fail me; so terrible did the cross appear, it seemed that I should not be able to hear it. Previous to my setting out to go to see him, so agitated was my mind, that my appetite for my daily food failed me entirely. Several times on my way there, I turned back again; but as often I felt my strength again renewed, and I soon found that the nearer I approached to the house of the minister, the less was my fear. Accordingly, as soon as I came to the door, my fears subsided, the cross was removed, all things appeared pleasant—I was tranquil.

I now told him, that the Lord had revealed it to me, that [I] must preach the gospel. He replied, by asking, in what sphere I wished to move in? I said, among the Methodists. He then replied, that a Mrs. Cook, a Methodist lady, had also some time before requested the same privilege; who, it was believed, had done much good in the way of exhortation, and holding prayer meetings; and who had been permitted to do so by the verbal license of the preacher in charge at the time. But as to women preaching, he said that our Discipline knew nothing at all about it—that it did not call for women preachers. This I was glad to hear, because it removed the fear of the cross—but no sooner did this feeling cross my mind, than I found that a love of souls had in a measure departed from me; that holy energy which burned within me, as a fire, began to be smothered. This I soon perceived.

O how careful ought we to be, lest through our by-laws of church government and discipline, we bring into disrepute even the word of life. For as unseemly as it may appear no-a-days for a woman to preach, it should be remembered that nothing is impossible with God. And why should it be thought impossible, heterodox, or improper for a woman to preach seeing the Saviour died for the woman as well as for the man.

If the man may preach, because the Saviour died for him, why not the woman? Seeing he died for her also. Is he not a whole Saviour, instead of a half one? As those who hold it wrong for a woman to preach, would seem to make it appear.

Did not Mary *first* preach the risen Saviour, and is not the doctrine of the resurrection the very climax of Christianity—hangs not all our hope on this, as argued by St. Paul? Then did not Mary, a woman, preach the gospel? For she preached the resurrection of the crucified Son of God.

But some will say that Mary did not expound the Scripture, therefore, she did not preach, in the proper sense of the term. To this I reply it may be that the term *preach* in those primitive times, did not mean exactly what it is now *made* to mean; perhaps it was a great deal more simple then, than it is now—if it were not, the unlearned fishermen could not have preached the gospel at all, as they had no learning.

To this it may be replied, by those who are determined not to believe that it is right for a woman to preach, that the disciples, though they were fishermen and ignorant of letters too, were inspired so to do. To which I would reply, that though they were inspired, yet that inspiration did not save them from showing their ignorance of letters, and man's wisdom; this the multitude soon found out, by listening to the remarks of the envious Jewish priests. If then, to preach the gospel, by the gift of heaven, comes by inspiration solely, is God straitened: must he take the man exclusively? May he not, did he not, and can he not inspire a female to preach the simple story of the birth, life, death, and resurrection of our Lord, and accompany it too with power to the sinner's heart. As for me, I am fully persuaded that the Lord called me to labor according to what I have received, in his vineyard. If he has not, how could he consistently bear testimony in favor of my poor labors, in awakening and converting sinners?

In my wanderings up and down among men, preaching according to my ability, I have frequently found families who told me that they had not for several years been to a meeting, and yet, while listening to hear what God would say by his poor female instrument, have believed with trembling—tears rolling down their cheeks, the signs of contrition and repentance towards God. I firmly believe that I have sown seed, in the name of the Lord, which shall appear with its increase at the great day of accounts, when Christ shall come to make up his jewels.

At a certain time, I was beset with the idea, that soon or late I should fall from grace and lose my soul at last. I was frequently called to the throne of grace about this matter, but found no relief; the temptation pursued me still. Being more and more afflicted with it, till at a certain time, when the spirit strongly impressed it on my mind to enter into my closet and carry my case once more to the Lord; the Lord enabled me to draw nigh to him, and to his mercy seat, at this time, in an extraordinary manner; for while I wrestled with him for the victory over this disposition to doubt whether I should persevere, there appeared a form of fire, about the size of a man's hand, as I was on my knees; at the same moment there appeared to the eye of faith a man robed in a white garment, from the shoulders down to the feet; from him a voice proceeded, saying:

"Thou shalt never return from the cross." Since that time I have never doubted, but believe that God will keep me until the day of redemption. Now I could adopt the very language of St. Paul, and say, that nothing could have separated me from the love of God, which is in Christ Jesus. Since that time, 1807, until the present, 1833, I have not even doubted the power and goodness of God to keep me from falling, through the sanctification of the spirit and belief of the truth.

My Marriage

In the year 1811, I changed my situation in life, having married Mr. Joseph Lee, pastor of a Society at Snow Hill, about six miles from the city of Philadelphia. It became necessary therefore for me to remove. This was a great trial at first, as I knew no person at Snow Hill, except my husband, and to leave my associates in the society, and especially those who composed the band of which I was one. None but those who have been in sweet fellowship with such as really love God, and have together drank bliss and happiness from the same fountain, can tell how dear such company is, and how hard it is to part from them.

At Snow Hill, as was feared, I never found that agreement and closeness in communion and fellowship, that I had in Philadelphia, among my young companions, nor ought I to have expected it. The manners and customs at this place were somewhat different, on which account I became discontented in the course of a year, and began to importune my husband to remove to the city. But this plan did not suit him, as he was the Pastor of the Society, he could not bring his mind to leave them. This afflicted me a little. But the Lord showed me in a dream what his will was concerning this matter.

I dreamed that as I was walking on the summit of a beautiful hill, that I saw near me a flock of sheep, fair and white, as if but newly washed; when there came walking toward me a man of a grave and dignified countenance, dressed entirely in white, as it were in a robe, and looking at me, said emphatically, "Joseph Lee must take care of these sheep, or the wolf will come and devour them." When I awoke I was convinced of my error, and immediately, with a glad heart, yielded to the right spirit in the Lord. This also greatly strengthened my faith in his care over them, for fear the wolf should by some means take any of them away. The following verse was beautifully suited to our condition, as well as to all the little flocks of God scattered up and down this land:

Us into Thy protec'ion take,
And gather wi'h Thine arm;
Unless the fold we first forsake,
The wolf can never harm.

After this, I fell into a state of general debility, and in an ill state of health, so much so, that I could not sit up: but a desire to warn sinners to flee the wrath to come, burned vehemently in my heart, when the Lord would send sinners into the house to see me. Such opportunities I embraced to press home on their consciences the things of eternity, and effectual was the word of exhortation made through the Spirit, that I have seen them fall to the floor crying aloud for mercy.

From this sickness I did not expect to recover, and there was but one thing which bound me to earth, and this was, that I had not as yet preached the gospel to the fallen sons and daughters of Adam's race, to the satisfaction of my mind. I wished to go from one end of the earth to the other, crying, Behold, behold the lamb! To this end I earnestly prayed to the Lord to raise me up, if consistent with his will. He condescended to hear my prayer, and to give me a token in a dream, that in due time I should recover my health. The dream was as follows: I thought I saw the sun rise in the morning, and ascend to an altitude of about half an hour high, and then become obscured by a dense black cloud, which continued to hide its rays for about one-third part of the day, and then it burst forth again with renewed splendor.

This dream I interpreted to signify my early life, my conversion to God, and this sickness, which was a great affliction, as it hindered me, and I feared would forever hinder me from preaching the gospel, was signified by the cloud; and the bursting forth of the sun, again, was the recovery of my health, and being permitted to preach.

I went to the throne of grace on this subject, where the Lord made this impressive reply in my heart, while on my knees: "Ye shall be restored to thy health again, and worship God in full purpose of heart."

This manifestation was so impressive, that I could but hide my face as if some one was gazing upon me, to think of the great goodness of the Almighty God to my poor soul and body. From that very time I began to gain strength of body and mind, glory to God in the highest, until my health was fully recovered.

For six years from this time I continued to receive from above, such baptisms of the Spirit as mortality could scarcely bear. About that time I was called to suffer in my family, by death—five, in the course of about six years, fell by his hand; my husband being one of the number, which was the greatest affliction of all.

I was now left alone in the world, with two infant children, one of the age of about two year, the other six months, with no other dependences than the promise of Him who hath said—I will be the widow's God, and a father to the fatherless. Accordingly, he raised me up friends, whose liberality comforted and solaced me in my state of widowhood and sorrows, I could sing with the greatest propriety the words of the poet.

He helps the stranger in distress,
The widow and the fatherless,
And grants the prisoner sweet release.

I can say even now, with the Psalmist, "Once I was young, but now I am old, yet I have never seen the righteous forsaken, not his seed begging bread." I have ever been fed by his bounty, clothed by his mercy, comforted and healed when sick, succored when tempted, and every where upheld by his hand.

The Subject of My Call to Preach Renewed

It was now eight years since I had made application to be permitted to preach the gospel, during which time I had only been allowed to exhort, and even this privilege but seldom. This subject now was renewed afresh in my mind; it was as a fire shut up in my bones. About thirteen months passed on, while under this renewed impression. During this time, I had solicited of the Rev. Bishop, Richard Allen, who at this time had become Bishop of the African Episcopal Methodists in America, to be permitted the liberty of holding prayer meetings in my own hired house, and of exhorting as I found liberty, which was granted me. By this means, my mind was relieved, as the house soon filled when the hour appointed for prayer had arrived.

[After her account of what Lee characterized as "a singular conversion of a very wicked young man," she continues with the account below.]

Soon after this, as above related, the Rev. Richard Williams was to preach at Bethel Church, where I with others were assembled.

He entered the pulpit, gave out the hymn, which was sung, and then addressed the throne of grace; took his text, passed through the exordium, and commenced to expound it. The text he took is in Jonah, 2d chap. 9th verse,—"Salvation is of the Lord." But as he proceeded to explain, he seemed to have lost the spirit; when in the same instant, I sprang, as by altogether supernatural impulse, to my feet, when I was aided from above to give an exhortation on the very text which my brother Williams had taken.

I told them I was like Jonah; for it had been then nearly eight years since the Lord had called me to preach his gospel to the fallen sons and daughters of Adam's race, but that I had lingered like him, and delayed to go at the bidding of the Lord, and warn those who are as deeply guilty as were the people of Nineveh.

During the exhortation, God made manifest his power in a manner sufficient to show the world that I was called to labor according to my ability, and the grace given unto me, in the vineyard of the good husbandman.

I now sat down, scarcely knowing what I had done, being frightened. I imagined, that for this indecorum, as I feared it might be called, I should be expelled from the church. But instead of this, the Bishop rose up in the assembly, and related that I had called upon him eight years before, asking to be permitted to preach, and that he had put me off; but that he now as much believed that I was called to that work, as any of the preachers present. These remarks greatly strengthened me, so that my fears of having given an offence, and made myself liable as an offender, subsided, giving place to a sweet serenity, a holy joy of a peculiar kind, untasted in my bosom until then.

The next Sabbath day, while sitting under the word of the gospel, I felt moved to attempt to speak to the people in a public manner, but I could not bring my mind to attempt it in the church. I said, Lord, anywhere but here. Accordingly, there was a house not far off which was pointed out to me; to this I went. It was the house of a sister belonging to the same society as myself. Her name was Anderson. I told her I had come to hold a meeting in her house, if she would call in her neighbors. With this request she immediately complied. My congregation consisted of but five persons. I commenced by reading and singing a hymn; when I arose I found my hand resting on the Bible, which I had not noticed till that moment. It now occurred to me to take a text. I opened the Scripture, as it happened, at the 141st Psalm, fixing my eye on the third verse, which reads: "Set a watch, O Lord, before my mouth, keep the door of my lips." My sermon, such as it was, applied wholly to myself, and added an exhortation. Two of my congregation wept much, as the fruit of my labor this time. In closing, I said to the few, that if any one would open a door, I would hold a meeting the next sixth-day evening: when one answered that her house was at my service. Accordingly I went, and God made manifest his power among the people. Some wept, while others shouted for joy. One whole seat of females, by the power of God, as the rushing of a wind, were all bowed to the floor, at once, and screamed out. Also a sick man and woman in one house, the Lord convicted them both; one lived, and the other died. God wrought a judgment—some were well at night, and died in the morning. At this place I continued to hold meetings about six months. During that time I kept house with my little son, who was very sickly. About this time I had a call to preach at a place about thirty miles distant, among the Methodists, with whom I remained one week, and during the whole time, not a thought of my little son came into my mind; it was hid from me, lest I should have been diverted from the work I had to do, to look after my son. Here by the instrumentality of a poor coloured woman, the Lord poured forth his spirit among the people. Though, as I was told, there were lawyers, doctors, and magistrates present, to hear me speak, yet there was mourning and crying among sinners, for the Lord scattered fire among them of his own kindling. The Lord gave his hand-maiden power to speak for his great name, for he arrested the hearts of the people, and caused a shaking amongst the multitude, for God was in the midst.

I now returned home, found all well; no harm had come to my child, although I left it very sick. Friends had taken care of it which was of the Lord. I now began to think seriously of breaking up housekeeping, and forsaking all to preach the everlasting Gospel.

[After presenting her accounts of living and working as a traveling preacher and occasionally a teacher, including her referencing of the challenges of balancing motherhood and work, Lee returns to Philadelphia.]

I now returned to Philadelphia, where I stayed a short time, and went to Salem, West Jersey. I met with many troubles on my journey, especially from the elder, who like many others, was averse to a woman's preaching. And here let me tell that elder, if he has not gone to heaven, that I have heard that as far back as Adam Clarke's time [Clarke, 1762–1832, was a British Methodist theologian and biblical scholar], his objections to female preaching were met by the answer—"If an ass reproved Balaam [a non-Israelite prophet who was considered to be wicked], and a barn-door fowl reproved Peter, why should not a woman reprove sin?" I do not introduce this for its complimentary classification of women with donkeys and fowls, but to give the reply of a poor woman, who had once been a slave. To the first companion she said—"May be a speaking woman is like an ass—but I can tell you one thing, the ass seen the angel when Balaam didn't."

Notwithstanding the position, we had a prosperous time at Salem. I had some good congregations, and sinners were cut to the heart. After speaking in the meeting house, two women came up into the pulpit, and falling upon my neck cried out "What shall I do to be saved?" One said she had disobeyed God, and he had taken her children from her—he had called often after her, but she did not hearken. I pointed her to the all-atoning blood of Christ, which is sufficient to cleanse from all sin, and left her, after prayer, to his mercy. From this place I walked twenty-one miles, and preached with difficulty to a stiff-necked and rebellious people, who I soon left without any animosity for their treatment. They might have respected my message, if not the poor weak servant who brought it to them with so much labor.

"If they persecute you in onc city, flcc to another," was the advice I had resolved to take, and I hastened to Greenwich, where I had a lively congregation, had unusual life and liberty in speaking, and the power of God was there. We also had a solemn time in the meeting house on Sabbath day morning, and a dwelling house in the evening; a large company assembled, when the spirit was with us, and we had a mighty shaking among the dry bones.

Figure 3.2: Harriet Ann Jacobs

Harriet Ann Jacobs

Harriet Ann Jacobs (1813–1897), born into slavery in Edenton, North Carolina, is recognized as the first African American woman to publish her memoirs. As documented by William L. Andrews in "Harriet A. Jacobs (Harriet Ann), 1813–1897)," *Documenting the American South* (Chapel Hill: University of North Carolina), Jacobs was a single woman who escaped slavery in 1842. She lived as a fugitive in New York, then Rochester, and ultimately Boston, where she made a home for her two children and gained her freedom in 1852 as a gift from her employer. During these years, Jacobs worked in circles where she was surrounded by writers, editors, and abolitionists, for example, Frederick Douglass, Amy Post, Lydia Marie Childs, and others, and she engaged actively in the work of the antislavery movement. At the behest of her white allies and advocates, she wrote her autobiography under the pseudonym Linda Brent, indicating a specific sensitivity to women's decorum and expectations for what it means to be "a lady." With emphasis on the sociopolitical imperative of telling the truth about the experiences of enslaved women, however, she put rhetorical stakes in the ground.

Despite a series of challenges in bringing her story to public visibility, Jacobs published it in 1861 as *Incidents in the Life of a Slave Girl*. Her narrative is a story of unpaid and exploited labor in plantation households (rather than in agricultural fields), often under cruel and oppressive conditions, which included persistent sexual abuse; the equally persistent inventiveness that she and her grandmother (a freed slave) needed to deploy to establish some layer of protection for her; the process by which she escaped to the North; and her entry into freedom. The excerpts below from *Incidents in the Life of a Slave Girl* confirm the sociopolitical imperatives and intentions of her autobiographical interests, with her intended audience being, as she states, white women of the North on behalf of thousands of enslaved women in the South.

Harriet Ann Jacobs

Excerpts from *Incidents in the Life of a Slave Girl* (1861), ed. Maria Child, The Schomburg Library of Nineteenth-Century Black Women Writers (New York: Oxford University Press, 1988).

Childhood

I was born a slave; but I never knew it till six years of happy childhood had passed away. My father was a carpenter, and considered so intelligent and skilful in his trade, that when buildings out of the common line were to be erected, he was sent for from long distances, to be head workman. On condition of paying his mistress two hundred dollars a year, and supporting himself, he was allowed to work at his trade, and manage his own affairs. His strongest wish was to purchase his children; but, though he several times offered his hard earnings for that purpose, he never succeeded. In complexion my parents were a light shade of brownish yellow, and were termed mulattoes. They lived together in a comfortable home; and though we were all slaves, I was so fondly shielded that I never dreamed I was a piece of merchandise, trusted to them for safe keeping, and liable to be demanded of them at any moment. I had one brother, William, who was two years younger than myself—a bright, affectionate child. I had also a great treasure in my maternal grandmother, who was a remarkable woman in many respects. She was the daughter of a planter in South Carolina, who, at his death, left her mother and his three children free, with money to go to Saint Augustine, where they had relatives. It was during the Revolutionary War; and they were captured on their passage, carried back, and sold to different purchasers. Such was the story my grandmother used to tell me; but I do not remember all the particulars. She was a little girl when she was captured and sold to the keeper of a large hotel. I have often heard her tell how hard she fared during childhood. But as she grew older she evinced so much intelligence, and was so faithful, that her master and mistress could not help seeing it was for their interest to take care of such a valuable piece of property. She became an indispensable personage in the household, officiating in all capacities, from cook and wet nurse to seamstress. She was much praised for her cooking; and her nice crackers became so famous in the neighborhood that many people were desirous of obtaining them. In consequence of numerous requests of this kind, she asked permission of her mistress to bake crackers at night, after all the household work was done; and she obtained leave to do it, provided she would clothe herself and her children from the profits. Upon these terms, after working hard all day for her mistress, she began her midnight bakings, assisted by her two oldest children. The business proved profitable; and each year she laid by a little, which was saved for a fund to purchase her children. Her master died, and the property was divided among his heirs. The widow had her dower in the hotel which she continued to keep open. My grandmother remained in her service as a slave; but her children were divided among her master's children. As she had five, Benjamin, the youngest one, was sold, in order that each heir might have an equal portion of dollars and cents. There was so little difference in our ages that he seemed more like my brother than my uncle. He was a bright, handsome lad, nearly white; for he inherited the complexion my grandmother had derived from Anglo-Saxon ancestors. Though only ten years old, seven hundred and twenty dollars were paid for him. His sale was a terrible blow to my grandmother; but she was naturally hopeful, and she went to work with renewed energy, trusting in time to be able to purchase some of her children. She had laid up three hundred dollars [roughly eleven thousand dollars in modern dollars], which her mistress one day begged as a loan, promising to pay her soon. The reader probably knows that no promise or writing given to a slave is legally binding; for, according to Southern laws, a slave, *being* property, can *hold* no property. When my grandmother lent her hard earnings to her mistress, she trusted solely to her honor. The honor of a slaveholder to a slave!

To this good grandmother I was indebted for many comforts. My brother Willie and I often received portions of the crackers, cakes, and preserves, she made to sell; and after we ceased to be children we were indebted to her for many more important services.

Such were the unusually fortunate circumstances of my early childhood. When I was six years old, my mother died; and then, for the first time, I learned, by the talk around me, that I was a slave. My mother's mistress was the daughter of my grandmother's mistress. She was the foster sister of my mother; they were both nourished at my grandmother's breast. In fact, my mother had been weaned at three months old, that the babe of the mistress might obtain sufficient food. They played together as children; and, when they became women, my mother was a most faithful servant to her whiter foster sister. On her death-bed her mistress promised that her children should never suffer for any thing; and during her lifetime she kept her word. They all spoke kindly of my dead mother, who had been a slave merely in name, but in nature was noble and womanly. I grieved for her, and my young mind was troubled with the thought who would now take care of me and my little brother. I was told that my home was now to be with her mistress; and I found it a happy one. No toilsome or disagreeable duties were imposed upon me. My mistress was so kind to me that I was always glad to do her bidding and proud to labor for her as much as my young years would permit. I would sit by her side for hours, sewing diligently, with a heart as free from care as that of any free-born white child. When she thought I was tired, she would send me out to run and jump; and away I bounded, to gather berries or flowers to decorate her room. These were happy days—too happy to last. The slave child had no thought for the morrow; but there came that blight, which too surely waits on every human being born to be a chattel.

When I was nearly twelve years old, my kind mistress sickened and died. As I saw the cheek grow paler, and the eye more glassy, how earnestly I prayed in my heart that she might live! I loved her; for she had been almost like a mother to me. My prayers were not answered. She died, and they buried her in the little churchyard, where, day after day, my tears fell upon her grave.

I was sent to spend a week with my grandmother. I was now old enough to begin to think of the future; and again and again I asked myself what they would do with me. I felt sure I should never find another mistress so kind as the one who was gone. She had promised my dying mother that her children should never suffer for any thing; and when I remembered that, and recalled her many proofs of attachment to me, I could not help having some hopes that she had left me free. My friends were almost certain it would be so. They thought she would be sure to do it, on account of my mother's love and faithful service. But, alas! We all know that the memory of a faithful slave does not avail much to save her children from the auction block.

After a brief period of suspense, the will of my mistress was read, and we learned that she had bequeathed me to her sister's daughter, a child of five years old. So vanished our hopes. My mistress had taught me the percepts of God's Word: "Thou shalt love thy neighbor as thyself." "Whatsoever ye would that men should do unto you, do ye even so unto them." But I was her slave, and I suppose she did not recognize me as her neighbor. I would give much to blot out from my memory that one great wrong. As a child, I loved my mistress; and, looking back on the happy days I spent with her, I try to think with less bitterness of this act of injustice. While I was with her, she taught me to read and spell; and for this privilege, which so rarely falls to the lot of a slave, I bless her memory.

She possessed but few slaves; and at her death those were all distributed among her relatives. Five of them were my grandmother's children, and had shared the same milk that nourished her mother's children. Notwithstanding my grandmother's long and faithful service to her owners, not one of her children escaped the auction block. These God-breathing machines are no more, in the sight of their masters, than the cotton they plant, or the horses they tend.

The New Master and Mistress

Dr. Flint, a physician in the neighborhood, had married the sister of my mistress, and I was now the property of their little daughter. It was not without murmuring that I prepared for my new home;

and what added to my unhappiness, was the fact that my brother William was purchased by the same family. My father, by his nature, as well as by the habit of transacting business as a skilful mechanic, had more of the feelings of a freeman than is common among slaves. My brother was a spirited boy; and being brought up under such influences, he early detested the name of master and mistress. One day, when his father and his mistress both happened to call him at the same time, he hesitated between the two; being perplexed to know which had the strongest claim upon his obedience. He finally concluded to go to his mistress. When my father reproved him for it, he said, "You both called me, and I didn't know which I ought to go to first."

"You are *my* child," replied our father, "and when I call you, you should come immediately, if you have to pass through fire and water."

Poor Willie! He was now to learn his first lesson of obedience to a master. Grandmother tried to cheer us with hopeful words, and they found an echo in the credulous hearts of youth.

When we entered our new home we encountered cold looks, cold words, and cold treatment. We were glad when the night came. On my narrow bed I moaned and wept, I felt so desolate and alone.

I had been there nearly a year, when a dear little friend of mine was buried. I heard her mother sob, as the clods fell on the coffin of her only child, and I turned away from the grave, feeling thankful that I still had something left to love. I met my grandmother, who said, "Come with me, Linda;" and from her tone I knew that something sad had happened. She led me apart from the people, and then said, "My child, your father is dead." Dead! How could I believe it? He had died so suddenly I had not even heard that he was sick. I went home with my grandmother. My heart rebelled against God, who had taken from me mother, father, mistress, and friend. The good grandmother tried to comfort me. "Who knows the ways of God?" said she. "Perhaps they have been kindly taken from the evil days to come." Years afterwards I often thought of this. She promised to be a mother to her grandchildren, so far as she might be permitted to do so; and strengthened by her love, I returned to my master's. I thought I should be allowed to go to my father's house the next morning; but I was ordered to go for flowers, that my mistress's house might be decorated for an evening party. I spent the day gathering flowers and weaving them into festoons, while the dead body of my father was lying within a mile of me.

What cared my owners for that? He was merely a piece of property. Moreover, they thought he had spoiled his children, by teaching them to feel that they were human beings. This was blasphemous doctrine for a slave to teach; presumptuous in him, and dangerous to the masters.

The next day I followed his remains to a humble grave beside that of my dear mother. There were those who knew my father's worth, and respected his memory.

My home now seemed more dreary than ever. The laugh of the little slave-children sounded harsh and cruel. It was selfish to feel so about the joy of others. My brother moved about with a very grave face. I tried to comfort him, by saying, "Take courage, Willie; brighter days will come by and by."

"You don't know any thing about it, Linda," he replied. "We shall have to stay here all our days; we shall never be free."

I argued that we were growing older and stronger, and that perhaps we might, before long, be allowed to hire our own time, and then we could earn money to buy our freedom. William declared this was much easier to say than to do; moreover, he did not intend to *buy* his freedom. We held daily controversies upon this subject.

Little attention was paid to the slaves' meals in Dr. Flint's house. If they could catch a bit of food while it was going, well and good. I gave myself no trouble on that score, for on my various errands, I passed my grandmother's house, where there was always something to spare for me. I was frequently threatened with punishment if I stopped there; and my grandmother, to avoid detaining me, often stood at the gate with something for my breakfast or dinner. I was indebted to *her* for all my comforts, spiritual or temporal. It was *her* labor that supplied my scanty wardrobe. I have a vivid recollection of the linsey-woolsey dress given me every winter by Mrs. Flint. How I hated it! It was one of the badges of slavery.

While my grandmother was thus helping to support me from her hard earning, the three hundred dollars she had lent her mistress were never repaid. When her mistress died, her son-in-law, Dr. Flint, was appointed executor. When Grandmother applied to him for payment, he said the estate was insolvent, and the law prohibited payment. It did not, however, prohibit him from retaining the silver candelabra, which had been purchased with that money. I presume they will be handed down in the family, from generation to generation.

My grandmother's mistress had always promised her that, at

her death, she should be free; and it was said that in her will she made good the promise. But when the estate was settled, Dr. Flint told the faithful old servant that, under existing circumstances, it was necessary she should be sold.

On the appointed day, the customary advertisement was posted up, proclaiming that there would be a "public sale of negroes, horses, &c." Dr. Flint called to tell my grandmother that he was unwilling to wound her feelings by putting her up at auction, and that he would prefer to dispose of her at private sale. My grandmother saw through his hypocrisy; she understood very well that he was ashamed of the job. She was a very spirited woman, and if he was base enough to sell her, when her mistress intended she should be free, she was determined the public should know it. She had for a long time supplied many families with crackers and preserves; consequently, "Aunt Marthy," as she was called, was generally known, and every body who knew her respected her intelligence and good character. Her long and faithful service in the family was also well known, and the intention of her mistress to leave her free. When the day of the sale came, she took her place among the chattels, and at the first call she sprang upon the auction-block. Many voices called out, "Shame! Shame! Who is going to sell *you*, aunt Marthy? Don't stand there! That is no place for *you*." Without saying a word, she quietly awaited her fate. No one bid for her. At last, a feeble voice said, "Fifty dollars." It came from a maiden lady, seventy year old, the sister of my grandmother's deceased mistress. She had lived forty years under the same roof with my grandmother; she knew how faithfully she had served her owners, and how cruelly she had been defrauded of her rights; and she resolved to protect her. The auctioneer waited for a higher bid; but her wishes were respected; no one bid above her. She could neither read nor write; and when the bill of sale was out, she signed it with a cross. But what consequence was that, when she had a big heart overflowing with human kindness? She gave the old servant her freedom.

At the time, my grandmother was just fifty years old. Laborious years had passed since then; and now my brother and I were slaves to the man who had defrauded her of her money, and tried to defraud her of her freedom. One of my mother's sisters, called Aunt Nancy, was also a slave in his family. She was a kind, good aunt to me; and supplied the place of both housekeeper and waiting maid to her mistress. She was, in fact, at the beginning and end of every thing.

Mrs. Flint, like many southern women, was totally deficient in energy. She had not strength to superintend her household affairs; but her nerves were so strong, that she could sit in her easy chair and see a woman whipped, till the blood trickled from every stroke of the lash. She was a member of the church; but partaking of the Lord's supper did not seem to put her in a Christian frame of mind. If dinner was not served at the exact time on that particular Sunday, she would station herself in the kitchen, and wait till it was dished, and then spit in all the kettles and pans that had been used for cooking. She did this to prevent the cook and her children from eking out their meagre fare with the remains of the gravy and other scrapings. The slaves could get nothing to eat except what she chose to give them. Provisions were weighed out by the pound and ounce, three times a day. I can assure you she gave them no chance to eat wheat bread from her flour barrel. She knew how many biscuits a quart of flour would make, and exactly what size they ought to be.

Dr. Flint was an epicure. The cook never sent a dinner to his table without fear and trembling; for if there happened to be a dish not to his liking, he would either order her to be whipped, or compel her to eat every mouthful of it in his presence. The poor, hungry creature might not have objected to eating it; but she did object to having her master cram it down her throat till she choked. . . .

When I had been in the family a few weeks, one of the plantation slaves was brought to town, by order of his master. It was near night when he arrived, and Dr. Flint ordered him to be taken to the work house, and tied up to the joist, so that his feet would just escape the ground. In that situation he was to wait till the doctor had taken his tea. I shall never forget that night. Never before, in my life, had I heard hundreds of blows fall, in succession, on a human being. His piteous groans, and his "O, pray don't massa," rang in my ear for months afterwards. There were many conjectures as to the cause of this terrible punishment. Some said master accused him of stealing corn; others said the slave had quarrelled with his wife, in presence of the overseer, and had accused his master of being the father of her child. They were both black, and the child was very fair.

I went into the work house next morning, and saw the cowhide still wet with blood, and the boards all covered with gore. The poor man lived, and continued to quarrel with his wife. A few months afterwards Dr. Flint handed them both over to a slavetrader. The guilty man put their value into his pocket, and had the satisfaction of knowing that they were out of sight and hearing. When the mother was delivered into the trader's hands, she said, "You *promised* to treat me well." To which he replied, "You have let your tongue run too far; damn you!" She had forgotten that it was a crime for a slave to tell who was the father of her child. . . .

The Trials of Girlhood

During the first years of my service in Dr. Flint's family, I was accustomed to share some indulgences with the children of my mistress. Though this seemed to me no more than right, I was grateful for it, and tried to merit the kindness by the faithful discharge of my duties. But I now entered on my fifteenth year—a sad epoch in the life of a slave girl. My master began to whisper foul words in my ear. Young as I was, I could not remain ignorant of their import. I tried to treat them with indifference or contempt. The master's age, my extreme youth, and the fear that his conduct would be reported to my grandmother, made him bear this treatment for many months. He was a crafty man, and resorted to many means to accomplish his purposes. Sometimes he had stormy, terrific ways, that made his victims tremble; sometimes he assumed a gentleness that he thought must surely subdue. Of the two, I preferred his stormy moods, although they left me trembling. He tried his utmost to corrupt the pure principles my grandmother had instilled. He peopled my young mind with unclean images, such as only a vile monster could think of. I turned from him with disgust and hatred. But he was my master. I was compelled to live under the same roof with him—where I saw a man forty years my senior daily violating the most sacred commandments of nature. He told me I was his property; that I must be subject to his will in all things. My soul revolted against the mean tyranny. But where could I turn for protection? No matter whether the slave girl be as black as ebony or as fair as her mistress. In either case, there is no shadow of law to protect her from insult, from violence, or even from death; all these are inflicted by fiends who bear the shape of men. The mistress, who ought to protect the helpless victim, has no other feelings towards her but those of jealousy and rage. The degradation, the wrongs, the vices, that grow out of slavery, are more than I can describe. They are greater than you would willingly believe. Surely, if you credited one half the truths that are told you concerning the helpless millions suffering in this cruel bondage, you at the north would not help to tighten the yoke. You surely would refuse to do for the master, on your own soil, the mean and cruel work which trained bloodhounds and the lowest class of whites do for him at the south.

Every where the years bring to all enough of sin and sorrow; but in slavery the very dawn of life is darkened by these shadows. Even the little child, who is accustomed to wait on her mistress and her children, will learn, before she is twelve years old, why it is that her mistress hates such and such a one among the slaves. Perhaps the child's own mother is among those hated ones. She listens to violent outbreaks of jealous passion, and cannot help understand what is the cause. She will become prematurely knowing in evil things. Soon she will learn to tremble when she hears her master's footfall. She will be compelled to realize that she is no longer a child. If God has bestowed beauty upon her, it will prove her greatest curse. That which commands admiration in the white woman only hastens the degradation of the female slave. I know that some are too much brutalized by slavery to feel the humiliation of their position; but many slaves feel it most acutely, and shrink from the memory of it. I cannot tell how much I suffered in the presence of these wrongs, nor how I am still pained by the retrospect. My master met me at every turn reminding me that I belong to him, and swearing by heaven and earth that he would compel me to submit to him. If I went out for a breath of fresh air, after a day of unwearied toil, his footsteps dogged me. If I knelt by my mother's grave, his dark shadow fell on me even there. The light heart which nature had given me became heavy with sad forebodings. The other slaves in my master's house noticed the change. Many of them pitied me; but none dared to ask the cause. They had no need to inquire. They knew too well the guilty practices under that roof; and they were aware that to speak of them was an offence that never went unpunished.

I longed for some one to confide in. I would have given the world to have laid my head on my grandmother's faithful bosom, and told her all my troubles. But Dr. Flint swore he would kill me, if I was not as silent as the grave. Then, although my grandmother was all in all to me, I feared her as well as loved her. I had been accustomed to look up to her with a respect bordering upon awe. I was very young, and felt shamefaced about telling her such impure things, especially as I knew her to be very strict on such subjects. Moreover, she was a woman of a high spirit. She was usually very quiet in her demeanor; but if her indignation was once roused, it was not very easily quelled. I had been told that she once chased a white gentleman with a loaded pistol, because he insulted one of her daughters. I dreaded the consequences of a violent outbreak; and both pride and fear kept me silent. But though I did not confide in my grandmother, and even evaded her vigilant watchfulness and inquiry, her presence in the neighborhood was some protection to me. Though she had been a slave, Dr. Flint was afraid of her. He dreaded her scorching rebukes. Moreover, she was known and patronized by many people; and he did not wish to have his villany made public. It was luck for me that I did not live on a distant plantation, but in a town not so large that the inhabitants were ignorant of each other's affairs. Bad as are the laws and customs in a slaveholding community, the doctor, as a professional man, deemed it prudent to keep up some outward show of decency.

O, what days and nights of fear and sorrow that man caused me! Reader, it is not to awaken sympathy for myself that I am telling you truthfully what I suffered in slavery. I do it to kindle a flame of compassion in your hearts for my sisters who are still in bondage, suffering as I once suffered.

I once saw two beautiful children playing together. One was a fair white child; the other was her slave, and also her sister. When I saw them embracing each other, and heard their joyous laughter, I turned sadly away from the lovely sight. I foresaw the inevitable blight that would fall on the little slave's heart. I knew how soon her laughter would be changed to sighs. The fair child grew up to be a still fairer woman. From childhood to womanhood her pathway was blooming with flowers, and overarched by a sunny sky. Scarcely one day of her life had been clouded when the sun rose on her happy bridal morning.

How had those years dealt with her slave sister, the little playmate of her childhood? She, also, was very beautiful; but the flowers and sunshine of love were not for her. She drank the cup of sin, and shame, and misery, whereof her persecuted race are compelled to drink.

In view of those things, why are ye silent, ye free men and women of the north? Why do your tongues falter in maintenance of the right? Would that I had more ability! But my heart is so full, and my pen is so weak! There are noble men and women who plead for us, striving to help those who cannot help themselves. God bless them! God give them strength and courage to go on! God bless those, every where, who are laboring to advance the cause of humanity!

Figure 3.3: Mary Ann Shadd Cary

Mary Ann Shadd Cary

Mary Ann Shadd Cary (1823–1893) was born free in Wilmington, Delaware, which at the time was a slaveholding state. She is best known for three achievements: (1) being the first African American woman to own, edit, and publish her own paper in North America, in Windsor, Canada, where she emigrated after the passing of the Fugitive Slave Act in 1850; (2) serving as a recruiter of African American volunteers for the Union Army, when she returned home after the start of the Civil War; and (3) being among the first African American women to earn a law degree—in 1883 from Howard University School of Law. Throughout her life, Cary was actively engaged in sociopolitical work, from the abolitionist movement to the woman suffrage movement.

The eldest of thirteen children, Cary started life in a high status politically active family who opened their home, even in a slaveholding state, as a station on the Underground Railroad. Her family also believed in the right of their children to education. With such opportunities not being available in a slaveholding state, her parents moved their family to Pennsylvania, where she was educated in a Quaker boarding school. Cary worked first as a teacher in Pennsylvania and New York and founded her own school in East Chester, Pennsylvania. With the passing of the Fugitive Act of 1850 and an opportunity to teach in Windsor, Canada, however, things changed. Cary moved with her brother Isaac to Windsor, where both she and her brother (who was an ally of white radical activist John Brown) continued to be highly engaged with sociopolitical issues.

In Windsor, Cary opened a racially integrated school, attended by both refugee children and white children. In addition, she started her own newspaper, the *Provincial Freeman*, the first woman of African descent to do so in the Western Hemisphere. Cary served as editor and publisher. Samuel Ringgold Ward, a greatly admired African American public speaker, was her coeditor, and her brother helped with business operations. The paper was published from three sites over the next few years (Windsor, Toronto, and Chatham, Ontario). With this scope of operations, she demonstrated significant potential for success. However, her ability to sustain success was affected by a persistent lack of funding, the death of her husband, and the start of the Civil War.

While she lived in Canada, Cary became a passionate advocate for African Americans leaving the United States. In 1852, she published a pamphlet entitled *A Plea for Emigration: Notes on Canada West*, in which she gathered data that she thought would help African Americans (free, freed, and enslaved) to see that their horizons in Canada West were much brighter than in the United States. To be noted about the form of her writing, given her emphasis on an evidence-based analysis, is that Cary did not choose a personal voice or an imaginative literary genre—poetry, personal narrative, or even the personal essay. She chose to use the voice of the serious researcher and to publish a pamphlet. She claimed agency, identity, and authority based on the presentation of evidence, with the imperative of allowing the facts, the data, to speak truth and to permit her readers to make reasonable decisions about their own lives and actions. Included below are excerpts from this publication.

Mary Ann Shadd Cary

Excerpts from Mary A. Shadd. *A Plea for Emigration, or, Notes of Canada West* (1852), ed. Richard Almonte (Toronto: Mercury, 1998).

Introductory Remarks

The increasing desire on the part of the coloured people to become thoroughly informed respecting the Canadas, and particularly that part of the Province called Canada West [now known as Ontario]—to learn of the climate, soil and productions, and of the inducements offered generally to emigrants, and to them particularly, since that the passage of the odious Fugitive Slave Law [which was passed by the US Congress on September 18, 1850, and provided for the seizure and return of fugitive slaves] has made a residence in the United States to many of them dangerous in the extreme—this consideration, and the absence of condensed information accessible to all, is my excuse for offering this tract to the notice of the public.

The people are in a strait. On the one hand, a pro-slavery administration, with its entire controllable force, is bearing upon them with fatal effect. On the other, the Colonization Society [organized to send free African Americans to Africa], in the garb of *Christianity* and *Philanthropy*, is seconding the efforts of the first named power, by bringing into the lists a vast social and immoral influence, thus making more effective the agencies employed. Information is needed. Tropical Africa, the land of promise of the colonizationists, teeming as she is with the breath of pestilence, a burning sun, and fearful maladies, bids them welcome; she feelingly invites to moral and physical death, under a voluntary escort of their most bitter enemies at home. Again, many look with dreadful forebodings to the probability of worse than inquisitional inhumanity in the Southern States from the operation of the Fugitive Law. Certain that neither a home in Africa, nor in the Southern States, is desirable under present circumstances, inquiry is made respecting Canada.

I have endeavoured to furnish information to a certain extent, to that end, and believing that more reliance would be placed upon a statement of facts obtained in the country, from reliable sources and from observation, than upon a repetition of current statements made elsewhere, however honestly made, I determined to visit Canada, and to there collect such information as most persons desire. These pages contain the result of much inquiry: matter obtained both from individuals and from documents and papers of unquestionable character in the Province.

M.A.S.

British America

British America, it is well known, is a country equal in extent, at least, to the United States, extending on the north to the Arctic

Ocean, from the Atlantic on the east, to the Pacific on the west, and the southern boundary of which is subject to the inequalities in latitude of the several Northern States and Territories belonging to the Unites States government. This vast country includes within its limits some of the most beautiful lakes and rivers on the Western Continent. The climate, in the higher latitudes, is extremely severe, but for a considerable distance north of the settled districts, particularly in the western part, the climate is healthy and temperate: epidemics are not of such frequency as in the United States, owing to a more equable temperature, and local diseases are unknown. The Province claiming especial attention, as presenting features most desirable in a residence, is Canada, divided into East and West; and of these Canada West is to be preferred.

The Canadas and Their Climate

Canada East, from geographical position and natural characteristics, is not so well-suited to a variety of pursuits as the more western part of the Province. The surface is generally uneven, and in many parts mountainous; its more northern location subjects the inhabitants to extremely cold, cheerless winters, and short but warm summers. The land is of good quality, and vegetation is of rapid growth, but the general healthiness of the country is inferior to some of the other districts. The State of Maine presents a fair sample of Lower Canada in general. Population (which is principally French) is confined chiefly to the valley of the St. Lawrence and the country contiguous.

In Canada West, the variations from a salubrious and eminently healthy climate is nowhere sufficient to cause the least solicitude; on the contrary, exempt from the steady and enfeebling warmth of southern latitudes, and the equally injurious characteristics of polar countries, it is highly conducive to mental and physical energy. Persons living in the vicinity of the Great Lakes and the neighbouring districts say that their winters are much less severe than when, in past years, vast forests covered that region—that very deep snows are less frequent than they were, and that owing to the great body of ice that accumulates in the Lakes, the people living in the States bordering suffer more severely from the cold than Canadians—the ice making more intense the north winds sweeping over it. If these statements admit of a doubt, we well know that many flourishing towns in Canada are farther south than a large portion of Maine, New Hampshire, Vermont, New York, Michigan and Oregon, and should, in considering this fact, have the full benefit of geographical position.

I have thought proper to allude to the cold, at first, for the reason that it is the feature in the climate most dwelt upon: the solicitude of friends, ignorant on this point, and of persons less disinterested, often appealing to fears having no foundation whatever, when the facts are fairly set forth. . . .

Labour and Trades

In Canada, as in other recently settled countries, there is much to do, and comparatively few for the work. The numerous towns and villages springing up, and the great demand for timber and agricultural products, make labour of every kind plentiful. All trades that are practiced in the United States are there patronized by whomsoever carries on: no man's complexion affecting his business. If a coloured man understands his business, he receives the public patronage the same as a white man. He is not obliged to work a little better, and at a lower rate. There is no degraded class to identify him with, therefore every man's work stands or falls according to merit, not as is his colour. Builders and other tradesmen of different complexions work together on the same building and in the same shop, with perfect harmony, and often the proprietor of an establishment is coloured, and the majority or all of the men employed are white. Businesses that in older communities have ceased to renumerate [remunerate], yield a large percentage of the money invested.

The mineral resources of the Canadas have not been developed to an extent, for fuel wood is generally used, and a profitable trade in that commodity is carried on. Besides lumber for buildings, the getting out of materials for staves, coopers' stuff, and various purposes, affords steady employment and at fair prices, for cash. This state of things must increase, and assume more importance in Canadian markets, as the increasing population of the western United States burns and otherwise appropriates their timber. Railroads are in process of construction—steamboats now ply between Toronto and the several towns on the lakes; and in process of time, iron and other works will be in operation, it is said, all requiring their quota, and of course keeping up the demand. Boards for home and foreign markets are successfully manufactured, and numerous mill-sites are fast being appropriated to saw and grist mills.

In some sections, coloured men are engaged in saw mills on their own account. At Dawn, a settlement on the Sydenham (of which hereafter), and at other points, this trade is prosecuted with profit to them. To enumerate the different occupations in which coloured persons are engaged, even in detail, would but fatigue, and would not further the end in view, namely: to set forth the advantage of a residence in a country in which chattel slavery is not tolerated, and prejudice of *colour* has no existence whatever—the adaptation of that country, by climate, soil, and political character, to their physical and political necessities; and the superiority of a residence there over their present position at *home*. It will suffice, that coloured men prosecute all the different trades; are storekeepers, farmers, clerks, and labourers; and are not only unmolested, but sustained and encouraged in any business for which their qualifications and means fit them; and as the resources of the country develop, new fields of enterprise will be opened to them, and consequently new motives to honourable effort.

Churches and Schools

In the large towns and cities, as in similar communities in other Christian countries, the means for religious instruction are ample. There are costly churches in which all classes and complexions worship, and no "negro pew," or other seat for coloured persons, especially. I was forcibly struck, when at Toronto, with the contrast the religious community there presented, to our own large body of American Christians. In the churches, originally built by the white Canadians, the presence of coloured persons, promiscuously seated, elicited no comment whatever. They are members, and visitors, and as such have their pews according to their inclination, near the door, or remote, or central, as best suits them. The number of coloured persons attending the churches with whites constitutes a minority, I think. They have their "own churches."

That that is the feature in their policy, which is productive of mischief to the entire body, is event enough; and the opinion of the best informed and most influential among them, in Toronto and the large towns, is decided and universal. I have heard men of many years residence, and who have, in a measure, been moulded by the better sentiment of society, express deep sorrow at the course of coloured persons, in pertinaciously refusing overtures of religious fellowship from the whites; and in the face of all experience to the contrary, erecting Coloured Methodist, and Baptist, and other

Churches. This opinion obtains amongst many who, when in the United States, were connected with coloured churches. Aside from their cast character, their influence on the coloured people is fatal. The character of the exclusive church in Canada tends to perpetuate ignorance, both of their true position as British subjects, and of the Christian religion in its purity. . . .

A goodly portion of the people in the western part of the Province (for there are but few in the eastern), are enjoying superior religious opportunities, but the majority greatly need active missionary effort: first, to teach them love to their neighbour; and again to give them an intelligent and correct understanding of the Sacred Scriptures. The missionary strength, at present, consists of but six preachers—active and efficient gentlemen, all of them, and self-sacrificing in the last degree; and several women engaged in teaching, under the same auspices. Much privation, suffering, opposition, and sorrow await the missionary in that field. . . . There are those who pretend to have been enlightened, and to have at heart the common good, whose influence and operations he will find designedly counteracting his conscientious efforts, the more effectively appealing to a common origin and kindred sufferings, secretly striking behind, and bringing his character as a missionary, and his operations, into discredit in the eyes of a sympathizing Christian community. This, and more awaits those who may be called into the field. But the case is not a hopeless one. The native good sense of the fugitives, backed by proper schools, will eventually develop the real character of their operations and sacrifices. They and their families, of all others, should have the support of Christians.

The refugees express a strong desire for intellectual culture, and persons often begin their education at a time of life when many in other countries think they are too old. There are no separate schools. At Toronto and in many other places, as in the churches, the coloured people avail themselves of existing schools; but in the western country, in some sections, there is a tendency to "exclusiveness." The coloured people of that section petitioned, when the School Law was under revision, that they might have separate schools. There were counter-petitions by those opposed, and to satisfy all parties, twelve freeholders among *them*, can, by following a prescribed form, demand a school for their children; but if other schools, under patronage of Government, exist, (as Catholic or Protestant), they can demand admission into them, if they have not one. They are not compelled to have a coloured school. . . .

As before said, the facilities for obtaining a liberal education are ample in the large towns and cities. In Toronto, students of all complexions associate together, in the better-class schools and colleges. The operations of missionaries being chiefly among coloured people, they have established several schools in connection with their labours, yet they are open to children without exception. The coloured common schools have more of a complexional character than the private, which, with no exception that I have heard of, are open to all. . . .

Settlements: Dawn, Elgin, the Institution, the Fugitive Home

Much has been said of the Canadian coloured settlements, and fears have been expressed by many that by encouraging exclusive settlements, the attempt to identify coloured men with degraded men of like colour in the States would result, and as a consequence, estrangement, suspicion, and distrust would be induced. Such would inevitably be the result, and will be, shall they determine to have entirely proscriptive settlements. Those in existence, so far as I have been able to get at facts, do not exclude whites from their vicinity; but that settlements may not be established of that character, is not so certain. . . .

Vancouver's Island and Concluding Remarks

This island is situated between 49° and 51° north latitude, or on the southern boundary of British America; and between 122° and 127° west longitudc. It is about three hundred miles long and between ninety and one hundred miles broad, and contains about twenty-eight thousand square miles. Though remotely situated, and comparatively uninhabited (there bcing not morc than twenty thousand persons on it), it will, it is said, be the first island in importance on the globe. It has a fine climate, being in the same latitude as the south of England, Germany, and the north of France. The soil is also of the best description.

But it is not as an agricultural island that it will surpass all others. The western continent, and particularly the northern part, say "wise men of the east," must eventually leave the eastern far in the distance (a fact that should not be lost sight of by coloured men), and that over the Pacific will the trade with eastern nations be prosecuted. It is important now as a stopping place for whale ships visiting the Northern Seas, and is directly in the route to the East Indies, Japan Isles, and China, from Oregon and British America.

The overland route to the Pacific terminating near that point, the great Atlantic trade of Western Europe and America will find there the most practicable outlet and the shortest distance to Eastern Asia; consequently the people there settled, of whatever complexion, will be the "merchant princes of the world," and under the protection of Great Britain.

Now, there are two weighty reasons why the people settled there should be coloured principally. The first, because by that means they would become more fully involved in the destiny of this continent: any eastern move of magnitude, as for instance to Africa, if possible, would appear a retrograde step, now that the current of affairs is so clearly setting west. And secondly, in no more effectual way could a check be given to the encroachments of slavery on free soil. The purely American sympathy for kith and kin only, would experience unmistakable obstacles to its free exercise, in the event of a contemplated annexation of that delightful Western country.

It will be seen that the possibility of a pretty extensive emigration to those countries has been the prominent feature throughout this tract, and for that reason direct reference has been made to other points under British jurisdiction, than Canada. The preference given to these (Canada, West Indies, and Vancouver's Island), over British Colonies elsewhere, has been because of their strong position and availability in every way. There would not be as in Africa, Mexico, or South America, hostile tribes to annoy the settler, or destroy at will towns and villages with their inhabitants: the strong arm of British power would summarily punish depredations made, of whatever character, and the emigrants would naturally assume the responsibility of British freemen.

The question of whether or not an extensive emigration by the free coloured people of the United States would affect the institution of slavery would then be answered. I have here taken the affirmative of that question, because that view of the case seems to me most clear. The free coloured people have steadily discountenanced any rational scheme of emigration in the hope that by remaining in the States, a powerful miracle for the overthrow of slavery would be wrought. What are the facts?

More territory has been given up to slavery, the Fugitive Law has passed, and a concert of measures, seriously affecting their personal liberty, have been entered into by several of the Free States. So subtle, unseen and effective have been their movements, that, were it not that we remember there is a Great Britain, we would be overwhelmed, powerless, from the force of such successive shocks. And the end may not be yet, if we persist in remaining for targets while they are strengthening themselves in the Northwest and in the Gulf. There would be more of the right spirit, and infinitely more of real manliness, in a peaceful but decided demand for freedom to the slave from the Gulf of Mexico, than in a miserable scampering from state to state, in a vain endeavour to gather the crumbs of freedom that a pro-slavery besom [a broom made of twigs tied around a stick] may sweep away at any moment.

May a selection for the best be made, now that there are countries between which and the United States a comparison may be instituted. A little folding of the hands, and there may be no retreat from the clutches of the slave power.

Figure 3.4: Frances Ellen Watkins Harper

Frances Ellen Watkins Harper

Frances Ellen Watkins Harper (1825–1911), born free in Baltimore, Maryland, was orphaned at three years old and raised by her uncle Reverend William Watkins and his wife, Henrietta, who were civil rights activists and abolitionists. While Harper worked over the course of her life as a seamstress, nursemaid, teacher, and public speaker, she also built a distinguished career as the best known African American woman writer of her times. Her first publications were poems in antislavery journals, but with the publication of her first poetry collection, *Forest Leaves* or *Autumn Leaves*, and *Poems on Miscellaneous Subjects*, in 1854 her career gained significant traction. In fact, over the remainder of the century Harper generated a considerable flow of success establishing herself nationally as a pioneering multigenre writer. Not only did she publish poems she published also short stories and a highly praised novel, *Iola Leroy, or Shadows uplifted* (1892).

Beyond this distinguished and prolific record as a creative writer, Harper was also very well known, especially among broadly based progressive audiences, for her published essays and speeches as a passionate activist and leader. She advocated publicly for several sociopolitical causes and held high offices in several organizations associated with these causes: abolitionism, education, woman suffrage, women's rights more generally, and temperance. Included below is one of Harper's best known poems, "Bury Me in a Free Land," first published in the *Anti-Slavery Bugle* in 1858, before the Civil War. Included also, as an indication of the continuity of her interests, concerns, and commitments as a sociopolitical actor, is the essay "We Are All Bound Up Together," which she presented in New York eight years later, after the Civil War, on May 1, 1866, at the Eleventh National Women's Rights Convention. In both documents and in two expressive forms, she demonstrates a dedication to speaking truth and casting light on critical and rational needs for action.

Frances Ellen Watkins Harper

Bury Me in a Free Land

Published in Harper's first collection of poetry, *Forest Leaves* (1845), https://poets.org/poem/bury-me-free-land.

Make me a grave where'er you will,
In a lowly plain, or a lofty hill;
Make it among earth's humblest graves,
But not in a land where men are slaves.

I could not rest if around my grave
I heard the steps of a trembling slave;
His shadow above my silent tomb
Would make it a place of fearful gloom.

I could not rest if I heard the tread
Of a coffle gang to the shambles led,
And the mother's shriek of wild despair
Rise like a curse on the trembling air.

I could not sleep if I saw the lash
Drinking her blood at each fearful gash,

And I saw her babes torn from her breast,
Like trembling doves from their parent nest.

I'd shudder and start if I heard the bay
Of bloodhounds seizing their human prey,
And I heard the captive plead in vain
As they bound afresh his galling chain.

If I saw young girls from their mother's arms
Bartered and sold for their youthful charms,
My eye would flash with a mournful flame,
My death-paled cheek grow red with shame.

I would sleep, dear friends, where bloated might
Can rob no man of his dearest right;
My rest shall be calm in any grave
Where none can call his brother a slave.

I ask no monument, proud and high,
To arrest the gaze of the passers-by;
All that my yearning spirit craves,
Is bury me not in a land of slaves.

We Are All Bound Up Together

A speech delivered by Harper at the Eleventh National Women's Rights Convention in New York, May 1, 1866. https://awpc.cattcenter.iastate.edu/2017/03/21/we-are-all-bound-up-together-may-1866.

I feel I am something of a novice upon this platform. Born of a race whose inheritance has been outrage and wrong, most of my life had been spent in battling against those wrongs. But I did not feel as keenly as others, that I had these rights, in common with other women, which are now demanded. About two years ago, I stood within the shadows of my home. A great sorrow had fallen upon my life. My husband had died suddenly, leaving me a widow, with four children, one my own, and the others stepchildren. I tried to keep my children together. But my husband died in debt; and before he had been in his grave three months, the administrator had swept the very milk crocks and wash tubs from my hands. I was a farmer's wife and made butter for the Columbus market; but what could I do, when they had swept all away? They left me one thing and that was a looking glass! Had I died instead of my husband, how different would have been the result! By this time he would have had another wife, it is likely; and no administrator would have gone into his house, broken up his home, and sold his bed, and taken away his means of support. I took my children in my arms, and went out to seek my living. While I was gone; a neighbor to whom I had once lent five dollars, went before a magistrate and swore that he believed I was a non resident, and laid an attachment on my very bed. And I went back to Ohio with my orphan children in my arms, without a single feather bed in this wide world, that was not in the custody of the law. I say, then, that justice is not fulfilled so long as woman is unequal before the law.

We are all bound up together in one great bundle of humanity, and society cannot trample on the weakest and feeblest of its members without receiving the curse in its own soul. You tried that in the case of the negro. You pressed him down for two centuries; and in so doing you crippled the moral strength and paralyzed the spiritual energies of the white men of the country. When the hands of the black were fettered, white men were deprived of the liberty of speech and the freedom of the press. Society can not afford to neglect the enlightenment of any class of its members. At the South, the legislation of the country was in behalf of the rich slaveholders, while the poor white man was neglected. What is the consequence today? From that very class of neglected poor white men, comes the man who stands today with his hand upon the helm of the nation. He fails to catch the watchword of the hour, and throws himself, the incarnation of meanness, across the pathway of the nation. My objection to Andrew Johnson is not that he has been a poor white man; my objection is that he keeps "poor white" all the way through. (Applause.) That is the trouble with him.

This grand and glorious revolution which has commenced, will fail to reach its climax of success, until throughout the length and brea[d]th of the American Republic, the nation shall be so color-blind, as to know no man by the color of his skin or the curl of his hair. It will then have no privileged class, trampling upon outraging the unprivileged classes, but will be then one great privileged nation, whose privilege will be to produce the loftiest manhood and womanhood that humanity can attain.

I do not believe that giving the woman the ballot is immediately going to cure all the ills of life. I do not believe that white women are dew-drops just exhaled from the skies. I think that like men they may be divided into three classes, the good, the bad, and the indifferent. The good would vote according to their convictions and principles; the bad, as dictated by preju[d]ice or malice; and the indifferent will vote on the strongest side of the question, with the winning party.

You white women speak here of rights. I speak of wrongs. I, as a colored woman, have had in this country an education which has made me feel as if I were in the situation of Ishmael, my hand against every man, and every man's hand against me. Let me go [to-morrow] morning and take my seat in one of your street cars—I do not know that they will do it in New York, but they will in Philadelphia—and the conductor will put up his hand and stop the car rather than let me ride.

A Lady—They will not do that here.

Mrs. Harper—They do in Philadelphia. Going from Washington to Baltimore this Spring, they put me in the smoking car. (*Loud Voices*—"Shame.") Aye, in the capital of the nation, where the black man consecrated himself to the nation's defence, faithful when the white man was faithless, they put me in the smoking car! They did it once; but the next time they tried it, they failed; for I would not go in. I felt the fight in me; but I don't want to have to fight all the time. Today I am puzzled where to make my home. I would like to make it in Philadelphia, near my own friends and relations. But if I want to ride in the streets of Philadelphia, they send me to ride on the platform with the driver. (Cries of "Shame.") Have women nothing to do with this? Not long since, a colored woman took her seat in an Eleventh Street car in Philadelphia, and the conductor stopped the car, and told the rest of the passengers to get out, and left the car with her in it alone, when they took it back to the station. One day I took my seat in a car, and the conductor came to me and told me to take another seat. I just screamed "murder." The man said if I was black I ought to behave myself. I knew that if he was white he was not behaving himself. Are there no wrongs to be righted?

In advocating the cause of the colored man, since the Dred Scott decision, I have sometimes said I thought the nation had touched bottom. But let me tell you there is a depth of infamy lower than that. It is when the nation, standing upon the threshold of a great peril, reached out its hands to a feebler race, and asked that race to help it, and when the peril was over, said, "You are good enough for soldiers, but not good enough for citizens. When Judge Taney said that the men of my race had no rights which the white man was bound to respect, he had not seen the bones of the black man bleaching outside of Richmond. He had not seen the thinned ranks and the thickened graves of the Louisiana Second, a regiment which went into battle nine hundred strong, and came out with three hundred. He had not stood at Olustee and seen defeat and disaster crushing down the pride of our banner, until words were brought to Col. Hallowell, "The day is lost; go in and save it," and black men stood in the gap, beat back the enemy, and saved your army. (Applause.)

We have a woman in our country who has received the name of "Moses," not by lying about it, but by acting out (Applause)—a woman who has gone down into the Egypt of slavery and brought out hundreds of our people into liberty. The last time I saw that woman, her hands were swollen. That woman who had led one of Montgomery's most successful expeditions, who was brave enough and secretive enough to act as a scout for the American army, had her hands all swollen from a conflict with a brutal conductor, who undertook to eject her from her place. That woman whose courage and bravery won a recognition from our army and from every black man in the land, is excluded from every thoroughfare of travel. Talk of giving women the ballot-box? Go on. It is a normal school, and the white women of this country need it. While there exists this brutal element in society which tramples upon the feeble and treads down the weak, I tell you that if there is any class of people who need to be lifted out of their airy nothings and selfishness, it is the white women of America. (Applause.)

Chapter 4

During the Civil War

For African Americans (enslaved, freed, or freeborn), the Civil War was a curious opportunity indeed. During this time period, regardless of their specific social status, they existed in interstitial space—without the presumption of agency, authority, or a predictable stability. They were perennially vulnerable within a context where laws, policies, and practices did not automatically position them as having either human or civil rights, and where their socioeconomic resources did not protect them from discrimination and inequity. With the advent of a war that challenged the nation to clarify its identity as one nation or two, the stakes for all African Americans were especially high, and certainly so for African American women.

Before the war, the United States was, of course, a slaveholding nation with a deeply gendered sociocultural context where there was little chance for African Americans of any status to expect brighter horizons without persistent advocacy and activism. With the coming of the war, it was not a stretch for them to see that a Confederate victory would mean disastrous consequences in terms of both life and liberty. Interestingly, it was also not a stretch to see that, with a Union victory, they still could not expect easy transitions. They presumed that the Union would need to reaffirm the core values of freedom, justice, equality, and the pursuit of happiness—for all. However, the political realities of the operational context did not suggest a comfortable victory but instead, once again, a cautionary tale.

The future landscape for reaffirmation was uncharted, with the devil being in the details. The nation would need to forge not only workable pathways but sustainable ones, in deepening and broadening the scope of the rights of citizenship and a set of accountabilities for the implementing and monitoring of the maintenance of these rights. In other words, African Americans, generally, and African American women in particular, recognized that the winner of the war did indeed matter in terms of establishing the potential of transformative change. However, they demonstrated also that they recognized the need to bring flesh to the frame even if the Union was victorious. Both men and women rose to the occasion to fight in whatever ways they were able for their own freedom and to be vigilant about securing justice and equality for their communities. Moreover, their commitments to action demonstrated an understanding that they would need to stand boldly, whenever possible, to declare and sustain a place going forward for their race in the definition of "citizen," with the full rights and privileges appertaining thereto.

A huge hindrance to enacting such commitments was, in fact, the war and the reality that the overwhelming numbers of African Americans were enslaved in the Deep South with limited mobility, limited resources, and limited leverage. Given the increasingly deteriorating conditions of war, this oppressed group needed to be inventive in taking care of themselves, reconnecting their families after emancipation in 1863, and getting themselves away from their enslaved circumstances. Generally, a critical task was the daunting challenge of surviving the war and thereby being able to exercise with valor the potential of new opportunities. For African Americans living in the northern and border states, they too had to survive, but they also understood the specific linkages of their own freedom to the freedom of their brothers and sisters enslaved in the South. Freedom might seem individual, but justice and equality had to be, quite necessarily, for the race as a whole.

The writers selected below exhibit ways in which African American women during the Civil War envisioned what it meant for them to work for freedom, justice, equality, and empowerment. There are two genres represented in these examples. One is the memoir with the focus of this genre on reminiscences in hindsight of a particular time, place, and situation. The other is the personal essay, where we gain a sense of the real time observations, perspectives, and insights of the writer. In both cases, these rhetorical choices offer examples of how African American women during this era (one born free, two born into slavery) took advantage of their available opportunities and chronicled the work that helped them to make a difference for others and for themselves.

Figure 4.1: Elizabeth Hobbs Keckley

Elizabeth Hobbs Keckley

Elizabeth Hobbs Keckley (1818–1907) was born enslaved in Virginia on the plantation of Colonel Armistead Burwell. At fourteen she was given to Burwell's son Reverend Robert Burwell, who lived in North Carolina. At the age of twenty Keckley was raped and gave birth to her son George in 1839. After her son's birth, she was given to Burwell's daughter, Ann Burwell Garland, who lived in Virginia with her husband, Hugh. In 1847 the Garland family moved to Saint Louis, Missouri, where Keckley was required to support the Garland family through her work as a seamstress. She had been trained as a seamstress by her mother and was excellent. As a slave who was hired out based on these skills, she successfully developed a large clientele. From the small percentage that she received from her earnings as a successful dressmaker, Keckley saved her money, and with some funds borrowed from her wealthy

Figure 4.2: Keckley gown for Mary Todd Lincoln

clients, she bought her freedom (and her son George's freedom). She was officially emancipated on November 15, 1855, at the age of thirty-one. Her son was sixteen. During this process of liberating herself, Keckley had married James Keckley in 1852, but the marriage was not a successful union. By 1860 she had paid back the funds that she had borrowed from her clients, left her husband, and moved to Washington, DC, on her own to make a better life for herself and her son.

In 1861, at the beginning of the Civil War, Keckley was building an excellent reputation as a gifted fashion designer and dressmaker and garnering a distinguished clientele at the most elite levels of Washington society. Her clients included, for example, Varina Davis, wife of Jefferson Davis, and ultimately Mary Todd Lincoln, with Keckley being in the prestigious position of personal dressmaker and confidante to the first lady of the United States (see figure 4.2). Symbolically, Keckley was demonstrating, as Alice Walker proclaims in "In Search of Our Mothers' Gardens" (1983), an expressive power in the rhetoric of adornment through fashion and design.

Although I do not focus in this volume on visual rhetorics, there is a story to be told about how the design expertise and excellence in craftsmanship of a former slave translated into fashion success in the stunning context of the American Civil War. Clearly, Keckley's work spoke well for her talents as an artist and a business woman, as well as for her unbridled spirit as a woman of African descent and a former slave, all of which, in Keckley's case, helped to make "her signature [on the world] clear" (A. Walker 1983, 243). At the height of her success during and immediately after the Civil War, Keckley ran a shop that employed twenty women. This success confirms that, although many who know about Keckley as a historic figure think of her mainly as the dressmaker, friend, and confidante of Mary Todd Lincoln, she was actually a very successful business woman, philanthropist, community activist, and leader.

In 1862 Keckley spoke as an advocate for African American refugees before her fellow church members in the Fifteenth Street Presbyterian Church. With their support, Keckley founded the Contraband Relief Association (later renamed the Ladies' Freedmen and Soldiers' Relief Association) in order to address the needs for food, clothing, shelter, and medical attention for the thousands of African American refugees who were flooding into Washington, DC, from the embattled southern states, and ultimately for the numbers of African American soldiers who were being wounded in the war. Keckley organized meetings and events in several cities, leading the effort to generate funds to support an array of critical activities. She was successful in raising funds and other contributions, including from African American communities across the Northeast, from among the refugees themselves, from Frederick Douglass, and from various antislavery societies in Great Britain. Moreover, with her broadly cast opportunities to leverage her relationships with the White House, Keckley was also able to garner funding not only from the Lincolns but also from luminaries within the white abolitionist communities, such as Wendell Phillips and Leonard Grimes. Thus, as a recognized leader in the African American community, Keckley and her organization became a key resource for the survival and sustainability of the refugees in the Washington, DC, area, providing important support in critical areas of need.

After the assassination of President Lincoln on April 15, 1865, Keckley was no longer at the White House, but she remained friends with Mary Todd Lincoln. In order to help support herself, she wrote *Behind the Scenes, Or, Thirty Years a Slave, and Four Years in the White House* (1868). The publication of this autobiography was controversial since it did indeed tell stories of life "behind the scenes at the White House." Keckley's relationship with Mary Todd Lincoln, who felt betrayed by the invasion of her privacy, was severed. Keckley continued to work as a seamstress, but with a declining client base from elite Washingtonians who no longer supported her business. In 1892 she moved to Zenia, Ohio, to accept a position as head of the Department of Sewing and Domestic Science Arts at Wilberforce University. At the end of her life, in failing health, she moved back to Washington. She lived in poverty in the National Home for Destitute Colored Women and Children, a resource that emerged, ironically, from the effort of the organization that she founded in 1862. Keckley died there in 1907 at the age of eighty-nine.

In *Behind the Scenes*, Keckley chronicles specific incidences from her early life, including the crushing moment when her father, who was enslaved on another plantation, was ripped from her and her mother. She heard from him in letters for several years, but she never saw him again. Among several stories of the horrors of slave experiences, she chronicles also the multiple times when she was brutally beaten as a young girl and woman, despite her determined efforts each and every time to physically defend herself, emphasizing to her readers that these attempts to break her spirit were unsuccessful.

Keckley speaks, as well, about the four years of sexual harassment and rape that she was compelled to endure, which resulted in the birth of her son. Much of the memoir, however, is about the process of her emancipation; her work in slavery in several households and also in freedom as a business woman (with several employees) and her ingenuity and leadership in support of her community. In the three excerpts below, Keckley speaks about her first meeting with Mary Todd Lincoln, explains the interconnections of her White House employment with her work as a community organizer and leader, and shares her view of the historical moment of Lincoln's presidential leadership and her privilege in witnessing it.

In casting light on Keckley's story of life and living during this turbulent era, her memoir offers far more than a one-dimensional view of her as a top tier fashion designer for elite women in Washington, DC, and as the confidante of the first lady of the United States of America. As distinctive as this view of her work may indeed be, there is a larger scope to be understood. Elizabeth Keckley was born a slave, with all the challenges that this sociopolitical status implies. However, with focus, persistence, and hard work she gained her own freedom (and her son's) and became a very successful entrepreneur. Notably, in addition to establishing a level of prosperity for herself for several decades, she also used her talents and her access to elite networks strategically to help address critical challenges in her community, to sustain those around her who were in dire need, and to participate actively in forging a vision of possibility for her people. Fundamentally, over the course of her life, even as a person who had been enslaved for several decades, she demonstrated a sense of self and agency that grounded her ability to work as an advocate, activist, and leader in support of herself and others—despite the challenges at the end of her life that left her, not without hope, but still in degraded financial circumstances.

Elizabeth Hobbs Keckley

Excerpts from *Behind the Scenes, Or, Thirty Years a Slave, and Four Years in the White House* (1868; Scotts Valley, CA: CreateSpace Independent Publishing Platform, 2011).

My Introduction to Mrs. Lincoln

Ever since arriving in Washington I had a great desire to work for the ladies of the White House, and to accomplish this end I was ready to make almost any sacrifice consistent with propriety. Work came in slowly, and I was beginning to feel very much embarrassed, for I did not know how I was to meet the bills staring me in the face. It is true, the bills were small, but then they were formidable to me, who had little or nothing to pay them with. While in this situation I called at the Ringolds, where I met Mrs. Captain Lee. Mrs. L. was in a state bordering on excitement, as the great event of the season, the dinner party given in honor of the Prince of Wales, was soon to come off, and she must have a dress suitable for the occasion. The silk had been purchased, but a dress-maker had not yet been found. Miss Ringold recommended me, and I received the order to make the dress. When I called on Mrs. Lee the next day, her husband was in the room, and handing me a roll of bank bills, amounting to one hundred dollars, he requested me to purchase the trimmings, and to spare no expense in making a selection. With the money in my pocket I went out in the street, entered the store of Harper & Mitchell, and asked to look at their laces. Mr. Harper waited on me himself, and was polite and kind. When I asked permission to carry the laces to Mrs. Lee, in order to learn whether she could approve my selection or not, he gave a ready assent. When I reminded him that I was a stranger, and that the goods were valuable, he remarked that he was not afraid to trust me—that he believed my face was the index to an honest heart. It was pleasant to be spoken to thus, and I shall never forget the kind words of Mr. Harper. I often recall them, for they are associated with the dawn of a brighter period in my dark life. I purchased the trimmings, and Mr. Harper allowed me a commission of twenty-five dollars on the purchase. The dress was done in time, and it gave complete satisfaction. Mrs. Lee attracted great attention at the dinner-party, and her elegant dress proved a good card for me. I received numerous orders, and was relieved from all pecuniary embarrassments. One of my patrons was Mrs. Gen. McClean, a daughter of Gen. Sumner. One day when I was very busy, Mrs. McC. drove up to my apartments, came in where I was engaged with my needle, and in her emphatic way said:

"Lizzie, I am invited to dine at Willard's on next Sunday, and positively I have not a dress fit to wear on the occasion. I have just purchased material, and you must commence work on it right away."

"But Mrs. McClean," I replied, "I have more work now promised than I can do. It is impossible for me to make a dress for you to wear on Sunday next."

"Pshaw! Nothing is impossible. I must have the dress made by Sunday;" and she spoke with some impatience.

"I am sorry," I began, but she interrupted me.

"Now don't say no again. I tell you that you must make the dress. I have often heard you say that you would like to work for the ladies of the White House. Well, I have it in my power to obtain you this privilege. I know Mrs. Lincoln well, and you shall make a dress for her provided you finish mine in time to wear at dinner on Sunday."

The inducement was the best that could have been offered. I would undertake the dress if I should have to sit up all night—every night, to make my pledge good. I sent out and employed assistants, and, after much worry and trouble, the dress was completed to the satisfaction of Mrs. McClean. It appears that Mrs. Lincoln had upset a cup of coffee on the dress she designed wearing on the evening of the reception after the inauguration of Abraham Lincoln as President of the United States, which rendered it necessary that she should have a new one for the occasion. On asking Mrs. McClean who her dress-maker was, that lady promptly informed her.

"Lizzie Keckley." . . .

The next Sunday Mrs. McClean sent me a message to call at her house at four o'clock P.M., that day. As she did not state why I was to call, I determined to wait till Monday morning. Monday morning came, and nine o'clock found me at Mrs. McC's house. The streets of the capital were thronged with people, for this was Inauguration day. A new President, a man of the people from the broad prairies of the West, was to accept the solemn oath of office, was to assume the responsibilities attached to the high position of Chief Magistrate of the United States. Never was such deep interest felt in the inauguration proceedings as was felt today; for threats of assassination had been made, and every breeze from the South came heavily laden with the rumors of war. Around Willard's hotel swayed an excited crowd, and it was with the utmost difficulty that I worked my way to the house on the opposite side of the street, occupied by the McCleans. Mrs. McClean was out, but presently an aide on General McClean's staff called, and informed me that I was wanted at Willard's. I crossed the street, and on entering the hotel was met by Mrs. McClean, who greeted me:

"Lizzie, why did you not come yesterday, as I requested? Mrs. Lincoln wanted to see you, but I fear that now you are too late."

"I am sorry, Mrs. McClean. You did not say what you wanted with me yesterday, so I judged that this morning would do as well."

"You should have come yesterday," she insisted. "Go up to Mrs. Lincoln's room"—giving me the number—"she may find use for you yet."

"You are Lizzie Keckley, I believe."

I bowed assent.

"The dress-maker that Mrs. McClean recommended?"

"Yes, madam."

"Very well; I have not time to talk to you now, but would like to have you call at the White House, at eight o'clock to-morrow morning, where I shall then be."

I bowed myself out of the room, and returned to my apartments.

The day passed slowly, for I could not help but speculate in relation to the appointed interview for the morrow. My long-cherished hope was about to be realized, and I could not rest.

[After some discussion of her qualifications and a confirmation that she would "work cheap," Keckley was hired.]

Tuesday evening came, and I had taken the last stitches on the dress. I folded it and carried it to the White House, with the waist for Mrs. Grimsly [a second order for Keckley]. When I went up-stairs, I found the ladies in a terrible state of excitement. Mrs. Lincoln was protesting that she could not go down, for the reason that she had nothing to wear.

"Mrs. Keckley, you have disappointed me—deceived me. Why do you bring my dress at this late hour?"

"Because I have just finished it, and thought I should be in time."

"But you are not in time, Mrs. Keckley; you have bitterly disappointed me. I have no time now to dress, and what is more, I will not dress, and go down-stairs."

"I am sorry if I have disappointed you, Mrs. Lincoln, for I intended to be in time. Will you let me dress you? I can have you ready in a few minutes."

"No, I won't be dressed. I will stay in my room. Mr. Lincoln can go down with the other ladies."

"But there is plenty of time for you to dress, Mary," joined in Mrs. Grimsly and Mrs. Edwards. "Let Mrs. Keckley assist you, and she will soon have you ready."

Thus urged, she consented. I dressed her hair, and arranged the dress on her. It fitted nicely, and she was pleased. Mr. Lincoln came in, threw himself on the sofa, laughed with Willie and little Tad, and then commenced pulling on his gloves quoting poetry all the while.

"You seem to be in a poetical mood to-night," said his wife.

"Yes, mother, these are poetical times," was his pleasant reply. "I declare, you look charming in that dress. Mrs. Keckley has met with great success." And then he proceeded to compliment the other ladies.

Mrs. Lincoln looked elegant in her rose-colored moiré-antique. She wore a pearl necklace, pearl ear-rings, pearl bracelets, and red roses in her hair. . . . Mrs. Lincoln took the President's arm, and with smiling face led the train below. I was surprised at her grace and composure. I had heard so much, in current and malicious report, of her low life, of her ignorance and vulgarity, that I expected to see her embarrassed on this occasion. Report, I soon saw, was wrong. No queen, accustomed to the usage of royalty all her life, could have comported herself with more calmness and dignity than did the wife of the President. She was confident and self-possessed, and confidence always gives grace.

The levee was a brilliant one, and the only one of the season. I became the regular modiste of Mrs. Lincoln. I made fifteen or sixteen dresses for her during the spring and early part of the summer. . . .

Washington in 1862–63

In the summer of 1862, freedmen began to flock into Washington from Maryland and Virginia. They came with a great hope in their hearts, and with all their worldly goods on their backs. Fresh from the bonds of slavery, fresh from the benighted regions of the plantation, they came to the Capital looking for liberty, and many of them not knowing it when they found it. Many good friends reached forth kind hands, but the North is not warm and impulsive. For one kind word spoken, two harsh ones were uttered; there was something repelling in the atmosphere, and the bright joyous dreams of freedom to the slave faded—were sadly altered, in the presence of that stern, practical mother, reality. Instead of flowery paths, days of perpetual sunshine, and bowers hanging with golden fruit, the road was rugged and full of thorns, the sunshine was eclipsed by shadows, and the mute appeals for help too often were answered by cold neglect. Poor dusky children of slavery, men and women of my own race—the transition from slavery to freedom was too sudden for you! The bright dreams were too rudely dispelled; you were not prepared for the new life that opened before you, and the great masses of the North learned to look upon your helplessness with indifference—learned to speak of you as an idle, dependent race. Reason should have prompted kinder thoughts. Charity is ever kind.

One fair summer evening I was walking the streets of Washington, accompanied by a friend, when a band of music was heard in the distance. We wondered what it could mean, and curiosity prompted us to find out its meaning. We quickened our steps, and discovered that it came from the house of Mrs. Farnham. The yard was brilliantly lighted, ladies and gentlemen were moving about, and the band was playing some of its sweetest airs. We approached the sentinel on duty at the gate, and asked what was going on. He told us that it was a festival given for the benefit of the sick and wounded soldiers in the city. This suggested an idea to me. If the white people can give festivals to raise funds for the relief of suffering soldiers, why should not the well-to-do colored people go to work to do something for the benefit of the suffering blacks? I could not rest. The thought was ever present with me, and the next Sunday I made a suggestion in the colored church, that a society of colored people be formed to labor for the benefit of the unfortunate freedmen. The idea proved popular, and in two weeks "the Contraband Relief Association" was organized with forty working members.

In September of 1862, Mrs. Lincoln left Washington for New York, and requested me to follow her in a few days, and join her at the Metropolitan Hotel. I was glad of the opportunity to do so, for I thought that in New York I would be able to do something in the interests of our society. Armed with credentials, I took the train for New York, and went to the Metropolitan, where Mrs. Lincoln had secured accommodations for me. The next morning I told Mrs. Lincoln of my project; and she immediately headed my list with a subscription of $200. I circulated among the colored people, and got them thoroughly interested in the subject, when I was called to Boston by Mrs. Lincoln, who wished to visit her son Robert, attending college in that city. I met Mr. Wendell Phillips, and other Boston philanthropists, who gave me all the assistance in their power. We held a mass meeting at the Colored Baptist Church, Rev. Mr. Grimes, in Boston, raised a sum of money, and organized there a branch society. The society was organized by Mrs. Grimes, wife of the pastor, assisted by Mrs. Martin, wife of Rev. Stella Martin. This branch of the main society, during the war, was able to send us over eighty large boxes of goods, contributed exclusively by the colored people of Boston. Returning to New York, we held a successful meeting at the Shiloh Church, Rev. Henry Highland Garnet, pastor. The Metropolitan Hotel at that time as now, employed colored help. I suggested the object of my mission to Robert Thompson, Steward of the Hotel, who immediately raised quite a sum of money among the dining-room waiters. Mr. Frederick Douglass contributed $200, besides lecturing for us. Other prominent colored men sent in liberal contributions. From England, a large quantity of stores was received. Mrs. Lincoln made frequent contributions, as also did the President. In 1863 I was re-elected President of the Association, which office I continue to hold. . . .

The Second Inauguration

Mrs. Lincoln came to my apartments one day towards the close of the summer of 1864, to consult me in relation to a dress. . . . After some conversation, she asked: "Lizzie, where do you think I will be this time next summer?"

"Why, in the White House, of course."

"I cannot believe so. I have no hope of the re-election of Mr. Lincoln. The canvass is a heated one, the people begin to murmur at the war, and every vile charge is brought against my husband."

"No matter," I replied, "Mr. Lincoln will be re-elected. I am so confident of it, that I am tempted to ask a favor of you."

"A favor! Well, if we remain in the White House I shall be able to do you many favors. What is the special favor?"

"Simply this, Mrs. Lincoln—I should like for you to make me a present of the right-hand glove that the President wears at the first public reception after his second inaugural."

"You shall have it in welcome. It will be so filthy when he pulls it off, I shall be tempted to take the tongs and put it in the fire. I cannot imagine, Lizabeth, what you want with such a glove."

"I shall cherish it as a precious memento of the second inauguration of the man who has done so much for my race. He has been a Jehovah to my people—has lifted them out of bondage, and directed their footsteps from darkness into light. I shall keep the glove, and hand it down to posterity."

"You have some strange ideas, Lizabeth. Never mind, you shall have the glove; that is, if Mr. Lincoln continues President after the 4th of March next."

I held Mrs. Lincoln to her promise. That glove is now in my possession, bearing the marks of the thousands of hands that grasped the honest hand of Mr. Lincoln on that eventful night. Alas! It has become a prouder, sadder memento than I ever dreamed—prior to making the request—it would be.

[A few weeks later, on April 14, 1865, President Lincoln was assassinated by John Wilkes Booth.]

Figure 4.3: Charlotte Forten Grimké

Charlotte Forten Grimké

Charlotte Forten Grimké (1837–1914) was born free in Philadelphia, Pennsylvania, into the wealthy, high achieving, abolitionist Forten-Purvis family. She became best known herself as an educator, writer, and poet, showing evidence of the nurturing intellectual and activist environment in which she was raised. Her circle of family, friends, and colleagues included many prominent figures of the day: Sarah Mapps Douglass, Charles Lenox Rémond, William Lloyd Garrison, Lydia Maria Child, John Greenleaf Whittier, Wendell Phillips, William Wells Brown, Sarah Parker Rémond, and more.

Forten was educated privately until her teen years when her father, abolitionist Robert Bridges Forten, made arrangements for her to live with friends (Charles Lenox Rémond and Amy Matilda Rémond) in Salem, Massachusetts, to attend the Higginson Grammar School. She was the only African American student. She continued her education in Salem at the Salem Normal School. After graduating in 1856, she was the first African American hired to teach in Salem, Massachusetts, at the prestigious Epes Grammar School.

During her years in Salem, Forten began keeping a diary, starting on May 24, 1854, and continuing through May 15, 1864, with other diaries in 1885 and in 1892. Her diaries are a remarkable record of her thoughts and experiences, as well as her efforts to develop her intellectual abilities and to use her talents for good in the world. Living in Salem, Forten records that she became very active in the Female Anti-Slavery Society, attending meetings and lectures and engaging in robust conversation and correspondence with prominent progressive leaders on the issues of the day. She also began publishing poetry in several abolitionist journals (e.g., *The Liberator*, the *National Anti-Slavery Standard*, and *The Evangelist*), with her diary entries confirming that her passion for justice was very strong.

When the opportunity arose for teachers to go South to teach newly liberated slaves, Forten was determined to go, and she became the first African American teacher to do so. Working through the Port Royal Relief Association, she was sent to Saint Helena Island, South Carolina, in 1862, where she taught the people there. In addition, however, she also volunteered to serve as a nurse for wounded soldiers from the Fifty-Fourth Massachusetts Regiment, an African American troop commanded by Colonel Robert Gould Shaw (memorialized in the film *Glory* in 1989). The soldiers had fought bravely in the battle of Fort Wagner, South Carolina, but lost. A particular highlight during these years was that Forten met Harriet Tubman and was thoroughly inspired by the stories that Tubman shared about her life.

During the two years that Forten worked as a teacher and nurse on Saint Helena Island, she continued to write. Distinctive among these texts were the letters about her experiences that she regularly sent to the *Atlantic Monthly*, where they published them. In 1864 she also wrote "Life on the Sea Islands," which this magazine published in two parts in the May and June issues of that year. In May of the same year, Forten became ill, resigned her position, and returned to Philadelphia, where she remained until the end of the war. In 1865 she accepted a position as secretary of the teachers committee of the New England branch of the Freedmen's Union Commission, and she moved to Boston where she recruited and trained teachers for the recently liberated slaves. In 1871 Forten accepted a teaching position in Charleston, South Carolina, and in 1872 she moved to Washington, DC, where she worked as a clerk in the US Treasury Department and where she was also hired to teach at the African American Preparatory School (later known as the M Street School and renamed, ultimately, the Paul Laurence Dunbar High School).

In 1878 Forten married Reverend Francis James Grimké (also from a prominent abolitionist family). He was pastor of the Fifteenth Street Presbyterian Church, a position that gave Forten the opportunity to become more involved in the missionary work of the church. Although she continued to write poetry, her activism in the community became ever sharper, with her spending considerable time and energy working with the African American women leaders of Washington. As an active member of this group, she became a founding member of the National Association of Colored Women and remained active in sociopolitical work until her death on July 23, 1914.

Below are excerpts from Parts I and II of "Life on the Sea Islands." The articles offered to the readers of *The Atlantic Monthly* a slice-of-life view of what it meant to live and work in the Sea Islands with the Civil War so close at hand. The account is mainly descriptive. However, in Forten's descriptions there is also a glimpse of the apparent diversity that she and her charges represented. She was a well-educated, elite, free born African American woman who had grown up in the North among very socially and politically conscious circles. The people whom she was teaching were the polar opposite. Forten's account suggests that she felt herself both alike and different from the recently liberated slaves who surrounded her.

In contrast to her fascination with the people and the place, Forten does not address very much her relationships with the two white women who were supposedly her fellow volunteers and colleagues. One might well imagine, given the fact that Forten is only referred to infrequently and in servant-like terms in the diary of her white colleague Laura Towne (Towne 1993), that Forten functioned within a biased framework where she may have been valued but not fairly or equitably so, even though she was remarkably well prepared, arguably well beyond her white colleagues, to perform the important educational activism that she was performing. Forten also did not directly address her apparent affection for Colonel Shaw, the white leader of the Fifty-Fourth regiment of African American troops. In this case as well, one might easily imagine that, beyond the cross-race taboos of admitting such affection, especially for a married man, the mores of the nineteenth century did not include the sharing of such personal sexualized content in public discourses—and especially not by "a lady."

In "Life on the Sea Islands," Forten's most persistent set of messages include: (1) her fascination with the cultural environment of the island, which was quite different from her own home context; (2) her admiration of the potential of the people to learn; (3) her disdain for the injustices so regularly cast against a race of people who had been so deliberately downtrodden. As generally the case with rhetorical performances, Forten's messages were informed by experiences and opportunities that were a function, not only of her race, gender, culture, and so forth in context but also by her class privileges as a freeborn African American woman from an elite activist family. To be acknowledged, the experience of class privilege was, of course, not typically shared by all of her fellow African American women activists—for example, her opportunities to publish in national magazines. Like other activists of her day, however, she demonstrated a consistent sense of social responsibility, in her case, exhibiting a twofold commitment both to help educate the newly freed people who were in dire need of opportunities to learn and to provide nursing care to African American soldiers in a field of war.

Forten demonstrated also sociopolitical sensibilities. She consistently used her rhetorical expertise to make it possible for the broad national audience of the *Atlantic Monthly* to gain a deeper understanding of formerly enslaved people as human beings with untapped potential. At this convergence of ideology and actions, she used her available means to advocate for a bold conclusion for her day and time. She suggested in a well-regarded venue that, as people with potential, this downtrodden group should be afforded not just education but the full rights of citizenship.

This period in Forten's life constitutes, thereby, a signal opportunity to document and understand an instructive example of the ways in which African American women deliberately interlinked their ideological beliefs, often with considerable courage, with their commitments to social change and social justice. Like other African American women, Forten stepped forward courageously to do her part and used her available resources to make a meaningful difference in the world around her. Metaphorically, through the work she did in the Sea Islands, in close proximity to the fighting in the Civil War and then afterward in several venues across the decades until her death, she lived the life she had hungered for as an ambitious young woman. In contrast, however, Forten's achievements also offer another instructive example. While many African American women were intellectually engaged with the issues of the day and wrote about their beliefs and work, they were a diverse group of women from different backgrounds. A basic point is that few of them gained access to venues, except in the African American periodical press, that would give their thoughts the light of day for consumption by national audiences in the general public sphere. Forten, on the other hand, had the unusual privilege of publishing in the *Atlantic Monthly*.

Charlotte Forten Grimké

Excerpts from "Life on the Sea Islands (Part I): A Young Black Woman Describes Her Experience Teaching Freed Slaves during the Civil War," *The Atlantic* (May 1864). https://theatlantic.com/magazine/archive/1864/05/life-on-the-sea-islands/308758.

It was nearly dark when we reached the island, and then we had a three-miles' drive through the lonely roads to the house of the superintendent. We thought how easy it would be for a band of guerrillas, had they chanced that way, to seize and hang us; but we were in that excited, jubilant state of mind which makes fear impossible, and sang "John Brown" with a will, as we drove through the pines and palmettos. Oh, it was good to sing that song in the very heart of Rebeldom! Harry, our driver, amused us much. He was surprised to find that we had not heard of him before. "Why, I thought eberybody at de Nort had heard o' me," he said, very innocently. We learned afterward that Mrs. F., who made the tour of the islands last summer, had publicly mentioned Harry. Some one had told him of it, and he of course imagined that he had become quite famous. Notwithstanding this little touch of vanity, Harry is one of the best and smartest men on the island.

Gates occurred, it seemed to us, at every few yards' distance, made in the oddest fashion—opening in the middle, like folding-doors, for the accommodation of horsemen. The little boy who accompanied us as gate-opener answered to the name of Cupid.

Arrived at the headquarters of the general superintendent, Mr. S., we were kindly received by him and the ladies, and shown into a large parlor, where a cheerful wood-fire glowed in the grate. It had a home-like look; but still there was a sense of unreality about everything, and I felt that nothing less than a vigorous "shaking-up," such as Grandfather Smallweed [a character in Charles Dickens's *Bleak House*] daily experienced, would arouse me thoroughly to the fact that I was in South Carolina.

The next morning L. and I were awakened by the cheerful voices of men and women, children and chickens, in the yard below. We ran to the window, and looked out. Women in bright-colored handkerchiefs, some carrying pails on their heads, were crossing the yard, busy with their morning work; children were playing, and tumbling around them. On every face there was a look of serenity and cheerfulness. My heart gave a great throb of happiness as I looked at them, and thought, "They are free! so long down-trodden, so long crushed to the earth, but now in their old homes, forever free!" And I thanked God that I had lived to see this day.

After breakfast Miss T. drove us to Oaklands, our future home. The road leading to the house was nearly choked with weeds. The house itself was in a dilapidated condition, and the yard and garden had a sadly neglected look. But there were roses in bloom; we plucked handfuls of feathery, fragrant acacia-blossoms; ivy crept along the ground and under the house. The freed people on the place seemed glad to see us. After talking with them, and giving some directions for cleaning the house, we drove to the school, in which I was to teach. It is kept in the Baptist Church,—a brick building, beautifully situated in a grove of live-oaks. These trees are the first objects that attract one's attention here: not that they are finer than our Northern oaks, but because of the singular gray moss with which every branch is heavily draped.

This hanging moss grows on nearly all the trees, but on none so luxuriantly as on the live-oak. The pendants are often four or five feet long, very graceful and beautiful, but giving the trees a solemn, almost funereal look. The school was opened in September. Many of the children had, however, received instruction during the summer. It was evident that they had made very rapid improvement, and we noticed with pleasure how bright and eager to learn many of them seemed. . . .

The first day at school was rather trying. Most of my children were very small, and consequently restless. Some were too young to learn the alphabet. These little ones were brought to school because the older children—in whose care their parents leave them while at work—could not come without them. We were therefore willing to have them come, although they seemed to have discovered the secret of perpetual motion, and tried one's patience sadly. But after some days of positive, though not severe treatment, order was brought out of chaos, and I found but little difficulty in managing and quieting the tiniest and most restless spirits. I never before saw children so eager to learn, although I had had several years' experience in New-England schools. Coming to school is a constant delight and recreation to them. They come here as other children go to play. The older ones, during the summer, work in the fields from early morning until eleven or twelve o'clock, and then come into school, after their hard toil in the hot sun, as bright and as anxious to learn as ever.

Of course there are some stupid ones, but these are the minority. The majority learn with wonderful rapidity. Many of the grown people are desirous of learning to read. It is wonderful how a people who have been so long crushed to the earth, so imbruted as these have been,—and they are said to be among the most degraded negroes of the South,—can have so great a desire for knowledge, and such a capability for attaining it. One cannot believe that the haughty Anglo-Saxon race, after centuries of such an experience as these people have had, would be very much superior to them. And one's indignation increases against those who, North as well as South, taunt the colored race with inferiority while they themselves use every means in their power to crush and degrade them, denying them every right and privilege, closing against them every avenue of elevation and improvement. Were they, under such circumstances, intellectual and refined, they would certainly be vastly superior to any other race that ever existed.

After the lessons, we used to talk freely to the children, often giving them slight sketches of some of the great and good men. Before teaching them the "John Brown" song, which they learned to sing with great spirit, Miss T. told them the story of the brave old man who had died for them. I told them about Toussaint, thinking it well they should know what one of their own color had done for the race. They listened attentively, and seemed to understand. We found it rather hard to keep their attention in school. It is not strange, as they have been so entirely unused to intellectual concentration. It is necessary to interest them every moment, in order to keep their thoughts from wandering. Teaching here is consequently far more fatiguing than at the North.

Excerpts from "Life on the Sea Islands" (Part II): A Young Black Woman Describes Her Experience Teaching Freed Slaves during the Civil War," *The Atlantic* (June 1864). https://theatlantic.com/magazine/archive/1864/06/life-on-the-sea-islands-continued/308759.

A few days before Christmas, we were delighted at receiving a beautiful Christmas Hymn from Whittier, written by request [i.e., by Forten's request of Whittier as a family friend], especially for our children. They learned it very easily, and enjoyed singing it. We showed them the writer's picture, and told them he was a very good friend of theirs, who felt the deepest interest in them, and had written this hymn expressly for them to sing,—which made them very proud and happy. Early Christmas morning, we were wakened by the people knocking at the doors and windows, and shouting, "Merry Christmas!" After distributing some little presents among them, we went to the church, which had been decorated with holly, pine, cassena, mistletoe, and the hanging moss, and had a very Christmas-like look. The children of our school assembled there, and we gave them the nice comfortable clothing, and the picture-books, which had been kindly sent by some Philadelphia ladies. There were at least a hundred and fifty children present. It was very pleasant to see their happy, expectant little faces. To them, it was a wonderful Christmas-Day,—such as they had never dreamed of before. There was cheerful sunshine without, lighting up the beautiful moss-drapery of the oaks, and looking in joyously through the open windows; and there were bright faces and glad hearts within. The long, dark night of the Past, with all its sorrows and its fears, was forgotten; and for the Future,—the eyes of these freed children see no clouds in it. It is full of sunlight, they think, and they trust in it, perfectly.

After the distribution of the gifts, the children were addressed by some of the gentlemen present. They then sang Whittier's Hymn, the "John Brown" song, and several of their own hymns, among them a very singular one, commencing,—

I wonder where my mudder gone'
Sing, O graveyard!
Graveyard ought to know me;

Ring, Jerusalem!
Grass grow in de graveyard;
Sing, O graveyard!
Graveyard ought to know me;
Ring, Jerusalem!

They improvise many words as they sing. It is one of the strangest, most mournful things I ever heard. It is impossible to give any idea of the deep pathos of the refrain,—

Sing, O graveyard!

In this, and many other hymns, the words seem to have but little meaning; but the tones,—a whole lifetime of despairing sadness is concentrated in them. They sing, also, "Jehovyah, Hallelujah," which we like particularly:—

De foxes hab holes,
An' de birdies hab nes,'
But de Son ob Man he hab not where
To lay de weary head.
Chorus.
Jehovyah, Hallelujah! De Lord He will purvide!
Jehovyah, Hallelujah! De Lord He will purvide!

They repeat the words many times. "De foxes hab holes," and the succeeding lines, are sung in the most touching, mournful tones; and then the chorus—"Jehovyah, Hallelujah"—swells forth triumphantly, in glad contrast.

Christmas night, the children came in and had several grand shouts. They were too happy to keep still.

"Oh, Miss, all I want to do is to sing and shout!" said our little pet, Amaretta. And sing and shout she did, to her heart's content.

She read nicely, and was very fond of books. The tiniest children are delighted to get a book in their hands. Many of them already know their letters. The parents are eager to have them learn. They sometimes said to me,—

"Do, Miss, let de chil'en learn eberything dey can. We nebber hab no chance to learn nuttin,' but we wants de chil'en to learn."

They are willing to make many sacrifices that their children may attend school. One old woman, who had a large family of children and grandchildren, came regularly to school in the winter, and took her seat among the little ones. She was at least sixty years old. Another woman—who had one of the best faces I ever saw—came daily, and brought her baby in her arms. It happened to be one of the best babies in the world, a perfect little "model of deportment," and allowed its mother to pursue her studies without interruption. . . .

No description of life on these islands would be complete without a word concerning the fleas. They appeared at the opening of spring, and kept constantly "risin,'" as the people said, until they reached a height the possibility of which we had never conceived. We had heard and read of fleas. We had never realized them before. Words utterly fail to describe the tortures we endured for months from these horrible little tyrants. Remembering our sufferings "through weary day and weary night," we warn everybody not gifted with extraordinary powers of endurance to beware of a summer on the Sea Islands.

Notwithstanding the heat, we determined to celebrate the Fourth of July as worthily as we could. The freed people and the children of the different schools assembled in the grove near the Baptist Church. The flag was hung across the road, between two magnificent live-oaks, and the children, being grouped under it, sang "The Star-Spangled Banner" with much spirit. Our good General could not come, but addresses were made by Mr. P.,—the noble-hearted founder of the movement for the benefit of the people here, and from first to last their stanch and much-loved friend,—Mr. L., a young colored minister, and others. Then the people sang some of their own hymns; and the woods resounded with the grand notes of "Roll, Jordan, roll." They all afterward partook of refreshments, consisting of molasses and water,—a very great luxury to them,—and hardtack.

Among the visitors present was the noble young Colonel Shaw, whose regiment was then stationed on the island. We had met him a few nights before, when he came to our house to witness one of the people's shouts. We looked upon him with the deepest interest. There was something in his face finer, more exquisite, than one often sees in a man's face, yet it was full of courage and decision. The rare and singular charm of his manner drew all hearts to him. He was deeply interested in the singing and appearance of the people. A few days afterwards we saw his regiment on dress-parade, and admired its remarkably fine and manly appearance. After taking supper with the Colonel we sat outside the tent, while some of his men entertained us with excellent singing. Every moment we became more and more charmed with him. How full of life and hope and lofty aspirations he was that night! How eagerly he expressed his wish that they might soon be ordered to Charleston! "I do hope they will give us a chance," he said. It was the desire of his soul that his men should do themselves honor,—that they should prove themselves to an unbelieving world as brave soldiers as though their skins were white. And for himself, he was like the Chevalier of old, "without reproach or fear." After we had mounted our horses and rode away, we seemed still to feel the kind clasp of his hand,—to hear the pleasant, genial tones of his voice, as he bade us good-bye, and hoped that we might meet again. We never saw him afterward. In two short weeks came the terrible massacre at Fort Wagner, and the beautiful head of the young hero and martyr was laid low in the dust. Never shall we forget the heart-sickness with which we heard of his death. We could not realize it at first,—we, who had seen him so lately in all the strength and glory of his young manhood. For days we clung to a vain hope; then it fell away from us, and we knew that he was gone. We knew that he died gloriously, but still it seemed very hard. Our hearts bled for the mother whom he so loved,—for the young wife, left desolate. And then we said, as we say now,—"God comfort them! He only can." During a few of the sad days which followed the attack on Fort Wagner, I was in one of the hospitals of Beaufort, occupied with the wounded soldiers of the Fifty-Fourth Massachusetts. The first morning was spent in mending the bullet-holes and rents in their clothing. What a story they told! Some of the jackets of the poor fellows were literally cut in pieces. It was pleasant to see the brave, cheerful spirit among them. Some of them were severely wounded, but they uttered no complaint; and in the letters which they dictated to their absent friends there was no word of regret, but the same cheerful tone throughout. They expressed an eager desire to get well, that they might "go at it again." Their attachment to their young colonel was beautiful to see. They felt his death deeply. . . . I think they truly appreciated the greatness of the sacrifice. May they ever prove worthy of such a leader! Already, they, and the regiments of freedmen here, as well, have shown that true manhood has no limitations of color.

Daily the long-oppressed people of these islands are demonstrating their capacity for improvement in learning and labor. What they have accomplished in one short year exceeds our utmost expectations. Still the sky is dark; but through the darkness we can discern a brighter future. . . .

While writing these pages I am once more nearing Port Royal. The Fortunate Isles of Freedom are before me. I shall again tread the flower-skirted wood-paths of St. Helena, and the somber pines and bearded oaks shall whisper in the sea-wind their grave welcome. I shall dwell again among "mine own people." I shall gather my scholars about me, and see smiles of greeting break over their dusk faces. My heart sings a song of thanksgiving, at the thought that even I am permitted to do something for a long-abused race, and aid in promoting a higher, holier, and happier life on the Sea Islands.

Figure 4.4: Susanna (Susie) Baker King Taylor

Susanna (Susie) Baker King Taylor

Susanna (Susie) Baker King Taylor (1848–1912) was born, as she stated in her memoir, "under the slave law" (Taylor 1988, 29) on the Grest Plantation in Midway, Liberty County, Georgia, near Savannah. As a young child, she was first taught to read by the plantation mistress. At seven, as the oldest living of nine children, she and her brother were sent to live with their grandmother Dolly Reed, in Savannah. Reed sent Baker (and presumably her brother as well) to secret schools taught by African American women: to Mrs. Woodhouse and her daughter Mary Jane for two years; to Mother Mathilda Beasley, the first African American Catholic nun in Georgia, until 1860 when Mother Beasley confirmed she had nothing more she could teach Baker; for lessons for four months with Baker's white playmate Katie O'Connor until O'Connor was sent to a convent; and then for lessons until 1861 from James Blouis, the son of her grandmother's landlord, before he was ordered to the Confederate battlefront.

In 1862 the Civil War came to the Savannah area with the battle of Fort Pulaski. Baker was sent back to her mother, Hagar Ann Baker, on the Grest Plantation. With Union success at Fort Pulaski, Baker escaped slavery with her mother's brother James and his family to the Union-occupied St. Catherine's Island. From there, Union forces transferred the group of about thirty escapees to St. Simon's Island, the event that transformed Baker's life. After Fort Pulaski, Major General David Hunter declared all of the African Americans in this area to be free and available to volunteer for service in the Union Army. He formed the First South Carolina Volunteers, the first group of African American freedmen to form a regiment. This infantry group was placed under the leadership of General Rufus Saxton in Port Royal, South Carolina, and functioned as a guerilla group along the coastlines of South Carolina, Georgia, and Florida. In 1864 the First South Carolina Volunteers were officially recognized as the Thirty-Third Infantry Regiment of the US Colored Troops.

At fifteen, Susie Baker was hired by Union officers as a laundress, to wash and iron, and as a cook. However, her duties soon grew with the recognition of her literacy skills. She became the first federally funded African American teacher in the state of Georgia, establishing a freedmen's school to teach openly and officially recently freed slaves, children and adults. To be noted, Baker's work as a teacher in the Sea Islands on St. Simon's Island off the coast of Georgia overlapped with the service of Charlotte Forten on St. Helena Island off the coast of South Carolina. Being in the same geographical area, they attended at least one event at the same time and knew some of the same people, including Harriet Tubman who was also working in the area. On January 1, 1863, both attended the reading of the Emancipation Proclamation and a barbeque. However, there is no documentation to date that they interacted socially with each other as African American women from different worlds—one a formerly enslaved southern woman, the other a freeborn northern woman; one working class, one affluent; one modestly educated, one college educated, and so on.

In 1863, after the First South Carolina Volunteer Infantry began fighting and accomplishing missions, Baker transitioned into a nurse for the troops, becoming the first African American woman nurse to be acknowledged in the United States for providing care on the battlefield to soldiers and for establishing a stellar record for the quality of care that she rendered to both the sick and wounded. As noted in her memoir, she considered both the First South Carolina Troops and the Fifty-Fourth Massachusetts Volunteers who fought bravely at the battle of Fort Wagner to be "our boys," African American men, freeborn and freed, who showed themselves to be courageous warriors (a viewpoint shared by Charlotte Forten who also served as a nurse for the troops after the battle of Fort Wagner).

During the war Baker married Sergeant Edward King of the Thirty-Third Regiment. They served together until the end of the war. After the regiment was mustered out on January 31, 1866, the Kings made their home in Savannah, where Baker opened a school and continued to teach until her husband died suddenly just a few months into their new life. At that point, Baker went back to Liberty County to give birth to their son. While she was there, she opened another school and continued to teach but soon moved back to Savannah where she opened a third school. Despite her commitment to this important work, however, Baker was unable to compete with the public schools for African Americans that were opening. Leaving her son with family, she moved to Boston where she worked as a domestic servant.

At the age of thirty-one, Baker married Russell L. Taylor. Even though she continued to work as a domestic, she also worked as a community organizer and an activist with the Woman's Relief Corps, a national organization for female Civil War veterans. In 1886 she and other African American women founded their own branch of the organization, Number 67, caring for the needs of African American soldiers and veterans, including sending care packages in 1898 to soldiers fighting in the Spanish American War. Over the years, however, Baker experienced many disappointments: the denial of her application in 1892 for a pension for her services as an army nurse during the Civil War; the lack of acknowledgment, respect, and support for African American veterans; the ruling by the US Supreme Court in 1896 in *Plessy v. Ferguson* that calcified the doctrine of separate but equal; the death in 1898 of her son who was denied medical care by white doctors in Shreveport, Louisiana, a trauma that was exacerbated by the Southern Railroad denying her the opportunity to purchase a train ticket to travel to obtain care for him in Cincinnati, Ohio.

In 1902 Baker wrote and self-published *Reminiscences of My Life in Camp with the 33rd U.S. Colored Troops, Late 1st South Carolina Volunteers* (republished in 1988 as *Reminiscences of My Life: A Black Woman's Civil War Memoirs*). In this volume, she paid tribute to the first African American regiments authorized to fight for their own freedom in the Civil War, and she shared her perspectives on her times. Her rhetorical imperative was to raise her voice to speak her own truths and to claim visibility via self-publication for herself and others like her, women and men, who served their country proudly and well. In doing so, Taylor claimed the right to agency and authority. She wrote herself into the American story, making it possible for subsequent generations to understand that there is more to the story of the Civil War than many citizens typically know and that African American women were part of this story.

Susanna (Susie) Baker King Taylor

Excerpts from *Reminiscences of My Life: A Black Woman's Civil War Memoirs*, ed. Patricia W. Romero and Willie Lee Rose (1902; Princeton, NJ: Markus Wiener Press, 1988).

My Childhood

I was born under the slave law in Georgia, in 1848, and was brought up by my grandmother in Savannah. There were three of us with her, my younger sister and brother. My brother and I being the two eldest, we were sent to a friend of my grandmother, Mrs. Woodhouse, a widow, to learn to read and write. She was a free woman and lived on Bay Lane, between Habersham and Price streets, about half a mile from my house. We went every day about nine o'clock, with our books wrapped in paper to prevent the police or white persons from seeing them. We went in, one at a time, through the gate, into the yard to the L kitchen, which was the schoolroom. She had twenty-five or thirty children whom she taught, assisted by her daughter, Mary Jane. The neighbors would see us going in sometimes, but they supposed we were there learning trades, as it was the custom to give children a trade of some kind. After school we left the same way we entered, one by one, when we would go to a square, about a block from the school, and wait for each other. We would gather laurel leaves and pop them on our hands, on our way home. I remained at her school for two years or more, when I was sent to a Mrs. Mary Beasley, where I continued until May, 1860, when she told my grandmother she had taught me all she knew, and grandmother had better get some one else who could teach me more, so I stopped my studies for a while.

I had a white playmate about this time, named Katie O'Connor, who lived on the next corner of the street from my house, and who attended a convent. One day she told me, if I would promise not to tell her father, she would give me some lessons. On my promise not to do so, and getting her mother's consent, she gave me lessons about four months, every evening. At the end of this time she was put into the convent permanently, and I have never seen her since.

A month after this, James Blouis, our landlord's son, was attending the High School, and was very fond of grandmother, so she asked him to give me a few lessons, which he did until the middle of 1861, when the Savannah Volunteer Guards, to which he and his brother belonged, were ordered to the front under General Barton. In the first battle of Manassas, his brother Eugene was killed, and James deserted over to the Union side, and at the close of the war went to Washington, D.C., where he has since resided.

I often wrote passes for my grandmother, for all colored persons, free or slaves, were compelled to have a pass; free colored people having a guardian in place of a master. These passes were good until 10 or 10:30 P.M. for one night or every night for one month. The pass read as follows:—

SAVANNAH, GA, MARCH 1ST, 1860
Pass the bearer__________from 9 to 10:30 P.M.
Valentine Grest.

Every person had to have this pass, for at nine o'clock each night a bell was rung, and any colored persons found on the street after this hour were arrested by the watchman, and put in the guard-house until next morning, when their owners would pay their fines and release them. I knew a number of persons who went out at any time at night and were never arrested, as the watchman knew them so well he never stopped them, and seldom asked to see their passes, only stopping them long enough, sometimes, to say "Howdy," and then telling them to go along.

About this time I had been reading so much about the "Yankees" I was very anxious to see them. The whites would tell their colored people not to go to the Yankees, for they would harness them to carts and make them pull the carts around, in place of horses. I asked grandmother, one day, if this was true. She replied, "Certainly not!" that the white people did not want slaves to go over to the Yankees, and told them these things to frighten them. "Don't you see those signs pasted about the streets? One reading, 'I am a rattlesnake, if you touch me I will strike!' Another reads, 'I am a wildcat! Beware,' etc. These are warnings to the North; so don't mind what the white people say." I wanted to see these wonderful "Yankees" so much, as I heard my parents say the Yankee was going to set all the slaves free. Oh, how those people prayed for freedom! I remember, one night, my grandmother went out into the suburbs of the city to a church meeting, and they were fervently singing this old hymn,—

Yes, we all shall be free,
Yes, we all shall be free,
Yes, we all shall be free,
When the Lord shall appear,—

when the police came in and arrested all who were there, saying they were planning freedom, and sang "the Lord," in place of "Yankee," to blind any one who might be listening. Grandmother never forgot that night, although she did not stay in the guard-house, as she sent to her guardian, who came at once for her; but this was the last meeting she ever attended out of the city proper.

On April 1, 1862, about the time the Union soldiers were firing on Fort Pulaski, I was sent out into the country to my mother. I remember what a roar and din the guns made. They jarred the earth for miles. The fort was at last taken by them. Two days after the taking of Fort Pulaski, my uncle took his family of seven and myself to St. Catherine Island. We landed under the protection of the Union fleet, and remained there two weeks, when about thirty of us were taken aboard the gunboat P______, to be transferred to St. Simon's Island, and at last, to my unbounded joy, I saw the "Yankee."

After we were all settled aboard and started on our journey, Captain Whitmore, commanding the boat, asked me where I was from. I told him Savannah, Ga. He asked if I could read; I said, "Yes!" "Can you write?" he next asked. "Yes, I can do that also," I replied, and as if he had some doubts of my answers he handed me a book and a pencil and told me to write my name and where I was from. I did this; when he wanted to know if I could sew. On hearing I could, he asked me to hem some napkins for him. He was surprised at my accomplishments (for they were such in those days), for he said he did not know there were any negroes in the South able to read or write. He said, "You seem to be so different from the other colored people who came from the same place you did." "No!" I replied, "the only difference is, they were reared in the country and I in the city, as was a man from Darien, Ga., named Edward King" [who was with the Thirty-Third regiment, and whom she married in 1862]. That seemed to satisfy him, and we had no further conversation that day on the subject.

In the afternoon the captain spied a boat in the distance, and as it drew nearer he noticed it had a white flag hoisted, but before it had reached the Putumoka he ordered all passengers between decks, so we could not be seen, for he thought they might be spies. The boat finally drew alongside of our boat, and had Mr. Edward Donegall on board, who wanted his two servants, Nick and Judith. He wanted these, as they were his own children. Our captain told him he knew nothing of them, which was true, for at the time they were on St. Simon's, and not, as their father supposed, on our boat. After the boat left, we were allowed to come up on deck again.

On St. Simon's Island, 1862

Next morning we arrived at St. Simon's. . . . After I had been on St. Simon's about three days, Commodore Goldsborough heard of me, and came to Gaston Bluff to see me. I found him very cordial. He said Captain Whitmore had spoken to him of me, and that he was pleased to hear of my being so capable, etc., and wished me to take charge of a school for the children on the island. I told him I would gladly do so, if I could have some books. He said I should have them, and in a week or two I received two large boxes of books and testaments from the North. I had about forty children to teach, besides a number of adults who came to me nights, all of them so eager to learn to read, to read above anything else. . . .

There were about six hundred men, women, and children on St. Simon's, the women and children being in the majority, and we were afraid to go very far from our own quarters in the daytime, and at night even to go out of the house for a long time; for there were not any soldiers on the island, only the marines were on the gunboats along the coast. The rebels, knowing this, could steal by them under cover of the night, and getting on the island would capture any persons venturing out alone and carry them to the mainland. Several of the men disappeared, and as they were never heard from we came to the conclusion they had been carried off in this way.

The latter part of August, 1862, Captain C.T. Trowbridge, with his brother John and Lieutenant Walker, came to St. Simon's Island from Hilton Head, by order of General Hunter, to get all the men possible to finish filling his regiment which he had organized in March 1862. He had heard of the skirmish on this island, and was very much pleased at the bravery shown by these men. He found me at Gaston Bluff teaching my little school, and was much interested in it. When I knew him better I found him to be a thorough gentleman and a staunch friend to my race.

Captain Trowbridge remained with us until October, when the order was received to evacuate, and so we boarded the Ben-De-Ford, a transport, for Beaufort, S.C. When we arrived in Beaufort, Captain Trowbridge and the men he had enlisted went to camp at Old Fort, which they named "Camp Saxton." I was enrolled as laundress.

The first suits worn by the boys were red coats and pants, which they disliked very much, for, they said, "The rebels see us, miles away."

The first colored troops did not receive any pay for eighteen months, and the men had to depend wholly on what they received from the commissary, established by General Saxton. A great many of these men had large families and as they had no money to give them, their wives were obliged to support themselves and children by washing for the officers of the gunboats and the soldiers, and making cakes and pies which they sold to the boys in camp. Finally, in 1863, the government decided to give them half pay, but the men would not accept this. They wanted "full pay" or nothing. They preferred rather to give their services to the state, which they did until 1864, when the government granted them full pay, with all the back pay due. . . .

In February, 1863, several cases of varioloid [a type of small pox] broke out among the boys, which caused some anxiety in camp. Edward Davis, of Company E (the company I was with), had it very badly. He was put into a tent apart from the rest of the men, and only the doctor and camp steward, James Cummings, were allowed to see or attend him; but I went to see this man every day and nursed him. The last thing at night, I always went in to see that he was comfortable, but in spite of the good care and attention he received, he succumbed to the disease.

I was not in the least afraid of the small-pox. I had been vaccinated, and I drank sassafras tea constantly, which kept my blood purged and prevented me from contracting this dread scourge, and no one need fear getting it if they will keep their blood in good condition with this sassafras tea, and take it before going where the patient is.

Camp Saxton—Proclamation and Barbecue, 1863

On the first of January, 1863, we held services for the purpose of listening to the reading of President Lincoln's proclamation by Dr. W.H. Brisbane, and the presentation of two beautiful stands of colors, one from a lady in Connecticut, and the other from Rev. Mr. Cheever. The presentation speech was made by Chaplain French. It was a glorious day for us all, and we enjoyed every minute of it, and as a fitting close and the crowning event of this occasion we had a grand barbecue. A number of oxen were roasted whole, and we had a fine feast. Although not served as tastily or correctly as it would have been at home, yet it was enjoyed with keen appetites and relish. The soldiers had a good time. They sang or shouted "Hurrah!" all through the camp, and seemed overflowing with fun and frolic until taps were sounded, when many, no doubt, dreamt of this memorable day. . . .

I taught a great many of the comrades in Company E to read and write, when they were off duty. Nearly all were anxious to learn. My husband taught some also when it was convenient for him. I was very happy to know my efforts were successful in camp, and also felt grateful for the appreciation of my services. I gave my services willingly for four years and three months without receiving a dollar. I was glad, however, to be allowed to go with the regiment, to care for the sick and afflicted comrades.

[At the end of the Civil War, King and her husband returned to Savannah to try to build a life for themselves. She was soon widowed, however, and left alone to raise their son, who was born after her husband's death. Although she was quite enterprising in trying to support herself, her ventures were not successful. She moved to Boston where she worked as a domestic servant, but she continued to be actively engaged with issues related to soldiers and veterans. As evidenced by the publication of her memoir, she

was particularly passionate that audiences should know there were large numbers of African American women who worked to support the Union and win the war. Ultimately, she married a second time—Russell L. Taylor. Her life continued to be filled with challenges of various kinds, however, confirming that, even though she was no longer enslaved, living in freedom was not a simple, easy, or just path—as she proclaims at the end of her memoir in the recognition of the rise in lynchings.]

Thoughts on Present Conditions

In this "land of the free": we are burned, tortured, and denied a fair trial, murdered for any imaginary wrong conceived in the brain of the negro-hating white man. There is no redress for us from a government which promised to protect all under its flag. It seems a mystery to me. They say, "One flag, one nation, one country indivisible." Is this true? Can we say this truthfully, when one race is allowed to burn, hang, and inflict the most horrible torture weekly, monthly, on another? No, we cannot sing, "My country 'tis of thee, Sweet land of Liberty"! It is hollow mockery. The Southland laws are all on the side of the white, and they do just as they like to the negro, whether in the right or not.

Chapter 5

After the Civil War

In the decades following the Civil War, members of the African American community continued to seize opportunities for civil rights and social justice whenever and however they could. Education became key leverage as men and women determined that the fight for true freedom continued in their passionate pursuits of the full rights of citizenship, access to opportunity, and equal treatment under the law. African American women were not silent in agitating for these causes. They spoke up and out as opportunities to do so became available. They also directed their energies toward action. They worked through existing organizations, created new organizations, sought collaborations with others, and more. They exhibited a desire to be recognized and appreciated for their talents, knowledge, and expertise. Sometimes they worked within their own communities, but quite often recognition and appreciation of them for their activism and leadership stopped at the borders of those communities. Whatever the case, as had been their commitments before and during the war, they kept working, doing whatever they were able to do to care for their communities and themselves, and to build the nation with African Americans included.

Rhetorically, their means and modes of expression were generally the same—literary genres such as poetry, short stories, and novels; personal genres such as letters, diaries, and journals; self-reflections such as memoirs and autobiographies; as well as more essayistic genres such as speeches, editorials, articles, book length analyses, and so on. Within this scope of possibilities, a specific change in horizons that became more evident was the expansion of their options as journalists. Their experiences with the periodical press as contributors, editors, business managers, owners, and consumers of these texts nurtured the development of robust communities of practice. These activities helped them to develop knowledge and expertise, and to exercise their rhetorical abilities as writers and speakers with opportunities to engage with ever-broadening audiences—locally, nationally, and internationally—within their own communities typically but, increasingly, sometimes beyond.

In essence, the nineteenth century moved forward, and so too did African American women. They went to schools, colleges, and universities. In growing numbers, they entered the professions and other arenas of work. As educators, health-care providers, businesswomen, community developers, and laborers of various kinds, they were persistently inventive in finding ways to participate in the community-building and nation-building agenda as advocates, activists, and leaders. With an expanded range of motion as women in freedom, they took advantage of opportunities—old and new—to show their talents and strengths and to care for themselves and others. They wrote and spoke their hearts and minds in social, institutional, and public settings, and they did so typically with passion and eloquence. As generations of women before them had done, they remained focused on getting things done, often against the odds, in the name of survival, progress, and change as they exercised their capacities to dream a world and then do the hard work of helping to build it.

Figure 5.1: Rebecca Davis Lee Crumpler

Rebecca Davis Lee Crumpler

Rebecca Davis Lee Crumpler (1831–1895) was born free in Christiana, Delaware, to Absolum Davis and Matilda Webber. Although little is known about her early years, it is known that she was raised in Pennsylvania by an aunt who was highly respected in her community as a caregiver, and she was educated as a special student in mathematics at the prestigious West Newton English and Classical School in Massachusetts. In 1852 Davis moved to Charlestown, Massachusetts, where she married Wyatt Lee that same year and where she apprenticed as a nurse for eight years until 1860, which was typical training for nurses in the United States. There were no schools for the formal professional training of nurses until after the Civil War and the demonstration of the value of professional nursing in the care of soldiers. To illustrate this point, note that the Bellevue Hospital School of Nursing was founded in New York City in 1873, based on the principles of nursing established by Florence Nightingale in her publication *Notes on Nursing*, drawn from Nightingale's experiences in coordinating care for wounded soldiers during the Crimean War.

After eight years of serving as a nurse in Charlestown, Davis was highly recommended for admission to the New England Female Medical College in 1860, where she earned a medical degree in 1864, specializing in the diseases of women and children. Davis's husband died of tuberculosis while she was a medical student, but she continued her studies, becoming the first and only African American woman to attend and to graduate from this college, which closed in 1873. She practiced first in Boston, Massachusetts, where she met and married Arthur Crumpler in 1865. They were active members of the Beacon Hill community before they moved to Richmond, Virginia, at the end of the Civil War.

Working with the Freedmen's Bureau, Davis provided medical services for freed slaves in this area despite resistance to her doing so. Not surprisingly, given the social norms of her times for both race and gender, she faced the presumption that women (and certainly African American women) would quite necessarily be expected to fill only limited roles in any of the professions. These arenas were defined as public spaces, the territory of men, with woman's place being in domestic arenas. Consequently, while it was not unheard of to see a woman working in a profession, it was still highly unusual and perhaps even more unusual for women working in these areas to receive anything but limited recognition for whatever excellence they managed to exhibit.

In 1869 Davis moved back to Boston to Beacon Hill where she continued to practice medicine. Later, she, her husband, and her daughter moved to Hyde Park, New York, where there is little evidence that she continued to practice medicine. However, in 1883, she published *A Book of Medical Discourses, In Two Parts*, a treatise dedicated to nurses and mothers that offered advice and guidance to women on how to provide quality care for themselves and their children. This volume is one of the earliest known medical book publications authored by an African American physician.

Although by today's standards Davis's advice in her treatise may seem conservative and outdated, in 1893 it was based on the best medical knowledge of the day and on her experiences. She combined autobiographical details with advice, establishing her own authority and credibility as a trained physician and drawing also from the journals she kept as a practicing physician. She exhibited, as well, a sensitivity to her audience (nurses and mothers) in using a language and style that was accessible and directly responsive to the needs of the communities she was dedicated to serving. By this means, Davis was distinctive and innovative as a participant in the specialized public discourses of health care. For subsequent generations of women, Davis stands as a leader and advocate for raising the knowledge of the community itself on health issues and raising the level of quality and excellence for those caring for both women and children.

The excerpts below, beginning with the introduction to *Medical Discourses*, declare the natural appropriateness of women to provide health care—whether doctors, nurses, or women in the community—but emphasize the urgency for care to be based on well-grounded health knowledge. With this framework, Davis stepped forward to underscore with both knowledge and precision that the imperative is to save lives unnecessarily lost or prevent injuries.

Rebecca Davis Lee Crumpler

Excerpts from *A Book of Medical Discourses, In Two Parts* (1883; Delhi: Facsimile, 2016).

Introduction

I now present to the public a few thoughts in book form, trusting that they will be accepted on their merits alone. The following pages contain a few simple appeals to common sense, and are addressed to mothers, nurses, and women generally. All honor is due to a far-seeing legislation which has recognized the importance of fitting woman for the great and natural office of nurse, or doctress of medicine; for by it facilities are offered to each member of a community for the promotion of Christian enlightenment. By frequent visits through various parts of the United States, at all seasons of the year, as well as by quite an extensive opportunity while in the capacity of family nurse, and subsequent practitioner, I have become quite familiar with those ailments and diseases which afflict many infants from birth to the close of the teething period, or till after the fifth year of their age.

It may be well to state here that, having been reared by a kind aunt in Pennsylvania, whose usefulness with the sick was continually sought, I early conceived a liking for, and sought every opportunity to be in a position to relieve the sufferings of others. Later in life, I devoted my time, when best I could, to nursing as a business, serving under different doctors for a period of eight years (from '52 to '60); most of the time at my adopted home in Charlestown, Middlesex County, Massachusetts. From these doctors I received letters commending me to the faculty of the New England Female Medical College, whence, four years afterward, I received the degree of Doctress of Medicine. I then practiced in Boston, but desiring a larger scope for general information, I travelled toward the British Dominion. On my return, after the close of the Confederate War, my mind centered upon Richmond, the capital city of Virginia, as the proper field for real missionary work, and one that would present ample opportunities to become acquainted with the diseases of women and children.

During my stay there nearly every hour was improved in that sphere of labor. The last quarter of the year 1866, I was enabled, through the agency of the Bureau under Gen. Brown, to have access each day to a very large number of the indigent, and others of different classes, in a population of over 30,000 colored. At the close of my services in that city I returned to my former home, Boston, where I entered into the work with renewed vigor, practicing outside, and receiving children in the house for treatment; regardless, in a measure, of remuneration. Although not now in a locality where my constant attendance is required, I do not fail to notice the various published records of the condition of the health of Boston and vicinity.

That woman should study the mechanism of the human structure to better enable her to protect life, before assuming the office of nurse, few will agree. But that good service has been performed by those who were entirely ignorant of it, every one must admit. In my own experience, there was much that to me was obscure, yet, strange to say, I never met with an accident. A kind Father directed every thought in behalf of the helpless.

I believe matrimony to be a divine institution; and that the results arising from a union of the sexes should be considered an important study for each party concerned. If we as intelligent beings sit still in this matter of physical security, premature decay must take the place of perfection. Since I have, with no small degree of diffidence, consented to submit my long-kept journal to the public in the form of a book, I desire to present the different subjects by the use of as few technical terms as possible; and to make my statements brief, simple, and comprehensive. Indeed I desire that my book shall be as a primary reader in the hands of every woman; and yet none the less suited to any who may be conversant with all branches of medical science. If women are permitted to read and reflect for themselves, it is hardly possible that they will say it is uninteresting to them, or that it should only be read by men.

In dealing with subjects that bring to mind thousands of premature mortalities, as, for instance, those from cholera infantum or pneumonia, I deem it expedient to speak only of what I know and to which I can testify. I have endeavored to give some domestic or ready palliative reliefs for the several cases described; thereby hoping to avoid the possibility of a remedy's being applied without an acquaintance with the character and phases of the complaint for which it is intended. There is no doubt that thousands of little ones annually die at our very doors, from diseases which could have been prevented, or cut short by timely aid. People do not wish to feel that death ensues through neglect on their part; indeed they speak of consumption, cholera infantum, and diphtheria, etc., as if sent by God to destroy our infants.

They seem to forget that there is a *cause* for every ailment, and that it may be in their power to remove it. My chief desire in presenting this book is to impress upon somebody's mind the possibilities of prevention.

The Present Modes of Washing and Dressing the New-Born

Usually, as soon as the birth of a child is announced, a basin or tub of hot water is ordered. The washing begins with a "wee bit of rag" and a great cake of perfumed soap purchased long, long before, for the occasion. Then follows wiping with a great linen towel, during which time the creature gets [well] aired, being indirectly exhibited to as many as have courage to look on and admire "the cunning little thing."

"The water must be hot, to get off the grease," said an old nurse. Aye, but with ignorant help would it be surprising if a little of the skin came off first? In more favored circles a nice bath tub is prepared, the water of an equal temperature with the room. Some fine soap is put in to make a suds, which is applied after the surface of the body is oiled. Some cold water adherents persist in using ice-cold water upon a new-born babe, depending on "rubbing it to get up a circulation." I once knew a divine (divines have rules sometimes) whose customs led him to have his only child washed in this way, and believing in the adage of "the hair of the dog curing the bite," he continued to doctor it himself for eighteen months, from its birth to its death, with cold water. The babe received a severe cold, stopping up its nostrils and air tubes, and rendering its little life wholly miserable. To the cause of all this suffering they gave the technical name, Catarrh. . . .

The methods of washing infants just described are more common even in this enlightened age of humanity than is generally known. The excuse for cold baths may exist in the mode of life of the erratic tribes, or among uncivilized nations whose minds are dark upon the construction and office of a nervous system. The several sad results that I myself have witnessed at times, and places, that it was not deemed my business to speak, have led me to adopt what seemed a more humane course. With the use of cold water some judgment is required, as many infants, when born, are weak, and ready to yield up life upon the application of the slightest sedative. The skin being so largely supplied with nerves which transmit all sensations to the internal organs, as telegraph wires do the electric current. Thus cold water may send a chill to some vital part, the result of which no effort in the power of man can counteract. It is next to impossible to keep a babe as warm as it should be going through with the customary routine. Indeed it is not at all uncommon for a babe to be laid beside its mother (if not alone in a crib) lips purple and cold as a lump of clay. I once looked upon a babe who from this cause had for three days resisted all attempts to get it warm. Thus I fear, many come and go. Does any desire to preserve the vitality of a new being? Then it will not suffice to be too self-assured or too oriental to seek to improve in the matter.

I deeply regret to have to state that I have heard many apparently intelligent persons express opposition to the continuation of the human species. But let me ask, What devastating visitations may we not expect if we seek to diminish God's images by any selfish or misguided motives?

The Use of Soap

There are many kinds of soap in use for the purpose of washing clothes, cleansing paint, etc. Then there are not a few advertised as superior for washing the skin. But the fact that water into which soap is rubbed turns white, or becomes sudsy, is sufficient evidence that it contains an alkali, or something having the nature of potash. To use it on the tender skin of infants is but to experiment for the benefit of the dealer, at the expense of the babe. Again, soap is irritating to the more tender surfaces, as the lips and eyelids. If the suds is sucked by the child while the sponge is passed over the face, severe purging may occur. Then if soap gets in the eyes, it is liable to cause sore or inflamed eyes, perhaps for life. I truly believe that more children are afflicted with sore eyes, ears, noses, and heads, whose friends took the precaution to have them washed with "pure baby soap," than could be counted in a hundred years. The germs of bronchitis, which means cold settled in the air-tubes leading to the lungs,—pneumonia, which means lung fever, indigestion, each or all, can be inducted into the system in the first washing. The male physician, unlike the woman physician, does not always remain long enough to see this important duty properly performed. This may be owing to the fact that, among the poorer classes, two or three women are present who are expected to be experts in baby-washing. But, as a fact, many old women sit around on such occasions who have almost as little knowledge what and how to do, as the babe whose expected advent has called them together. Therefore we cannot too strongly protest against the practice of many physicians,—that of leaving a woman in the hands of an inexperienced person as soon as the navel cord is severed. For it is not at all reasonable to conclude, that because a woman is the mother of many children, she is an expert in the matter of washing and dressing the new-born, or of relieving the various ailments incident upon child-bearing. . . .

Born with a Caul

It is no uncommon thing, in hasty labor, for the bag of water to break and remain close around the face and neck of the child. This is done by the quick, rolling motion in coming into the world. The force of the descent breaks the thin skin or bag, and the same force packs the face into it; so that it remains over the face, partly around the neck, and sometimes over the head as well. Were it not removed, the child must suffocate. This circumstance at a birth has given rise to the sayings, "Born with a caul," "Born with a veil," etc. The proper way to remove this bag or membrane is, from over the head down, as lifting it may pull open the eyes; thereby bringing the eyeball in contact with the fluid or the chalk-like substance, thus laying the foundation for sore eyes. After twenty minutes or more, beating having ceased in the cord,—which may be known by pressing closely between the fingers that part nearest the belly of the child,—it should be tied by means of a flat knot, with lamp wicking, or many strands of white spool cotton, about a finger's length from the belly. In case of twins, there should be a second tie the same length from the first, and the cord cut between the two ties. There have been times when women depended largely upon each other, in their helpless hours of confinement; it may be so again, but with a far greater chance of successful results.

The Better Mode of Washing the New-Born

Washing is the name given to the old method. Cleansing is the proper one for the new.

How to proceed: A soft, white, all wool blanket, about two yards square, should be always in readiness when a birth is expected. Not necessarily new, but pure, never having been used about fever patients, or about the dead. A metallic slop-pail with cover, that all secundine particles may be put out of sight; the same serving as a vessel for the woman to sit over. As soon as the babe is freed from the mother, it should be wrapped in the blanket and laid aside in a comfortable place. After the mother's safety is assured of, prepare thus to clean and dress the babe: Secure a comfortable position, with plenty of light and ventilation, as far from the confinement bed as possible. Have a stand or covered chair, upon which to place the half of a small teacupful of fresh hog's lard or sweet oil. If in a cold room, warm the grease by setting the cup in hot water for a few minutes. Have a piece of soft, all-wool flannel, about the size of your pocket-handkerchief, another piece half as large, and two pieces of soft linen or cotton about as large as your hand. A piece of lamp wicking or several strands of white spool cotton, to be used in re-tying, in case of bleeding from the cut end of the cord. The infant may then be brought forth, held on the lap, or laid on two chairs. As many babes have open eyes as soon as born, it is best to dip a small piece of the soft linen or cotton in the grease, and wipe the inner edges of the lids first of all, as the drying on of the chalky substance or other matter with which the child's face may have had contact, while coming in to the world, may, as I have before said, be the first cause of sore or inflamed eyes. Then proceed with the small piece of flannel, well saturated with oil, to clean the face, ears, nose,—avoiding the eyes,—neck, chest, under the arms and between the fingers. Wipe dry with the clean, large piece of flannel. Those parts can then be covered with a part of the blanket, and the lower extremities cleaned with care. Should there be dried blood from the cut end of the cord, moisten with warm water, and wipe it off. Then proceed to clean and examine well all the private parts. When done, cut a hole in the piece of cotton, linen or batting, as it may suit, about the size of your hand, through which slip the cord, fold it closely, but flat and smooth, and lay it over to the left side of the belly, that it may not intercept the circulation of the liver, which is situated on the right side. Then secure it with an all-wool flannel band. The band should be made so as to include a shirt with long sleeves. It should extend from over the teats down below the hips. There never would be swelling of the breasts of infants if the bands were purposely made wide. The natural office of the mama in girl-children, has been destroyed by repeated pressing of the teats with the mistaken purpose of "getting out the milk." Narrow bands are worthless. If they shrink they should be pieced out or replaced with new. The band securely placed,—a flannel roller, plain slip and napkin, is all that is required for the first dressing. It often happens that, after "washing" and dressing by present methods, blood oozes from the cut end of the cord. Seldom does this happen by the new method,—I should say, my method. Sometimes the fault is in the manner of tying, or from imperfection of the cord itself. In any case the cord should be re-tied, or the bleeding otherwise stopped, and the infant kept warm till medical aid can be summoned. To return to first dressing: After the wraps have been drawn up over the feet, the head should be thoroughly greased and cleaned, taking care not to press the bones in the least. Pressure upon the head at birth may be the means of stupidity, or even idiocy, during life. The baby's mouth should then be swabbed out with a clean, wet cloth, and the little one laid down in quiet. Babies usually sleep during the procedure, as does the mother, she waking only to find her babe by her side, "all warm, sweet and clean," and "mamma didn't even hear it cry once." One trial of this method is convincing of its benefits. If soap is used with grease, it acts the same as suds into which new cotton cloth is put. No good laundress will meet with such an accident, if possible to avoid it. And surely no careful nurse will allow her little charge to suffer by having to stop and change the water. Moreover, in the absence of soap, there is no liability to chapped skin, glandular sores, sore eyes, ears, and crusty scalp. Especially should the scalp be well cleaned, and kept so; as it not only adds to the tidy appearance of the child, but favors an even, healthy growth of the hair bulbs. The foundation for a love of cleanliness can best be laid in infancy. There are many adults who desire good hair, yet do not or will not know that combing the hair daily, and keeping the scalp clean and cool, promotes a healthy growth of the hair.

Figure 5.2: Frances (Fanny) Jackson Coppin

Frances (Fanny) Jackson Coppin

Frances (Fanny) Jackson Coppin (1837–1913) was born enslaved in Washington, DC, living with her grandmother (and her mother, Lucy) until her aunt Sarah Orr Clark was able to purchase her freedom for $125. She was sent to New Bedford, Massachusetts, to live with another aunt who secured a job for her as a domestic servant, an opportunity that made it possible for her to obtain a bit of schooling. At fourteen, she moved to Newport, Rhode Island, to live with an aunt by marriage, Elizabeth Orr, where she found a job, again as a domestic servant, and also better opportunities for schooling at a public school for African Americans. With a successful examination, she entered the Rhode Island State Normal School, where she discovered her interests in teaching as a career and her commitment to helping the children of her race to learn. After completing this course of study, she heard about Oberlin College, enrolled with support from her Aunt Sarah and Bishop Daniel Payne of the AME Church, and became the second African American woman to earn a bachelor's degree in the United States (with Mary Jane Patterson being the first).

While at Oberlin in her fourth year, Coppin was the first African American student to be invited to teach in the Oberlin Academy, the preparatory school. In 1866, after graduation, she received an appointment at the Institute for Colored Youth in Philadelphia to teach Greek, Latin, and mathematics. With this appointment Coppin became the second African American woman to become a professor at a college or university. The first one was Sarah Jane Woodson Early, also an Oberlin graduate, who was hired to teach English at Wilberforce University in 1858. At the institute (now Cheyney University), Coppin had a remarkable thirty-seven-year career, serving in multiple administrative leadership roles, as principal of the Ladies' Department and, in 1869, as principal of the institute. Her leadership included also her establishing important innovations that advanced excellence in the teacher training program and her establishing the institute's Industrial Department, an innovation that broadened significantly the career opportunities for African Americans without negating the simultaneous need for the institute to sustain a strong academic unit as well. Throughout this period of her life, Coppin reached broader and broader audiences; she was a frequent public speaker in a range of venues and a contributor to several African American newspapers. This level of public engagement secured her reputation as an intellectual leader and an expert in education and teacher training.

In 1881 Coppin married Reverend Levi J. Coppin who became a bishop in the AME Church. As a leading woman of the church, she served as president of the Women's Home and Foreign Missionary Society. Her reputation in this arena grew nationally and internationally, as evidenced, for example, by her being invited to speak at the Centenary of Missions, held in London in 1888, and by her work in education, temperance, and women's issues during the years that she spent in Africa during her husband's appointment as bishop for South Africa. Over the full course of her life, Coppin was noted for the quality and excellence of her work. A marker of her success and influence came in 1926 when a teacher training school in Baltimore, Maryland, was named the Fanny Jackson Coppin Normal School (now Coppin State University) in honor of her outstanding leadership in teacher education.

In her autobiography, *Reminiscences of School Life, and Hints on Teaching*, Coppin focused on her pathway to education, her pedagogical vision, experiences, and practices, and the acknowledgment of the long line of high achieving students whose lives she encouraged. The excerpt below is taken from Part I of this volume.

Fanny Jackson Coppin

Excerpts from *Reminiscences of School Life, and Hints on Teaching* (1913; Emeryville: Franklin Classics, 2018).

Autobiography: A Sketch

Passing over years, I distinctly remember having chills and fever. Sometimes I would be taken with a shaking ague on the street, and would have to sit down upon a doorstep until I would stop shaking enough to go on my way. Then, I would have to go to bed, as I could not endure the fever and headache that would follow. When my aunt had finally saved up the hundred and twenty-five dollars, she bought me and sent me to New Bedford, Mass., where another aunt lived, who promised to get me a place to work for my board, and get a little education if I could. She put me out to work, at a place where I was allowed to go to school when I was not at work. But I could not go on wash day, nor ironing day, nor cleaning day, and this interfered with my progress. There were no Hamptons [a university in Virginia founded to educate African American students], and no night schools then.

Finally, I found a chance to go to Newport with Mrs. Elizabeth Orr, an aunt by marriage, who offered me a home with her and a better chance at school. I went with her, but I was not satisfied to be a burden on her small resources. I was now fourteen years old, and felt that I ought to take care of myself. So I found a permanent place in the family of Mr. George H. Calvert, a great grandson of Lord Baltimore, who settled Maryland. His wife was Elizabeth Stuart, a descendant of Mary, Queen of Scots. Here I had one hour every other afternoon in the week to take some private lessons, which I did of Mrs. Little. After that, I attended for a few months the public colored school which was taught by Mrs. Gavitt. I thus prepared myself to enter the examination for the Rhode Island State Normal School, under Dana P. Colburn; the school was then located at Bristol, R.I. Here, my eyes were first opened on the subject of teaching. I said to myself, is it possible that teaching can be made so interesting as this! But, having finished the course of study there, I felt that I had just begun to learn; and hearing of Oberlin College, I made up my mind to try and get there. I had learned a little music while at Newport, and had mastered the elementary studies of the piano and guitar. My aunt in Washington still helped me, and I was able to pay my way to Oberlin, the course of study there being the same as that at Harvard College. Oberlin was then the only College in the United States where colored students were permitted to study.

The faculty did not forbid a woman to take the gentleman's course, but they did not advise it. There was plenty of Latin and Greek in it, and as much mathematics as one could shoulder. Now, I took a long breath and prepared for a delightful contest. All went smoothly until I was in the junior year in College. Then, one day, the Faculty sent for me—ominous request—and I was not slow in obeying it. It was a custom in Oberlin that forty students from the junior and senior classes were employed to teach the preparatory classes. As it was now time for the juniors to begin their work, the Faculty informed me that it was their purpose to give me a class, but I was to distinctly understand that if the pupils rebelled against my teaching, they did not intend to force it. Fortunately for my training at the normal school, and my own dear love of teaching, tho there was a little surprise on the faces of some when they came into the class, and saw the teacher, there were no signs of rebellion. The class went on increasing in numbers until it had to be divided, and I was given both divisions. One of the divisions ran up again, but the Faculty decided that I had as much as I could do, and it would not allow me to take any more work.

When I was within a year of graduation, an application came from a Friends' school in Philadelphia for a colored woman who could teach Greek, Latin, and higher mathematics. The answer returned was: "We have the woman, but you must wait a year for her." . . .

I had been so long in Oberlin that I had forgotten about my color, but I was sharply reminded of it when, in a storm of rain, a Philadelphia street car conductor forbid my entering a car that did not have on it "for colored people," so I had to wait in the storm until one came in which colored people could ride. This was my first unpleasant experience in Philadelphia. Visiting Oberlin not long after my work began in Philadelphia, President Finney asked me how I was growing in grace; I told him that I was growing as fast as the American people would let me. When told of some of the conditions which were meeting me, he seemed to think it unspeakable.

At one time, at Mrs. Peck's [spouse of Professor H. E. Peck and in whose home Coppin lived for a time when a student at Oberlin], when we girls were sitting on the floor getting out our Greek,

Miss Sutherland, from Maine, suddenly stopped, and, looking at me, said: "Fanny Jackson, were you ever a slave?" I said yes; and she burst into tears. Not another word was spoken by us. But those tears seemed to wipe out a little of what was wrong. . . .

I went to Oberlin in 1860, and was graduated in August, 1865, after having spent five and a half years.

The years 1860 and 1865 were years of unusual historic importance and activity. In '60 the immortal Lincoln was elected, and in '65 the terrible war came to a close, but not until freedom for all the slaves in America had been proclaimed, and that proclamation made valid by the victorious arms of the Union party. In the year 1863 a very bitter feeling was exhibited against the colored people of the country, because they were held responsible for the fratricidal war then going on. The riots in New York especially gave evidence of this ill feeling. It was in this year that the faculty put me to teaching. . . .

And now came the time for me to leave Oberlin, and start in upon my work at Philadelphia.

In the year 1837, the Friends of Philadelphia had established a school for the education of colored youth in higher learning. To make a test whether or not the Negro was capable of acquiring any considerable degree of education. For it was one of the strongest arguments in the defense of slavery, that the Negro was an inferior creation; formed by the Almighty for just the work he was doing. It is said that John C. Calhoun [former vice president of the United States, 1825–1832, and staunch defender of slavery] made the remark, that if there could be found a Negro that could conjugate a Greek verb, he would give up all his preconceived ideas of the inferiority of the Negro. Well, let's try him, and see, said the fair-minded Quaker people. And for years this institution, known as the Institute for Colored Youth [later renamed Cheyney University], was visited by interested persons from different parts of the United States and Europe. Here I was given the delightful task of teaching my own people. . . .

[Over the next decades, Coppin rose in regard as an academic administrator and educational leader in the liberal arts, in the professional training of teachers, and in the preparation of African American students for business and the trades. Notably, as the spouse of a bishop in the AME Church, she also gained visibility as a leader in the church, the community, and particularly in women's organizations, all of which led to her being

a frequent participant, locally, nationally, and internationally, as a speaker in public arenas and as a journalist in the periodical press. Coppin documents this expertise in the excerpt below.]

Within the past ten years we have made almost no advance in getting our youth into industrial and business occupations. It is just as hard to get a boy into a printing office now as it was ten years ago. It is simply astonishing when we consider how many of the common vocations of life colored people are shut out of. Colored men are not admitted to the Printers' Trade Union, nor, with very rare exceptions, are they employed in any city of the United States in a paid capacity as printers or writers, one of the rare exceptions being the employment of H. Price Williams, on the Sunday Press of this city. We are not employed as salesmen, or pharmacists, or saleswomen, or bank clerks, or merchants' clerks, or tradesmen, or mechanics, or telegraph operators, or to any degree as State or Government officials, and I could keep on with the string of "ors" until tomorrow morning, but the patience of the reader has its limit.

Slavery made us poor, and its gloomy, malicious shadow tends to keep us so. I beg to say, kind reader, that this is not spoken in a spirit of recrimination; we have no quarrel with our fate, and we leave your Christianity to yourself. Our faith is firmly fixed in that "Eternal Providence," that in its own good time will "justify the ways of God to man." But, believing that to get the right men into the right places is a "consummation most devoutly to be wished," it is a matter of serious concern to us to see our youth, with just as decided diversity of talent as any other people, all herded together into three or four occupations. It is cruel to make a teacher or a preacher of a man who ought to be a printer or a blacksmith, and that is exactly what we are now obliged to do. The most advance that has been made since the war has been done by political parties, and it is precisely into political positions that we think it least desirable that our youth should enter. We have our choice of the professions, but, as we have not been endowed with a monopoly of brains, it is not probable that we can contribute to the bar a great lawyer, except once in a great while. The same may be said of medicine; nor are we able to tide over the "starving time," between the reception of a diploma and the time that a man's profession becomes a paying one.

Being determined to know whether this industrial and business ostracism was "in ourselves or in our stars," we have from time to time, knocked, shaken and kicked at these closed doors of work. A cold, metallic voice from within replies, "We do not employ colored people." Ours not to make reply, ours not to question why. Thank heaven, we are not obliged to do and die, having the preference to do or die, we naturally prefer to do. But we can not help wondering if some ignorant or faithless steward of God's work and God's money hasn't blundered. It seems necessary that we should make known to the good men and women who are so solicitous about our souls and our minds that we haven't quite got rid of our bodies yet, and until we do we must feed and clothe them; and this thing of keeping us out of work forces us back upon charity. That distinguished thinker, Mr. Henry C. Carey [a leading nineteenth century economist and advisor to President Lincoln], in his valuable works on Political Economy, has shown by the truthful and irresistible logic of history that the elevation of all peoples to a higher moral and intellectual plane, and to a fuller investiture of their civil rights has always steadily kept pace with the improvements in their physical condition. Therefore we feel that resolutely and in unmistakable language, yet in the dignity of moderation, we should strive to make known to all men the justice of our claims to the same employments as other men under the same conditions. We do not ask that any one of our people shall be put into a position because he is a colored person, but we do most emphatically ask that he shall not be kept out of a position because he is a colored person. "An open field and no favors" is all that is requested. The time was when to put a colored boy or girl behind a counter would have been to decrease custom; it would have been a tax upon the employer, and a charity that we were too proud to accept; but public sentiment has changed. I am satisfied that the employment of a colored clerk or a colored saleswoman wouldn't even be a "nine days' wonder." It is easy of accomplishment, and yet it is not done. To thoughtless and headstrong people who meet duty with impertinent dictation I do not now address myself; but to those who wish the most gracious of all blessings, a fuller enlightenment as to their duty, to those I beg to say, think of what is said in this appeal.

Figure 5.3: Ida B. Wells-Barnett

Ida B. Wells-Barnett

Ida B. Wells-Barnett (1862–1931) was born enslaved in Holly Springs, Mississippi, to parents who were deeply involved in social activism and community development. She was the eldest of eight children (two of whom died in early childhood). In 1878 there was a yellow fever epidemic in the United States, with the Mississippi River serving as its epicenter. Because of this devastating disease, Wells and her five remaining siblings lost both parents and her youngest sibling. At sixteen Wells stepped in to take care of the family. Having begun classes at Rust College, where her father had been a trustee, she dropped out to take the teacher's examination and begin a career teaching in the public schools of the state. Obtaining a position near Holly Springs, she began a grueling schedule to generate an income that helped her to keep her younger brothers and sisters together as a family. In 1880, at the age of eighteen, she was invited by her mother's sister, Belle (who had been widowed in the epidemic), to move to Memphis, Tennessee, where economic opportunities were better.

In Memphis, Wells joined another community that was also active sociopolitically and became herself vibrantly engaged in work on behalf of the race, including various church activities and the activities of a lyceum where the membership included several of her fellow teachers in the public schools. Through these activities, Wells's talents as a writer emerged. She became, first, a contributor and editor of the lyceum's newspaper, the *Evening Star*; a contributor to a weekly newspaper, the *Living Way*; and in 1889 co-owner and editor of the *Free Speech and Headlight*, shortened subsequently to the *Free Speech*. During this time, after controversial articles that she wrote about the school system, Wells was pushed out of teaching. Preferring her journalistic work anyway, she was free to devote her full attention to writing, editing, and investigative analyses, and to her entrepreneurial efforts as a business woman. She was successful in building a robust readership in the region and a well-deserved reputation as an outspoken social critic on issues of importance to the African American community.

On May 21, 1892, Wells wrote a very short but powerful editorial, "Eight Men Lynched," raising critical questions about what she considered to be the true nature of lynching cases. It was published while she was attending a church conference in Philadelphia. According to her autobiography, *Crusade for Justice* (published posthumously in 1970), after the publication of the editorial, a "committee of leading [white] citizens" in Memphis ran her co-owner J. L. Fleming out of town, destroyed the offices of her paper, and issued a death threat against her if she ever set foot in Memphis again. With this series of events, Wells was relegated to living in exile from the South. However, being in exile permitted her to launch a national and international anti-lynching campaign. Dedicated to the mission of social justice, Wells came to be recognized as a compelling writer and a critically astute public speaker, forging a career over her lifetime as a steadfast and relentless crusader for justice.

Wells's first public speech was sponsored by Maritcha Lyons and Victoria Earle Matthews, African American women in New York City and Brooklyn who were highly respected leaders and community activists. They hosted a testimonial dinner in honor of Wells on October 5, 1892, at Lyric Hall in New York. The event raised five hundred dollars to support the publication of Wells's first pamphlet, *Southern Horrors: Lynch Law in All Its Phases*, so that she could share her insights and experiences more broadly. After this event, Wells gave another speech, similarly entitled, "Lynch Law in

All Its Phases." It was the first speech that she gave before a white audience, delivered at Tremont Temple in the Boston Monday Lectureship on February 13, 1893. Before an audience composed of prominent men and women in the Boston community, Wells exhibited the stance that would mark her presentational style going forward—that is, as an investigative reporter who investigates situations herself, but who, in making her case, quotes also the investigations of more conservative white papers as well. For generations to come, this speech established, quite powerfully, a fundamental argument for the rights of citizenship and the obligation of the oppressed to resist discrimination and abuse. This argument included her underscoring the need for African Americans to keep the waters troubled and not to let the people forget the inescapable presence of injustice in a country that proclaims to uphold truth, justice, and equality for all.

Ida B. Wells-Barnett

Excerpt from "Lynch Law in All Its Phases (1893)," in *With Pen and Voice: A Critical Anthology of Nineteenth-Century African-American Women*, ed. Shirley Wilson Logan (Carbondale: Southern Illinois University Press, 1995), 80–99.

I am before the American people to-day through no inclination of my own, but because of a deep-seated conviction that the country at large does not know the extent to which lynch law prevails in parts of the Republic, nor the conditions which force into exile those who speak the truth. I cannot believe that the apathy and indifference which so largely obtains regarding mob rule is other than the result of ignorance of the true situation. And yet, the observing and thoughtful must know that in one section, at least, of our common country, a government of the people, by the people, and for the people, means a government by the mob; where the land of the free and the home of the brave means a land of lawlessness, murder and outrage; and where liberty of speech means the license of might to destroy the business and drive from home those who exercise this privilege contrary to the will of the mob. Repeated attacks on the life, liberty and happiness of any citizen or class of citizens are attacks on distinctive American institutions; such attacks imperiling as they do the foundation of government, law and order, merit the thoughtful consideration of far-sighted Americans; not from a standpoint of sentiment, not even so much from a standpoint of justice to a weak race, as from a desire to preserve our institutions.

The race problem or negro question, as it has been called, has been omnipresent and all-pervading since long before the Afro-American was raised from the degradation of the slave to the dignity of the citizen. It has never been settled because the right methods have not been employed in the solution. It is the Banquo's ghost of politics, religion, and sociology which will not down at the bidding of those who are tormented with its ubiquitous appearance on every occasion. Times without number, since invested with citizenship, the race has been indicted for ignorance, immorality and general worthlessness—declared guilty and executed by its self-constituted judges. The operations of law do not dispose of negroes fast enough, and lynching bees have become the favorite pastime of the South. As excuse for the same, a new cry, as false as it is foul, is raised in an effort to blast race character, a cry which has proclaimed to the world that virtue and innocence are violated by Afro-Americans who must be killed like wild beasts to protect womanhood and childhood.

Born and reared in the South, I had never expected to live elsewhere. Until this past year I was one among those who believed the condition of the masses gave large excuse for the humiliations and proscriptions under which we labored; that when wealth, education and character became more general among us, the cause being removed the effect would cease, and justice be accorded to all alike. I shared the general belief that good newspapers entering regularly the homes of our people in every state could do more to bring about this result than any agency. Preaching the doctrine of self-help, thrift and economy every week, they would be the teachers to those who had been deprived of school advantages, yet were making history every day—and train to think for themselves our mental children of a larger growth. And so, three years ago, last June, I became editor and part owner of the *Memphis Free Speech*. As editor, I had occasion to criticize the city School Board's employment of inefficient teachers and poor school buildings for Afro-American children. I was in the employ of the board at the time, and at the close of that school-term one year ago, was not re-elected to a position I had held in the city schools for seven years. Accepting the decision of the Board of Education, I set out to make a race newspaper pay—a thing which older and wiser heads said could not be done. But there were enough of our people in Memphis and surrounding territory to support a paper, and I believed they would do so. With nine months hard work the circulation increased from 1,500 to 3,500; in twelve months it was on a good paying basis. Throughout the Mississippi Valley in Arkansas, Tennessee and Mississippi—on plantations and in towns, the demand for the interest in the paper increased among the masses. The news boys who would not set it on the trains, voluntarily testified that they had never known colored people to demand a paper so eagerly.

To make the paper a paying business I became advertising agent, solicitor, as well as editor, and was continually on the go. Wherever I went among the people, I gave them in church, school, public gatherings, and home, the benefit of my honest conviction that maintenance of character, money getting and education would finally solve our problem and that it depended on us to say how soon this would be brought about. This sentiment bore good fruit in Memphis. We had nice homes, representatives in almost every branch of business and profession, and refined society. We had learned that helping each other helped all, and every well-conducted business by Afro-Americans prospered. With all our proscription in theatres, hotels and on railroads, we had never had a lynching and did not believe we could have one. There had been lynchings and brutal outrages of all sorts in our own state and those adjoining us, but we had confidence and pride in our city and the majority of its laws. So far in advance of other Southern cities was ours, we were content to endure the evils we had, to labor and to wait.

But there was a rude awakening. On the morning of March 9, the bodies of three of our best young men were found in an old field horribly shot to pieces. These young men had owned and operated the "People's Grocery," situated at what was known as the Curve—a suburb made up almost entirely of colored people—about a mile from city limits. Thomas Moss, one of the oldest letter-carriers in the city, was president of the company, Calvin McDowell was manager and Will Stewart was a clerk. There were about ten other stockholders, all colored men. The young men were well known and popular and their business flourished, and that of Barrett, who kept store there before the "People's Grocery" was established, went down. One day an officer came to the "People's Grocery" and inquired for a colored man who lived in the neighborhood, and for whom the officer had a warrant. Barrett was with him and when McDowell said he knew nothing as to the whereabouts of the man for whom they were searching, Barrett, not the officer, then accused McDowell of harboring the man, and McDowell gave the lie. Barrett drew his pistol and struck McDowell with it; thereupon McDowell, who was a tall, fine-looking six-footer, took Barrett's pistol from him, knocked him down and gave him a good thrashing, while Will Stewart, the clerk, kept the special officer at bay. Barrett went to town, swore out a warrant for their arrest on a charge of assault and battery. McDowell went before the Criminal Court, immediately gave bond and returned to his store. Barrett then threatened (to use his own words) that he was going to clean out the whole store. Knowing how anxious he was to destroy their business, these young men consulted a lawyer who told them they were justified in defending themselves if attacked, as they were a mile beyond city limits and police protection. They accordingly armed several of their friends—not to assail, but to resist the threatened Saturday night attack.

When they saw Barrett enter the front door and a half dozen men at the rear door at 11 o'clock that night, they supposed the attack was on and immediately fired into the crowd, wounding three men. These men, dressed in citizen's clothes, turned out to be deputies who claimed to be hunting another man for whom they had a warrant, and whom any of them could have arrested without trouble. When these men found they had fired upon officers of the law, they threw away their firearms and submitted to arrest, confident they should establish their innocence of intent to fire upon officers of the law. The daily papers in flaming headlines roused the evil passions of the whites, denounced these poor boys in unmeasured terms, nor permitted them a word in their own defense.

The neighborhood of the Curve was searched next day, and about thirty persons were thrown into jail, charged with conspiracy. No communication was to be had with friends any of the three days these men were in jail; bail was refused and Thomas Moss was not allowed to eat the food his wife prepared for him. The judge is reported to have said, "Any one can see them after three days." They were seen after three days, but they were no longer able to respond to the greetings of friends. On Tuesday following the shooting at the grocery, the papers which had made much of the sufferings of the wounded deputies, and promised it would go hard with those who did the shooting, if they died, announced that the officers were all out of danger, and would recover. The friends of the prisoners breathed more easily and relaxed their vigilance. They felt that as the officers would not die, there was no danger that in the heat of passion the prisoners would meet violent death at the hands of the mob. Besides, we had such confidence in the law. But the law did not provide capital punishment for shooting which did not kill. So the mob did what the law could not be made to do, as a lesson to the Afro-American that he must not shoot a white man, no matter what the provocation. The same night after the announcement was made in the papers that the officers would get well, the mob, in obedience to a plan known to every prominent white man in the city, went to the jail between two and three o'clock in the morning, dragged out these young men, hatless and shoeless, put them on the yard engine of the railroad which was in waiting just behind the jail, carried them a mile north of city limits and horribly shot them to death while the locomotive at a given signal let off steam and blew the whistle to deaden the sound of the firing.

"It was done by unknown men," said the jury, yet the *Appeal-Avalanche*, which goes to press at 3 a.m., had a two-column account of the lynching. The papers also told how McDowell got hold of the guns of the mob, and as his grasp could not be loosened, his hand was shattered with a pistol ball and all the lower part of his face was torn away. There were four pools of blood found and only three bodies. It was whispered that he, McDowell, killed one of the lynchers with his gun, and it is well known that a policeman who was seen on the street a few days previous to the lynching, died very suddenly the next day after.

"It was done by unknown parties," said the jury, yet the papers told how Tom Moss begged for his life, for the sake of his wife, his little daughter and his unborn infant. They also told us that his last words were, "If you will kill us, turn our faces to the West."

All this we learned too late to save these men, even if the law had not been in the hands of their murderers. When the colored people realized that the flower of our young manhood had been stolen away at night and murdered, there was a rush for firearms to avenge the wrong, but no house would sell a colored man a gun; the armory of the Tennessee Rifles, our only colored military company, and of which McDowell was a member, was broken into by order of the Criminal Court judge, and its guns taken. One hundred men and irresponsible boys from fifteen years and up were armed by order of the authorities and rushed out to the Curve, where it was reported that the colored people were massing, and at point of the bayonet dispersed these men who could do nothing but talk. The cigars, wines, etc. of the grocery stock were freely used by the mob, who possessed the place on pretence of dispersing the conspiracy. The money drawer was broken into and contents taken. The trunk of Calvin McDowell, who had a room in the store, was broken open, and his clothing, which was not good enough to take away, was thrown out and trampled on the floor.

These men were murdered, their stock was attached by creditors and sold for less than one-eighth of its cost to that same man Barrett, who is to-day running his grocery in the same place. He had indeed kept his word, and by aid of the authorities destroyed the People's Grocery Company root and branch. The relatives of Will Stewart and Calvin McDowell are bereft of their protectors. The baby daughter of Tom Moss, too young to express how she misses her father, toddles to the wardrobe, seizes the legs of the trousers of his letter-carrier uniform, hugs and kisses them with evident delight and stretches up her little hands to be taken up into the arms which will nevermore clasp his daughter's form. His wife holds Thomas Moss, Jr., in her arms, upon whose unconscious baby face the tears fall thick and fast when she is thinking of the sad fate of the father he will never see, and of the two helpless children who cling to her for the support she cannot give. Although these men were peaceable, law-abiding citizens of this country, we are told there can be no punishment for their murderers nor indemnity for their relatives.

I have no power to describe the feeling of horror that possessed every member of the race in Memphis when the truth dawned upon us that the protection of the law which we had so long enjoyed was no longer ours; all this had been destroyed in a night, and the barriers of the law had been thrown down, and the guardians of the public peace and confidence scoffed away into the shadows, and all authority given into the hands of the mob, and innocent men cut down as if they were brutes—the first feeling was one of utter dismay, then intense indignation. Vengeance was whispered from ear to ear, but sober reflection brought the conviction that it would be extreme folly to seek vengeance when such action meant certain death for the men, and horrible slaughter for the women and children, as one of the evening papers took care to remind us. The power of the State, country and city, the civil authorities and the strong arm of the military power were all on the side of the mob and of lawlessness. Few of our men possessed firearms, our only company's guns were confiscated, and the only white man who would sell a colored man a gun, was himself jailed, and his store closed. We were helpless in our great strength. It was our first object lesson in the doctrine of white supremacy; an illustration of the South's cardinal principle that no matter what the attainments, character or standing of an Afro-American, the laws of the South will not protect him against a white man.

There was only one thing we could do, and a great determination seized upon the people to follow the advice of the martyred Moss, and "turn our faces to the West," whose laws protect all alike. The *Free Speech* supported by our ministers and leading business men advised the people to leave a community whose laws did not protect them. Hundreds left on foot to walk four hundred miles between Memphis and Oklahoma. A Baptist minister went to the territory, built a church, and took his entire congregation out in less than a month. Another minister sold his church and took his flock to California, and still another has settled in Kansas. In two months, six thousand persons had left the city and every branch of business began to feel this silent resentment of the outrage, and failure of the authorities to punish the lynchers. There were a number of business failures and blocks of houses were for rent. The superintendent and treasurer of the street railway company called at the office of the *Free Speech*, to have us urge the colored people to ride again on the street cars. A real estate dealer said to a colored man who returned some property he had been buying on the installment plan: "I don't see what you 'niggers' are cutting up about. You got off light. We first intended to kill every one of those thirty-one 'niggers' in jail, but concluded to let all go but the 'leaders.'" They did let all go to the penitentiary. These so-called rioters have since been tried in the Criminal Court for the conspiracy of defending their property, and are now serving terms of three, eight, and fifteen years each in the Tennessee State prison.

To restore the equilibrium and put a stop to the great financial loss, the next move was to get rid of the *Free Speech*, the disturbing element which kept the waters troubled; which would not let the people forget, and in obedience to whose advice nearly six thousand persons had left the city. In casting about for an excuse, the mob found it in the following editorial which appeared in the Memphis *Free Speech*, May 21, 1892:

> Eight negroes lynched in one week. Since last issue of the *Free Speech* one was lynched at Little Rock, Ark., where the citizens broke into the penitentiary and got their man; three near Anniston, Ala., and one in New Orleans, all on the same charge, the new alarm of assaulting white women and three near Clarksville, Ga., for killing a white man. The same program of hanging then shooting bullets into the lifeless bodies was carried out to the letter. Nobody in this section of the country believes the old threadbare lie that negro men rape white women. If Southern white men are not careful they will overreach themselves, and public sentiment will have a reaction. A conclusion will then be reached which will be very damaging to the moral reputation of their women.

Commenting on this, *The Daily Commercial* of Wednesday following said:

> Those negroes who are attempting to make lynching of individuals of their race a means for arousing the worst passions of their kind, are playing with a dangerous sentiment. The negroes may as well understand that there is no mercy for the negro rapist, and little patience with his defenders. A negro organ printed in this city in a recent issue published the following atrocious paragraph: "Nobody in this section believes the old threadbare lie that negro men rape white women. If Southern white men are not careful they will overreach themselves and public sentiment will have a reaction. A conclusion will be reached which will be very damaging to the moral reputation of their women." The fact that a black scoundrel is allowed to live and utter such loathsome and repulsive calumnies is a volume of evidence as to the wonderful patience of Southern whites. There are some things the Southern white man will not tolerate, and the obscene intimidation of the foregoing has brought the writer to the very utter-most limit of public patience. We hope we have said enough.

The *Evening Scimitar* of the same day copied this leading editorial and added this comment: "Patience under such circumstances is not a virtue: If the negroes themselves do not apply the remedy without delay, it will be the duty of those he has attacked, to tie the wretch who utters these calumnies to a stake at the intersection of Main and Madison streets, brand him in the forehead with a hot iron and—"

Such open suggestions by the leading daily papers of the progressive city of Memphis were acted upon by the leading citizens and a meeting was held at the Cotton Exchange that evening. *The Commercial* two days later had the following account of it:

Atrocious Blackguardism.

There will be no Lynching and no Repetition of the Offense.

In its issue of Wednesday *The Commercial* reproduced and commented upon an editorial which appeared a day or two before in a negro organ known as the *Free Speech*. The article was so insufferably and indecently slanderous that the whole city awoke to a feeling of intense resentment which came within an ace of culminating in one of those occurrences whose details are so eagerly seized and so prominently published by Northern newspapers. Conservative counsels, however, prevailed, and no extreme measures were resorted to. On Wednesday afternoon a meeting of citizens was held. It was not an assemblage of hoodlums or irresponsible fire-eaters, but solid, substantial business men who knew exactly what they were doing and who were far more indignant at the villainous insult to the women of the South than they would have been at any injury done themselves. This meeting appointed a committee to seek the author of the infamous editorial and warn him quietly that upon repetition of the offense he would find some other part of the country a good deal safer and pleasanter place of residence than this. The committee called a negro preacher named Nightingale, but he disclaimed responsibility and convinced the gentlemen that he had really sold out his paper to a woman named Wells. This woman is not in Memphis at present. It was finally learned that one Fleming, a negro who was driven out of Crittenden Co. during the trouble there a few years ago, wrote the paragraph. He had, however, heard of the meeting, and fled from a fate which he feared was in store for him, and which he knew he deserved. His whereabouts could not be ascertained, and the committee so reported. Later on, a communication from Fleming to a prominent Republican politician, and that politician's reply were shown to one or two gentlemen. The former was an inquiry as to whether the writer might safely return to Memphis, the latter was an emphatic answer in the negative, and Fleming is still in hiding. Nothing further will be done in the matter. There will be

> no lynching, and it is very certain there will be no repetition of the outrage. If there should be Friday, May 25.

The only reason there was no lynching of Mr. Fleming who was business manager and half owner of the *Free Speech*, and who did not write the editorial, was because this same white Republican told him the committee was coming, and warned him not to trust them, but get out of the way. The committee scoured the city hunting him, and had to be content with Mr. Nightingale who was dragged to the meeting, shamefully abused (although it was known he had sold out his interest in the paper six months before). He was struck in the face and forced at the pistol's point to sign a letter which was written by them, in which he denied all knowledge of the editorial, denounced and condemned it as slander on white women. I do not censure Mr. Nightingale for his action because, having never been at the pistol's point myself, I do not feel that I am competent to sit in judgment on him, or say what I would do under such circumstances.

I had written that editorial with other matter for the week's paper before leaving home the Friday previous for the General Conference of the A.M.E. Church in Philadelphia. Conference adjourned Tuesday, and Thursday, May 25, at 3 p.m., I landed in New York City for a few days' stay before returning home, and there learned from the papers that my business manager had been driven away and the paper suspended. Telegraphing for news, I received telegrams and letters in return informing me that the trains were being watched, that I was to be dumped into the river and beaten, if not killed; it had been learned that I wrote the editorial and I was to be hanged in front of the court-house and my face bled if I returned, and I was implored by my friends to remain away. The creditors attached the office in the meantime and the outfit was sold without more ado, thus destroying effectually that which it had taken years to build. One prominent insurance agent publicly declares he will make it his business to shoot me down on sight if I return to Memphis in twenty years, while a leading white lady had remarked that she was opposed to the lynching of those three men in March, but she did wish there was some way by which I could be gotten back and lynched.

I have been censured for writing that editorial, but when I think of the five men who were lynched that week for assault on white women and that not a week passes but some poor soul is violently ushered into eternity on this trumped-up charge, knowing the many things I do, and part of which I tried to tell in the *New York Age* of June 25, (and in the pamphlets I have with me) seeing that the whole race in the South was injured in the estimation of the world because of these false reports, I could no longer hold my peace, and I feel, yes, I am sure, that if it had to be done over again (provided no one else was the loser save myself) I would do and say the very same again.

The lawlessness here described is not confined to one locality. In the past ten years over a thousand colored men, women and children have been butchered, murdered and burnt in all parts of the South. The details of these horrible outrages seldom reach beyond the narrow world where they occur. Those who commit the murders write the reports, and hence these lasting blots upon the honor of a nation cause but a faint ripple on the outside world. They arouse no great indignation and call forth no adequate demand for justice. The victims were black, and the reports are so written as to make it appear that the helpless creatures deserved the fate which overtook them. . . .

It is no wonder in my mind that the party which stood for thirty years as the champion of human liberty and human rights, the party of great moral ideas, should suffer overwhelming defeat when it has proven recreant to its professions and abandoned a position it created: when although its followers were being outraged in every sense, it was afraid to stand for the right, and appeal to the American people to sustain them in it. It put aside the question of a free ballot and fair count of every citizen and gave its voice and influence for the protection of the coat instead of the man who wore it, for the product of labor instead of the laborer; for the seal of citizenship rather than the citizen, and insisted upon the evils of free trade instead of the sacredness of free speech. I am no politician but I believe if the Republican party had met the issues squarely for human rights instead of the tariff it would have occupied a different position to-day. The voice of the people is the voice of God, and I long with all the intensity of my soul for the Garrison, Douglas[s], Sumner, W[h]ittier and Phillips who shall rouse this nation to a demand that from Greenland's icy mountains to the coral reefs of the Southern seas, mob rule shall be put down and equal and exact justice be accorded to every citizen of whatever race, who finds a home within the borders of the land of the free and the home of the brave.

Then no longer will our national hymn be sounding brass and a tinkling cymbal, but every member of this great composite nation will be a living, harmonious illustration of the words, and all can honestly and gladly join in singing:

> My country! 'tis of thee, Sweet land of liberty
> Of thee I sing.
> Land where our fathers died,
> Land of the Pilgrim's pride,
> From every mountain side
> Freedom does ring.

Figure 5.4: Lucy E. Parsons

Lucy E. Parsons

Lucy E. Parsons (1851–1942), born to an enslaved woman in Virginia, migrated with her family to Waco, Texas, during the Civil War. Parsons's early life, however, remains cloaked in mystery as a function, significantly, of two basic factors. One factor was that her physical appearance as a mixed race person made her ethnic identity unclear. Another was that, despite her visibility as a public figure, she sustained a steadfast commitment to not sharing personal details about herself and her personal situation, preferring instead to focus attention on the issues and ideas about which she was so passionate.

What is clear about Parsons's personal history is that, by the early 1870s, she had met and married Albert Parsons who was white. He was a former Confederate soldier who became a Radical Republican. To be noted, Parsons's marriage was likely illegal because of the miscegenation laws of the time period that essentially banned the marriage of African Americans to anyone other than another African American. Such laws were not overturned in the United States until the US Supreme Court ruling in 1967 in the *Loving versus Virginia* case that deemed laws against miscegenation to be unconstitutional.

By 1872—with the rise of Jim Crow laws across the South, their interracial marriage, and their active involvement in various sociopolitical causes—the Parsonses were living under considerable threat in Texas. In 1873 they moved to Chicago, where Albert Parsons worked as a journalist and printer. In their new context, both Albert and Lucy remained active in sociopolitical issues, becoming especially well known for their full partnership as a highly engaged couple in the anarchist and labor movements. With this level of radicalism, Albert Parsons soon lost his job, and Lucy Parsons opened a dressmaking business in their home to support her family, which by that point included two children. Even with this setback, she continued her activities, which included hosting union meetings for the International Ladies' Garment Workers Union, serving as an organizer and speaker for the Working Women's Union, organizing seamstresses like herself as members of the Knights of Labor, and in 1883 being among the founders of the International Working People's Association.

Over this time period, Parsons built a reputation as an outspoken and uncompromising activist. She was a contributor to the radical periodical press (for example, *The Socialist*, a publication of the Socialist Labor Party, and *The Alarm*, edited by her husband, a publication of the International Working People's Association); and a public speaker, both nationally and internationally. She focused on issues related to the impoverished (for example, hunger, unemployment, homelessness), workers' rights (for example, her advocacy of an eight-hour work day), free speech, and more.

On May 3, 1886, Parsons experienced a catalytic event. There was a strike at McCormick Harvest Works in Chicago. Police disrupted the event and several workers were killed. The next day labor activists organized a protest that was peaceful until, again, police were called in. The gathering, known subsequently as the Haymarket Riot, became violent. An unidentified person threw a bomb, and both policemen and workers were killed and injured. Albert Parsons was one of eight anarchists who were accused as conspirators in the bombing. They were convicted and sentenced to death for inciting violence and for murder. Lucy Parsons was not charged as a conspirator, but she was constantly surveilled and harassed.

After seeing the injustices of the verdict, Parsons waged a national campaign from the fall of 1886 through the spring of 1887 that covered seventeen states. Her imperative was to raise funds and advocacy for a new trial for the eight men who were perceived in the labor movement to be martyrs. She was unsuccessful, however, in preventing their executions and was ultimately jailed herself while four of the men, her husband included, were executed. This situation left her and her two children in poverty, with Parsons, as a radical African American woman, facing resistance to her leadership not only from external power elites but also from other leaders within the labor movement as well. Still, she persevered and her activism continued.

In 1889 she published *The Life of Albert R. Parsons*, a collection of her husband's letters, articles, and speeches. In 1890 she became the founder and coeditor of *Freedom: A Revolutionary Anarchist-Communist Monthly*. In 1905 she was one of two women delegates at the founding convention of the Industrial Workers of the World, and the only woman invited to speak. That year she also became editor of *The Liberator*, one of this organization's newspapers published in Chicago. Over the next decades until her death, she continued to work with many radical organizations and remained an outspoken public advocate on various issues related to labor, freedom, equity, and justice. Among her broad range of activities, she wrote a column about famous working women and a history of the working class, and she supported international issues, as well, which included her advocacy in 1910 of the Mexican Revolution.

Over the decades, it became more evident that Parsons was a supporter of an array of causes and active in many radical organizations, with her commitment to action anchored still by issues related to labor, class, social justice, and sociopolitical reform. She was an advocate for women's issues, including a woman's right to divorce, remarry, and have access to birth control. She was outspoken against lynching. In this case, while issues directly related to race were not evident as a top priority for her, she included these concerns, nevertheless, within her scope, as evidenced in 1931 by the work that she did with the Coalition for International Labor Defense of the Communist Party on their clemency campaign, which was focused on the Scottsboro Boys, a group of young African

American men and boys who were sentenced to death for the rape of two white women.

An important point to underscore is that, unlike most of the women highlighted in this volume, Parsons was not associated with or active in the National Association of Colored Women (NACW). While NACW became an operational base for many African American women advocates, activists, and leaders, such just was not the case for all, especially if they did not identify as members of the educated elite, as women who worked in highly regarded professions, or as elite members of their African American communities based on other markers of status. In Parsons's case, NACW did not become an operational base. She allied herself most explicitly with working class people, labor issues, and poverty as an oppressive condition. Even though she was sociopolitically active in Chicago at the same time that other African American women leaders in this city were also active, for example, Ida B. Wells-Barnett and Fannie Barrier Williams, she functioned in a different circle.

Parsons's inclusion as an exemplar in this showcase, therefore, is not by ideological alignment with the emergence of the Black Clubwomen's Movement by the end of the nineteenth century but by the imperative of bringing to bolder relief the point that African American women leaders and activists are not and have never been monolithic. Historically and currently, they represent a range of experiences, ideologies, patterns of interests, patterns of practice, alliances, and coalitions. In the nineteenth century, this assertion was clear both within the Black Clubwomen's Movement (as illustrated, for example, by Wells-Barnett and Williams who varied in sociopolitical regard) and also beyond it, as illustrated by Parsons as a striking example of activism and leadership by means of a different path. A fuller history of leadership and activism among African American women—whether militant, radical, working-class, affluent, progressive, conservative, or by other identity markers—remains very much opaque as a collective story. The point to emphasize, therefore, is that the landscape of sociopolitical leadership and action across the range of African American women was a vibrant one that deserves caring and careful critical attention.

Parsons's speech below, "I Am an Anarchist," is a compelling exhibition of a radical perspective on freedom, justice, and social reform. It takes on the basic challenge of explaining what an "anarchist" is and the nature of the work that anarchists perform. It was published in the *Kansas City Journal* on December 21, 1886, amid

Parsons's six-month seventeen-state campaign for a new trial for the Haymarket martyrs and her efforts to prevent the execution of her husband. While her critical framework extends beyond many of the issues espoused by the leaders of the Black Clubwomen's Movement, even as those issues are diversely rendered, the speech below demonstrates the thought-provoking ways in which Parsons's viewpoints animate the concept of freedom and justice. This critical framework formed the foundation for her work throughout her life and stands as an exemplification of her passionate commitments and her rhetorical prowess as a sociopolitical leader and activist.

Lucy E. Parsons

"I Am an Anarchist" (1886). https://blackpast.org/african-american-history/1886-lucy-parsons-i-am-anarchist.

I am an anarchist. I suppose you came here, the most of you, to see what a real, live anarchist looked like. I suppose some of you expected to see me with a bomb in one hand and a flaming torch in the other, but are disappointed in seeing neither. If such has been your ideas regarding an anarchist, you deserved to be disappointed. Anarchists are peaceable, law abiding people. What do anarchists mean when they speak of anarchy? Webster gives the term two definitions chaos and the state of being without political rule. We cling to the latter definition. Our enemies hold that we believe only in the former.

Do you wonder why there are anarchists in this country, in this great land of liberty, as you love to call it? Go to New York. Go through the byways and alleys of that great city. Count the myriads starving; count the multiplied thousands who are homeless; number [of] those who work harder than slaves and live on less and have fewer comforts than the meanest slaves. You will be dumbfounded by your discoveries, you who have paid no attention to these poor, save as objects of charity and commiseration. They are not objects of charity, they are the victims of the rank injustice that permeates the system of government, and of political economy that holds sway from the Atlantic to the Pacific. Its oppression, the misery it causes, the wretchedness it gives birth to, are found to a greater extent in New York than elsewhere. In New York, where not many days ago two governments united in unveiling a statue of liberty, where a hundred bands played that hymn of liberty, "The Marseillaise." But almost its equal is found among the miners of the West, who dwell in squalor and wear rags, that the capitalists, who control the earth that should be free to all, may add still further to their millions! Oh, there are plenty of reasons for the existence of anarchists.

But in Chicago they do not think anarchists have any right to exist at all. They want to hang them there, lawfully or unlawfully. You have heard of a certain Haymarket meeting. You have heard of a bomb. You have heard of arrests and of succeeding arrests effected by detectives. Those detectives! There is a set of men, nay, beasts for you! Pinkerton detectives! They would do anything. I feel sure capitalists wanted a man to throw that bomb at the Haymarket meeting and have the anarchists blamed for it. Pinkerton could have accomplished it for him. You have heard a great deal about bombs. You have heard that the anarchists said lots about dynamite. You have been told that Lingg made bombs. He violated no law. Dynamite bombs can kill, can murder, so can Gatling guns. Suppose that bomb had been thrown by an anarchist. The constitution says there are certain inalienable rights, among which are a free press, free speech and free assemblage. The citizens of this great land are given by the constitution the right to repel the unlawful invasion of those rights. The meeting at Haymarket square was a peaceable meeting. Suppose, when an anarchist saw the police arrive on the scene, with murder in their eyes, determined to break up that meeting, suppose he had thrown that bomb; he would have violated no law. That will be the verdict of your children. Had I been there, had I seen those murderous police approach, had I heard that insolent command to disperse, had I heard Fielden say, "Captain, this is a peaceable meeting," had I seen the liberties of my countrymen trodden under foot, I would have flung the bomb myself. I would have violated no law, but would have upheld the constitution.

If the anarchists had planned to destroy the city of Chicago and to massacre the police, why was it they had only two or three bombs in hand? Such was not their intention. It was a peaceable meeting. Carter Harrison, the mayor of Chicago, was there. He said it was a quiet meeting. He told Bonfield [Captain John Bonfield, commander of Desplaines Police Station] to send the police to their different beats. I do not stand here to gloat over the murder of those policemen. I despise murder. But when a ball from the revolver of a policeman kills it is as much murder as when death results from a bomb.

The police rushed upon that meeting as it was about to disperse. Mr. Simonson talked to Bonfield about the meeting. Bonfield said he wanted to do the anarchists up. Parsons went to the meeting. He took his wife, two ladies and his two children along. Toward the close of the meeting, he said, "I believe it is going to rain. Let us adjourn to Zeph's hall." Fielden said he was about through with his speech and would close it at once. The people were beginning to scatter about, a thousand of the more enthusiastic still lingered in spite of the rain. Parsons, and those who accompanied him started for home. They had gone as far as the Desplaine's street police station when they saw the police start at a double quick. Parsons stopped to see what was the trouble. Those 200 policemen rushed on to do the anarchists up. Then we went on. I was in Zeph's hall when I heard that terrible detonation. It was heard around the world. Tyrants trembled and felt there was something wrong.

The discovery of dynamite and its use by anarchists is a repetition of history. When gun powder was discovered, the feudal system was at the height of its power. Its discovery and use made the middle classes. Its first discharge sounded the death knell of the feudal system. The bomb at Chicago sounded the downfall of the wage system of the nineteenth century. Why? Because I know no intelligent people will submit to despotism. The first means the diffusion of power. I tell no man to use it. But it was the achievement of science, not of anarchy, and would do for the masses. I suppose the press will say I belched forth treason. If I have violated any law, arrest me, give me a trial, and the proper punishment, but let the next anarchist that comes along ventilate his views without hindrance.

Well, the bomb exploded, the arrests were made and then came that great judicial farce, beginning on June 21. The jury was impaneled. Is there a Knight of Labor here? Then know that a Knight of Labor was not considered competent enough to serve on that jury. "Are you a Knight of Labor?" "Have you any sympathy with labor organizations?" were the questions asked each talisman. If an affirmative answer was given, the talisman was bounced. It was not are you a Mason, a Knight Templar? O, no! [Great applause.] I see you read the signs of the times by that expression. Hangman Gary, miscalled judge, ruled that if a man was prejudiced against the defendants, it did not incapacitate him for serving on the jury. For such a man, said Hangman Gary, would pay closer attention to the law and evidence and would be more apt to render a verdict for the defense. Is there a lawyer here? If there is he knows such a ruling is without precedent and contrary to all law, reason or common sense.

In the heat of patriotism the American citizen sometimes drops a tear for the nihilist of Russia. They say the nihilist can't get justice, that he is condemned without trial. How much more should he weep for his next door neighbor, the anarchist, who is given the form of trial under such a ruling.

There were "squealers" introduced as witnesses for the prosecution. There were three of them. Each and every one was compelled to admit they had been purchased and intimidated by the prosecution. Yet Hangman Gary held their evidence as competent. It came out in the trial that the Haymarket meeting was the result of no plot, but was caused in this wise. The day before the wage slaves in McCormick's factory had struck for eight hours labor, McCormick, from his luxurious office, with one stroke of the pen by his idle, be ringed fingers, turned 4,000 men out of employment. Some gathered and stoned the factory. Therefore they were anarchists, said the press. But anarchists are not fools; only fools stone buildings. The police were sent out and they killed six wage slaves. You didn't know that. The capitalistic press kept it quiet, but it made a great fuss over the killing of some policemen. Then these crazy anarchists, as they are called, thought a meeting ought to be held to consider the killing of six brethren and to discuss the eight-hour movement. The meeting was held. It was peaceable. When Bonfield ordered the police to charge those peaceable anarchists, he hauled down the American flag and should have been shot on the spot.

While the judicial farce was going on the red and black flags were brought into court, to prove that the anarchists threw the bomb. They were placed on the walls and hung there, awful specters before the jury. What does the black flag mean? When a cable gram says it was carried through the streets of a European city it means that the people are suffering—that the men are out of work, the women starving, the children barefooted. But, you say, that is in Europe. How about America? The Chicago Tribune said there were 30,000 men in that city with nothing to do. Another authority said there were 10,000 barefooted children in mid winter. The police said hundreds had no place to sleep or warm. Then President Cleveland issued his Thanksgiving proclamation and the anarchists formed in procession and carried the black flag to show that these thousands had nothing for which to return thanks. When the Board of Trade, that gambling den, was dedicated by means of a banquet, $30 a plate, again the black flag was carried, to signify that there were thousands who couldn't enjoy a 2 cent meal.

But the red flag, the horrible red flag, what does that mean? Not that the streets should run with gore, but that the same red blood courses through the veins of the whole human race. It meant the brotherhood of man. When the red flag floats over the world the idle shall be called to work. There will be an end of prostitution for women, of slavery for man, of hunger for children.

Liberty has been named anarchy. If this verdict is carried out it will be the death knell of America's liberty. You and your children will be slaves. You will have liberty if you can pay for it. If this verdict is carried out, place the flag of our country at half mast and write on every fold "shame." Let our flag be trailed in the dust. Let the children of workingmen place laurels to the brow of these modern heroes, for they committed no crime. Break the two fold yoke. Bread is freedom and freedom is bread.

Chapter 6

At the Turn of the Century

By the turn of the century, it was more evident than ever that African American women were not monolithic in their thinking or in their problem-posing and -solving strategies. Some were more politically minded than others; some more outer-focused to the general society than inner-focused on African American communities; some held more radical views regarding governance, race, gender, cultural connections than others. Collectively, in fact, they demonstrated the diverse ways that sociopolitical actors might come to action agenda, but with all participating actively in civic enterprises of various kinds and engaged in complementary fashion in the institutional operations of these enterprises. With the rise of the Black clubwomen's movement, several of these variously connected women from across a range of experiences and perspectives came together as leaders to set a coherent national action agenda and to vie for national leadership.

One thing that this particular set of women's groups held in common was a recognition of the need to establish a sustainable infrastructure to support sociopolitical action. The question was one of design, whether the infrastructure would be inner-directed toward strengthening the race or outer-directed toward strengthening the place of the race on a larger stage, nationally and internationally, or perhaps better, a balancing of both with the possibility of approaches that might be even more innovative—in the hands of women. These ideological divides were enacted in ways that set the pace for African American women's sociopolitical work at the turn of the nineteenth century, and as their activism, advocacy, and leadership continued to evolve in the twentieth and now the twenty-first centuries.

By the turn of the twentieth century, African American women's rhetorical choices flourished across different genres of expression. Their achievements were escalating as creative writers, journalists, academics, and leaders in their various professions. Of particular note, however, is that by 1900, the cohort of clubwomen included ninety-nine clubs in twenty-eight states and the District of Columbia, drawing into the organization several hundred women. This concentration of energy for sociopolitical change constituted a distinctive milestone for both the individual women and their various groupings not only for advocacy and activism but also for a diversifying and flourishing display of visionary leadership going forward.

Figure 6.1: Anna Julia Haywood Cooper

Anna Julia Haywood Cooper

Anna Julia Haywood Cooper (1858–1964) was born enslaved in Raleigh, North Carolina, to Hannah Stanley and slaveowner George Washington Haywood. She built a distinctive career as a renowned educator, scholar, philosopher, community advocate and activist and as a civic and highly respected intellectual leader. Her interests were focused on education, the status of women, and civil rights for all, anchored by her belief that uplifting women was necessary not only for the advancement of a downtrodden race but also to take advantage of the diverse perspectives, talents, and abilities of a broadly defined citizenry in a nation that must face an array of challenges in a complex world.

Cooper began her formal education after the Civil War at Saint Augustine Normal School and Collegiate Institute (now Saint Augustine University) in North Carolina, earning the equivalent of a high school education and completing the Normal Collegiate School in 1877. During that year, she married fellow student George A. G. Cooper, who became an Episcopal priest. Both continued to teach at Saint Augustine. However, just two years later, George Cooper died. After his death Cooper enrolled in Oberlin College in Ohio, graduating in 1884 (the same year as Mary Church Terrell and Ida A. Gibbs Hunt) with a Bachelor of Science degree in mathematics. Upon graduation, Cooper was appointed chair of languages and science at Wilberforce University. In 1885 she returned to North Carolina, accepting a position at Saint Augustine College, where she taught math, Latin, Greek, and German. These experiences as a college teacher formed the basis for her being awarded a master's degree in mathematics from Oberlin in 1887.

In that same year Cooper was recruited to join the faculty of the M Street School in Washington, DC (the same year that Mary Church Terrell joined this faculty), where she taught mathematics, science, and Latin. The M Street School, established in 1870 as the Preparatory High School for Negro Youth, was one of the first public high schools in the United States for African Americans. It has counted among its faculty some of the best and brightest of the African American intellectual elite. Between 1891 and 1916, it was known as the M Street School, and in 1916 it was renamed in tribute to the esteemed poet Paul Lawrence Dunbar. In 1902 Cooper was named principal of the school, joining a distinctive line of leaders who shepherded generations of academic success for the student body—a reputation securely held by this institution until the integration of public schools in the 1950s, the broadening of educational opportunities for African American students, and the general downturn in subsequent decades in urban development in historic African American communities, especially with regard to differential investments in public schooling.

The era of Cooper's leadership of the M Street School at the turn of the century occurred during the rise and ultimate dominance of the philosophies of Booker T. Washington, who championed the ideology that vocational and industrial training was the most appropriate for African American students rather than a classical liberal arts education. Cooper, however, subscribed to the view, more aligned with W. E. B. Du Bois, that African American students should have full access to all opportunities—including both a college preparatory education and vocational or industrial training. Her emphasis was on creating a strong infrastructure within the community constituted by both professionals and a range of other workers in order to optimize the progress, sustainability, and productivity of the race within the larger society.

As principal of the M Street School, Cooper was steadfast in her commitment to continue the legacies of the school and to offer an excellent college preparatory curriculum in support of higher educational goals for the students, even though other more vocationally oriented courses were also offered. This stance was in opposition to powerful members of the Washington Board of Education who did not support a classical curriculum for African American students. These ideological disagreements fueled a multiyear public battle between Cooper and the board. This battle—coupled with a campaign of personal attacks on her moral character and her leadership abilities as an educator—meant that Cooper was constantly under siege professionally. Despite the strong support that she held among teachers and the Principals' Association, the M Street Alumni Association, and the African American community generally, in 1905 the school board decided not to renew Cooper's contract as principal. Instead of returning to a teaching position at M Street, however, Cooper accepted an invitation to teach at Lincoln University in Jefferson City, Missouri, where she remained until her return to Washington in 1910. At that point, she was rehired at M Street as a teacher and remained there until 1930 when she was named president of Frelinghuysen University, an institution in Washington, DC, that was dedicated to working-class adults.

To be brightly underscored is that Cooper's story went well beyond educational leadership and activism. Throughout these years she engaged actively in research, scholarship, and a range of public discourses. She was invited to deliver talks, for example, at a convocation of Black Episcopal ministers, at meetings of the American Negro Academy, and at the Pan African Conference that was held in 1900 in London. She contributed essays to the periodical press. She published her highly regarded volume *A Voice from the South* (1892) and published, as well, a substantial list of other studies related to sociopolitical concerns (e.g., *The Social Settlement: What It Is, and What It Does*, 1913). Through such activities, Cooper built a stellar and well-deserved reputation as an intellectual leader. In addition, in light of her very active engagement throughout her life in community organizations (e.g., the Bethel Literary and Historical Association, the Phyllis Wheatley YWCA, the Colored Settlement House, the Colored Women's League of Washington, and more), she also built an excellent reputation as a community organizer, leader, and activist. As confirmed by Vivian M. May in *Anna Julia Cooper, Visionary Black Feminist* (2012), throughout this time period Cooper deepened her reputation as an educator and academic administrator, as a public intellectual who contributed to the periodical press, as a very active community leader, and particularly as a leader in women's organizations.

To be noted, however, even with her prominence as an intellectual and community leader, Cooper never gave up on her own ambitious educational goals. In 1911 she enrolled at Columbia University. Her desire for a higher degree had been interrupted over the decades by her life, including family obligations. In the 1880s, she became guardian of John and Lula Love after the death of their parents who were her close friends. After she enrolled at Columbia, she adopted her brother's five grandchildren. Even with such disruptions, Cooper persevered, and in 1924 at sixty-seven years of age, she completed her doctoral work at the Sorbonne in Paris, becoming the fourth African American woman to earn a doctorate. Her dissertation on slavery was written in French but published in English as *Slavery and the French Revolution, 1788–1805.*

In 1892, with the publication of *A Voice from the South*, Cooper clearly established herself as the premier African American woman intellectual of her day and, as asserted by the *Stanford Encyclopedia of Philosophy*, well situated historically as an intellectual leader equivalent to W. E. B. Du Bois, Ralph Ellison, Frantz Fanon, and Toni Morrison. In *A Voice from the South*, Cooper offers a remarkable display of her intellectual depth and breadth and invokes referential connections throughout her volume that underscore how very well educated she was and how nimble she was as a thinker. With regard to her conceptual anchors, Cooper's focus on African American women is richly articulated, drawing attention to the unique position of African American women with regard to race, gender, class, and intellectual development; to their human and civil rights; and to what the race, nation, and world loses without the inclusion of their talents and abilities. In retrospect, this volume has been deemed the first book-length text on Black feminist thought.

In the context of the sexist, racist, and political frameworks in which she existed, and the long-standing issues related to visibility, audibility, and intelligibility for African American women's achievements, it is not surprising that Cooper is not as well known in contemporary culture as some others. In her own day, however, her words were especially inspiring to African American women, as confirmed by the ways in which they embraced her proclamation in *A Voice from the South* that the last decade of the century marked the emergence of a "woman's era," and a time especially well-suited for African American women themselves to claim the agency and authority to be far more aggressive in community-building and nation-building enterprises and to claim space in the world for themselves. In the chapter from *A Voice from the South*, "The Higher Education of Women," presented below, Cooper sets new terms of engagement for African American women, while she acknowledges the need for women and girls to expand their horizons despite ever-present and ongoing challenges, as this generation entered at that moment a new century and a new woman's era.

Anna Julia Haywood Cooper

Excerpt from "The Higher Education of Women," in *A Voice from the South*, The Schomburg Library of Nineteenth Century Black Women Writers (1892; New York: Oxford University Press, 1988), 48–79.

In the very first year of our century, the year 1801, there appeared in Paris a book by Silvain Marechal, entitled "Shall Woman Learn the Alphabet." The book proposes a law prohibiting the alphabet to women, and quotes authorities weighty and various, to prove that the woman who knows the alphabet has already lost part of her womanliness. The author declares that woman can use the alphabet only as Moliere predicted they would, in spelling out the verb *amo*; that they have no occasion to peruse Ovid's *Ars Amoris*, since that is already the ground and limit of their intuitive furnishing; that Madame Guion [a seventeenth-eighteenth-century French mystic] would have been far more adorable had she remained a beautiful ignoramus as nature made her; that Ruth, Naomi, the Spartan woman, the Amazons, Penelope, Andromache, Lucretia, Joan of Arc, Petrarch's Laura, the daughters of Charlemagne, could not spell their names; while Sappho, Aspasia, Madame de Maintenon, and Madame de Stael could read altogether too well for their good; finally, that if women were once permitted to read Sophocles and work with logarithms, or to nibble at any side of the apple of knowledge, there would be an end forever to their sewing on buttons and embroidering slippers.

Please remember this book was published at the beginning of the Nineteenth Century. At the end of the first third, (in the year 1833) one solitary college in America decided to admit women within its sacred precincts, and organized what was called a "Ladies' Course" as well as the regular B.A. or Gentlemen's course.

It was felt to be an experiment—rather dangerous experiment—and was adopted with fear and trembling by the good fathers, who looked as if they had been caught secretly mixing explosive compounds and were guiltily expecting every moment to see the foundations under them shaken and rent and their fair superstructure shattered into fragments.

But the girls came, and there was no upheaval. They performed their tasks modestly and intelligently. Once in a while one or two were found choosing the gentlemen's course. Still no collapse; and the dear, careful, scrupulous, frightened old professors were just getting their hearts out of their throats and preparing to draw one good free breath, when they found they would have to change the names of those courses; for there were as many ladies in the gentlemen's course as in the ladies,' and a distinctively Ladies' Course, inferior in scope and aim to the regular classical course, did not and could not exist.

Other colleges gradually fell into line, and to-day there are one hundred and ninety-eight colleges for women, and two hundred and seven coeducational colleges and universities in the United States alone offering the degree of B.A. to women, and sending out yearly into the arteries of this nation a warm, rich flood of strong, brave, active, energetic, well-equipped, thoughtful women—women quick to see and eager to help the needs of this needy world—women who can think as well as feel, and who feel none the less because they think—women who are none the less tender and true for the parchment scroll they bear in their hands—women who have given a deeper, richer, nobler and grander meaning to the word "womanly" than any one-sided masculine definition could ever have suggested or inspired—women whom the world has long waited for in pain and anguish till there should be at last added to its forces and allowed to permeate its thought the complement of that masculine influence which has dominated it for fourteen centuries.

Since the idea of order and subordination succumbed to barbarian brawn and brutality in the fifth century, the civilized world has been like a child brought up by his father. It has needed the great mother heart to teach it to be pitiful, to love mercy, to succor the weak and care for the lowly.

Whence came this apotheosis of greed and cruelty? Whence this sneaking admiration we all have for bullies and prize-fighters? Whence the self-congratulation of "dominant" races, as if "dominant" meant "righteous" and carried with it a title to inherit the earth? Whence the scorn of so-called weak or unwarlike races and individuals, and the very comfortable assurance that it is their manifest destiny to be wiped out as vermin before this advancing civilization? As if the possession of the Christian graces of meekness, non-resistance and forgiveness, were incompatible with a civilization professedly based on Christianity, the religion of love! Just listen to this little bit of Barbarian brag:

> As for Far Orientals, they are not of those who will survive. Artistic attractive people that they are, their civilization is like their own tree flowers, beautiful blossoms destined never to bear fruit. If these people continue in their old course, their earthly career is closed. Just as surely as morning passes into afternoon, so surely are these races of the Far East, if unchanged, destined to disappear before the advancing nations of the West. Vanish, they will, off the face of the earth, and leave our planet the eventual possession of the dwellers where the day declines. Unless their newly imported ideas really take root, it is from this whole world that Japanese and Koreans, as well as Chinese, will inevitably be excluded. Their Nirvana is already being realized; already, it has wrapped Far Eastern Asia in its winding sheet.–*Soul of the Far East,* P. Lowell

Delightful reflection for "the dwellers where day declines." A spectacle to make the gods laugh, truly, to see the scion of an upstart race by one sweep of his generalizing pen consigning to annihilation one-third the inhabitants of the globe—a people whose civilization was hoary headed before the parent elements that begot his race had advanced beyond nebulosity.

How like Longfellow's Iagoo, we Westerners are, to be sure! In the few hundred years, we have had to strut across our allotted territory and bask in the afternoon sun, we imagine we have exhausted the possibilities of humanity. Verily, we are the people, and after us there is none other. Our God is power; strength, our standard of excellence, inherited from barbarian ancestors through a long line of male progenitors, the Law Salic permitting no feminine modifications.

Says one, "The Chinaman is not popular with us, and we do not like the Negro. It is not that the eyes of the one are set bias, and the other is dark-skinned; but the Chinaman, the Negro is weak—*and Anglo Saxons don't like weakness.*"

The world of thought under the predominant man-influence, unmollified and unrestrained by its complementary force, would become like Daniel's fourth beast: "dreadful and terrible, and *strong* exceedingly"; "it had great iron teeth; it devoured and brake in pieces, and stamped the residue with the feet of it"; and the most independent of us find ourselves ready at times to fall down and worship this incarnation of power.

Mrs. Mary A. Livermore, a woman whom I can mention only to admire, came near shaking my faith a few weeks ago in my theory of thinking woman's mission to put in the tender and sympathetic chord in nature's grand symphony, and counteract, or better, harmonize the diapason of mere strength and might.

She was dwelling on the Anglo-Saxon genius for power and his contempt for weakness, and described a scene in San Francisco which she had witnessed.

The incorrigible animal known as the American small-boy had pounced upon a simple, unoffending Chinaman, who was taking home his work, and had emptied the beautifully laundried contents of his basket into the ditch. "And," said she, "when that great man stood there and blubbered before that crowd of lawless urchins, to any one of whom he might have taught a lesson with his two firsts, *I didn't much care.*"

This is said like a man! It grates harshly. It smacks of the worship of the beast. It is contempt for weakness, and taken out of its setting it seems to contradict my theory. It either shows that one of the highest exponents of the Higher Education can be at times untrue to the instincts I have ascribed to the thinking woman and to the contribution she is to add to the civilized world, or else the influence she wields upon our civilization may be potent without being necessarily and always direct and conscious. The latter is the case. Her voice may strike a false note, but her whole being is musical with the vibrations of human suffering. Her tongue may parrot over the cold conceits that some man has taught her, but her heart is aglow with sympathy and loving kindness, and she cannot be true to her real self without giving out these elements into the forces of the world. . . .

There is, then, a real and special influence of woman. An influence subtle and often involuntary, an influence so intimately interwoven in, so intricately interpenetrated by the masculine influence of the time that it is often difficult to extricate the delicate meshes and analyze and identify the closely clinging fibers. And yet, without this influence—so long as woman sat with bandaged eyes and manacled hands, fast bound in the clamps of ignorance and inaction, the world of thought moved in its orbit like the revolutions of the moon: with one face (the man's face) always out, so that the spectator could not distinguish whether it was disc or sphere.

Now I claim that it is the prevalence of the Higher Education among women, the making it a common everyday affair for women to reason and think and express their thought, the training and stimulus which enable and encourage women to administer to the world the bread it needs as well as the sugar it cries for; in short it is the transmitting the potential forces of her soul into dynamic factors that has given symmetry and completeness to the world's agencies. So only could it be consummated that Mercy, the lesson she teaches, and Truth, the task man has set himself, should meet together: that righteousness, or rightness, man's ideal,—and *peace*, its necessary "other half," should kiss each other. . . .

Now please understand me. I do not ask you to admit that these benefactions and virtues are the exclusive possession of women, or even that women are their chief and only advocates. It may be a man who formulates and makes them vocal. It may be, and often is, a man who weeps over the wrongs and struggles for the amelioration: but that man has imbibed those impulses from a mother rather than from a father and is simply materializing and giving back to the world in tangible form the ideal love and tenderness, devotion and care that have cherished and nourished the helpless period of his own existence..

All I claim is that there is a feminine as well as a masculine side to truth; that these are related not as inferior and superior, not as better or worse, not as weaker and stronger, but as complements—complements in one necessary and symmetric whole. That as the man is more noble in reason, so the woman is more quick in sympathy. That as he is indefatigable in pursuit of abstract truth, so is she in caring for the interests by the way—striving tenderly and lovingly that, not one of the least of these "little ones" should perish. That while we not unfrequently see women who reason, we say, with the coolness and precision of a man, and men as considerate of helplessness as a woman, still there is a general consensus of mankind that the one trait is essentially masculine and the other as peculiarly feminine. That both are needed to be worked into the training of children, in order that our boys may supplement their virility by tenderness and sensibility, and our girls may round out their gentleness by strength and self-reliance. That, as both are alike necessary in giving symmetry to the individual, so a nation or a race will degenerate into mere emotionalism on the one hand, or bullyism on the other, if dominated by either exclusively; lastly, and most emphatically, that the feminine factor can have its proper effect only through woman's development and education so that she may fitly and intelligently stamp her force on the forces of her day, and add her modicum to the riches of the world's thought.

> For woman's cause is man's: they rise or sink
> Together, dwarfed or godlike, bond or free:
> For she that out of Lethe scales with man
> The shining steps of nature, shares with man
> His nights, his days, moves with him to one goal.
> If she be small, slight-natured, miserable,
> How shall men grow?
> * * * Let her make herself her own
> To give or keep, to live and learn and be
> All that not harms distinctive womanhood.
> For woman is not undeveloped man
> But diverse: could we make her as the man
> Sweet love were slain; his dearest bond is this,
> Not like to like, but like in difference.
> Yet in the long years liker must they grow;
> The man be more of woman she of man;
> He gain in sweetness and in moral height,
> Nor lose the wrestling thews that throw the world:
> She mental breadth, not fail in childward care,
> Nor lose the childlike in the larger mind;
> Till at the last she set herself to man
> Like perfect music unto noble words.

Now you will argue, perhaps, and rightly, that higher education for women is not a modern idea, and that, if that is the means of setting free and invigorating the long desired feminine force in the world, it has already had a trial and should, in the past, have produced some of these glowing effects. Sappho, the bright sweet singer of Lesbos, "the violet-crowned, pure, sweetly smiling Sappho" as Alcaeus calls her, chanted her lyrics and poured forth her soul nearly six centuries before Christ, in notes as full and free, as passionate and eloquent as did ever Archilochus or Anacreon.

Aspasia, that earliest queen of the drawing room, a century later ministered to the intellectual entertainment of Socrates and the leading wits and philosophers of her time. Indeed, to her is attributed, by the best critics, the authorship of one of the most noted speeches ever delivered by Pericles.

Later on, during the Renaissance period, women were professors in mathematics, physics, metaphysics, and the classic languages in Bologna, Pavia, Padua, and Brescia. Olympia Fulvia Morata, of Ferrara, a most interesting character, whose magnificent library was destroyed in 1553 in the invasion of Schweinfurt by Albert of Brandenburg, had acquired a most extensive education. It is said that this wonderful girl gave lectures on classical subjects in her sixteenth year, and had even before that written several very remarkable Greek and Latin poems, and what is also to the point, she married a professor at Heidelberg, and became a *help-meet for him*.

[Cooper continues to amplify points regarding a more holistic view of the capacities of women and men and to emphasize the need for opportunities for development with both so that the world can benefit from the contributions and collaborations of all, regardless of gender.]

Now I would that my task ended here. Having shown that a great want of the world in the past has been a feminine force; that that force can have its full effect only through the untrammelled development of woman; that such development, while it gives her to the world and to civilization, does not necessarily remove her from the home and fireside; finally that while past centuries have witnessed sporadic instances of this higher growth, still it was reserved for the latter half of the nineteenth century to render it common and general enough to be effective; I might close with a glowing prediction of what the twentieth century may expect from this heritage of twin forces—the masculine battered and toil worn as a grim veteran after centuries of warfare, but still strong, active, and vigorous, ready to help with his hard-won experience the young recruit rejoicing in her newly found freedom, who so confidently places her hand in his with mutual pledges to redeem the ages.

And so the twain upon the skirts of Time,
Sit side by side, full-summed in all their powers,
Dispensing harvest, sowing the To-be,
Self-reverent each and reverencing each.

Fain would I follow them, but duty is nearer home. The high ground of generalities is alluring but my pen is devoted to a special cause: and with a view to further enlightenment on the achievements of the century for THE HIGHER EDUCATION OF COLORED WOMEN, I wrote a few days ago to the colleges which admit women and asked how many colored women had completed the B.A. course in each during its entire history. These are the figures returned: Fisk leads the way with twelve; Oberlin next with five; Wilberforce, four; Ann Arbor and Wellesley three each, Livingstone two, Atlanta one, Howard, as yet none.

I then asked the principal of the Washington High School [the M Street School] how many out of a large number of female graduates from his school had chosen to go forward and take a collegiate course. He replied that but one had ever done so, and she was then in Cornel.

Others ask questions too, sometimes, and I was asked a few years ago by a white friend, "How is it that the men of your race seem to outstrip the women in mental attainment?" "Oh," I said, "so far as it is true, the men, I suppose, from the life they lead gain more by contact; and so far as it is only apparent, I think the women are more quiet. They don't feel called to mount a barrel and harangue by the hour every time they imagine they have produced an idea."

But I am sure there is another reason which I did not at that time see fit to give. The atmosphere, the standards, the requirements of our little world do not afford any special stimulus to female development.

It seems hardly a gracious thing to say, but it strikes me as true, that while our men seem thoroughly abreast of the times on almost every other subject, when they strike the woman question they drop back into sixteenth century logic. They leave nothing to be desired generally in regard to gallantry and chivalry, but they actually do not seem sometimes to have outgrown that old contemporary of chivalry—the idea that women may stand on pedestals or live in doll houses, (if they happen to have them) but they must not furrow their brows with thought or attempt to help men tug at the great questions of the world. I fear the majority of colored men do not yet think it worth while that women aspire to higher education. Not many will subscribe to the "advanced" ideas of Grant Allen already quoted. The three R's, a little music and a good deal of dancing, a first rate dress-maker and a bottle of magnolia balm, are quite enough generally to render charming any woman possessed of tact and the capacity for worshipping masculinity.

My readers will pardon my illustrating my point and also giving a reason for the fear that is in me, by a little bit of personal experience. When a child I was put into a school near home that professed to be normal and collegiate, i.e. to prepare teachers for colored youth, furnish candidates for the ministry, and offer collegiate training for those who should be ready for it. Well, I found after a while that I had a good deal of time on my hands. I had devoured what was put before me, and, like Oliver Twist, was looking around to ask for more. I constantly felt (as I suppose many an ambitious girl has felt) a thumping from within unanswered by any beckoning from without. Class after class was organized for these ministerial candidates (many of them men who had been preaching before I was born). Into every one of these classes I was expected to go, with the sole intent, I thought at the time, of enabling the dear old principal, as he looked from the vacant countenances of his sleepy old class over to where I sat, to get off his solitary pun—his never-failing pleasantry, especially in hot weather—which was, as he called out "Any one!" to the effect that "any one" then meant "Annie one."

Finally a Greek class was to be formed. My inspiring preceptor informed me that Greek had never been taught in the school, but that he was going to form a class *for the candidates for the ministry*, and if I liked I might join it. I replied—humbly I hope, as became a female of the human species—that I would like very much to study Greek, and that I was thankful for the opportunity, and so it went on. A boy, however meager his equipment and shallow his pretentions, had only to declare a floating intention to study theology and he could get all the support, encouragement and stimulus he needed, be absolved from work and invested beforehand with all the dignity of his far away office. While a self-supporting girl had to struggle on by teaching in the summer and working after school hours to keep up with her board bills, and actually to fight her way against positive discouragements to the higher education; till one such girl one day flared out and told the principal "the only mission opening before a girl in his school was to marry one of those candidates." He said he didn't know but it was. And when at last that same girl announced her desire and intention to go to college it was received with about the same incredulity and dismay as if a brass button on one of those candidate's coats had propounded a new method for squaring the circle or trisecting the arc.

Now this is not fancy. It is a simple unvarnished photograph, and what I believe was not in those days exceptional in colored schools, and I ask the men and women who are teachers and co-workers for the highest interests of the race, that they give the girls a chance! We might as well expect to grow trees from leaves as hope to build up a civilization or manhood without taking into consideration our women and the home life made by them, which must be the root and ground of the whole matter. Let us insist then on special encouragement for the education of our women and special care in their training. Let our girls feel that we expect something more of them than that they merely look pretty and appear well in society. Teach them that there is a race with special needs which they and only they can help; that the world needs and is already asking for their trained, efficient forces. Finally, if there is an ambitious girl with pluck and brain to take the higher education, encourage her to make the most of it. Let there be the same flourish of trumpets and clapping of hands as when a boy announces his determination to enter the lists; and then, as you know that she is physically the weaker of the two, don't stand from under and leave her to buffet the waves alone. Let her know that your heart is following her, that your hand, though she sees it not, is ready to support her. To be plain, I mean let money be raised and scholarships be founded in our colleges and universities for self-supporting, worthy young women, to offset and balance the aid that can always be found for boys who will take theology.

The earnest well trained Christian young woman, as a teacher, as a home-maker, as wife, mother, or silent influence even, is as potent a missionary agency among our people as is the theologian; and I claim that at the present stage of our development in the South she is even more important and necessary.

Let us then, here and now, recognize this force and resolve to make the most of it—not the boys less, but the girls more.

MRS. JOSEPHINE ST. PIERRE RUFFIN,
Prominent Woman of Boston, Leader of the Club Movement Among Colored Women.

Figure 6.2: Josephine St. Pierre Ruffin

Josephine St. Pierre Ruffin

Josephine St. Pierre Ruffin (1842–1924) was the youngest of six children born into what during this era was termed an "amalgamated" family (African, European, French, British, and Narragansett), a family that had been living free for several generations in Taunton, Massachusetts, and then in Boston. Her father was John St. Pierre, a successful clothier whose family was originally from Martinique, and her mother was an English-born white woman, Elizabeth Matilda Menhenick, from Cornwall, England. They were actively engaged within a lively circle of abolitionists and transcendentalists. For example, her father was a founding member of the African Methodist Episcopal Zion Church, with its own activist roots, and her parents fought for the desegregation of Boston public schools.

Ruffin was educated in the integrated public schools of Salem, Massachusetts, rather than in Boston where there was no such opportunity. Subsequently, she attended a finishing school in Boston and received two years of private tutoring in New York. In 1858 at the age of sixteen, Ruffin married George Lewis Ruffin, himself both freeborn and multiracial. He was the first African American graduate of Harvard University Law School and ultimately the first African American judge in the state of Massachusetts. Even though Ruffin married at this young age, she had already been giving speeches in abolitionist circles. Her activist pursuits continued after marriage and throughout the births of their five children, four of whom lived to adulthood.

Shortly after their marriage, the Ruffins moved to England to escape the restrictions of a slaveholding society. They returned, however, with the advent of the Civil War to work for freedom. During the Civil War, Ruffin and her husband engaged in a range of civic services. For example, she recruited soldiers for the Fifty-Fourth and Fifty-Sixth Union regiments and volunteered to care for sick and wounded Union soldiers through the US Sanitary Commission, which later became the Red Cross. After the war, her commitments continued. In 1875, she established and headed the West End Relief Association to aid destitute children. She was cofounder and first president of the Colored Women's Refugee Aid Society to assist African American refugees fleeing the post-Reconstruction South, and in 1879, she organized the Boston Kansas Relief Association to send clothing and money to African Americans fleeing from the South to Kansas.

Beyond such organizational activities, the Ruffin home was a gathering place for the African American students at Harvard University, her husband's alma mater. She hosted regularly opportunities for the students to build community among themselves and, in the company of such others, to sharpen their critical perceptions of the world around them. A member of this group who would go on to achieve national and international prominence as an academic and intellectual leader was W. E. B. Du Bois. Included in Ruffin's long list of sociopolitical advocacy and leadership was her growing experience and expertise as a journalist. She was a contributor to the *Boston Courant*, an African American newspaper, and developed a reputation for excellence in this arena, becoming ultimately the first African American woman member of the New England Women's Press Association. In like manner, she was a member of the New England Women's Club, where she interacted with white clubwomen such as Julia Ward Howe, Lucy Stone, Ednah Cheney, and Abby Morton Diaz, and she was actively involved, as well, with the Massachusetts State Federation of Women's Clubs and the

General Federation of Women's Clubs, where her cross-race network was broadened even more.

In 1886 Ruffin's husband, George, died, but she didn't cut back on her activist agenda. In 1887 she was elected president of the West End League of the Massachusetts Woman Suffrage Association. In 1889 she was a member of the executive committee of Boston's Colored National League, a nonpartisan organization devoted to the welfare of the race. In 1893, however, she made the most impactful move of her career as activist and leader. She attended the tri-state gathering for Ida B. Wells at Lyric Hall in New York. After this event Ruffin hosted Wells in Boston, creating a springboard from which she, her daughter Florida Ruffin Ridley, and her friend Maria Baldwin took the lead in founding Boston's Woman's Era Club (ultimately renamed the New Era Club). Under the umbrella of that organization, Ruffin started the *Woman's Era* newspaper. Owned, edited, and published by Ruffin herself, this newspaper was the first one in the United States to be designed by, for, and about African American women.

In other words, by 1893 at the age of fifty-one, Ruffin had built a public reputation as a highly respected sociopolitical leader with professional expertise and as a person with a diverse social network—locally, nationally, and internationally. As a well-connected and very experienced warrior for civil and human rights, she had demonstrated over the decades since she was a teenage speaker for abolitionism that she was a clever and passionate rhetor who was very much accustomed to working across races for social action and reform. With this array of knowledge, experience, and expertise, she was well positioned (and had the personal financial resources) to push the momentum of African American women's sociopolitical activism and leadership forward into the twentieth century. As illustrated below by the two editorial selections from her newspaper, *Woman's Era*, and by her opening address as the convener of the first national gathering of African American women in Boston in 1896, Ruffin had a facility for organized strategic action and a compelling vision of a future in which African American women are able to participate in society with all the rights of citizenship and with the freedom and encouragement to use their talents and abilities fully, including in community-building and nation-building enterprises—arenas where she herself was, quite obviously, outstanding.[1]

Chapter 6

Josephine St. Pierre Ruffin

"Greeting," *Woman's Era* 1.1 (March 24, 1894)

Of the makers of papers there be not a few, and an additional one may seem a superfluity unless a vacant spot is found in an apparently already overgrown field.

Such a void, we think, exists, and it is to help fill it that we presume to make our first bow as editors of THE WOMAN'S ERA, to a long suffering but indulgent public. The need of such a journal has long been felt as a medium of intercourse and sympathy between the women of all races and conditions; especially true is this, of the educated and refined, among the colored women, members of which class may be found in every state from Maine to Florida, but in nearly all of these places an important factor, and one that receives little or no recognition, and the one more than all others which prevents her from making the most of herself and taking her legitamate [*sic*] place among the advanced women, is the limitation of—her surroundings and the circumscribed sphere in which she must move. The impossibility of mingling freely with people of culture and learning, and so carrying on the mental growth begun in schools and colleges, shuts her in with her books but shuts her out of physical touch with the great world of art, science and letters which is open to all other ambitious women. In fact the stumbling block in the way of even the most cultured colored woman is the narrowness of her environment. But let the fact be emph[asized] that in the [undecipherable] a large and growing factor in the intellectual as well as industrial life of the country; and the strength of the chain of woman's advancement will be determined by the strength of this weak link. It is to help strengthen this link by hastening on the day when a keener appreciation of the hindrances of this class and a better understanding between all classes shall exist that this little venture is sent out on its mission.

"Let Us Confer Together," *Woman's Era* 2.3 (June 1895)

The coming together of our women from all over the country for consultation, for conference, for the personal exchange of greeting, which means so much in the way of encouragement and inspiration, has been a burning desire in the breasts of the colored women in every section of the United States.

The matter has been discussed and re-discussed. Of some things all are convinced—the need of such a conference is great, the benefit to be derived inevitable and inestimable. In view of this, we, the women of the Woman's Era Club of Boston, send forth a call to our sisters all over the country, members of all clubs, societies, associations, or circles to meet with us in conference in this city of Boston.

And we urge upon all clubs, societies, associations and circles to take immediate action, looking towards the sending of delegates to this convention.

Boston has been selected as a meeting place because it has seemed to be the general opinion that here, and here only can be found the atmosphere which would best interpret and represent us, our position, our needs and our aims. One of the pressing needs of our cause is the education of the public to a just appreciation of us, and only here can we gain the attention upon which so much depends.

It is designed to hold the convention three days, the first of which will be given up to business, the second and third to the consideration of vital questions concerning our moral, mental, physical and financial growth and well-being, these to be presented through addresses by representative women.

Although this matter of a convention has been talked over for some time, the subject has been precipitated by a letter to England, written by a southern editor, and reflecting upon the moral character of all colored women; this letter is too indecent for publication, but a copy of it is sent with this call to all the women's bodies throughout the country. Read this document carefully and use discriminatingly and decide if it be not time for us to stand before the world and declare ourselves and our principles.

The time is short, but everything is ripe; and remember, earnest women can do anything.

A circular letter will be sent you in the meantime. Let us hear at once from you.

"Address of Josephine St. P. Ruffin, President of Conference," *Woman's Era* 2.5 (August 1895)

It is with especial joy and pride that I welcome you all to this, our first conference. It is only recently that women have waked up to the importance of meeting in council, and great as has been the advantage of women *generally*, and important as it is and has been that they should confer, the necessity has not been nearly so great, matters at stake not nearly so vital, as that we, bearing peculiar blunders, suffering under especial hardships, enduring peculiar privations, should meet for a "good talk" among ourselves. Although rather hastily called, you as well as I can testify how long and how earnestly a conference has been thought of and hoped for and even prepared for. These women's clubs, which have sprung up all over the country, built and run upon broad, strong lines, have all been a preparation, small conferences in themselves, and their spontaneous birth and enthusiastic support have been little less than inspirational on the part of our women and a general preparation for a large union such as it is hoped this conference will lead to. Five years ago we had no colored women's clubs outside of those formed for special work; to-day, with little over a month's notice, we are able to call representatives from more than twenty clubs. It is a good showing, it stands for much, it shows that we are truly American women, with all the adaptability, readiness to seize and possess our opportunities, willingness to do our part for good as other American women.

The reasons why we should confer are so apparent that it would seem hardly necessary to enumerate them, and yet there is none of them but demand our serious consideration. In the first place we need to feel the cheer and inspiration of meeting each other. We need to gain the courage and fresh life that comes from the mingling of congenial souls, of those working for the same ends. Next, we need to talk over not only those things which are of vital importance to us as women, but also the things that are of especial interest to us as colored women, the training of our children, openings for our boys and girls, how they can be prepared for occupations and occupations may be found or opened for them, what we especially can do in the moral education of the race with which we are identified, our mental elevation and physical development, the home training it is necessary to give our children in order to prepare them to meet the peculiar conditions in which they shall find themselves, how to make the most of our own, to some extent, limited opportunities, these are some of our own peculiar questions to be discussed. Besides these are the general questions of the day, which we cannot afford to be indifferent to: temperance, morality, the higher education, hygienic and domestic questions. If these things need the serious consideration of women more advantageously placed by reason of all the aid to right thinking and living with which they are surrounded, surely we, with everything to pull us back, to hinder us in developing, need to take every opportunity and means for the thoughtful consideration which shall lead to wise action.

I have left the strongest reasons for our conferring together until the last. All over America there is to be found a large and growing class of earnest, intelligent, progressive colored women, women who, if not leading full useful lives, are only waiting for the opportunity to do so, many of them warped and cramped for lack of opportunity, not only to do more but be more; and yet, if an estimate of the colored women of America is called for, the inevitable reply, glibly given, is "For the most part ignorant and immoral, some exceptions, of course, but these don't count."

Now, for the sake of the thousands of self-sacrificing young women teaching and preaching in lonely southern backwoods for the noble army of mothers who have given birth to these girls, mothers whose intelligence is only limited by their opportunity to get at books, for the sake of the fine cultured women who have carried off the honors in school here and often abroad, for the sake of our own dignity, the dignity of our race, and the future good name of our children, it is "mete, right and our bounded duty" to stand forth and declare ourselves and principles, to teach an ignorant and suspicious world that our aims and interests are identical with those of all good aspiring women. Too long have we been silent under unjust and unholy charges; we cannot expect to have them removed until we disprove them through ourselves. It is not enough to try to disprove unjust charges through individual effort, that never goes any further. Year after year southern women have protested against the admission of colored women into any national organization on the ground of the immorality of these women, and because all refutation has only been tried by individual work the charge has never been crushed, as it could and should have been at the first. Now with an army of organized women standing for purity and mental worth, we in ourselves deny the charge and open the eyes of the world to a state of affairs to which they have been blind, often willfully so, and the very fact that the charges, audaciously and flippantly made, as they often are, are of so humiliating and delicate a nature, serves to protect the accuser by driving the helpless accused into mortified silence. It is to break this silence, not by noisy protestation of what we are not, but by a dignified showing of what we are and hope to become that we are impelled to take this step, to make of this gathering all object lesson to the world. For many and apparent reasons, it is especially fitting that the women of the race take the lead in this movement but for all this we recognize the necessity of the sympathy of our husbands, brothers and fathers.

Our woman's movement is woman's movement in that it is led and directed by women for the good of women and men, for the benefit of *all* humanity, which is more than any one branch or section of it. We want, we ask the active interest of our men, and, too, we are not drawing the color line; we are women, American women, as intensely interested in all that pertains to us as such as all other American women; we are not alienating or withdrawing, we are only coming to the front, willing to join any others in the same work and cordially inviting and welcoming any others to join us.

If there is any one thing I would especially enjoy upon this conference it is union and earnestness. The questions that are to come before us are of too much import to be weakened by my trivialities or personalities. If any differences arise let them be quickly settled, with the feeling that we are all workers to the same end, to elevate and dignify colored American womanhood. This conference will not be what I expect if it does not show the wisdom, indeed the absolute necessity of a national organization of our women. Every year new questions coming up will prove it to us. This hurried, almost informal convention does not begin to meet our needs, it is only a beginning, made here in dear old Boston, where the scales of justice and generosity hang evenly balanced, and where the people "dare be true" to their best instincts and stand ready to lend aid and sympathy to worthy struggles. It is hoped and believed that from this will spring an organization that will in truth bring in a new era to the colored women of America.

Figure 6.3: Mary Church Terrell

Mary Church Terrell

Mary Eliza Church Terrell (1863–1954) was born in Memphis, Tennessee, the daughter of former slaves. Her mother, Louisa Ayres Church, was the owner of a hair salon, and her father, Robert Reed Church, was a leader in business and real estate and one of the first African American millionaires in the United States. As one of two children, Terrell lived a life of privilege even though her parents divorced early during her childhood.

Terrell attended elementary school at the Antioch College Laboratory School in Yellow Springs, Ohio, and high school at Oberlin Academy. She earned a bachelor of arts degree in classical languages at Oberlin College in 1884 (the same year as Anna Julia Cooper) and earned a master's degree in education from Oberlin in 1888. With this record, Terrell was among the first cohort of African American women in the United States to earn degrees from a US institution of higher education.

After earning the bachelor's degree, Terrell taught for two years at Wilberforce University in Ohio before moving to Washington, DC, in 1887 to join the faculty of the highly respected M Street School (the same year that Cooper joined). There she met and married Robert Terrell in 1891, a colleague who ultimately became the principal of the school. Robert Terrell was a magna cum laude graduate of Harvard University (1884). He earned an LLB in 1889 and an LLM in 1893 from the Howard University School of Law. He left the M Street School to practice law, became a friend and associate of Booker T. Washington, and ultimately became the first African American municipal judge in Washington, DC.

Active in many civic services as a member of the African American elite in Washington, in 1892 Terrell was motivated to become even more active sociopolitically when a friend from her hometown of Memphis, Tennessee, was murdered. Thomas Moss was a successful business owner. Along with two of his partners, he was targeted by white citizens and lynched in a horrific manner, a case of terrorism that was made famous by Ida B. Wells-Barnett. At the time Wells-Barnett was living and working as a journalist in Memphis. This case launched her rise as a national and international crusader for justice.

Over the decades that followed, Terrell's activism and leadership included her collaboration in 1892 with other African American women leaders of Washington to form the Colored Women's League. In addition, she participated actively in the National American Woman Suffrage Association, where she spoke out against sexism, racism, and issues at the intersections of these two challenges in both national and international venues. She also participated in the Republican Party, serving as president of the Women's Republican League in Washington, DC. She was the first African American woman to be appointed to the Washington Board of Education, serving from 1895 to 1901 and again from 1906 to 1911.

In 1895, in response to the call by Josephine St. Pierre Ruffin for a national conference for African American women leaders, the Colored Women's League joined hands with the New Era Club of Boston and sixteen other clubs across the nation, with the result that the National Federation of Afro-American Women was formed. In 1896, in an effort not to have competing national organizations, the Colored Women's League and the National Federation of Afro-American Women merged to form the National Association of Colored Women (NACW). Terrell was elected the first president of the new organization in a very competitive race among women leaders of the time. Below is her inaugural address as president, titled "The Duty of the National Association of Colored Women to the Race."

In this speech, Terrell acknowledges the hard and consistent work that women of the race had been doing and were continuing to do to make sure that their organized collective efforts for community support and social change were solidly grounded, and she shared a vision of present and future action. With this vision, she set in motion an ambitious agenda for the ongoing work of her group, recognizing the limitations in the United States of woman's sphere as well as long-standing constraints to agency and authority for people of African descent. Terrell's focus was on advocacy, activism, and leadership for African American women of consequence, on any and all issues affecting their race and gender. In effect, in 1896 through the work of the NACW, Terrell took the helm in launching a legacy of leadership and action that continues now into the twenty-first century.

Mary Church Terrell

"The Duty of the National Association of Colored Women to the Race," in *Quest for Equality: The Life and Writings of Mary Aliza Church Terrell, 1863–1954*, ed. Beverly Washington Jones (1900; Brooklyn: Carlson, 1990), 139–50.

The National Association of Colored Women had at its second convention every reason to rejoice and be exceedingly glad. From its birth in July, 1896, till the present moment its growth has been steady and its march ever onward and upward to the goal of its ambition.

An infant of but three years is this organization, over which I have had the honor to preside, ever since it first saw the light of day in the Capital of the Nation, and yet in those short years it has accomplished a vast amount of good. So tenderly has this child of the organized womanhood of the race been nurtured, and so wisely ministered unto by all who have watched prayerfully and waited patiently for its development, that it comes before you to-day a child hale, hearty and strong, of which its fond mothers have every reason to be proud.

As individuals, colored women have always been ambitious for their race. From the day when shackles first fell from their fettered limbs till now, they have often, single-handed and alone, struggled against the most desperate and discouraging odds, in order to secure for their loved ones and themselves that culture of the head and heart for which they hungered and thirsted so long in vain. But it dawned upon them finally, that individuals working alone, or scattered here and there in small companies, might be ever so honest in purpose, so indefatigable in labor, so conscientious about methods, and so wise in projecting plans, yet they would accomplish little, compared with the possible achievement of many individuals, all banded together throughout the entire land, with heads and hearts fixed on the same high purpose and hands joined in united strength. As a result of a general realization of this fact, the National Association of Colored Women was born.

Though we are young in years, and have been unable to put into execution some plans on which we had built high hopes, the fruits of organized effort are already apparent to all. If in the short space of three years the National Association had done nothing but give an impressive object lesson in the necessity for, and the efficacy of, organization, it would have proved its reason for existence and its right to live; but, seriously handicapped though we have been, both because of the lack of experience and lack of funds, our efforts have for the most part been crowned with success.

In the kindergartens established by some of our organizations, children have been cultivated and trained. A sanatorium with a training school for nurses has been set on such a firm foundation in a Southern city, and has given such abundant proof of its utility and necessity, that the municipal government has voted it an annual appropriation of several hundred dollars. To our poor benighted sisters in the black belt of Alabama we have gone, and have been both a help and a comfort to these women, through the darkness of whose ignorance of everything that makes life sweet or worth the living, no ray of light would have penetrated but for us. We have taught them the A, B, C, of living, by showing them how to make their huts more habitable and decent with the small means at their command, and how to care for themselves and their families more in accordance with the laws of health. Plans for aiding the indigent, orphaned and aged have been projected and in some instances have been carried to a successful execution. Mother's meetings have been generally held and sewing classes formed. Abuses like lynching, the convict lease system and the Jim Crow car laws have been discussed with a view of doing something to remedy these evils. In Chicago, magnificent work has been done by the Illinois Federation of Colored Women's Clubs through whose instrumentality schools have been visited, truant children looked after, parents and teachers urged to co-operate with each other, public institutions investigated, rescue and reform work engaged in to reclaim unfortunate women and tempted girls, garments cut, made and distributed to the needy poor. In short, what our hands have found to do, that we have cheerfully done. It is not, therefore, because I feel that the National Association of Colored Women has been derelict, or has failed, that I shall discuss its duty to our race, but because I wish to emphasize some special lines of work in which it is already engaging, but to which I would pledge its more hearty support.

The more closely I study the relation of this Association to the race, the more clearly defined becomes its duty to the children.

Believing in the saving grace of the kindergarten for our little ones, at our first convention, as some may remember, I urged with all the earnestness that I could command, that the Association should consider the establishment of kindergartens as the special mission it is called upon to fulfill. The importance of engaging extensively in this effort to uplift the children, particularly those to whom the opportunity of learning by contact what is true and good and beautiful could come through no other source, grows on me more and more every day. Through the kindergarten alone, which teaches in lessons in the most impressionable years of childhood, shall we be able to save countless thousands of our little ones who are going to destruction before our very eyes. To some the task of establishing kindergartens may seem too herculean for the Association to undertake, because of the great expense involved. Be that as it may, we shall never accomplish the good it is in our power to do, nor shall we discharge our obligation to the race, until we engage in this work in those sections at least where it is most needed.

In many cities and towns the kindergarten has already been incorporated in the public school system. Here it may not be necessary for the Association to work. But wherever the conditions are such that our children are deprived of the training which they can receive from the kindergarten alone, deprived of that training which from the very nature of the case, they so sorely need, there the Association should establish these schools, from which so much benefit to our little ones will accrue.

Side by side in importance with the kindergarten stands the day nursery, a charity of which there is an imperative need among us. Thousands of our wage-earning mothers with large families dependent upon them for support are obliged to leave their infants all day to be cared for either by young brothers or sisters, who know nothing about it, or by some good-natured neighbor, who promises much, but who does little. Some of these infants are locked alone in a room from the time the mother leaves in the morning until she returns at night. Their suffering is, of course, unspeakable. Not long ago, I read in a southern newspaper that an infant thus locked alone in a room all day, while its mother went out to wash, had cried itself to death. Recently I have had under direct observation a day nursery, established for infants of working women, and I have been shocked at some of the miserable little working women, and I have been shocked at some of the miserable little specimens of humanity brought in by mothers, who had been obliged to board them out with either careless or heartless people. In one instance the hands and legs of a poor little mite of only fourteen months had been terribly drawn and twisted with rheumatism contracted by sleeping in a cold room with no fire during the severe winter, while the family with whom it boarded enjoyed comfortable quarter overhead. And so I might go on enumerating cases, showing how terrible is the suffering of infants of working women, who have no one with whom to leave them, while they earn their daily bread. Establishing day nurseries is clearly a practical charity, of the need of which there is abundant proof in every community where our women may be found.

What a vast amount of good would be accomplished, if by every branch of the Association, a home were provided for the infants of working women, who no matter how tender may be their affection for their little ones, are forced by stern necessity to neglect them all day themselves, and at best, can only entrust them to others, from whom, in the majority of cases, they do not receive the proper care. It would not only save the life, and preserve the health of many a poor little one, but it would speak eloquently of our interest in our sisters, whose lot is harder than our own, but to whom we should give unmistakable proof of our regard, our sympathy, and our willingness to render any assistance in our power. When one thinks of the slaughter of the innocents which is occurring with pitiless persistency every day, and reflects upon how many are maimed for life through neglect, how many there are whose intellects are clouded because of the treatment received during their helpless infancy, establishing day nurseries can seem neither unnecessary nor far-fetched; but must appeal directly to us all. No great amount is required to establish a day nursery, and part of the money necessary for its maintenance might be secured by charging each of the mothers who take advantage of it a small sum. In no other way could the investment of the same amount of money bring such large and blessed returns.

To each and every branch of the Association, then, I recommend the establishment of a day nursery, as a means through which it can render one of the greatest services possible to humanity and the race. . . .

Let us remember that we are banded together to do good, to work most vigorously and conscientiously upon that which will redound most to the welfare and progress of the race. If that be true, I recommend to you, I plead to you, for the children, for those who will soon represent us, for those by whom as a race we shall soon stand or fall in the estimation of the world, for those upon whom the hope of every people must necessarily be built. As an Association, let us devote ourselves enthusiastically, conscientiously, to the children, with their warm little hearts, their susceptible little minds, their malleable, pliable characters. Through the children of to-day, we must build the foundation of the next generation upon such a rock of integrity, morality, and strength, both of body and mind, that the floods of proscription, prejudice, and persecution may descend upon it in torrents, and yet it will not be moved. We hear a great deal about the race problem, and how to solve it. This theory, that and the other, may be advanced, but the real solution of the race problem, both so far as we, who are oppressed and those who oppress us are concerned, lies in the children.

Let no one suppose that I would have a large organization like ours, a body of one idea, with no thought, plan or purpose except that which centers about the children. I am an optimist, because I see how we are broadening and deepening out into the various channels of generosity and beneficence, which indicates what a high state of civilization we have already reached. Homes for the orphaned and aged must be established; sanatoriums, hospitals, and training schools for nurses founded; unfortunate women and tempted girls encircled by the loving arms of those who would woo them back to the path of rectitude and virtue; classes formed for cultivating the mind; schools of domestic science opened in every city and village in which our women and girls may be found. All this is our duty, all this is an obligation, which we should discharge as soon as our means will permit. But in connection with such work let us not neglect, let us not forget, the children, remembering that when we love and protect the little ones, we follow the footsteps of Him, who when He wished to paint the most beautiful picture of Beulah land it is possible of the human mind to conceive, pointed to the children and said—"Of such is the kingdom of heaven."

It is frequently charged against the more favored among us who have been blessed with advantages of education and moral training superior to those enjoyed by the majority, that they hold themselves too much aloof from the less fortunate of their people. Without discussing the reasons for such a condition of things, it must be patent to the most careless observer that the more intelligent and influential among us do not exert themselves as much as they should to uplift those beneath them, as it is plainly their duty to do.

It has been suggested, and very appropriately, I think, that this Association should take as its motto—*Lifting as we climb*. In no way could we live up to such a sentiment better than by coming into closer touch with the masses of our women, by whom, whether we will nor not, the world will always judge the womanhood of the race. Even though we wish to shun them, and hold ourselves entirely aloof from them, we cannot escape the consequences of their acts. So, that, if the call of duty were disregarded altogether, policy and self-preservation would demand that we go down among the lowly, the illiterate, and even the vicious to whom we are bound by the ties of race and sex, and put forth every possible effort to uplift and reclaim them.

It is useless to talk about elevating the race if we do not come into close touch with the masses of our women, through whom we may correct many of the evils which militate so seriously against us, and inaugurate the reforms without which, as a race, we cannot hope to succeed. It is often difficult, I know, to persuade people who need help most to avail themselves of the assistance offered by those who wish to lift them to a higher plane . . . we should nevertheless work unceasingly to this end until we win their confidence so that they will accept our aid. . . . Let us explain the situation as we may, the fact remains that trades and avocations, which formerly by common consent belonged almost exclusively to our men and women are gradually slipping from their grasp.

Whom does such a condition of things affect more directly and disastrously than the women of the race? As parents, teachers and guardians, we teach our children to be honest and industrious, to cultivate their minds, to become skilled workmen, to be energetic and then to be hopeful. It is easy enough to impress upon them the necessity of cultivating their minds, and of becoming skilled workmen, of being energetic, honest and industrious, but how difficult it is for colored women to inspire their children with hope, or offer them an incentive for their best endeavor under the existing condition of things in this country.

As a mother of the dominant race looks into the sweet innocent face of her babe, her heart thrills not only with happiness in the present, but also with joyful anticipations of the future. For well she knows that honor, wealth, fame and greatness in any vocation he may choose, are all his, if he but possess the ability and determination to secure them. She knows that if it is in him to be great, all the exterior circumstances, which can help him to the goal of his ambition, such as the laws of his country, the public opinion of his countrymen and manifold opportunities, are all his, without the asking. From his birth he is king in his own right, and is no suppliant for justice.

But how bitter is the contrast between the feelings of joy and hope which thrill the heart of the white mother and those which stir the soul of her colored sister. As a mother of the weaker race clasps to her bosom the babe which she loves with an affection as tender and deep as that the white mother bears her child, she cannot thrill with joyful anticipation of the future. For before her babe she sees the thorny path of prejudice and proscription his little feet must tread. She knows that no matter how great his ability, or how lofty his ambition, there are comparatively few trades and avocations in which any one of his race may hope to succeed. She knows that no matter how skillful his hand, how honest his heart, or how great his need, trade unions will close their doors in his face and make his struggle for existence desperate indeed. So rough does the way of her infant appear to many a poor colored mother, as she thinks of the hardships and humiliations to which he will be subjected, when he tries to earn his daily bread, that instead of thrill with joy and hope, she trembles with apprehension and despair.

This picture, though forbidding to look upon, is not overdrawn, as those who have studied the labor question in its relation to our race can testify. What, then, shall we do? Shall we sit supinely by, with folded hands, drooping heads, and weeping eyes, or shall we be up and doing, determined to smooth out the rough roads of labor over which tiny feet that now patter in play, will soon stumble and fall? . . .

As individuals, we have presented our case again and again. Let us now try the efficacy of organized effort; on this, I build great hope. Organization is one of the most potent forces in the world to-day, and the good it is possible for the National Association to accomplish has not yet been approximated by those most sanguine of its success.

And now, I must briefly call your attention to a subject fraught with interest to us all. The health of our race is becoming a matter of deep concern to many who are alarmed by statistics showing how great is the death rate among us as compared with that of the whites.

There are many reasons why this proportion is so great among us—chief of which are poverty and ignorance of the laws of health. . . . I must not neglect to mention another duty which the Association owes the race, and which it must not fail to discharge. Creating a healthful, wholesome public opinion in every community in which we are represented, is one of the greatest services we can render. The duty of setting a high moral standard and living up to it devolves upon us as colored women in a peculiar way. . . .

If I were called upon to state in a word where I thought the Association should do its most effective work, I should say unhesitatingly, "in the home." The purification of the home must be our first consideration and care. It is in the home where woman is really queen, that she wields her influence with the most telling effect. . . .

And now, finally, let us be up and doing wherever a word may be spoken for principle, or a hand lifted to aid. We must study carefully and conscientiously the questions which affect us most deeply and directly. Against lynching, the convict lease system, the Jim Crow car laws, and all other barbarities and abuses which degrade and dishearten us, we must agitate with such force of logic and intensity of soul that the oppressor will either be converted to principles of justice or be ashamed to openly violate them. Let loyalty to race, as displayed by employing and patronizing our own, in refusing to hold up our own to public ridicule and scorn, let allegiance to those whose ability, character and general fitness qualify them to lead, be two of the cardinal principles by which each and every member of this Association is guided. If we are to judge the future by the emancipation, there is no reason why we should view it with despair. Over almost insurmountable obstacles as a race we have forged ahead until today there is hardly a trade, a profession, or an art in which we have not at least one worthy representative. I challenge any other race to show such wonderful progress along all lines in so short a time, under circumstances so discouraging as that made by the ex-slaves of the United States of America. And though today some of us are cast down by the awful barbarities constantly inflicted upon some of our unfortunate race in the South who have been shot and burned to death by mobs which took no pains to establish the guilt of their victims, some of whom were doubtless innocent, we must remember that the darkest hour is just before the dawn.

As an Association, by discharging our duty to the children, by studying the labor question in its relation to our race, by coming into closer touch with the masses of our women, by urging parents and teachers to protect the health of our boys and girls, by creating a wholesome, healthful public sentiment in every community in which we are represented, by setting a high moral standard and living up to it, and purifying the home, we shall render the race a service, whose magnitude and importance it is not in my power to express.

Let us love and cherish our Association with such loyalty and zeal, that it will wax strong and great, that it may soon become that bulwark of strength and source of inspiration to our women that it is destined to be.

> In spite of rock and tempest's roar,
> In spite of false lights on the shore,
> Sail on, nor fear to breast the sea!
> Our heart, our hopes are all with Thee,
> Our heart, our hopes, our prayers, our tears,
> Our faith, triumphant o'er our fears,
> Are all with Thee, are all with Thee.

Part III

Intelligibility

Chapter 7

Recasting Frameworks for Engagement and Regard

The ultimate challenge for African American women as sociopolitical advocates, activists, and leaders is for their stories to be intelligible within our narratives of nation. The imperative is to develop mechanisms that enable this group to be discernable as women of substance, impact, and consequence and as worthy of respect and regard. Traditionally, however, power elites have defaulted analytical and interpretive frameworks for engagement and appreciation toward their own lives and achievements without a systemically inclusive consideration of those citizens who may be definable by other factors—for example, by race, gender, class, culture, condition, place of origin, and so forth. Our habitual storytelling and history-telling processes and practices (including, for example, the terms of engagement and recognition that we utilize, the policies and practices that dominate in our sociocultural ecosystem, and the operational frameworks of our economic and political systems) have not functioned with an inclination to see and respect the complexities of the lives, work, and achievements of all citizens regardless of sociopolitical identities, including African American women.

At a fundamental level, therefore, the struggle for intelligibility by this group, as women quite far removed historically from the central circles of power and authority, has been intense and continues still. Nevertheless, as evidenced by the documentation and analyses presented here, African American women have been vigilant in their resistance to disempowering conditions and effects. They have been resilient in their pursuit of truth, freedom, justice, equality, and empowerment. They have been relentless in their dedication to making the world a better place for themselves and others.

Given this framing of intelligibility as an extreme challenge, I focus in this chapter on using the expanding knowledge base on African American women's sociopolitical activity over time to shift the habitual analytical and interpretive paradigms by which we can develop a deeper understanding of this group as agents of progress and change. By design, the propositions that I have drawn forward in this shifting process are multidimensional and intersectional in the sense that they have emerged as points in relationship to each other at the intersections of a collective body of evidence from multiple sources. From this point of view, a preliminary assertion is the idea that what we can see as currently operational in sociopolitical environments with regard to social justice and social change has not evolved by magic or by happenstance but, rather, because of prior investments of time, energy, talents, and intentions by a fuller range of highly engaged actors than we have habitually acknowledged in our national narratives.

With emphasis on African American women as the case in point, in earlier chapters I have cast attention on this group's actions mostly as individuals—on who some of the women specifically were, on the ecosystems in which they functioned, and to some extent on the interests and occasions that inspired their work and the relationships and networks that supported or undermined it. In this chapter, I shift perspectives to a higher level of generality in order to focus more directly on the women as a cohort, via the example of their club work. The focus is on the pattern of the group's mandates, what those mandates entailed, what the women took responsibility for as a collective, and what their strategies were for managing and leading positive change, typically, amid inhospitable conditions and circumstances. The operational goal here has been to enhance the documentation, analysis, and interpretation of how persistently this group of women have found ways to create their own room for participating in sociopolitical work.

With this agenda, attention refocuses in kaleidoscopic fashion to bring to the foreground a more richly rendered view. The task is to examine patterns of practice rather than singular achievements by individual women viewed one by one; to look at the women's visibility and audibility in the various causes that they were pursuing; and to pay particular attention to their visionary thinking and their strategic planning and action. This refocusing permits the preliminary assertion that progress and change emerged from work rather than by magic to be linked to a second set of assertions. African American women have engaged in sociopolitical work over time. In doing so, they have demonstrated a long-standing and continuous desire to engage as robustly as possible in actions that they have deemed helpful to themselves, their families and friends, their communities, their nation, and beyond. Most interestingly, perhaps, the women have consistently determined that many hands (i.e., women working together) make for lighter work and greater impact.

A third assertion is that, at the turn of the eighteenth century, the founding of the United States of America as a deliberately democratic nation for all its citizens offered African American women a signal opportunity to imagine a better world and to figure out ways, large and small, to engage more energetically in actions that might help to bring the world of their dreams into reality. The brightened light of this kairotic moment permits us to enhance our capacity to see the nineteenth century as a powerful and inspirational landscape for this group. The whole century becomes, in effect, an extended runway upon which the women took advantage of opportunities, in whatever ways they were able, to build strength and capacity for meaningful, positive, and transformative change for themselves and others as fully fledged citizens of the nation. From some points of view, this runway was an excruciatingly slow walk. However, in terms of a longer view of impact and consequence, the decades from 1776 to 1900 proved to be a vibrant ecosystem within which African American women managed ultimately to live free and to work as women in a nation that proclaimed itself to be democratic. Moreover, as a specific group of women, they lived and worked, not randomly or passively, but with intention and purpose as they negotiated their ways forward toward prosperity, respect, and peace. Along the way, they gained a broader array of experiences, enhanced their levels of knowledge and expertise, and exercised their abilities to deploy an evolving and expanding set of actions (by word and deed) in response to and in defiance of the acute array of challenges and constraints that continued to surround them.

In this chapter, then, I build upon the pentadic interrogation of African American women in various contexts during the long nineteenth century and on the examples of a substantial slate of women showcased in Chapters 3–6. This documentation and analysis enable us to sharpen the visibility and audibility of this cohort as agents of change and to gain a deeper understanding of the ways in which they worked to support survival, progress, and sustainability. In a complementary manner, I deploy the practice of listening rhetorically (see Ratcliffe 2005) with conscious awareness of the women's sociocultural environments, as well as with care and caring about their actual ideas and expressions as a particular cohort of women who wrote and spoke in public venues. With regard to intelligibility, listening well puts us in a much better position to understand how individual women found ways to participate in various public discourses that mattered to them. In committing ourselves to hearing their words and ideas, interrogating their expressiveness in richly rendered contexts, and responding to their rhetorical events respectfully and thoughtfully, we have specific opportunities to appreciate their insights, experiences, and rhetorical expertise. We can appreciate also their enterprising spirits in being audacious enough to share their visions, voices, intentions, and strategies for transformative change—even against the odds—as their opportunities permitted.

Beyond the ongoing goal of enhancing our ability to document, analyze, and interpret the work of African American women, in this chapter the specific task at hand is to bring two of the analytical lenses together—visibility and audibility—in context in order to enrich the sight line for intelligibility. The purpose is to craft a more vibrant vista from which to increase both the level and the quality of the interpretations that can be derived about African American women's identity, agency, authority, performances, and excellence. Using this more kaleidoscopic approach, the desired outcome is to move beyond quick, simple, and sometimes superficial analyses to take a bolder step toward understanding with greater depth what the women were doing and trying to do, both individually and collectively, how and why. In other words, when the actual ways and means of the women's labor as advocates, activists, and leaders over time become the more direct subject of inquiry, it makes sense that the framework for inquiry might reasonably shift, beyond a confirming (or not) of traditional measures and expectations to looking again more carefully and more caringly to see what is actually there and not there and what might be there instead, a process of inquiry that has become a rather basic definition of critical thinking. The anticipated outcome is that the assertions that emerge might have a greater opportunity to be more richly, fairly, and respectfully articulated than in the past.

Fundamentally, I am suggesting that documenting, analyzing, and interpreting women's individual achievements is, of course, critically important, but quite simply, I am also saying that remaining at the level of individual impact is not enough to yield a fully rendered accounting of the nature, ways, and means or the importance of African American women's sociopolitical work. A fourth assertion, therefore, is that interrogations of these records of action and achievement benefit from more multilectical analyses—that is, analyses that take into account a range of ways of thinking, seeing, saying, and sense making, with the intention of gaining a more vibrant understanding of African American women's sociopolitical work as an intentional and self-determined enterprise. With an eye toward the rise of the Black Clubwomen's Movement at the end of the nineteenth century, the critical opportunity is to figure out how, as posited earlier, the nineteenth century actually functioned as a runway for clubwomen to launch a well-grounded, coherent, and bold mechanism for collective sociopolitical action.

Some of the questions are basic. How did the women create such a robust organization? What was the operational infrastructure? How did its various operations function as a professional training ground for leadership and action? How did this organization become a nationwide framework for collective action, presumably, so organically and so quickly? How could African American women—as a group of citizens clearly encumbered during this time period by their race, gender, and class—plan, control, and manage such a bold and dynamic agenda? How did the women sustain focus on the range of their sociopolitical desires? How was that focus defined, shaped, and redefined during the formative years of the organization?

To begin addressing such questions, contemporary researchers and scholars have an opportunity to fine-tune their points of view and to take seriously what advocacy, activism, and leadership have looked like and functioned as, not by traditional expectations in mainstream society, but in the hands of African American women over time. With the women's general framework for engagement made more visible, our vista for analysis and interpretation gains more capacity to evolve. Essentially, across the first twelve decades of the nation's formation, these women enhanced their capacities to engage in action—step by step, day by day, decade by decade. They exhibited visionary strength and an escalating set of skills. Many among this group spoke for themselves, exemplifying a bold sense of self, agency, and authority. Their efforts resulted in a substantial documentary record of their participation in various public discourses, and they generated quite a list of individual accomplishments. A central analytical task, therefore, is to focus on this documentary record to track, using their own words, their patterns of thought and action in context. The purpose of these types of interrogations is to determine the ways in which African American women's patterns of rhetorical behavior permit us to see, better understand, and appreciate the musculature of their intellectual and operational prowess in their pursuits of a very ambitious common goal—making the world a better place.

One benefit of moving beyond singular explorations of African American women's performances to a more kaleidoscopic set of interrogations is that we enhance our capacity to dismantle ungrounded myths and presumptions. Especially challenging have been the presumptions that have characterized these earlier generations of women as silent on race and gender issues and not really politically engaged. The discomforting questions are these: If nineteenth-century African American women were not engaged in sociopolitical activism by defaulted habitual definitions for determining the existence of activism and leadership, then what were they doing instead? What did they consider themselves to be doing? How should we clarify and name or rename what they were doing? How do these actions fit in or connect with the larger scope of developing and sustaining their communities and helping to build a nation that lives up to its bedrock values?

The intention of this more multilectical approach is to gather what we know about the visibility and audibility of African American women's sociopolitical actions in context in order to reimagine the women with far more specificity and materiality as active agents of change—in order to make them more intelligible historically as advocates, activists, and leaders. With this perspective, the task is to interrogate their intellectual grounding, their rhetorical prowess, their culturally informed habits of engagement, the ways and means of their participation in public discourses, and the multilayered dimensions of them as enterprising and innovative leaders. In moving forward with this analytical agenda, we have an obligation to look for the actual evidence of their work with the presumption that, just because this evidence has been previously unseen or unacknowledged, it does not mean that the evidence does not exist. The advantage in this case of looking with an enhanced critical awareness at these twelve decades in particular (1776 through 1900) is that we have an opportunity to cast a brighter, more powerful light as we envision this historical era, not just as a chunk of time, but as an ecosystem for the women's lives and their possibilities. In this particular instance, we leverage our capacity, perhaps exponentially, to determine the worthiness of African American women as women of substance and consequence who deserve to be recognized, acknowledged, and appreciated, not just in their own communities, but by the nation.

So, what do we know about the public performances of African American women? One thing that we know is that African American women had a tendency to speak their minds, even when they were not invited to do so. They told their stories. They shared their perspectives and experiences. They put forward their visions of reality and their hopes for change. They also directed a considerable amount of labor toward transformative change, such that, metaphorically, they created a view of themselves as warrior women taking on the responsibility for making the change that they wanted to see. They articulated strategic actions of various kinds with a weather eye on the current survival and the future prosperity of their families, communities, race, and nation—all against the odds since the society did not perceive them as capable or consequential given their status as women who were constrained by race, gender, class, access, and opportunity. Regardless of what others thought, however, the women often exhibited a capacity to both support and lead in carrying out various actions that they considered to be important. They demonstrated persistently that, despite a world that expected nothing of them, they defined themselves to be agents of change who felt obligated to resist oppression, to advocate for safety, survival, and progress, and to be proactive in doing whatever was possible to do in finding or making a way to forward freedom, truth, justice, equality, empowerment, and peace—for all, including themselves.

For all practical purposes, however, African American women were not the ones in control. Typically, they were present but they existed within an environment of deep disregard. Whether their participation in and contributions to society were ordinary or extraordinary, it is not news to note that they were not always recognized publicly for their work and achievements or given credit for their ideas. In effect, given the sociocultural expectations, policies, and practices of this time period, their presence in public arenas has been filtered, restricted, or proscribed. Their work as strategic thinkers, problem-solvers, and actors has been habitually disregarded even if that work has been used. Their value, impact, and consequence in these spaces has regularly been hidden and ignored.[1]

An obvious outcome of this inhospitable context is that, even though we are now in the twenty-first century and know more about our national past than we have ever known (and in more diverse terms than we have ever acknowledged before), the specific participation and accomplishments of African American women remain largely unknown, underacknowledged, under-researched, and misinterpreted. In response to this dilemma, I draw forward the slowly but steadily mounting evidence of their visions, voices, and actions in order to bring these women into bolder relief. A basic methodological strategy has been to look for what they managed to do, where, and how, and to listen to what they had to say about what they were seeing and doing. In using their own words, the effort is to understand the ways in which their words indemnify their actions. Without a doubt, this approach to analysis and interpretation seeks to render a fuller view of the sociopolitical work of African American women. Of equal importance, however, this approach also seeks to underscore far more boldly the proposition that the specific frameworks and methodologies that we use to judge the presence, participation, and excellence of African American women in sociopolitical work really do matter.

Gaining Rhetorical Strength

By the latter half of the nineteenth century, African American women were gaining strength as a recognizable group of writers, distinguishable because of the ecosystem within which they were functioning and the ways in which this environment shaped and directed their strategic actions and rhetorical decision-making processes. As a complement to their African American brethren such as Frederick Douglass, T. Thomas Fortune, Alexander Crummell, Kelly Miller, Booker T. Washington, W. E. B. Du Bois, and others who were being anointed as the voices of the people, African American women also envisioned and seized upon the post–Civil War, post-chattel slavery, Reconstruction, and post-Reconstruction era as a kairotic occasion to pursue ambitious social, political, and nation-building goals. With writing and speaking in public an important part of their escalating strengths, one element that deserves more focused attention is their use of the African American periodical press.

Over the decades many of the women—from various walks of life, but most especially those who had taken advantage of educational opportunities and were working as professional women (teachers, nurses, doctors, lawyers, business women, community organizers, etc.)—chose to write for the African American periodical press as an operational medium of choice for getting things said and done. Their focal point was social reform. Their vision was to forward the development, prosperity, and sustainability of their people—locally, nationally, and internationally to the extent that they were able. Their basic desire was to do their part in shifting the horizons for themselves and for their people through active engagement in the complex public discourses of their day. Their passion was to seize the moment. The available means was the flexible medium of the press. As women in an era when the action horizons for women were limited, and even more so for African American women, they were able to see that the periodical press was a flexible medium in which they might more assertively show and share their thinking and problem-solving prowess and engage as advisors and leaders in the ongoing quest for freedom, justice, equality, and empowerment.

An examination of the journalistic participation of these women clarifies both their rhetorical productivity as a distinctive group and also the extent to which their activities functioned as part of a social action framework, thus marking this time period as a transformative operational moment in the history of African American women's activism. In order to clarify this assertion, we need to map the rise of the African American periodical press before and after the American Civil War (from 1827 to 1900). The focus centers on the ways in which the rhetorical actions of late nineteenth-century African American women are linked to this expressive tradition and on the sociopolitical ecosystem in which the African American public sphere functioned. The general task is to present a lively view of the landscape of the women's journalistic engagement. In more specific terms, the task is to direct attention to the texts and contexts of their expressive practices and to the social networks within which they were able to set a national agenda for agency, action, and leadership; to hone their talents and develop rhetorical expertise, and to create circles of relationships that inspired, enabled, and sponsored agency and action—with the formation of NACW at the end of the century being a distinctive material result.

The basic hypothesis is that, by the end of the nineteenth century, African American women writers had ushered into being, as they themselves proclaimed, a "new woman's era." They had pursued educational opportunities and developed and enhanced their individual skills and abilities as rhetors and sociopolitical actors. They took advantage of the periodical press and created mechanisms not simply for individual achievement but, quite importantly, for collective action. Within this ecosystem, they emerged as a new generation of women with professional expertise, and as highly engaged thinkers and problem solvers whose patterns of leadership, rhetorical action, and social activism were innovative and distinctive.

At this point in our national history, it has become a commonplace to state that African Americans have waged a long-standing quest for truth, justice, equality, and empowerment with regard to both human and civil rights.[2] One basic dimension of our knowledge-making processes has been, in fact, to acknowledge that both men and women have engaged passionately in pursuing a tripartite agenda—freedom, justice, equality. They have pursued, as well, various strategies for empowerment in the interest of forwarding community progress and sustainability with regard to social, economic, and political reforms. This quest has persistently occasioned an imperative to claim spaces, again for both men and women, within which to advocate for freedom and justice, counter social domination and discrimination, resist oppressions, celebrate achievements, advance community-building and nation-building agendas, and generally make reasonable and prosperous lives for themselves.

From a more nuanced perspective, the African American periodical press constituted kairotic space for rhetorical invention. It provided arenas for contributors to generate ideas and strategies and within which they could construct a more empowering sense of agency, identity, and authority as human beings. Having access to the periodical press provided both African American men and women opportunities to exercise their potential in advocating for their specific social and political interests. These venues were platforms from which to build up their experiences in creating impact regarding various problems and issues, and from which to sustain a positive momentum for change on behalf of the community at large. In this regard the African American periodical press, like African American churches, constituted an accommodating space for various negotiations within the national public sphere, with the press serving in particular as the social medium of choice for these times. These venues functioned as a set of self-determined and community-controlled environments, providing African Americans fertile ground for the development of their own public sphere—a Black public sphere, as compared with their limited access to the more traditional national public sphere. In essence, contributors were able to use literacy and rhetorical expertise to address concerns, problems, and issues and to advance their various causes.

From a historical perspective, to understand this asset in more explicit terms, we can mark March 16, 1827, as the key historical moment. This date was the publication date for the first issue of *Freedom's Journal*, the first newspaper in the United States that was African American owned and edited. It was founded by Reverend Peter Williams Jr., John B. Russwurm, and Samuel B. Cornish, with Russwurm and Cornish serving as the pioneering coeditors. Before *Freedom's Journal*, many free and freed African American men and women were contributors, supporters, and leading voices for abolitionist papers that were owned, edited, and operated by whites. A striking example was Frederick Douglass, of course, who was a regular contributor to William Lloyd Garrison's *Liberator*. Early exemplars of Garrison's publication also included women writers such as Maria Miller Stewart, Sarah Mapps Douglass, Charlotte Forten, and others who, in complementary fashion to their male counterparts, published articles and creative writing in this paper.

Publishing in the periodicals of others, however, was not enough.[3] African Americans had a compelling desire to speak for themselves. In their very first editorial, Russwurm and Cornish stated:

> In presenting our first number to our patrons we feel all the diffidence of persons entering upon a new and untried line of business. But a moment's reflection upon the noble object we have in view by the publication of this journal; the expediency of its appearance at this time when so many schemes are in action concerning our people—encourage us to come boldly before an enlightened public. For we believe that a paper devoted to the dissemination of useful knowledge among our brethren, and to their moral and religious improvement, must meet with the cordial approbation of every friend of humanity. . . . We wish to plead our own cause. Too long have others spoken for us. Too long has the public been deceived by misinterpretations, in things that concern us dearly. . . . It is our earnest wish to make our Journal a medium of intercourse between our brethren in the different states of this great confederacy; that through its columns an expression of our sentiments, on many interesting subjects that concern us, may be offered to the public: that plans which apparently are beneficial may be candidly discussed and properly weighed; if worthy receive our cordial approbation; if not, our marked disapprobation. (*Freedom's Journal* 1.1, March 16, 1827)

With the launch of a paper both owned and operated by African Americans, the periodical press (newspapers, magazines, journals, and so forth) moved beyond being just an inventive space. It became a critical tool, a means to help members of a chronically marginalized and oppressed community speak for themselves. With this asset, the community could:

> articulate its own problems, deliberate its own needs, celebrate its own achievement, and identify strategies capable of effecting change in the larger sociopolitical context. In this specific function, the periodical press has been a magnetizing force in generating knowledge about the range of issues and concerns affecting the group and in directing this knowledge toward available strategies. . . . Periodical publications have served as a constant forum for the voices of African Americans to be heard. They have constituted a counterforce to the more dominant "official" voices that defined the public agenda in a manner that essentially excluded African American interests. (Royster 2000, 218–19)

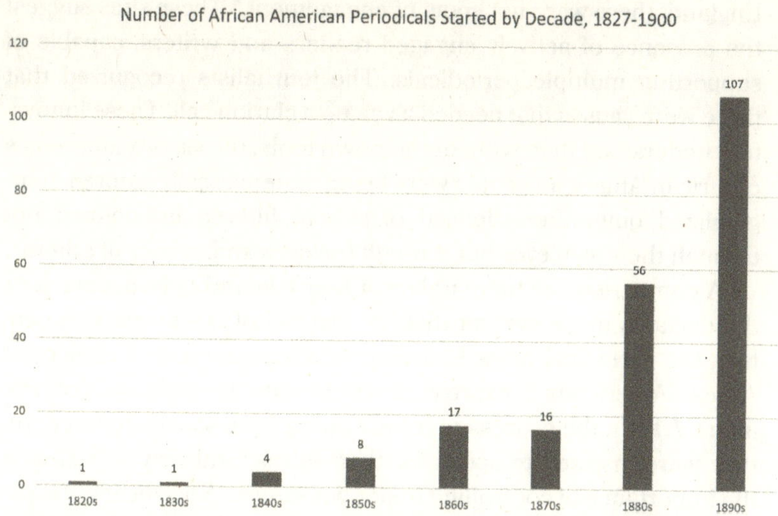

Figure 7.1: Number of African American Periodicals Started by Decade, 1827–1900

Freedom's Journal was circulated through eleven US states, Canada, Europe, and Haiti.[4] By March 28, 1829, it had ceased its weekly publication, although Cornish restarted and renamed it *The Rights of All*, which he maintained for one additional year. The impact of this starting point is that the trend toward using the periodical press for direct engagement in sociopolitical action had been set in motion. By the Civil War, dozens of African American–owned and –operated papers had been established across twenty-five states and the District of Columbia.[5] More were to come, as social and political exigencies continued to diversify and evolve throughout the nineteenth century, over the next century, and beyond. Early exemplars include the *Mirror of Liberty* in New York and the *National Reformer* in Philadelphia (1838); the *African Methodist Episcopal Church Magazine* in Brooklyn (1841); *The Elevator* in Albany, New York (1842); the *North Star* in Rochester, New York (1847); the *Anglo-African* in New York (1859). The first paper to be owned and operated by African Americans in the South was the *Colored American*, in Augusta, Georgia. It was published by J. T. Shuften. The first issue appeared on December 16, 1865.

The African American periodical press served local communities across the nation and constituted a network of interests and concerns. In specific geographical sites such as Kansas and New

England, there were hot spots of engagement.[6] These sites suggest the presence of actively engaged readers and writers, capable of supporting multiple periodicals. The journalists recognized that there were causes that needed a voice—a clarion call. These innovators understood that, without their own tools, the visions and voices of African American people were being systematically ignored, marginalized, quite often silenced, or at best, filtered and defined, not through their own eyes but through the eyes and agency of others.

A comparison of the number of journals and newspapers over the decades make evident that, by the end of the nineteenth century, the periodical press had become an instrument of choice for African Americans to express themselves in the public sphere (see figure 7.1). In the process of transitioning from slavery to freedom, they were inspired to speak for themselves, and they saw clearly the importance of controlling their own venues. Specifically, the periodical press became a key tool to enable the blossoming of their rights to freedom before and during the Civil War. After the Civil War the press gained even more traction as an asset in advancing their quest for truth, freedom, justice, equality, and empowerment as fully recognized citizens of the nation.

After the Civil War, periodicals owned and operated by African Americans increased the visibility and viability of African American communities at large and amplified the voices of contributors at both local and national levels. Gaining strength in the numbers of periodicals and in the scope of participants gave rise to a vibrant public sphere and also to a national organization, the National Colored Press Association, which was first convened in Louisville, Kentucky, in 1881. The story that remains to be more thoroughly documented, however, is the contributions of women in this nation-building project. Like their male counterparts African American women were passionate to speak for themselves, to be treated as valuable and valued assets in strategic planning and action, and to have the opportunity to be consequential in creating brighter horizons for African American needs and interests.

The Landscape for African American Women's Civic Engagement

In recognizing, as I did in chapter 2 (see figure 2.4), that African American women were writing for periodicals in several cities across the nation, we can infer that, during this time of growth in their journalistic experience, the women were laying the groundwork for their formation of a nationwide social and professional network. With a national scope, their emerging set of relationships reveals the breadth and density of African American women's circles of civic engagement, with each contributor to a particular press representing, presumably, the tip of a proverbial iceberg of readers, including women readers. Using this type of data-driven perspective shows more clearly how African American women were active in what was arguably the second most persistently available forum of the Black public sphere—with the church being the first. To be noted, the presence and roles of women in the church is yet another data point that is coming under greater scrutiny for recalibration as well.[7] With the generation of more data-driven analyses of African American women's social and professional networks, the next step in building and magnifying knowledge and understanding is to think more critically about the ways in which the work that the women were doing in these circles was being informed by their ideological and sociopolitical interests and by the roles that they were taking on in their communities as advocates, activists, and leaders (see figure 2.4).

Connecting such dots shows us where African American women who were actively engaged in public discourses were located geographically. The obvious conclusion is that at these locations the women were using journals and newspapers as a primary medium for public engagement. Examinations of extant texts from this era can confirm that they were civically engaged and focused on issues and concerns about race, gender, class, community, and nation. The core questions are why these locations? What were the nature, ways, and means of their civic engagement? What were the cultural expectations for their participation in public arenas? And how, by the last decade of the nineteenth century, did these activities give rise to a more comprehensive and coherent model for African American women's social networking and sociopolitical action?

In 1994 Elsa Barkley Brown offered an important insight in addressing such questions. In "Negotiating and Transforming the Public Sphere," she discusses her study of civic engagement in post–Civil War communities in Richmond, Virginia, with reference to other areas in the South. She directs attention to patterns of participation in mass political meetings, many of which occurred in church settings. She considers the ways in which operational patterns evolved over the latter half of the nineteenth century and puts forward a more elaborately defined operational schema than was typical in historical accounts at that time. She starts by making a case for the church community's internal habits of engagement: "Central to African Americans' construction of a fully democratic notion of political discourse was the church as a foundation of the black public sphere. . . . As a political space occupied by men, women and children, literate and nonliterate, ex-slave and formerly free, church members and nonmembers, the availability and use of First African [Baptist Church] for mass meetings enabled the construction of political concerns in democratic space. . . . Afro-Richmonders challenged liberal bourgeois notions of rational discourse" (Barkley Brown 1994, 110).

Barkley Brown documents that attendees at political meetings at the First Baptist Church (as exemplary of meeting sites across the South) were diverse across all of these categories. African American churches, as distinctive culturally defined spaces, typically embraced a more diverse circle of participants than churches of the more dominant society. These more community-controlled environments tended to operate interactively and dialogically. Barkley Brown posits that in such worship spaces civic engagements were infused with these habits of practice. Using church records, she confirms that, throughout the era of Reconstruction, the variety of attendees at the political meetings mirrored attendees at church meetings, with these participants exercising the privilege of sharing their voices and their visions openly, actively, and often audibly—in keeping, for example, with what we appreciate in rhetorical studies as the African American practice of call and response.

Adapting a model for public discourse and political action from their existing habitual worship practices permitted the attending community to construct an African American–infused public sphere that was shaped by the particulars of this preexisting worship infrastructure. According to Barkley Brown this alternative approach for the Black public sphere positioned the practices to be devalued in the context of dominant public sphere patterns. Essentially, African American ways were perceived to be inappropriate. For example, dominant American frameworks were defined by individual-centered rather than community-centered needs and goals. The dominant operational practices were constrained significantly by the social, economic, and gendered hierarchies of this time period, with specific regard to race, gender, and socioeconomic class participation. Within such frameworks, African American civic practices quite simply violated normalized boundaries of mainstream civic discourse—with regard in particular for who could attend meetings, who could speak, whose viewpoints were valued and incorporated, and who might be assumed to participate in shaping conversations and making critical decisions. The more diverse and inclusive democratic political engagements of African Americans just seemed "unorthodox" (Barkley Brown 1994, 110), disorderly, and outside the masculinist norms of the day. The meetings demonstrated that political discourses in the African American community were not yet acculturated to the dominant masculinist system and functioned with more open space for a broader range of participation, including the visions and voices of African American women—who, by cultural practice, considered themselves to have a rightful place in these enterprises and to be deep stakeholders in these critical processes.

Barkley Brown suggests that, inside the Black public sphere, participants assumed that all attendees had the right to be present and to engage actively. By their habits of practice, the community envisioned civic participation to be a "collective" enterprise rather than the performances of anointed individuals. A striking example is that, typically, participants in these rhetorical events considered the vote, though exercised by men, to be a socially responsible process in support of the common good—rather than an individualistic one. Barkley Brown confirms the distinctiveness of this discourse framework during the early decades after the Civil War before the disfranchisement processes and the disempowering social and political practices emerged so dramatically during the post-Reconstruction era and the rise of Jim Crow practices. Notably, African American women were fully present in these political meetings, highly engaged in the discourses, and very much committed to exercising a sense of agency and authority as key stakeholders in these nation-building processes.

Note, however, that with these broad comparisons of audience and participation patterns comes a cautionary tale. A closer interrogation confirms that the collectively defined African American practices were also gendered. Fundamentally, amid the more stringent gendered practices of the dominant culture, the agency and authority of African American women within sociopolitical spaces in African American communities were on a declining trajectory. In order for African American men to be taken more seriously by white men in public discourses and not be seen as unorthodox and disorderly, African American discourse practices were drifting toward a stronger alignment with the dominant practices where women were not expected to participate. For example, Barkley Brown's account of the political meetings suggests that African American women attendees, in keeping with habitual expectations, might regularly provide commentary on the ideas and information that emerged in the discussion. They might respond to whatever was being discussed, audibly and sometimes quite argumentatively. In contrast, however, they may not have expected to dictate the conversation itself or to lead the decision-making processes on their own authority. These expectations for African American women can be characterized more likely as the right to participate in full voice rather than to lead, such that the model of engagement might be more accurately articulated as collaborative and equitable—but not necessarily equal—in role performance.

Even so, the women's expectations were still that their viewpoints were to be respected, considered seriously, and valued in the process—not ignored and dismissed, which indeed in mainstream public discourses they regularly were. In reflecting on the preceding examples, under the laws of the United States and by sociocultural practices, the core observation is that men held the vote. Within the African American community, however, holding the vote was not considered an individual right for men alone. The men were, instead, the *trustees* of voting rights on behalf of the community's freedom and self-actualization. African American men were obligated thereby to be attentive to the community's views and opinions in exercising their own rights—but obligated specifically to do so in the interest of all. What is impossible to escape, though, is that at the end of the day, from the perspective of African American women, men still held the vote, based on the nation's policies and practices. Women did not.

For African American women's activism, these realities informed the spirit of their independent civic engagement, even as the horizons for their public political participation continued to deteriorate by the end of the century—in keeping with the double jeopardy of the racialized and gendered societal norms of that period. By the 1880s African American civic practices were aligning far more closely with mainstream masculinist norms, with African American women increasingly being positioned, in similar fashion to their white women counterparts, as more "organically" at the periphery of political participation and decision-making. In order to recover the status that they had habitually occupied, therefore, African American women were called upon to reinvent strategies for more active engagement to reestablish what they considered to be their rightful presence, agency, authority, and indeed their rightful positioning as assets for their communities, their race, and the nation. By this reckoning, voting rights and woman's suffrage, as specifically defined within their lived experiences, were for African American women a crucial and quintessenially core issue.

Exigencies for Rhetorical Action

Barkley Brown's explanation of the intersections between cultural practices in the African American church and the emergence of inclusive democratic practices in the Black public sphere offers a springboard for understanding the ways in which African American women envisioned themselves as rightful stakeholders in sociopolitical action, as active participants in public discourses, and as assets for the caring and sustainability of their communities—in local and national scope. Over the history of Africans in the Americas, the exigencies of slave culture and racial domination (and then the remnants of these cultural practices after the American Civil War) dictated that by necessity African American women would need to partner with their male counterparts in the passionate quest of African peoples for freedom, justice, and equality. In the construction and exercise of innovative strategies in their resistance to oppression, the church offered an environment within which women occupied a place of respect as well as an opportunity to be in full voice when it came to ideas, issues, and concerns. This sense of agency, identity, and authority positioned them as strategic actors to collaborate with African American men in support of common causes and also to seize opportunities in the use of new technologies (such as the rise of the periodical press during the nineteenth century and the creation of a Black public sphere) as powerful tools in fomenting the reforms that they wanted to see.

The ecosystem for this quest, however, was complex. Under the pressure of a general narrowing of freedoms for African American communities during post-Reconstruction and the rise of segregation, Jim Crow laws, and other disempowering policies and practices, the drift away from the African American community's unorthodox community-centered patterns made a difference. To reiterate the challenge, the dominant culture considered these practices unintelligible. Ultimately in response to this categorization, the community moved toward a more "normalized" individualistic masculinist framework in closer alignment with the "American" model.

The consequence for African American women was that their active participation in sociopolitical work was increasingly cast in shadow and their achievements were left out of the story in favor of a male-dominated master narrative. With these changing external and internal contexts, the women were called upon to recalibrate the ways and means of their participation. They were determined not to be pushed aside, but they needed to clarify and reclaim status within the community; to establish visibility, audibility, and intelligibility beyond the community; and to invent strategies for civic engagement that permitted them to exercise their own visions and voices and to develop a wider range of motion and impact—for themselves. Their imperative, therefore, was twofold: first, to shift their trajectories toward better opportunities for their own development, action, and leadership; and second, to take advantage of innovative opportunities that might facilitate the work they considered theirs to do as community assets in moving an activist agenda forward for the community, the race, and the nation.

One critical strategic pattern was that they brought forward from their long-standing habits in their communities the culturally informed habit of unorthodoxy. It was evident that, with the constraints of their societal context, African American women needed to be willing to think outside the box in order to perform the work they wanted and needed to perform. Their mission was twofold, as declared during the rise of the Black Clubwomen's Movement. The thematic task, as articulated by Mary Church Terrell, was "Lifting as We Climb." Thus, it was with two imperatives (both climbing and simultaneously lifting) that this generation of women clearly felt well equipped to achieve. A key instrument in accomplishing their goals (and in launching NACW as their enabling organizational effort) was their community-controlled, woman-defined uses of the periodical press.[8]

Building Communities of Practice

In her introduction to *A Voice from the South* (1892), Anna Julia Cooper seeks to bring African American women out of the shadows and into full voice:

> In the clash and clatter of our American Conflict, it has been said

> that the South remains Silent. Like the Sphinx she inspires vociferous disputation, but herself takes little part in the noisy controversy. One muffled strain in the Silent South, a jarring chord and a vague and uncomprehended cadenza has been and still is the Negro. And of that muffled chord, the one mute and voiceless note has been the sadly expectant Black Women. . . . If these broken utterances can in any way help to a clearer vision and a truer pulse-beat in studying our Nation's Problem, this Voice by a Black Woman of the South will not have been raised in vain. (Cooper 1988, i, iii)

Framing her argument with astute analyses of race and gender issues, Cooper goes on to make additional points about educational opportunity and training and about embracing women as assets for the nation. As she states in "The Higher Education of Women": "All I claim is that there is a feminine as well as a masculine side to truth; that they are related not as inferior and superior, not as better and worse, not as weaker and stronger, but as complements—complements in one necessary and symmetric whole" (Cooper 1988, 60). Cooper articulated well what many women of her generation believed: African American women should develop their talents and abilities and use them the best that they can as people fully capable of making meaningful contributions to their communities, the nation, and the world. She spoke poignantly about the obligation of the communities in which the women lived to support them (as they would men with talents and desires to achieve), and she warned that, without the values added by women to the world, we are left at a distinct disadvantage.

Cooper published her book at the end of the nineteenth century in 1892, establishing a place for herself as a highly respected intellectual and as a distinctive voice in public discourses. Other women, however, had been similarly inspired to speak and write for several decades from the formation of the nation through the end of the century and the publication of Cooper's book. The nineteenth century bore witness to the emergence of a growing cohort of well-educated (often college-educated) women advocates, activists, and leaders who were prepared to function as professional women in public space. By the last decade of the nineteenth century, they had been building communities of practice for well over a hundred years, taking advantage of opportunities to acquire knowledge, experience, and rhetorical expertise in both institutional and social settings—in schools, churches, social clubs, and community organizations, for example. They had been exhibiting deep-seated desires for and passionate commitments to making the changes they wanted to see in their world, such that the roles they performed in their various and sundry undertakings served them well in their efforts to build and enhance their skills and abilities, and to showcase the value that they wished to add in sociopolitical enterprises.

Given recent scholarship in multiple disciplines (women's studies, historical studies, literary studies, and rhetorical studies), we have come to know much more about the professional accomplishments of these early cohorts of women with journalists identified as a specific case in point. Two examples that stand out from the ones that I showcase in this analysis are Mary Shadd Cary, the first African American woman in North America to own, write, and edit her own newspaper, the *Provincial Freeman*, in Toronto and Chatham, Ontario (see chapter 3), and Ida B. Wells-Barnett, co-owner, writer, and editor of the *Free Speech* in Memphis, Tennessee (see chapter 5). These two journalists—one from before and one from after the Civil War—are far from the only examples of African American women during this era who were actively engaging in journalistic activities (see figure 2.4), as confirmed in this analysis. This preliminary documentation confirms that in national scope at least sixty-five women from 1853 to 1900 were using the periodical press frequently as an expressive instrument of choice.

Again, starting with the crucial acknowledgment that the visualizations included here (see figure 2.5) are neither comprehensive nor complete but based on a small data set, key points to be highlighted are that (1) even as a small data set, evidence confirms that African American women were visible and audible in the public venues that were available to them; (2) given the oppressive conditions that surrounded the women during this era, evidence also confirms that they were consistently engaged in civic enterprises; (3) over the decades these pioneering women constituted a growing social and professional network that stretched from San Francisco, north to Yankton and south to Houston, and then to the east coast; (4) their active participation in journalistic enterprises suggests they were energized by both their own personal desires as writers and their ideological commitments as women who cared about and for their communities; and (5) by the last decade of the century, African American women had produced a body of writing that now constitutes a lens for illuminating the point that this era was not marked simply and solely by the accomplishments of hardworking individual women but also by communities of practice within this group who endowed their capacity to be agents of progress and change with both words and deeds.

Over the decades, African American women used the periodical press as a means to fulfil their expressive desires, to engage collaboratively with their compatriots in public discourses, and to comment on issues, problems, and concerns of particular interest to them (such as children, culture, and the viability and prosperity of their communities), concerns that certainly did not leave out their awareness of racialized and gendered issues and implications. Quite evidently, African American women were determined to make space for themselves in this evolving public sphere, and they raised their voices persistently to do so. They articulated their own visions and the collective vision of their identity groups. By this means they were able to broaden their range of motion as activists, engaging various audiences with the challenges and opportunities that they deemed critical. They could participate, from many walks of life, in forwarding an agenda for the progress and sustainability of their downtrodden people and focus with agency and authority on the activism and leadership of women in enabling freedom, equality, justice, and empowerment—for all, including themselves.

Loosely defined, by the end of the nineteenth century, these pioneering women constituted a community of professional practice, women who were regularly using their expressive expertise in the public sphere as writers and speakers. The work in the 1890s, therefore, was not a beginning for their sociopolitical activity in public arenas but, rather, an enhancing of their operational strengths and an expanding of their opportunities to claim space as agents of transformative change. They succeeded in signaling with a more commanding presence that African American women were assets for their communities, for their race, and for their nation. They also succeeded in putting their own stakes in the ground for declaring that they themselves were using their own potential to make a better world.

With this landscape as backdrop, we might reimagine the nature and means of African American women's civic identity and engagement. Many among this group of women writers, if not all of them, were women who were not only sharp observers but also outspoken rhetors and bold intersectional thinkers fully capable of connecting dots among race, class, and gender oppressions as they tackled thorny problems that were affecting the safety, peace, and prosperity of the race. They were thoughtful problem posers and problem solvers who engaged regularly with the challenges and concerns of their day. They had available to them expressive platforms, such as newspapers, journals, magazines, and so on, for sharing insights and observations with others. We might surmise, then, that some, if not all, among this group were excited and enthusiastic about an innovative moment in the evolution of the Black public sphere.

In 1884 the African Methodist Episcopal Church sponsored the launching of the *A.M.E. Church Review* (the first journal owned and edited by African Americans to be focused explicitly on the analysis and engagement of African American problems by African American intellectuals of the day). Surely, the women had to be excited about the possibility of having their intellectual strengths recognized and about the reinstatement of a rightful place for themselves in community-building and nation-building enterprises. What they found, however, is that, although they were indeed included in the journal, their circle of agency and authority in this space was not ample enough to satisfy their desires. They wanted more.

By the 1880s masculinist operational frameworks were already in motion within the African American community. In keeping with dominant societal expectations, the presumption for women's presence and participation was geared toward the notion that women deserved respect but intellectuals were overwhelmingly male and, thereby, had priority in the journal. Despite this pattern, women were actually recognized by both the community and the journal as having a valued place in social reform and as deserving of race pride. In effect, though, African American women were perceived, apparently, not to be at the center of African American intellectual strength or sociopolitical action itself. Instead, they were positioned, as suggested by the conception of the journal's mission and objectives, as creative writers, as reviewers, or as writers who might address issues of import for the domestic sphere rather than the public sphere—in keeping with dominant societal expectations. Issues that were considered appropriate for women's engagement, for example, related to health care, or education, or the training of children—again, in keeping with prevailing ideologies of true womanhood, where distinctions between public and private domains were crystalized as gendered expectations. Only upon specific and special occasions were African American women included as intellectuals in the larger sociopolitical work of the journal. Consider in this light the journal's statement of mission on the back cover of its third issue:

> The object aimed at in the publication of the AFRICAN METHODIST EPISCOPAL CHURCH REVIEW is to give outlet to the negro scholarship a) of the A.M.E. Church, b) and of the world. At present this scholarship is practically hedged in. The white Magazines and Reviews stand in no need of it, and are in no humor or condition to try experiments. Their publishers are satisfied, in so far as it relates to themselves, to let well enough alone. Nothing remains but for the negro to open a channel for himself. The men of this organization are prepared to lead off in the work of cutting the ditch. They only ask that the negro scholars of the country, of the West Indies, of Africa and of the world come to their help. And yet, to accomplish this, we were obliged to lay over no less than five articles already in type and ready for the press, to wit. . . . The comfort is that each of these five articles is good enough to keep." Rev. B. T. Tanner, DD., 631 Pine Street, Philadelphia. (*A.M.E. Church Review* 1.3, January 1885)

With the drift in African American public discourses to align with the gendered frameworks of broader American public discourses, Rev. Tanner, the editor, normalized intellectual authority among African Americans as linked directly to the "men" of the organization. The first issue (volume 1.1) focused generally on two sets of interests: the history and critical rationale for the founding of the journal and political issues in both national and global scope, with the first issue directed toward information and insights about the nominees of the Republican National Convention and about the racist and ethnocentric crusade that was being waged against the Chinese by California labor leader Dennis Kearney. Women writers included in this issue were Martha E. Tyson, who contributed a book review, and Frances E. W. Harper, who contributed a poem.

In the second issue (volume 1.2), one of the concerns raised was the question of women's authority to enter the pulpit and their right to preach.[9] Rev. James H. A. Johnson, D. D., presented the argument in his article "Female Preachers" (102–5), concluding that:

"The pulpit is no place in which there should be a commingling of the sexes . . . woman has no more right to enter the pulpit, or go forth as a preacher than Uzzah had to touch the ark. . . . Surely then no good can come of such a subversion of the sacred principles which have been ordained for the extension of the church, and the welfare of the world" (105). This view of intellectual authority and the right to speak in public arenas counters the pioneering accomplishments of Jarena Lee (see chapter 3), Zilpha Elaw, Julia Foote, Amanda Berry Smith, Rebecca Cox Jackson, and others who pursued their goals as divinely inspired religious leaders. To be noted, in this issue of the *A.M.E. Church Review*, women were not invited to share their own perspectives on the issue or to respond to the controversy. Instead, they were invited to contribute a poem, an essay on education, and a book review.

Volume 1.3 offers more details that are instructive about the journals view of gender differences. Rev. Tanner advertised this issue in the following way:

> **Negro Scholarship: Its Only Outlet**
>
> The January number of The Review with other matters of interest, will contain a Symposium on the Democratic Restoration to Power. Papers will be there found from the pen of Frederick Douglass, P.B.S. Pinchback, George T. Downey, Peter H. Clark, T.T. Fortune, John H. Green, Wm. Still and others of our well-known leaders. In a sense, this January number may also be called a Ladies' number, containing poems from Mrs. M.E. Lambert and Miss Cordelia Ray; also papers from Mrs. F.E.W. Harper, Miss Frazelia Campbell, Miss Josephine J. Turpin and Miss A.E. Geary. . . . Everybody should subscribe. . . . B.T. Tanner, Box 906, Philadelphia, Pa.

In this volume Rev. Tanner was emphasizing that women writers were being included in the journal as both substantial and respectable, suggesting that the issue "may also be called a Ladies' number." He brought attention to their contributions, which was affirming. However, with one exception their contributions were not in the section dedicated to African American intellectual agency and authority. The women leaders contributed three poems and two short essays: Cordelia Ray, "Die Beiden Piccolomini"; M. E. Lambert, "Dante"; Frazelia Campbell, "Hymn to the New Year"; Josephine E. Turpin, "The Origin and Progress of the English Language"; and Anna Everett Geary, "Shadow Men." The one exception was an essay by Frances E. W. Harper. Harper was the most famous woman intellectual, writer, and activist of the era. In volume 1.3, she was the only female African American intellectual invited to offer her insights for the symposium. The essay was entitled "The Democratic Restoration of Power."

This examination of the *A.M.E. Church Review* is limited in scope to the first three issues. Even so, we can draw five conclusions from a preliminary analysis. (1) The journal focused on "Negro scholarship" with issues and problems thematically defined with an awareness of national and global issues. (2) The list of contributors to the three issues is not composed exclusively of men. (3) The women contributors were not generally included as intellectual leaders being invited to address the issues of the day—with Harper's essay being the exception in this set. (4) By their inclusion in other sections, however, women writers and leaders were recognized as having talents and expertise and as deserving of an honorable place. (5) Generally, the women's texts are positioned as peripheral to the core intellectual task and presented by the editor as "also included." The basic conclusion is that, despite the ways in which the journal included the intellectual voices of African American women at the turn of the century, during this time period women's visions and voices were mostly marginalized with regard to the journal's core mission. At its conceptual center, the *A.M.E. Church Review* was focused quite specifically on intellectual leadership, with that leadership being defined and shaped by African American men. It was not holistically informed by a collective view of leadership that fully included women as well.

A National Agenda for Women's Agency and Leadership

The proposition here is that African American women readers of the *A.M.E. Church Review* were likely pleased to see that women were included in this important journal and that the women chosen were clearly women of distinction. However, just six years after the appearance of the journal, in her signature volume *A Voice from the South* (1892), Cooper raised as persistently problematic the reality that African American women did not have adequate opportunity, agency, or authority to participate more fully in society to any extent in keeping with their talents and abilities. Cooper articulated the lingering issue that the existing roles that women were able to fill in public arenas, as people who were highly engaged in civic and sociopolitical pursuits, were not satisfying enough to them compared with the ways in which African American women leaders were viewing their own potential and actually performing sociopolitical work. Cooper captures the spirit of this viewpoint as follows:

> Everything to this race is new and strange and inspiring. There is a quickening of the pulses and a glowing of its self-consciousness. Aha, I can rival that! I can aspire to that! I can honor my name and vindicate my race! . . . Such is the colored woman's office. She must stamp weal or woe on the coming history of this people. May she see her opportunity and vindicate her prerogative. (Cooper 1988, 144–45)

It seems fair to say, given the rhetorical pursuits of African American women, that at the last decade of the century this cohort of high-performing women hungered still for a wider range of motion. They wanted to be more. They wanted to do more. As Cooper stated: "Let us then, here and now, recognize this force and resolve to make the most of it—not the boys less, but the girls more" (79). With regard to the rhetorical expertise exhibited in this statement as the crowning advice in a powerful essay, Cooper appealed to logos (in connecting this idea rationally to the rising importance and necessity of woman's voice in society, as well as in suggesting the urgency of using available talents to address crucial problems); to pathos (in recognizing the yearning of African American women for opportunities to show what they can do and to be a value added for society); and to ethos (in underscoring the need in African American communities across the nation and in the larger community to be ethically responsible in honoring talents and abilities regardless of gender or race or class).

Her appeals hit home. Cooper demonstrated with considerable prowess that African American women writers in this era had built up both expertise and experience in expressing their perspectives, desires, ideas, and strategies for transformative action. The outlets that embraced and encouraged the full exercising of their rhetorical talents and intellectual capacity were few, however, even as the exigencies for sociopolitical work and the need for transformative change in the nation remained strong.

Over the decades, when there were compelling imperatives to reset possibilities for action (with special regard for the survival and prosperity of the whole race), individual women stepped out to create their own opportunities, instead of waiting for others to acknowledge them and invite them in. In 1853 Mary Shadd Cary recognized the need for a platform to compete with rivals in political debates about immigration to Canada. She founded the *Provincial Freeman*. Amelia L. Tilghman, in Montgomery, Alabama, and later in Washington, DC, was concerned with expanding the cultural knowledge and appreciation of African American music. In 1886 she founded the *Musical Messenger*, which also included literature and articles on timely issues. Ida B. Wells in Memphis, Tennessee, was concerned that the community should have access to the truth about political and economic issues and problems that affected community members. In 1889 she purchased part ownership in the newspaper the *Free Speech*. Julia Ringwood Coston of Cleveland, Ohio, thought that African American women should have good information about fashion, style, and other issues of particular and practical relevance to the quality of women's lives. In 1891 she founded *Ringwood's Afro-American Journal of Fashion*, which is a particularly instructive example because it was a more collective enterprise. Coston solicited essays as well as poetry and stories, and her journal became a training ground for significant numbers of African American women writers to gain publishing experience as journalists and to be authorized, thereby, to write on various subjects and in various genres.

Notably, in 1891, *Ringwood's* was the only fashion magazine dedicated to the interests of African American women. In keeping with the analysis put forward by Noliwe Rooks in *Ladies' Pages: African American Women's Magazines and the Culture that Made Them* (2004), the priorities of the journal were to offer advice and council to African American women about homemaking, proper etiquette, and fashion. In setting this mission, *Ringwood's* recognized the challenges facing African American women who wanted to remake themselves and to take care of their families in freedom, even under trying socioeconomic conditions. Coston also recognized the desire of these women to do so with both practicality and style within the contexts and opportunities of the era. She acknowledged other sorts of imperatives for African American women, as well, such as those related to the often harsh realities of African American women's lives and experiences during this time period and the compelling challenges that needed to be addressed if the women were to have a better chance at improving themselves. *Ringwood's* included, therefore, articles that showcased examples of outstanding women, as well as those who showed promise. It also published articles that educated readers about the ill treatment of African American women, especially in the South.

The most instructive example of nineteenth-century African American women using the periodical press to leverage sociopolitical action is Josephine St. Pierre Ruffin, who founded *Woman's Era*. By the end of the nineteenth century, she had forged a distinctive record as a journalist and community activist who enthusiastically supported race and gender equality. Because of these activities, she was also able to form a large national and international network across races and among other women activists. In founding *Woman's Era*, Ruffin joined African American women journalists before her who recognized the need to create their own opportunities for agency and action, inventing their own public platform, and as in this case, participating with consequence in the public discourses of the day. Above and beyond a sparkling array of accomplishments, Ruffin demonstrated that she was a master strategist. With the founding of *Woman's Era*, she created an enabling infrastructure that successfully corralled the energies and strengths of a geographically diverse group of African American women as agents of transformative change. She created a sense of unfettered scope for their activism and leadership, establishing with this group of high-performing women an expanded sense of intellectual and professional viability and a broader range of motion for their sociopolitical labor.

This trajectory for sociopolitical work contributed tremendously to the rise of the National Association of Colored Women (NACW), a cohort that leveraged to excellent effect their individual and collective abilities to address the challenges and issues plaguing African American communities. The members of the newly formed national organization, both individually and collectively, were innovative in finding ways to generate impacts and consequences that mattered in support of freedom, justice, equality, and empowerment for their fellow citizens and for themselves, taking African American women's sociopolitical work to a different, more comprehensive, and more coherent national level.

By bringing more clarification to the confluence of actors, actions, and contexts of African American women's work, a key takeaway is that over the decades of the nineteenth century, African American women demonstrated a belief that their commitments and their work mattered, not simply for multileveled survival but as sociopolitical work in making a better world—regardless of whether the power brokers around them disregarded them or not. In point of fact, they brought to the table their visions of possibility as master strategists. They worked relentlessly to transform the circumstances and conditions around them for themselves and for others. They consistently raised their voices in the contexts that were open to them, using available resources and taking advantage of the expanding audience base. They understood the leverage provided by organized collective action in common cause—that there is strength in many hands doing the work.

At the same time, in being persistently excluded from existing white women's organizations and very much barred from or marginalized within men's enterprises, including the enterprises of African American men, they clearly understood the importance of having their own organizations. These women were not to be deterred from their sociopolitical interests and priorities. They chose to develop plans and processes for making their own, which they carried out with their own robust agenda, although they never relented in their efforts to continue working simultaneously with any others who were willing. The core consequence of their actions is that they became torchbearers, as indicated by the work of the Black Clubwomen's Movement, for generations to come, and through such work they left behind legacies of belief and action to inform ongoing sociopolitical work. We rest now in the arms of these angels, strengthened by their expectation that the need for vigilance is ever present.

Chapter 8

Shifting Interpretive Paradigms

In order to shift sight lines for interpreting African American women's sociopolitical engagement in public discourses, I have anchored the framework for this analysis with an examination of their experiences and achievements as speakers and writers in public space. I have taken into account most especially the rise of the African American periodical press during the nineteenth century as a prime tool for facilitating social and political change, in recognition of the assertion that this tool evolved to become the most available means for African America women advocates, activists, and leaders to exhibit rhetorical prowess and generate impact for the sociopolitical reforms that they wished to see. By their persistent engagement in this arena, the women themselves identified the press as fertile ground for nurturing their abilities to negotiate mandates for action and to function with consequence. With this analytical focus on the women's rhetorical prowess and on their ability to use this strength to meaningful, and often powerful, effect, my core priority has been to go beyond a simple recognition of their participation in rhetorical arenas. My goal has been to refine the analytical framework so that inferences and interpretations do not start at the end of the story in celebration mainly of the public presence of the women but, rather, at earlier moments with regard to the ways and means of how their stories of engagement and achievement evolved over the nineteenth century as the women took advantage of opportunities and created space for themselves to speak out and to make a positive difference in their world.

This analytical choice casts a brighter light on the need to dismantle myths about the presumed silence of African American women during this era on political concerns and their presumed lack of engagement with race and gender issues in particular within the broader scope of public discourses at the national level. As a more direct counterpoint to these mythological presumptions, my effort has been to design this framework to cast light on the rationality of taking into account the patterns, processes, and conditions of the women's actions—particularly as they articulated their own operational strategies themselves and worked conscientiously to operationalize them. My intention in this approach has been to clarify the point that the work of African American women in the public venues that were available to them was thoughtful, strategic, and meaningful in addressing an array of needs and concerns within their environment. With this intention, I have identified a twofold analytical agenda. On one hand, the effort is to appreciate the women's adaptability in using available resources to be assertive in working for change. On the other, the effort is to recognize that, from their own points of view, these women were very much aware that their sociopolitical context was dynamic and complex, rather than simple, and they were explicitly concerned with forwarding an ambitious agenda for social reform.

The basic goal of shifting analytical and interpretive paradigms in these ways is to magnify the possibility of more generative interpretations of what the women were actually doing and trying to do. My effort has been to recognize the ways in which African American women's journalistic endeavors leveraged the level, scope, and quality of their sociopolitical actions with particular regard for their identifying platforms for participation in an ambitious agenda and for gaining access to larger audiences for their ideas and strategies for change. The hypothesis has been that the inferences to be drawn from a more fully rendered set of inquiries confirm that African American women have earned the right to be acknowledged and appreciated for the quality and excellence of their work in narratives of nation.

Shifting paradigms for analysis and interpretation in making African American women more visible, audible, and intelligible is not simply a kindness offered to these women and their race. In broader scope, this process offers leverage for the nation itself, in keeping with our bedrock values, to function with greater credibility and capacity as a diverse and inclusive democracy, exhibiting rather than just declaring our national commitments to truth, justice, equality, and empowerment—for all. The imperative in this case is to resist upholding the dilemma, as so powerfully proclaimed by renowned philosopher and sociologist W. E. B. Du Bois, of viewing the women "through the eyes of others, of measuring [their souls] by the tape of a world that looks on in amused contempt and pity" (1994, 5). By these types of frameworks, the advantage of repositioning African American women's ways of working as agents of change is palpable. We foreground the opportunity to take into account their locations, societal status, points of view, experiences, and expertise. We add depth and texture in rendering more fully their actual ways and means of working, as well as the ways in which this work was able to connect with and enriched the broader activist landscape. We see in bolder relief that African American women were not just passively hoping for change but actively working to the extent that they were able to make it so.

Dismantling Myths

Shifting the analytical framework (in terms of visibility, audibility, and intelligibility) to make the sociopolitical actions of African American women more corporeal is a critical first step in dismantling myths. Another critical step calls for enriching interpretive frameworks to make better sense of what emerges through such analyses and, subsequently, calls for presenting and re-presenting this information credibly in knowledge-making enterprises in support of making the women more intelligible. To begin this second step of interpreting what we see, the task is to examine where we are now in interpreting, presenting, and re-presenting African American women's sociopolitical behavior during the nineteenth century—or, more likely, their perceived lack of sociopolitical behavior. A useful essay to help with this endeavor is Mia Bay's "The Battle for Womanhood Is the Battle for Race: Black Women and

Nineteenth-Century Racial Thought," as well as the coedited volume in which the essay is published, *Toward an Intellectual History of Black Women*. Bay and her coeditors deserve credit for accepting the notion that African American women do indeed have an intellectual history, an assertion that I consider to be both reasonable and appropriate even though I recognize that this view is not always presumed to be viable in anointed circles of power, authority, and credibility.

Bay starts her account of African American women's intellectual history with the public speaking career of Maria W. Stewart, whom she identifies as one of a few African American women in the 1830s who engaged in public discourse concerning race. She acknowledges the negative public response to Stewart's participation, caused by what was perceived during this era to be the impropriety of her presence as a woman in public and caused also by disagreements with her critiques of race relations and the conditions for African American people in the United States. Bay notes that, after Stewart, African American women did not speak out on race. She asserts that they were silent: "In the decades that followed [meaning the decades following Stewart's two-year career as a public speaker, from October 8, 1831, to September 21, 1833], it was not, in fact, black women who spoke out to counter the reproach of people of color. In contrast to African American men, who published a voluminous literature on the subject of ethnology—the nineteenth-century 'science of the races'—even educated black women remained conspicuously silent on the subject of race and racial differences right up until the turn of the century [which is the era of the rise of the Black Clubwomen's Movement]" (Bay 2015, 76; parenthetical comments are mine).

To explain how she accounts for this gap, Bay recognizes the gendered and racialized space occupied by African American women in the nineteenth century and the social constraints that surrounded them in terms of both identities (as African Americans and as women). She raises the question: "How do you write the history of a silence?" Bay asserts that silences are "rarely complete" and declares a need to know more about these women's interests and participation:

> As black women found their voice [i.e., as they began to have a public presence in dominant American public discourses], they also acknowledged their long history of silence and shame. The women

> who gathered for the inaugural meeting of the National Association of Colored Women Clubs in 1895 celebrated their embrace of female racial self-defense as a new goal. . . . [T]he conference's organizer, Josephine Ruffin, noted that black women could no longer be reduced to "mortified silence" by charges of a "delicate and humiliating" nature. The new organization's motto ["Lifting as We Climb"] reflected the fight these embattled women envisioned, as well as the dilemmas their forebears had faced: "The battle for womanhood is the battle for race." (Bay 2015, 89–90; parenthetical comments are mine)

The most profound conclusions that Bay draws in her analysis are her acknowledgment of an intellectual history for African American women and her recognition of the challenges for researchers and scholars to know and understand more about African American women during this time period. Most certainly, what has been most regularly documented and confirmed is the fact that between 1831 (when Stewart was published in *The Liberator*, the abolitionist newspaper founded by white progressives William Lloyd Garrison and Isaac Knapp) and 1895 (when the first national organizing meeting of African American women convened in Boston), African American women both socially and politically were indeed systemically and systematically constrained from freely exercising their intellectual capacities. Without argument, such material conditions in the United States were very much in motion well before 1831, and they have been persistently operating ever since.

With regard to the question that Bay raises about African American women's interests and participation in discourses on race, the opportunity for discovery is to shift the analytical paradigm in keeping with the model of inquiry suggested here. The task is to expand and reexamine more carefully and critically the evidence of the women's intellectualism and their sociopolitical work in order to enrich the conclusions that we might draw forth. The proposition is that a more expansive inquiry framework offers a possibility of additional insights about the patterns, nature, and history of their intellectual frameworks, leadership, and action. The effort is to take the opportunity to think critically about the women's ways of thinking and working in longer scope from the first public engagement of Phillis Wheatley in 1773 to Stewart's essay in 1831 and from Stewart's essay to the launching of the Black Clubwomen's Movement in 1896. In other words, when we look with greater expectations and more open minds at what African American women actually said within the public arenas that were open to them and what they did as actors in their lived environments, then we might be able to articulate more richly informed judgments.

In taking this stance, one might imagine that an enriched analysis might yield different conclusions. For example, we might see more evidence to suggests that intellectual frameworks for African American women were not anchored simply in the "science of race" and racial differences but, given their own lives and conditions, anchored instead more complexly at the convergence of race with other constructs such as gender, sexuality, class, culture, ideology, geographical location, and more. An expanded viewpoint pushes researchers and scholars to reconsider the advantage of a more kaleidoscopically rendered sight line. This broader conceptual perspective shifts the ground for interrogation. The contrasting opportunity becomes to understand that what we might view through race as a unifocal lens (with the conclusion that African American women were "conspicuously silent on race and racial differences" [Bay 2015, 76]) is quite likely not the women's silence at all but, perhaps, the women's more proactive decision to convey the conspicuous realities of their own critical vision at the intersection of social challenges and conditions, as confirmed not by a unifocal lens but by a multifocal lens.

Arguably, with a shifting of analytical and interpretive paradigms, in this case from unifocal to multifocal viewpoints, the inquiry turns more deliberately toward an interrogation of a fuller slate of interests as these focal points converge in lived experiences. Along these lines, it would make sense that African American women's intellectual frameworks and activist concerns are quite necessarily informed by their own multifocal points of view, with the question of race and racial differences morphing to connect more vibrantly with a broader range of factors—whether their engagement with these matrices of concerns happens in prestigious mainstream circles or in the discourses of counter-publics, such as the African American periodical press. Questions might include: What in addition to race are factors that matter to women? What is the value added by a multifocal viewpoint at a convergence of concerns rather than a singular viewpoint? Why were dominant discourses directed so singularly to race and racial differences as the appropriate and prime subjects for public priorities rather than there being a combination of factors that shape and direct public priorities? In putting forth the science of race and racial differences as of singular interest, what was the extent to which this narrow focal point left room for considerations of other sorts of factors, for example, gender and gender differences, or class and class differences, and so forth? How do unifocal and multifocal viewpoints help the nation to sustain commitments to national bedrock values—truth, freedom, justice, equality, and empowerment for all? How might the choice of viewpoint disrupt or facilitate progress and change? Does giving priority attention to race and racial differences suggest a hierarchy of importance, a hierarchy of needs, or a decision-making process that casts some things in light and others in shadow?

To reemphasize the point, the suggestion is that, in the hands of African American women, attention to race and racial differences is neither exclusive nor prime. What appears to be at the center of the women's viewpoints, both in contrast and complement to their brethren, is the notion that the concept of biologically determined racial differences (which seem inevitably to cluster around phenotype) seems to capture only a limited scope and substance for the array of issues about which the women were concerned. Multifocally, we might consider their views to connect, not so much to the idea of the science of race in relation to social justice and social reform, but more to the science of *Homo sapiens* in the sense of our contemporary understanding that the mapping of the human genome confirms that all human beings are quintessentially the same genetically. We might imagine, then—without assuming that their thinking was informed by our own understanding of the human genome—that the women were generally just starting their analysis at a different point on the ideological landscape. We might imagine that they considered race and racial differences alone not to make enough of a difference for social action and that speaking out about such theories seemed inadequate to define and address the pressing problems that they more urgently wanted to address.

Fundamentally, given the work of these early generations of women, the concept of race as biologically determined seems to flatten out in light of race as a social construction when we consider critically the ease with which race combines in social contexts with other identities and when we pay attention to the gravity of the impact of these combinations in the lives of African American people. By such glossing of terms, one might say that nineteenth-century African American women may have been ahead of their time in understanding that race was not a simple unifocal concern but quite a complex one and that they need not limit themselves to thinking well solely about race and racial differences as the prime and central leverage for change. Their effort instead during this time period was to concern themselves with several issues: fashioning speaking and writing selves and developing the expertise to elaborate in specific terms the dilemmas they were seeing around them, finding venues to display their expressive prowess, and using their intellectual abilities to articulate and exercise an agenda for meaningful action. By this reckoning, it is not a stretch to conclude that they were not actually ignoring the science of race but were honing in on a different viewpoint.

Given the range of topics that drew the women's attention (from racialized implications in education, health, gender, economic prosperity, and so forth), these women had a more nuanced multidimensional view of the connections between theory and action. A challenging question becomes, therefore, not: Why were they silent and unengaged about issues of race? But rather: How do the complexities of identity and status really matter in various arenas of action? In thinking through challenges and concerns, how do intellectual vision and power, critical thinking, innovative problem posing and problem solving work? For African American women in particular, how does the imperative to be bold and courageous in the pursuit of truth, freedom, justice, equality, and empowerment for all actually work when the task of speaking up and out occurs in arenas of power that are inhospitable to them?

To begin addressing Bay's call for more information about African American women's interests and participation, I propose the resetting of inquiries with patterns of questioning like the ones above that take into account visibility, audibility, and intelligibility. With these types of shifts, two quite different conclusions emerge. First, African American women were not silent on sociopolitical topics such as race and inequality—neither before 1831 nor in the six decades afterward and the launching of the Black Clubwomen's Movement in 1895. Second, we can imagine that Ruffin, in her opening address at the Boston conference in 1895 (see chapter 6), was not really apologizing or acknowledging that African American women were guilty of a history of silence and shame. Quite likely, she was clarifying something altogether different.

A key assertion in this instance is that researchers and scholars benefit from distinguishing between the dominant public sphere, as a nationally sanctioned set of venues, and other public spheres that were unsanctioned and not dominant. In effect, nineteenth-century mainstream arenas were defined, designed, and controlled as prestigious societal venues (for example, highly regarded periodicals, public lecture halls, churches, judicial courts, and so on) from the defaulted view of white elites and their preferences. In contrast, nondominant sites were unauthorized venues that were defined, designed, and controlled by people who did not function in central circles of power and prestige. These unanointed participants were often viewed as operating in inappropriate and unorthodox ways outside of standard expectations, for example, in terms of appropriate topics, contributors, and desired audiences. Typically, these nondominant sites could be more easily ignored and relegated to the counter-public sphere as present but not very consequential in national scope in terms of respect and regard. The implication of distinguishing between the spheres of public power and prestige and counter-public discourses (in this case the Black public sphere) highlights the importance of being intentional in bringing clarity to whether and how African American women might have been participating in public discourses—that is, in actually interrogating what might have constituted a venue for public discourse for this group.

The analytical and interpretive opportunity is to broaden the vista in order to move beyond traditional sites for public discourses in order to encompass a fuller range of venues. The idea is to be deliberate in expanding definitions of the public sphere as a multivariant set of opportunities for civic engagement rather than as a set of sanctioned sites that function in elite circles of power and prestige. From this perspective, in African American communities, venues for public discourse included the churches and, after 1827, the African American periodical press. This shift in defining what constitutes public discourse suggests that the critical question for African American women might more instructively be: What have we come to understand about the participation of African American women in nineteenth-century public discourses, around what issues, and with what audiences? In other words, the effort would be to examine more carefully what is there, rather than what is not there, and to consider more critically what might be there instead. What might performance, productivity, engagement, impact look like with these women's activities in mind rather than with them excluded or relegated to the periphery?

This type of shift in the paradigms for inquiry, documentation, analysis, interpretation, presentation, and representation enables a resetting of presumptions. In the case of African American women, the presumptions are fundamental: African American women, like other citizens of the United States with urgent mandates (such as the pursuit of truth, freedom, justice, equality, and empowerment) were speaking out publicly about things that mattered to them. The question is where were they speaking out? Who was listening? What level of consequence were they able to garner? With these paradigmatic shifts, we can focus more explicitly on the ways and means of the women's own intellectual visions and rhetorical choices rather than having them filtered through the visions, expectations, and actions of others. In this way, interrogations are focused on who, what, where, how, why, and under what circumstances the women were engaged and not engaged with regard to their chosen range of sociopolitical concerns.

With better grounded presumptions, we can direct attention more precisely, for example, to the presence and participation of African American women other than Maria Miller Stewart in the abolitionist movement, such as, for example, Elizabeth Freeman, Mary Prince, Sarah Mapps Douglass, Sarah Forten, Sarah Parker Rémond, Ellen Craft, and more. With the particularly racialized agenda of the abolitionist movement, where the imperative is to end the enslavement of people of African descent, we can begin anew to account for the evidence of African American women's visions, commitments, advocacy and activism. Even when Stewart remains the rhetor of interest, we can appreciate the need to seek a more nuanced view of her public performances, her networks, her rhetorical environments, and her own words. For example, a frequency count of her terms of engagement confirms that her conceptual framing was multifocal not unifocal, with her terms of engagement including issues related to race, gender, authority, education, economics, the nature of work, civic participation, ethical action, and more.

Given this regrounding of possibilities, I agree still with Bay regarding the constraints that related to racial oppression and white domination during this era. Barriers dictated that the African American women who were even in a position to speak out boldly in public venues were more typically northern women (or at least women who were living away from the South) such as Harriet A. Jacobs or Victoria Earle Matthews, rather than southern women who for most of the nineteenth century were overwhelmingly either enslaved or living under extremely oppressive conditions. The point, however, is that, regardless of barriers and constraints, African American women resisted oppression as they could. Some of them were indeed abolitionists, with several (for example, Sarah Mapps Douglass and Sarah Forten in Philadelphia, Sarah Parker Rémond in Salem, Massachusetts, and more) living in geographical sites beyond Boston, where Stewart lived. Like Stewart, though, all of the women just named were published in *The Liberator*.

A point not to be overlooked is that *The Liberator* was not a mainstream publication. It was an abolitionist newspaper, a specialized publication that profited from the patronage of African American communities. It is not surprising, therefore, that this paper made the atypical choice to offer both African American men and women opportunities for publication. Nevertheless, by all accounts, African American women had very limited access to the white periodical press, although there were a few exceptions such as Charlotte Forten's letters and essays from Saint Helena Island (see chapter 4) in the highly regarded *Atlantic Monthly*. Given the social expectations of their day, African American women could not count on white-owned venues to be an enabling mechanism for their civic engagement, as compared with specialized venues. With those realities being highlighted, we are brought back to the point that African American women participated in whatever venues they could, as opportunities became available.

A basic conclusion, then, is not that African American women were silent on race. They were not. They spoke out persistently and quite boldly, as public sites became available and opportunities permitted. The evidence of their words suggests that African American women advocates, activists, and leaders across the nineteenth century cast their arguments in values-centered ways, with emphasis on concepts such as truth, freedom, justice, equality, and peace, and from a problems-based perspective, with emphasis on issues and concerns related to education, health, poverty, working conditions, human and civil rights, and so on. Often, their viewpoints were intersectional, with race being inextricably linked to other aspects of their identity, to specific problems in their communities, and to the misalignments between national values and the urgent need to address pressing community concerns. The one thing that African American women were not is silent. A more troubling question, though, is whether anyone was listening and responding.

In recasting presumptions and generating better insights about African American women's work—that is, about what they actually said and did—what remains still is the darkness that surrounds: their intellectualism, the conceptual and operational visions that guided their work, their terms of engagement, matrices of concern and interests, operational practices, and communities of practice. A fundamental point that is emerging from expanding research agenda and scholarly practices is that the history of African American women's intellectualism is viscerally connected to their histories of practice, interwoven, quite inextricably it seems, with their beliefs and actions. To move forward, if we expect to advance both knowledge building and the quality and inclusiveness of our narratives of nation, then we have work to do to take more seriously the means, mechanisms, and processes of these women's productivity and impact as they sought, found, and created ways to enact their own beliefs and visions and to share their own voices in getting their sociopolitical work done. In other words, we need better heuristics for inquiry, documentation, analysis, interpretation, presentation, and representation.

With regard to matters of belief, then, let us return to Josephine St. Pierre Ruffin's welcoming keynote address at the 1895 convention in Boston. The gathering itself was a remarkable activist event, bringing together African American women leaders from across the nation. As an experienced rhetor and a declared agent of social and political change, Ruffin volunteered to be the leader in this organizational process. Her logistical work in coordinating arrangements for this first of its kind event offers a critical opportunity to think about the nature, ways, and means of this moment as a signature example of sociopolitical action. With attention directed specifically to her welcoming address, we can position it as a marker of dramatic change in the trajectory of African American women's activism, not locally, but as a national enterprise. Some basic questions come to bear: What were her imperatives in presenting this specific speech at the convention? What were her intentions and purposes? What was her message? Who was her audience? How did she anchor her message with her listeners who, even as a group of African American women, were still ideologically and operationally diverse? How was her message received? What

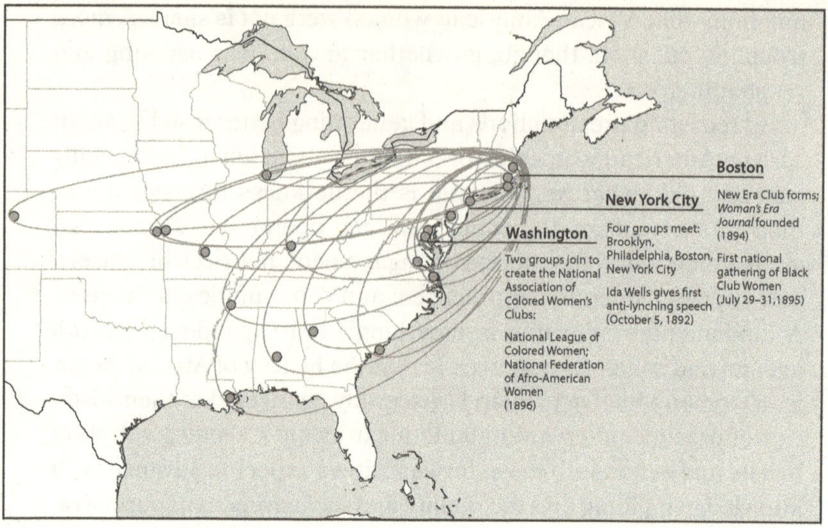

Figure 8.1: African American Clubwomen: Connections, 1892–1896

subsequent actions did she set in motion? One might quite easily conclude that none of the answers to these questions was that her intention was to apologize for or foreground African American women as previously silent and politically unengaged on race.

In her leadership role, Ruffin chose to gather African American women who were known from various social networks as leaders in their communities who were themselves engaged in a range of civic activities in more than twenty sites across the nation. These sites mapped directly onto the places where African American periodicals existed and the Black public sphere was vibrant (see figure 7.1). With regard to Ruffin's logistical planning, the Boston meeting (see figure 8.1) was nestled among a slate of three events that formed a major collaboration with women across three cities: New York, the gathering to pay tribute to Ida B. Wells; Boston, the convention organized by Ruffin to bring together leaders from over twenty African American women's organizations; and Washington, DC, the follow-up conventions to the 1896 Boston meeting that permitted two groups who were moving toward national organization to combine their efforts.

As the coordinator of the Boston event, Ruffin started her welcoming address by thanking a geographically diverse group of women organizational leaders for attending (see chapter 6 for the full text of this address). She recognized the value that would be derived from the meeting: "we [African American clubwomen from across the nation], bearing peculiar blunders, suffering under especial hardships, enduring peculiar privations, should meet for a 'good talk' among ourselves." She emphasized the wealth of knowledge, expertise, and experience these leaders were bringing to the conversation, in terms of their viewpoints of community action, educational preparation, operational competence, and organizational experience gained from their locally shaped activities, as well as their personal demonstrations of ingenuity as problem solvers, their expertise as speakers and writers, and the accomplishments that resulted from their strong work ethic.

Ruffin shared the imperatives for their gathering, emphasizing the privilege of refreshing their courage and spirit from "the mingling of congenial souls"; the opportunity to sort through "our own peculiar questions"; but most of all, to put forward far more assertively than they had chosen to do collectively in the past their own strengths and capacities—that is, in her words, "to stand forth and declare ourselves and principles, to teach an ignorant and suspicious world that our aims and interests are identical with those of all good aspiring women." This framework for Ruffin's address does not suggest "silence" or "shame" or even "apology." In contrast, she makes a powerful case for understanding the systemic efforts in American culture to promote "unjust and unholy charges" about African American women's character and their work, "audaciously and flippantly made," to push the women into "mortified silence," a viewpoint that underscores their "being silenced" (a verb) rather than "being silent" (an adjective).

This argumentative framing suggests that, with astute intellectual understanding, Ruffin recognized that the rhetorical situation required transformative action and did not benefit from the distraction of devoting any time at all to trying to create an alternate description of themselves in the face of "unholy charges" (most specifically the highly offensive charges raised against Ida B. Wells that spurred on the call for a meeting). In her argument, the "silence" these women needed to break was the silencing efforts against them—not a silence embraced and enacted by them. Moreover, the breaking process was that, in inviting her network of leaders for a "good talk," Ruffin merged thought and action and called for a collective effort from the women to defend themselves with more assertive declarations of who they were, not who they were not—which indicates a specific ideological stance. Ruffin's call was for collective transformative leadership and action in the hands of the group, rather than the individual actions that might be easily absorbed and dismissed, as was the habitual process of containment regularly exercised by the systems of oppression. She declared that this group of leaders was very much up to the task, and she extended her call for them to resist the persistently vile accusations of others against them—with proactive strategies rather than reactive ones.

Ruffin's welcoming speech, therefore, was indeed a "keynote," a bold message underscoring the ideological perspective that this group of African American women leaders had remarkable strength in numbers at this point in history and that they constituted thereby "an army of organized women . . . [to] open the eyes of the world to a state of affairs to which they [the world] have been blind, often willfully so." She ended by declaring this group of women to be the leaders of the resistance, warrior women, but very much open to allies (African American men, white women, white men, whoever was willing to join them in common cause), and declaring, as Anna Julia Cooper had declared in 1892, that the new organization they would form would be capable of ushering in "a new era to the colored women of America."

Using shifted paradigms for interrogation, we can examine Ruffin's address more closely, with attention on the considerable evidence she provides related to her expertise as an astute rhetor. Her speech confirms her view that, even in the face of the trauma of race, gender, and class oppressions, African American women were not responsible for the systemic efforts of the society either to silence or to shame them. Her argumentative structure shows that she understood both value constructs to have been imposed on them by policies and practices that operated and were often sanctioned well beyond their own political authority and control. Ruffin determined that, in their defense of themselves, their resistance should reasonably be focused on amplifying their own visions and voices, on being bold about fashioning their own operational paradigm, and being meticulous about not falling into the trap of twirling within paradigms constructed by others to constrain and distract them or to position them as somehow inferior. Appealing to logos, ethos, and pathos, Ruffin endowed the challenges before the group with the corporeality of their experiences, talents, and abilities, and moved them toward a different interpretive paradigm and a different pathway for transformative action.

A fundamental consequence of Ruffin resetting disempowering presumptions about African American women—away from a view of them as unworthy and passive and away from the notion that they were finally coming out of decades of silence and shame to find their voice—is actually a good step toward garnering greater intelligibility. With more data about their actual words and deeds, contemporary researchers and scholars are better positioned than ever before to notice and understand a basic point. The inescapable fact of oppressive conditions does not automatically mean that African American women were unaware of the complexities of their sociopolitical context nor that they were not engaged in public discourses and sociopolitical actions that mattered to their race, to the nation, and to themselves. Certainly, societal policies and practices have relentlessly pushed African American women—as a cloaked, muted, and unconsidered group—to the periphery of value and regard. Certainly, both the women and their work have been cast historically in dark shadows such that the group and their labor have inevitably been made invisible, inaudible, and unintelligible. Just as certainly, though, using a different set of analytical and interpretive lenses can enhance our capacity to see all the same that there is more to stories of African American women's lives, labor, and consequence than had been previously valued and told.

As suggested by my bringing the three paradigmatic anchors in this analysis forward (visibility, audibility, intelligibility), I acknowledge that, when we look with more care and caring over the decades from the founding of the nation throughout the nineteenth century, it really is not difficult to see African American women's intellectual vibrancy and the inventive ways in which they exercised a robust multilayered action agenda. As usual, however, there is a persistent cautionary tale. To understand their presence and consequence in public spaces, we must pay close attention to a double-edged sword. African American women were barred from circles of participation and regard by the power dynamics of the era. They were deemed to be unworthy of inclusion and regard. In circular fashion, their being categorized as unworthy meant that they were marked systemically as inferior, shameful, without potential, merit, or voice, a positioning that gave them little if any potential to demonstrate, as people with intellectual capacities, expertise, and experience, that they were actually worthy and deserved to be present. Ultimately, this operational pattern was easily normalized within the sociocultural environment by persistent practices of low expectations and disregard, even though such viewpoints from the women's perspectives were not actually true. With shifted inquiry paradigms, we can see that their being barred did not mean that they were uninterested in or unengaged in meaningful action.

In other words, African American women's actions and achievements suggest that they did not really believe in the disempowering views that were persistently ascribed to them. They did not think of themselves as inferior, or filled with shame, or silent on race or anything else. In her logistical planning for the Boston conference, Ruffin put that dilemma aside. What she considered to be far more urgent than worrying about how persistently they were surrounded by impossible constraints was the need for an operational tool to facilitate the breaking of those bonds. She determined that they needed their own African American women's public sphere. They needed their own platform to be free to speak their own vision, proclaim their own agenda, and not be dependent on others for inclusion or regard. By extension, the imperative for contemporary researchers and scholars about their work is not to think of the scholarly effort as a need to write "the history of a silence" but, rather, to reclaim the history of African American women's intellectualism, to recalibrate their sociopolitical work, and to write their history of resilience, despite the relentless racialized and gendered practices that have made both African American women and their work invisible, inaudible, and unintelligible.

With her leadership in organizing the first national political meeting, Ruffin was successful in articulating a touchstone for African American women's intellectual history that has resounded through the decades since 1895. As a case in point, an example of the legacies of this leadership and action happened a hundred years later, in 1993, after the Hill/Thomas hearings that were connected to the appointment of conservative African American judge Clarence Thomas to the Supreme Court of the United States and the charge of sexual harassment brought against him by Anita Hill. After the publication of the "Statement of African American Women in Defense of Ourselves" in the *New York Times* and eight other newspapers across the nation, there was another call for women of African descent to convene at the Massachusetts Institute of Technology in Cambridge, Massachusetts, on January 13–15, 1994.[1]

The title of the conference was "Black Women in the Academy: Defending Our Name, 1894–1994." In attendance were almost two thousand women of African descent from across Africa, Europe, and North America. They gathered to sort through an array of critical issues for the African American community and to address the special issues of women of African descent in the academy. This conference mirrored remarkably well the 1895 conference convened by Ruffin. As reported in *SAGE: A Scholarly Journal on Black Women*, over the course of the century between the two meetings, there was considerable evidence of a continuity of both concerns and responses to those concerns by the women in attendance:

> Despite a steady stream of remarkable contributions and achievements by African American women across many fields of endeavor, we find ourselves one hundred years later being brought again to a seemingly ever present reality. The more things change; the more they stay the same. . . . What we urge, however, is that all African American women, and others who might be encouraged to join us, be ever vigilant in the struggle for equity, power, and justice. What has become quite apparent to us, as we enter the twenty-first century and begin a second century of vigilance, is that defending our name is ultimately in the interest of defending the names of women everywhere. We must not be silent. We must never be silent. (Royster and Hammonds 1995, 8)

The 1994 conference recognized a century of struggle and the need "to feel the cheer and inspiration of meeting each other . . . to gain thc courage and fresh life that comes from the mingling of congenial souls, of those working for the same ends" (Royster and Hammonds 1995, 8). At the end of the conference, the group sent forward a five-point resolution addressed to the president of the United States, President William Jefferson Clinton. The resolution appealed to the president to "commission a blue-ribbon panel on race relations; promote black women's research and extend the Glass Ceiling Commission to address the women of color in academia; extend funding for community-based social service organizations for the poor; end covert actions against Haiti and restore President Aristide to power, and continue to support democracy in South and Southern Africa."[2] The sociopolitical work of the women in 1994 continued just as the work of the women in 1895 continued.

In Search of a Different Paradigmatic Approach

The paradigmatic shift proposed here functions to enable and encourage deeper insights, as is beautifully articulated in Alice Walker's "In Search of Our Mothers' Gardens."[3]

> What did it mean for a Black woman to be an artist in our grandmothers' time? In our great-grandmothers' day? It is a question with an answer cruel enough to stop the blood. . . . How was the creativity of the Black woman kept alive, year after year and century after century, when for most of the years Black people have been in America, it was a punishable crime for a Black person to read or write? And the freedom to paint, to sculpt, to expand the mind with action did not exist. Consider, if you can bear to imagine it, what might have been the result if singing, too, had been forbidden by law. Listen to the voices of Bessie Smith, Billie Holiday, Nina Simone, Roberta Flack, and Aretha Franklin, among others and imagine those voices muzzled for life. (Walker 1983, 233–34)

Walker paints a provocative image of the creative, intellectual, and sociopolitical impulses of African American women. Her basic argument is that, despite the bonds of slavery, despite laws that forbade the development of even basic literacy skills, despite incomprehensible barriers in all dimensions of their lives, African American women have still been bold enough to find ways to express their thoughts and desires, to raise their visions and voices, and to keep raising them by whatever means available. In doing so, African American women have fashioned a creative and innovative intellectual authority, a garden that continues to be productive and to yield ongoing legacies of action and leadership.

In 1983, when Walker published this essay collection, her assertions were bold in that they made visible and audible the need for serious interrogation of African American women's creative, intellectual, and sociopolitical work. Since then, there has been considerable research and scholarship that has confirmed the validity of Walker's claims. With what has now become an ever-expanding knowledge base, one might assume that, by now, we should have a more multidimensional understanding of African American women's creative and intellectual impulses, their sociopolitical work, and the nature, impact, and consequences of their leadership and activism. Seemingly, after almost four decades of knowledge generation, we should have created a rightful place in intellectual and activist history—both nationally and globally—for their productivity and achievements. However, while we do in fact know more than we did in 1983, we remain strikingly limited in the ways in which these discoveries have constituted a more substantive and insightful view of African American women's lives and work. In essence, we have added to the mound of historical knowledge, but the question remains about whether our collecting of more data has gone far enough in informing our thinking about leadership and action. The question is whether we have recalibrated and reset history-telling and storytelling paradigms to articulate more diverse and inclusive patterns and frameworks. What is evident still, even in contemporary discourses, are perceptions of African American women more as compassionate and hardworking, and less as intellectually strong strategic thinkers and communicators, with logistical expertise as leaders of transformative change (see Royster 2022).

Historically, during the horrors of the slave era the habitual practice of viewing African Americans as beasts of the earth rather than as human beings with the potential for excellence served to undermine expectations for the whole race. African American women were particularly vulnerable. One example of ill treatment from this era goes beyond the typical stories of beatings, rape, overwork, and the lack of self-autonomy to include the fact that African American women were also subjected to medical experimentation as though they were lab animals available for use by medical researchers without consequence or accountability (Axelsen 1985). With such unfettered policies and practices, it has been a constant struggle over the generations to move beyond deeply seated presumptions of low or no value. In reflection, one can easily imagine the intensity of their challenge in seeking to garner respect and dignity before, during, and after the Civil War in order to be perceived as human beings with talents and abilities, or intellectuals and philosophers, or strategic thinkers and problem solvers, or, more simply, as women of substance, integrity, and consequence. From this perspective, while it might be affirming that African American women may have come to be envisioned as compassionate, caring, and hardworking people, what remains problematic is an acknowledgment of them as talented women who exhibit high performance as advocates, activists, and leaders.

Some of the most compelling interrogations of the inequitable assignment of low status and regard to African American women have been presented by African American women themselves in bringing visibility to their own lives and experiences. A well-known example from the nineteenth century is Sojourner Truth who established a critical stance with regard to her own capacities and possibilities in her infamous "Ain't I a Woman?" speech delivered at the Women's Rights Convention in Akron, Ohio, in 1851. An example from the twentieth century is Zora Neal Hurston. In her novel, *Their Eyes Were Watching God* (first published in 1937), Hurston spoke eloquently through her central character, Janie, as Janie iconically proclaimed that African American women were the mules of the world. These examples suggest that the contrast in conceptual positioning is the difference between the women being assigned a disempowering status as compared with their own perceptions of themselves.

To reemphasize the point, there has been an impressive amount of research, as cited throughout this volume, that has been successful in recovering and reinscribing counter stories to the presumptions of limited level of excellence for African American women. We know a good deal more about the work and achievements of individual women, but we still do not have a strong enough hold of the innovative processes that these women developed to enable their actions. We know more about what the women had to say in various public spaces, but not so much about the deeper terrain of their intellectual grounding or the inventive operational frameworks they fashioned to engage in various decision-making enterprises, to express their viewpoints and to carry out their action goals. Sadly, despite the growing mound of knowledge, we have not really shifted analytical and interpretive paradigms enough to normalize the presence of African American women as consequential in various action arenas or to stabilize in the national imaginary the strength of their intellectual capacities, the excellence of their sociopolitical work, or a more substantive view of the quality of their accomplishments. Essentially, we know that they were there, which is good. In the United States, they've always been there. The question is what were they really doing, how, and why—not just in terms of what was happening, but what was really going on? How can we see, know, and understand the dimensions of their mandates and imperatives, their vision, agency, authority, and impact?

An important step in building a more substantive response to such questions is to shift the analytical gaze from viewing nineteenth-century African American women as *feminists* or *protofeminists* to seeing them as *race women*, the labeling that they used more often to name themselves. The terms *race men* and *race women* came into frequent use in the nineteenth century after the American Civil War in connection with a core group of men and women who had set a remarkable pace based on their activism in the Black abolitionist movement. They were staunch and steadfast advocates and leaders in the ongoing pursuit of freedom and civil rights. After emancipation, they quickly determined that freedom was not enough. They needed social justice and equity within the law. They brought a brighter light to the connections between civil rights and human rights as they identified an often urgent need not simply for the equitable application of existing law but for more and different laws and policies, ones that explicitly honored the national values of freedom, justice, equality, and empowerment for all citizens rather than for some.

During this era, African American women leaders aligned themselves regularly with the term *race women*. The basic question is what the term meant to them in their own day and time, rather than to us in ours. The range of interrogations might include the following: Who were the race women? Where did they come from? What sorts of things did they manage to do to enact their ideological commitments? Have we been paying close enough attention to this group of activists from their own points of view and in their own operational spaces? Have we have taken enough care in connecting various dots? What do we lose by using our contemporary terms and concepts rather than theirs? What were the factors that distinguished them as actors during their own day? How do we notice, value, and appreciate what we may not have noticed before?

In fundamental terms, we know that these women were born before or around the Civil War—some freeborn, some not. We know that they were the first generations of African American women to live in a slavery free nation, the first cohorts of college-educated women, the first cohorts of women in the professions, and among the first groups of women to reach critical mass and critical capacity—with the skills, training, experiences, and networks to shape and inform leadership and strategic action, whether they were working locally, nationally, or internationally. In addition, because their words and actions verified their view of themselves as race women (or as the leading women of the race), we also know that the members of this cohort were socially and politically aware of the need for respectability—and very much aware of the practices of dissemblance that might be necessary for their own protection in public space.

Given the era, it also goes without saying that these women were culturally identified and deeply rooted in African American communities, regardless of the various configurations of their personal identities. For example, by phenotype, Charlotte Forten, Josephine St. Pierre Ruffin, Mary Church Terrell, and Gertrude Bustill Mossell were sometimes considered to be from an "amalgamated" cross-race heritage. They were also privileged to hold a socioeconomic status that was more clearly elite than most African American women of their generation. The group as a whole represented a continuum of social identities, but more to the point, regardless of the various differences among the race women, as a whole they proclaimed an urgent need for all in their race to participate fully in the rights of US citizenship. Recovery processes in historical research and scholarship have confirmed, in fact, that, as the women of the race, they were committed to doing their parts the very best they could to respond to urgent needs with their own strengths and through long-standing habits of action in their communities. What researchers and scholars highlight less frequently in their documentation and analysis is the consistency with which, in doing their parts, these women were typically being deliberate in orchestrating vital and vibrant connections among their intellectual interests and concerns, their strategic actions in context, and the critical dimension of their sociopolitical awareness.

A more critical perspective of the evidence available, in keeping with the approach articulated in this volume, suggests that shifting analytical and interpretive paradigms helps us to gain a clearer perspective on all of the above. The basic proposition is not just that we have not been paying close enough attention to the women from their own points of view and in their own operational spaces but also that we have not taken enough care in our documenting processes to connect various points at the convergence of visibility and audibility. The questions are: How do we make better sense of what we are discovering? How might new interpretations emerge, if what the women have appeared to be doing from twenty-first-century perspectives was just one piece of what they imagined themselves to be doing or capable of doing? What were the factors that distinguished them intellectually and operationally as actors? Again, how do we notice, value, and appreciate what we have not noticed before?

To think again about the race women, we can restart the viewpoint by fleshing out a few more critical details, starting with the highlighting of two patterns for who some of the leading women categorized as race women were. In several cases, with examples such as Harriet Tubman, Charlotte Forten, Frances E. W. Harper, Mary Shadd Cary, and Josephine St. Pierre Ruffin, the women had come of age before the American Civil War. They held the distinction of already living free, and typically were already frontline activists before and during the war. Another pattern is based on women whose souls had been fired in forward-thinking activist communities, whether they were born before, during, or immediately after the war; born free, freed, or enslaved; and whether they were living in the North or the South. Among this set were women such as Maritcha Lyons, Mary Church Terrell, Fannie Jackson Coppin, Selena Sloan Butler, Josephine Silone Yates, Ida B. Wells, and Anna Julia Cooper. However, there is yet another set of sensibilities to add to the mix.

For the women who lived in the latter part of the nineteenth century, especially, they were living and working in a time of new hopes for freedom. They were the first generations of African American women to grow up and live in the newly united American nation, a society in which, after the war, slavery was deemed to be against the law of the land. The sobering point is that across these cohorts, the race women found that their work, hopes, and expectations were not automatically recognized by power elites—and they were not regularly called upon (as was the case for generations of African American women before them) to lead the resistance. Nevertheless, they remained resilient over the decades after the Civil War and true to the ongoing fight, against the odds, for both human and civil rights.

Embodying the Idea of a Woman's Era

What the characteristics of these "new era" women suggest is that, by the post-Reconstruction era of the 1880s, both race men and race women were painfully and inevitably aware of being ensnared in a complicated sociopolitical web of race, class, and gender. These entanglements required more than ever their holding on to their hopes for a better horizon. The dilemma of being free but not free, especially given the multiple oppressions of African American women (race, gender, class, and more), was a daunting challenge—expressed articulately and boldly for African American women by Anna Julia Cooper in *A Voice from the South*, as illustrated by a series of quotations from this publication. She says, for example: "I see two dingy little rooms with 'FOR LADIES' swinging over one and 'FOR COLORED PEOPLE' swinging over the other . . . while wondering under which head I come" (1988, 96). She also wrote: "Only the Black Woman can say 'when and where I enter, in the quiet, undisputed dignity of my womanhood, without violence and without suing or special patronage, then and there the whole Negro race enters with me'" (31). In the same volume Cooper carried her thoughts forward to appeal for a *woman's era*, stating:

> no woman can possibly put herself or her sex outside any of the interests that affect humanity. All departments in the new era are to be hers. . . . In the last decade of our century, changes of such moment are in progress. . . . To be a woman in such an age carries with it a privilege and an opportunity never implied before. But to be a woman of the Negro race in America, and to be able to grasp the deep significance of the possibilities of the crisis, is to have a heritage, it seems to me, unique in the ages. (143–44)

With these words Cooper took on the challenges of her day as inspiration, opportunity, and obligation, a sentiment echoed a year later by Frances E. W. Harper in her speech titled "Woman's Political Future," which she presented at the World Congress of Representative Women held during the World's Columbian Exhibition in Chicago in May 1893. Harper stated: "Through weary, wasting years men have destroyed, dashed in pieces, and overthrown, but today we stand on the threshold of woman's era, and woman's work is grandly constructive. In her hand are possibilities whose use or abuse must tell upon the political life of the nation, and send their influence for good or evil across the track of unborn ages" (1995, 43).

The theoretical framings in Harper's statement are richly endowed with declarations, claims, contrasts, and calls for action. The sentiments of both Cooper and Harper resonated through the ages, and one hundred years later, in 1996, Kimberlé Crenshaw, in *Critical Race Theory: The Key Writings that Focused the Movement*, reaffirmed the challenges and opportunities that have persisted for African American women at the convergence of oppressive forces. Crenshaw underscores, for example, that *feminism* at its best is not just woman-centered. It is most compellingly defined at the intersections of our multiple identities and in view of our multiple oppressions.

So, how did nineteenth-century African American women think about and theorize their positionality—when their lived realities were that they were free (but not free), that all citizens had equal rights under the law (but not really everyone), that the nation was just (but not just for all)? How did their theorizing and strategizing inform the patterns of their actions? In considerations of this positionality, research and scholarship have come up short in getting beyond an acknowledgment of the physical presence of civically engaged African American women during this era (Yes, they were there); and beyond the fact of their remarkable slate of individual achievements (Yes, many of the women were high performing in their communities). The challenge remains for knowledge-making, history-telling, and storytelling to connect the various dots of their excellence in creating a fuller account of their contributions and achievements. In shifting perspectives to be more deliberately kaleidoscopic in analysis and interpretation, the need, thereby, is for robust interrogations of the women's ideas, analyses, and critiques as their intellectual work—with an eye toward connecting their visions to belief, experience, and action; and for our use of multifocality, multivocality, and multilecticality in seeing and understanding their civic engagement as having breadth, depth, substance, and consequence.

This approach suggests that these women: (1) exhibited the intellectual capacity to see themselves as having agency, authority, and the right to voice even within a complex inhospitable context; (2) showed a tendency to use richly layered critiques in interrogating their worlds, in keeping with the dynamic intersections of their concerns and interests; (3) tended to be inventive in posing problems and developing strategies to address them; (4) used their beliefs and sensibilities about their identities, roles, and responsibilities to fashion springboards for meaningful action; and (5) exhibited a lively understanding of the notion that sustaining effective action in complex inhospitable contexts requires critical, creative, and innovative thought, commitment, vigilance, accountability, and often courage. In other words, as researchers and scholars, we are called upon to notice that the legacies of nineteenth-century African American women's sociopolitical action and leadership did not emerge by happenstance but, rather, at the dynamic convergence of their intellectualism, strategic actions, and passionate commitments to making a better world.

From this perspective, just as the Civil War constitutes a useful touchstone in fleshing out African American women's work at mid-century, so too does the Black Clubwomen's Movement constitute a useful touchstone for measuring progress and change by the end of the century. When we look at what was going on during these last decades, one point quickly becomes clearer. This cohort of women were not monolithic in their ideological frameworks, their experiences, or their alliances. Not surprising for human interactions, a central implication of their diversity is that they also did not all share the same preferences for how to achieve progress and change. This basic observation means that we need to think about what African American women's diversity, even among elite women, entailed and how it worked in civic arenas.

In *Beyond Respectability* (2017), Brittney Cooper focuses on this challenge. Her analysis suggests that we might cluster ideological differences in two quite specific ways, with the two clusters representing centers of gravity for what might be considered a continuum of African American women's patterns of leadership and action. On one end of the continuum, we can place an ideological stance that supports a framework of respectability and dissemblance. On the other end, we can position patterns that are more supportive of the idea of "undisputed dignity," in keeping with the ideological positioning of Anna Julia Cooper. In Brittney Cooper's analysis, racial respectability and dissemblance emphasizes the need to elevate the race in order to normalize the movement of African Americans in public space. In this case, strategic actions are centered in more inner-directed fashion on the internal development and conveyance of racial respectability so that African Americans—and African American women in particular—might be granted by the nation better mobility in geographical, social, political, and cultural space.

In contrast, Brittney Cooper's explanation of Anna Julia Cooper's notion of "undisputed womanhood" sets forth an approach that, in similar terms, also values respect and the elevation of the race. This stance centers, however, on the other end of the ideological continuum with strategic actions that are more explicitly outer-directed on social justice and social change. In this case, the right of respectability is presumed to be in evidence among members of the race, such that the energy for change is directed more toward the application of human and civil rights for citizens that, by their undisputed status, deserve justice and equality. Brittney Cooper's analysis offers an insightful springboard for understanding more specifically that the existence of this ideological continuum was a lively element in the NACW ecosystem. Recognizing the existence of diversity in preferred action agenda among the members permits us to gain a clearer hold of the ways in which the women were both similar and different. In particular, the recognition of variability sheds light on the ways in which the leadership of NACW, as a broad and diverse national organization, became very much a contested space, with tensions that played themselves out in interesting ways during the formative years of the organization.

To summarize the fundamental assertion here, given the type of analyses and interpretations that I have been presenting in this volume, what becomes more evident by the final decade of the nineteenth century is that the formation of NACW constitutes a dramatic case in point for understanding the evolution of African American women's advocacy, activism, and leadership as a many splendored enterprise. Over the course of the long nineteenth century (from the founding of the nation in 1776 to the end of the next century), this cohort of women had been fashioning more coherently and assertively their own creative and innovative intellectual agency and authority. They grounded their points of view at the convergence of their identities as women of substance with intellectual capacities; the specific array of their experiences, talents, skills, and networks; the consistency of their strategic actions over the decades; and their common commitments to live up to their sociocultural responsibilities as leading women of their race who had benefited from the opportunities available to them.

Using their various strengths, this group was committed to working hard for their causes. They demonstrated that, while they were not monolithic in vision, word, or deed, they were consistent in their dedication to an ongoing quest for truth, freedom, justice, equality, and empowerment. As leaders with local strength and national scope, they shared in the collective knowledge of the continuity of their experiences within a persistently oppressive society, and they vigorously embraced the common goal of making the world a better place. They exhibited intellectual strength, as well as prowess as strategic thinkers, astute communicators, and quite capable logistical experts. They were innovative in defining and solving problems and in fashioning and carrying out well-grounded action goals. With these traits and factors in hand, the members of NACW across their operational preferences brought corporeality to the belief that their era was a woman's era and that African American women from across the spectrum of potential and possibilities were determined and able to collaborate in making their work count for good.

Unorthodox Designs

The discussion to this point has focused on developing sight lines that cast brighter light on African American women as agents of change and on the contexts in which they were engaging. From this point forward, the imperative is to sharpen the analytical and interpretive paradigm to reveal the women's operational frameworks and particularly, with NACW members as the case in point, to take into account their ways of being as leaders at work. To be sure, the assertion that the launching of the Black Clubwomen's Movement was a powerful moment in African American women's intellectual history is now a familiar story to many researchers and scholars who work on this era or this cultural group. A baseline fact is that, just thirty-one years after the Civil War, this group of race women successfully established the NACW, a national organization. In doing so, they created deep and long-lasting roots for an organization that is now older than the NAACP (1909) and the National Urban League (1910), organizations within which these women were also active. In 2021 NACW (now the National Association of Colored Women's Clubs) celebrated its 125th anniversary as the first secular organization with national scope in the country deliberately and explicitly designed to support the progress and advancement of the African American community. Questions that linger are not about whether this cohort of women created this success. The evidence for that fact is clear. They did create it. The questions are: How did they do it? In doing this work, what did they imagine themselves, in fact, to be doing? What was the critical advantage that their creation set in motion for their race, their communities, themselves?

The focus here is not only on the leaders of the movement but also on the processes and actions by which these leaders created a movement and built organizational momentum. Consider Josephine St. Pierre Ruffin, the founder of the Woman's Era Club and the *Woman's Era* newspaper, and the managing organizer of the first national-level convention of African American women leaders. To be noted, when utilized as a continuum that enables closer and more direct analysis of the sociopolitical actions of NACW, Brittney Cooper's explanation of *respectability and dissemblance* and *undisputed womanhood* becomes very useful. On one end of the continuum, agenda setting focuses on respectability and mobility as a more internally defined conservative stance. Farther along the continuum, the stance is a less conservative, more policy-oriented viewpoint that combines the internal directives of respectability and mobility with external directives for social justice and social change. On the other end of the continuum, the agenda-setting view is more radically designed with emphasis on aggressive and dramatic sociopolitical action and change.

By this reckoning, Ruffin certainly wanted African American women to be safe, to have mobility across arenas of action, and to be respected in public space. However, her own history as an activist who regularly worked in multiple arenas and across racial boundaries suggests that, by 1894, she was far more concerned with creating a more hospitable space for the work she was willing and able to do than with creating more room mainly to improve herself. Essentially, the backdrop of her life and work suggests that Ruffin was aware that respectability had not always "saved" her or helped her to enter some arenas of action with the expectation of hospitality (which over the centuries has been quite a precarious concept for African American women). Her actions suggest, instead, that what African American women leaders really wanted and needed was a different world, not just stronger folks in an oppressive world. So, the basic questions in considering the ways and means of her approach to leadership are: Who was Josephine St. Pierre Ruffin? What was her ideological grounding? What did she do and encourage others to do? What were the results of her strategic preferences for NACW work?

Ruffin was a multiracial woman born on August 31, 1842, into a politically active family who had been living free for several generations in Taunton, Massachusetts, and then in Boston (see chapter 6). By the last two decades of the nineteenth century, she was considered to be among the top African American women leaders in the nation. She was actively involved in clubwomen's work through the white women's organizations in which she participated, as well as the newly formed organizations emerging during this era in the African American community. By 1893, at the age of fifty-one, Ruffin had demonstrated that she was a clever and passionate rhetor who was accustomed to working with others across various lines for social action and reform. She had a vision of the future that fired her passions. She was an experienced warrior for civil and human rights who demonstrated a remarkable facility for organizing strategic action, and she was well connected across several networks—locally, nationally, and internationally. Her accomplishments show that she engaged actively in public space as a leader with professional expertise, and through this work, by the 1890s, she had built a formidable reputation. With a focus on her actions after the gathering at Lyric Hall in New York, this time period in her leadership suggests that, like many African American women of her cohort, she did indeed believe in internal development, but it also suggests, simultaneously, that she had other interests and desires as well.

The recalibration of African American women's legacies of leadership and action in launching the Black Clubwomen's Movement begins, as many researchers and scholars have marked it, with a kairotic occasion for collective action, the hosting of journalist Ida B. Wells's first public lecture. Victoria Earle Matthews (journalist and community organizer) and Maritcha Rémond Lyons (school principal and community organizer) were two prominent women leaders in New York and Brooklyn who partnered regularly in community development initiatives (see chapter 2). With the attention across the African American community generated by Wells's exile from Memphis, it made sense that these two leaders would again work together to sponsor and organize a lecture by Wells to tell her story of terrorism. The event took place on October 5, 1892, at Lyric Hall in New York City. Given their long-standing sociopolitical activities and work in community development, Matthews and Lyons had developed a broad social network that brought together 250 African American women of renown from the three states of New York, Massachusetts, and Pennsylvania.

This event was not just the social event of the year. The women were not at the gathering simply to attend a banquet or a party or a fashion showcase—although we might well imagine that elements of social interaction and celebration were indeed a compelling part of the occasion. The women were there to engage instead in a serious sociopolitical act. They came to learn about the details of Ida B. Wells's anti-lynching campaign, her experiences as a journalist and civil rights activist in Memphis, Tennessee, and what she wanted to do next. At the end of this successful event, these women gave Wells a gift of five hundred dollars for her to continue her activist work, to publish a pamphlet, and to launch what would become her lifelong anti-lynching campaign, becoming an initial funder of Wells's activism.

With the Lyric Hall event as a signature occasion for action, Ruffin was visible as a prime candidate for an invitation from Matthews and Lyons. She attended the event and was inspired. After the dinner she demonstrated that she was a master strategist at work. She hosted Wells for a lecture in Boston, and she gathered her core team of allies, which consisted of her daughter, Florence Ruffin Ridley, a teacher also recognized for her expertise as a writer, and her good friend Maria L. Baldwin, a legendary educator and headmistress of the Agassiz School in Cambridge who was recognized in her own right for her abilities as a public speaker for educational and activist causes. Together, these three women organized the Woman's Era Club (which ultimately became the New Era Club). This organization was the first of its kind in Boston and among the first in the United States. The moment was catalytic.

Ruffin, Ridley, and Baldwin in the company of other friends (not all of them African American) not only founded the Woman's Era Club, they went a step farther. To take advantage of the opportunity to move a robust sociopolitical agenda at what Ruffin recognized to be an opportune time, she determined it was critical to build a platform for leveraging the momentum she had observed at Lyric Hall. The available means for accomplishing this goal was the periodical press, and she used her own resources to found a newspaper. She became the first African American woman journalist in the United States (as contrasted with Mary Shadd Cary who founded her paper in Canada) to be the sole owner of and to write for, edit, and publish her own politically focused periodical. In Ruffin's case, her focus was on issues of particular concern to African American women, and she directed it explicitly to an audience primarily of African American clubwomen across the nation who defined themselves as agents of change.

Ruffin called the newspaper *Woman's Era*, inspired by sentiments expressed by Anna Julia Cooper and Frances E. W. Harper. The mission of *Woman's Era*, as articulated in the first volume of the paper, was to fill what Ruffin perceived to be a void. The paper was to serve as a medium of "discourse and sympathy" between the women of all races and conditions, as a vehicle for African American women to take their places among "advanced women," and as a mechanism for "expanding the narrowness of their environment"—in art, science and letters. Ruffin's ultimate goal was to build up the knowledge, experiences, strengths, and capacities of African American women in order to enhance their abilities to "make the most of themselves" (editorial, *Woman's Era* 1.1). Simply put, like other African American women leaders of her era, Ruffin felt deeply the special qualities of their opportunities and just as deeply an obligation to take supreme advantage of these opportunities, doing whatever they were able to do to advance the race and to demonstrate that they were a value added for the nation. They did well. The first issue was published on March 24, 1894.

Quite innovatively, *Woman's Era* embraced national organization as a critical need. In the opening greeting of the paper (see the full text in chapter 6), Ruffin and Ridley, the editors, stated their intention to address "a long suffering but indulgent public," meaning the unmet needs of African American women. They acknowledged their own class interests and ambitions, and also their desire to create alliances in common cause with women of other racial groups and class interests. They declared that, beyond the need for *Woman's Era* to be an instrument of engagement for multiple stakeholders, there was a special need for "discourse and sympathy" among the women themselves, stating: "especially true is this, of the educated and refined, among the colored women, members of which class may be found in every state from Maine to Florida, but in nearly all of these places an important factor, and one that receives little or no recognition." The editors asserted their capacity as educated women to grow beyond their schooling and ambitious leanings, and they declared the paper to be a magnifier for African American women's viewpoints, interests, progress, and development.

Keeping their eyes sharply focused on the importance of national organization, Ruffin and Ridley and a network of club leaders used the paper to build community, promulgate progress—social, political, economic, intellectual, and so forth. In volume 1.2, they refined the idea that the work of the paper was to bind the clubs together, with all of their variations included, rather than absorbing them. The imperative was to help the individual clubs to grow and advance and also to bring women leaders together for a "great and powerful" national organization to support the growth and progress of the race. In the end the path toward national organization was a convergence of a range of complexities in social space, but what is also evident is that, in the organizing process, *Woman's Era* played a crucial role in enabling a collective convergence of the visionary spirit of the women leaders and the articulation of the activist agenda that they wished to set in motion at a national level.

Using *Woman's Era* as a forum for communication, education, and strategic planning, African American women from across the nation built a considerable momentum (see figure 8.1). The newspaper functioned as a convenient, multidimensional, and flexible tool as this network of clubs knitted themselves together, gained traction from their collective agency and action, and in 1896 facilitated the formation of the NACW. The organization then excelled as a highly engaged, highly productive group of women who got many things done, not only in the internal development of their local communities but also, collectively, in their national imperative for progress and change—for example, in woman's suffrage, anti-lynching, community safety, community health, education, and other issues. During the formative years of NACW, *Woman's Era* became the official voice not just of the Boston club but of the new organization, until 1897, as this fast-growing collective set in place a momentum that would take them into the next century and well beyond.

A total of three volumes of *Woman's Era* were published between March 1894 and January 1897. Over this short span in the formation of the national network, at least 112 African American women were actively engaged in writing for this paper, with thousands more in the reading audience, which was composed mostly of African American women but also of progressive African American men, white women, and white men. The various sections of the paper addressed the broad interests of the network of clubs, from issues-related articles to club news, to announcements, to advertisements of direct interest. Among the authors were some of the most highly respected African American women writers and leaders of the day: Josephine St. Pierre Ruffin in Boston, Ida B. Wells in Chicago, Victoria Earle Matthews in New York, Fannie Barrier Williams in Chicago, Mary Church Terrell in Washington, DC, Alice Ruth Moore in New Orleans, Josephine Silone Yates in Saint Louis, Charlotte Forten Grimké in Washington, DC, Gertrude Bustill Mossell in Philadelphia, Selena Sloan Butler in Atlanta, and many more. See the cluster of figures below about the authors (8.2, 8.3, and 8.4)

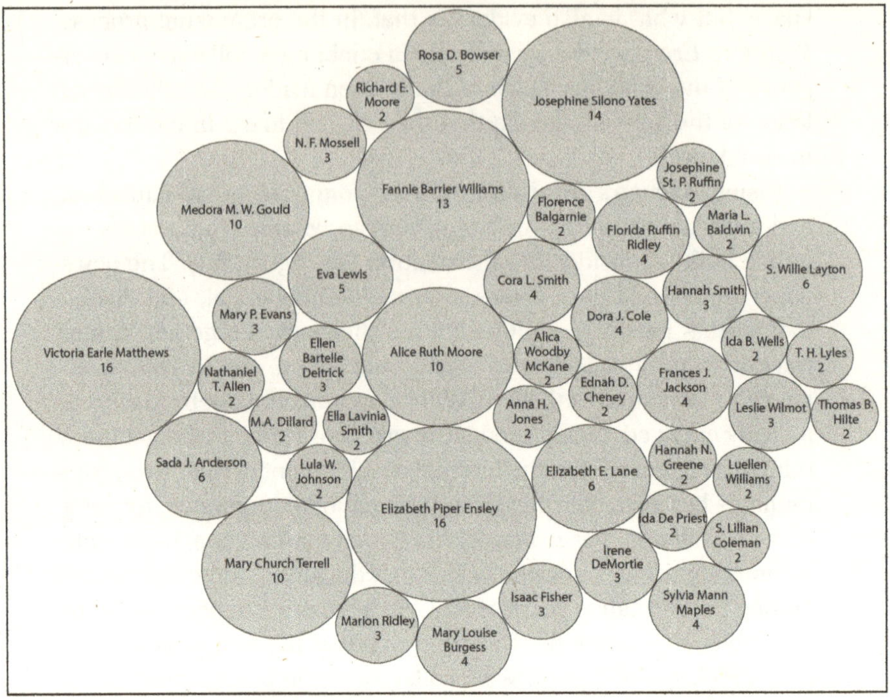

Figure 8.2: *Woman's Era* Authors of More than Two Articles

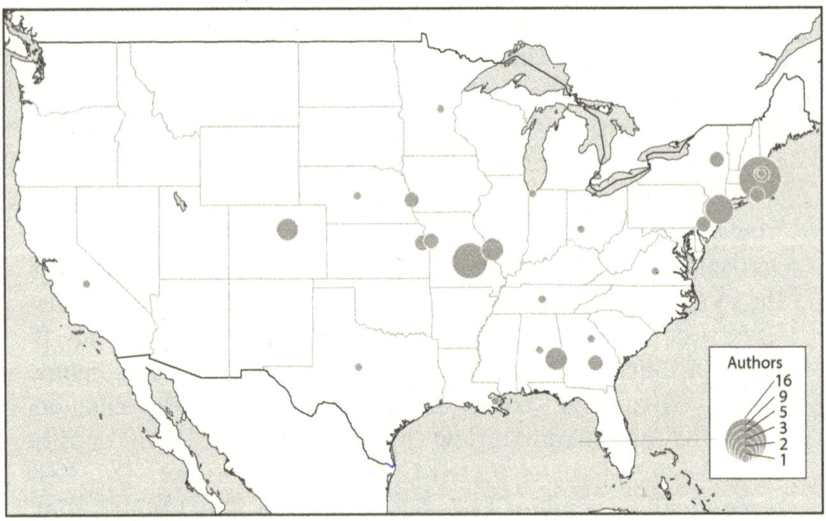

Figure 8.3: Geographic Locations of *Woman's Era* Authors with Number of Authors per Location

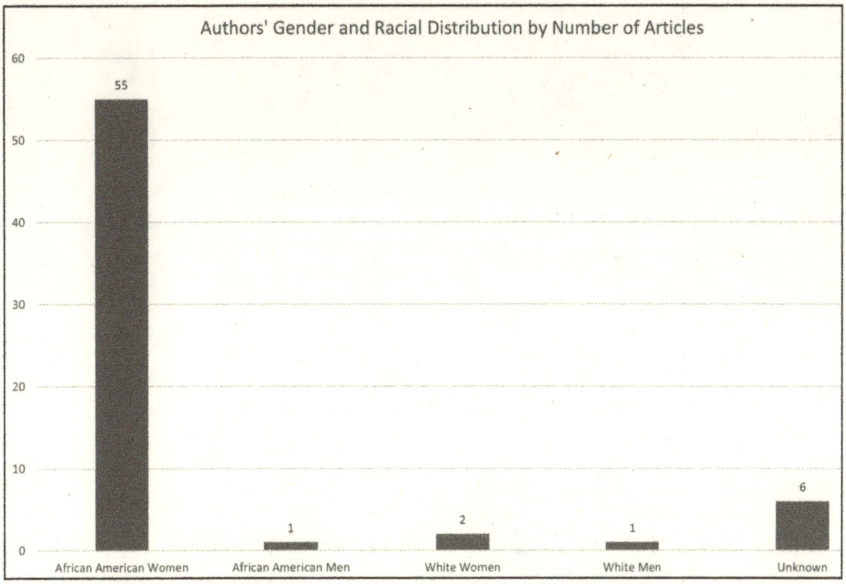

Figure 8.4: Authors' Gender and Racial Distribution by Number of Articles

The clubs regularly reported on their local actions and accomplishments through club news and announcements, but simultaneously the articles in the paper raised key issues for discussion. Frequent topics included cultural issues such as art, literature, and music; social issues such as education, crime and violence, poverty, religion, labor, health, and children's well-being; and policy and political issues such as gender equality, race equality, and social progress.[4] See the cluster of figures below about the topics addressed (8.5, 8.6, and 8.7) for specific details.

These visualizations of the *Woman's Era* data sets (see figures 8.2–8.7) demonstrate that Ruffin's local network of clubwomen formed a strong cohort of discussion leaders. There were fifty-one editorials related to network building, policy and politics, and various sociocultural issues and opportunities—including race equality, gender equality, crime and violence, social progress and engagement, labor and the arts. Other women leaders across the nation picked up on this pace-setting activity through their own articles and through letters to Ruffin and Ridley, the paper's coeditors. *Woman's Era* quickly became a vibrant arena for, of, and about African American women's sociopolitical concerns. See the cluster of figures below about the topics addressed (Figures 8.5, 8.6, and 8.7) for specific details.

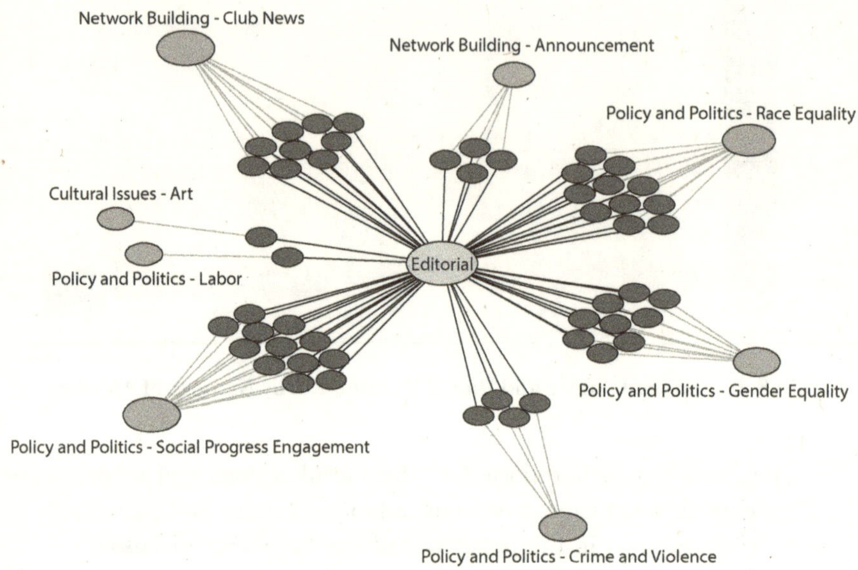

Number of Editorials by Topic		
Network Building	Club News	9
	Announcement	4
Policy and Politics	Race Equality	11
	Gender Equality	9
	Crime and Violence	4
	Social Progress Engagement	12
	Labor	1
Cultural Issues	Art	1
Total		51

Figure 8.5: *Woman's Era* Editorials by Subtopics

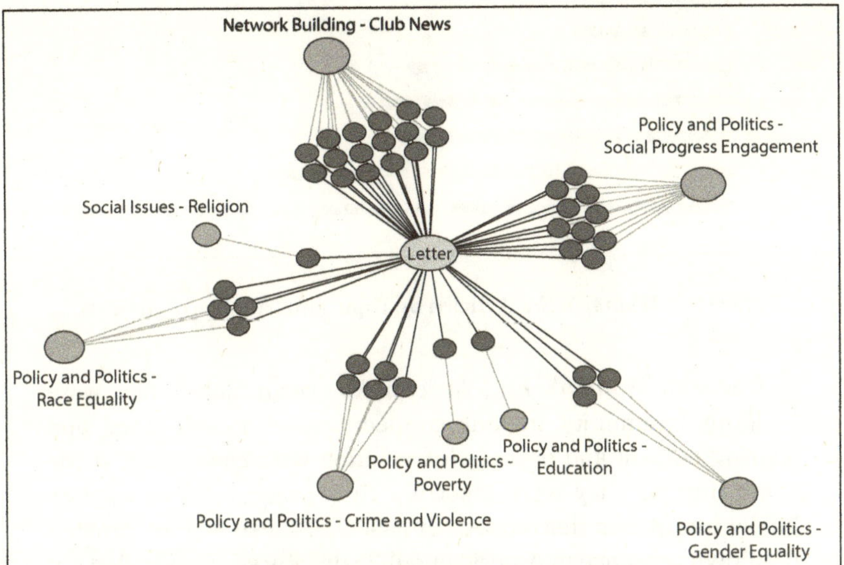

Number of Letters by Topic		
Network Building	Club News	16
Policy and Politics	Race Equality	4
	Gender Equality	3
	Crime and Violence	5
	Social Progress Engagement	10
	Education	1
	Poverty	1
Social Issues	Religion	1
Total		51

Figure 8.6: *Woman's Era* Letters to the Editor by Subtopic

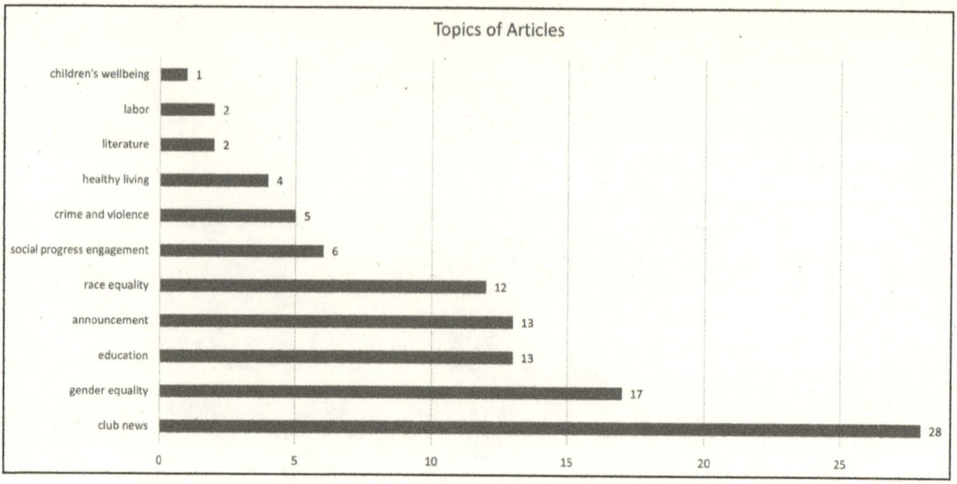

Figure 8.7: *Woman's Era* Articles by Topic and Number of Articles

Through *Woman's Era*, African American clubwomen were building community, making connections with each other, and sharing content and process information with each other, at the same time as they were inserting their voices and viewpoints boldly into public discourses. In essence, these women created their own presence in American public discourse. They called out a cluster of issues and challenges that they deemed worthy of action, and they set a core agenda for women's leadership, one that continues to prevail through contemporary times. The NACW was incorporated in 1904 as the National Association of Colored Women's Clubs, having been an operational model for an array of women-led organizations—social, religious, political, cultural, educational, professional, and various combinations of the above—through which African American women continued to raise their visions and voices and to engage in sociopolitical actions.

With the combination of an organization (the New Era Club) and a tool for communication and community building (the *Woman's Era* newspaper), Ruffin breathed life into an innovative conceptual framework. Arguably, she demonstrated that she was the right woman with the right vision and imagination at the right time. Being well positioned as a well-educated woman with expertise, experience, and resources, as well as with a national and international social network, she was able to use the mechanisms available to her to encourage, enable, and sustain African American women's collective action for social reform at a critical moment in the history of their intellectualism and activism. Through the New Era Club, Ruffin corralled women in the Boston area. Through the *Woman's Era* newspaper, she gathered clubwomen from across the nation, many of whom were fellow journalists and already actively participating in the periodical press. She engaged the group's intellectual energy, and she focused and catalyzed their social, political, economic, and cultural action in two explicitly dynamic ways:

> At the local level, she offered opportunities for these women leaders to talk about what was going on within their communities and how these activities resonated with similar activities across the nation, underscoring that they were not alone but, rather, part of a community of serious leaders and part of a sociopolitical movement.
>
> At a national level, she enabled and facilitated a remarkable arena for African American women's professional development in the company of others and provided a mechanism for conveying to audiences of various kinds that their leadership and actions were meaningful, substantial, and powerful in fomenting change on the ground—and worthy of serious attention.

In fashioning an unorthodox design for this time period, Ruffin's fundamental goal, in keeping with imperatives for respectability and social mobility, was to build up the knowledge, experiences, strengths, and capacities of African American women in support of the core internal actions that she determined were within the control of African American women themselves—the enhancement of their own abilities to "make the most of themselves" (editorial, *Woman's Era* 1.1). She also recognized, however, that because of their strengths and advantages they had the obligation to do more, as they were able, with whatever resources were available to them to address the needs of their communities. In carrying out these obligations, the success of the clubs that functioned under the banner of the NACW is legendary, especially within their own communities.

One example is the Neighborhood Union in Atlanta, organized in 1908 by fifty well-respected women under the leadership of Lugenia Burns Hope (February 19, 1871–August 14, 1947). Hope was an experienced community activist and organizer, originally from Chicago, who had moved to Atlanta in 1898 with her husband, John Hope, who had been appointed, first, as a faculty member at Morehouse College, then as president of Morehouse, and ultimately, in 1929, as president of Atlanta University. The Neighborhood Union was incredibly effective and pace-setting in addressing a sparkling array of needs in Atlanta well into the modern Civil Rights Movement. Their activities included working with the social work program at Atlanta University to set the watermarks for well-structured, well-documented, and robustly implemented social work and to develop innovative designs, based on their surveys, for building and sustaining strong communities around common goals and aspirations. They were leaders in advocating for kindergartens and safe play spaces for children and youth, conducting voter registration projects, establishing the first high school for African American students in the city and the region, establishing the first public park for African American citizens in the city, establishing health clinics and resources for African American communities that exist still within the municipal system of Atlanta, and more.[5]

In other words, the Black clubwomen across the nation were successful in their efforts to broaden horizons for both themselves and their communities. They built their own strengths and capacities both individually and as a group. They provided care and support for the critical needs of their fellow citizens. They were, in fact, relentless in articulating and implementing robust agenda that were shaped and informed by the specific needs of the communities in which they lived. To reemphasize the point, Ruffin and the clubwomen did well in getting good work done in their communities. Ruffin, however, wanted more.

Envisioning Matters of Choice

At the same time that Ruffin's goal was to enhance the strengths of African American women, she demonstrated, simultaneously, a commitment to social justice and social change. From the beginning, she conveyed a desire to organize a national meeting where women leaders could formulate ambitious agenda for more coherent and assertive woman-led reform. In order to accomplish this twofold goal, Ruffin was strategic in planning and implementation. With the New Era Club building momentum, she reached out to Mary Church Terrell, the leader of the Colored Women's League, a group based in Washington, DC. This group was also interested in national organization. In conversation with each other, both groups considered it more productive to join hands in this enterprise than to compete.

In the first issue of *Woman's Era*, Ruffin presented the paper to her reading audience as the communication platform for the Woman's Era Club (with the reminder that the club was renamed New Era Club). Club member Ellen Battelle Deitrick wrote "Editorial Notes," a report on the first public meeting of the Woman's Era Club. The last paragraph of this report states: "A Congress of the colored women's leagues and clubs of the Country was suggested long ago. Should we not be moving in the matter now? Such a convention could not but prove a delightful as well as profitable occasion; the Washington Women's League by virtue of its superior age, size and power should be the first to move in the matter" (*Woman's Era* 1.1). In response to the question of convening, in the very next issue (*Woman's Era* 1.2), Josephine Silone Yates, a correspondent for *Woman's Era* from the Kansas City Women's League in Missouri, was granted the lead in responding.

Yates was one of the first African American professors to be hired at Lincoln University in Jefferson City, Missouri, in 1881. Proving her excellence in teaching chemistry, elocution, and literature, in 1886 she was promoted to full professor, one of the first African American women to be granted such an appointment in a US university. With her reputation for excellence becoming increasingly evident, she was named head of the Natural Sciences Department, where she continued until 1889 and her marriage to William W. Yates (principal of the Wendell Phillips School in Kansas City). This profile of Yates's achievements suggests an important point for the horizons of women during this era. More often than not, marriage shifted the range of motion for women's professional development and for the expectation of ongoing high performance as leaders and activists, especially in institutional and public space, rather than the domestic sphere. In general, well-educated elite women, such as Yates, might have been able and willing to get good things of various kinds done. However, in keeping with notions of "true womanhood," elite married women in particular were expected to focus priorities on being "helpmates" for their husbands, caretakers for the moral development and general welfare of their children, and advocates in supporting (rather than orchestrating and leading) efforts to secure the well-being of their communities.

In contrast, there was little expectation that this cohort of women might harbor (or continue to harbor after marriage) a rightful sense of agency and authority as women with professional identities and desires, or that they might wish to exercise visionary insights, deliberate intentions, or passionate commitments of their own. By societal habits, their lives came to be defined, shaped, and directed by their husbands' lives and horizons. The general expectation was that their range of motion might likely be mediated, in the main, only by widowhood (as was the case in their own ways for Anna Julia Cooper and Josephine St. Pierre Ruffin). Clearly, this framework was operational for elite white women. Interestingly, however, with the drift of practices in the African American community toward conformity with mainstream practices, the framework also became operational for well-educated and well-prepared African American women as well. In reflection of the ways that social and political systems were changing the horizon of expectations within African American communities, they had to contend with the gendered expectations of their day.

That said, to the extent that we know and recognize Yates as a high-performing professional woman, basically, by the last decade of the century, she had become less known because of her academic work, as distinctive as it was, than she was for her visibility and leadership as a clubwoman. In her own community in Missouri, Yates had built an excellent reputation as a community advocate, activist, and leader. From a more holistic view, she was a well-respected educator, a highly engaged participant in vibrant social networks, and a frequent contributor to the periodical press. Through her social networks and journalistic visibility, she was also recognized by other leading African American women as a leader of distinction. In her article "Shall We Have a Convention of the Colored Women's Clubs, Leagues and Societies?" (*Woman's Era* 1.2), she aptly took the lead in providing the critical springboard by which the newspaper launched its advocacy for a national convention and its efforts to solicit and publish the views of "influential women" on three questions: Do you favor a convention of the colored women's clubs, leagues and societies? What in your opinion is the most available place and time for such a congress? State why you do or do not favor a convention.

The responses to the survey were to convene. The place chosen for the convention was Berkeley Hall in Boston, and the dates were July 29–31, 1895. The editors issued a "Call to Confer" (*Woman's Era* 2. 3). It is clear that they felt an urgency to act:

> Although this matter of a convention has been talked over for some time, the subject has been precipitated by a letter to England, written by a southern editor, and reflecting upon the moral character of

> all colored women [an incendiary article was published in England by James W. Jacks, president of the Missouri Press Association, about the character of African American women during the international anti-lynching speaking tour of Ida B. Wells]; this letter is too indecent for publication, but a copy of it is sent with this call to all the women's bodies throughout the country. Read this document carefully and use discriminatingly and decide if it be not time for us to stand before the world and declare ourselves and our principles. . . . The time is short, but everything is ripe; and remember, earnest women can do anything. (Parenthetical comments are mine.)

In 1895, as Ruffin had hoped, the first national meeting of African American women leaders occurred in Boston, with the collaboration of the New Era Club and the Colored Women's League. Ruffin served as the host and organizer. The gathering assembled delegates from ten states, representatives from twenty clubs, and large numbers of individual women from sixteen states and Washington, DC (Wesley 1984). In her welcoming keynote on Monday evening, July 29, 1895, Josephine St. Pierre Ruffin stated (see chapter 6 for a copy of the full address and note that in this excerpt the parenthetical statement is mine): "It is with special joy and pride that I welcome you all to this, our first conference. It is only recently that women have waked up to the importance of meeting in council, and great as has been the advantage to women generally, and important as it is and has been that they should confer, the necessity has not been nearly so great, matters at stake not nearly so vital, as that we [as African American women], bearing peculiar blunders, suffering under especial hardships, enduring peculiar privations, should meet for a 'good talk' among ourselves."

The agenda for the two-day meeting was not focused on being ashamed of their presumed silence on key issues, or on bemoaning their lack of a publicly acknowledged and appreciated presence, or on spending their time being reactive against the outrageous charges published by Jacks. By their attendance and active participation, they declared, instead, that they were not waiting and hoping for others to like them better or to act in their interests. They focused more proactively on defending themselves through their own work, based on the concerns of the community as they saw those concerns—on organizing themselves, on gathering ideas, and on putting their heads together around issues such as supporting justice and equality, encouraging mental elevation and industrial training, learning about and appreciating race literature, and encouraging social purity and temperance. The critical observation to make, therefore, is that the story of African American women's intellectualism and activism is a story in context. It is also a proactive story that is far more than what might superficially meet the eye by the metrics, viewpoints, and practices of the dominant culture.

With this type of recalibration, we see that neither organizational development nor sustainability, as a general enterprise, is simple or easy. The same was true for the NACW. A reminder is that the clubwomen were not ideologically monolithic. The women leaders shared common goals and desires for progress and change, but they were diverse in their beliefs, and their preferred actions. Essentially, with so many capable women becoming involved in collective action after the first national meeting, ongoing leadership was vibrantly in contention. Several women vied for the presidency of the group. The major contest was between Ruffin in Boston and Mary Church Terrell in Washington, DC. Using the ideological continuum suggested by Brittney Cooper offers a springboard for understanding the dynamism of the core differences that were in motion. To repeat, on one end of the continuum are respectability and social mobility, with priorities for action focused on internal community action as the driving force in enabling progress for the race. At the other end of the continuum is undisputed dignity, with a focus more explicitly on law, policy, and practices within the larger society. In this latter case, activism is directed on behalf of the race toward the advancement of social justice and social change from the outside inward; in the former case, activism is directed toward developing internal strength and then moving, in recognition of this enhanced capacity, more gradually toward social justice and social change from the inside outward.

The process for agenda setting in NACW was generally lively, but Ruffin's strategies for change constitute a productive starting point from which to direct a more focused and thorough analysis. Using Brittney Cooper's theoretical perspectives as a key lens for interrogation, we can bring forward for closer examination (1) the activities that Ruffin used to launch *Woman's Era*; (2) the analysis of her public addresses during the early days of organization; and (3) her efforts to position her newspaper as the official voice of the organization. These three focal points help to reveal the ways that Ruffin's strategic approach supported a balancing of both ends of the ideological continuum. Her activities demonstrate that Ruffin was concerned with creating a platform for the women to engage with each other and to build coherence and sustainability around strategies designed to address community needs. At the same time, she was also laser focused on national organization. By word and deed, she demonstrated a desire to provide leverage for raising African American women's visions and voices and having them recognized, heard, and included in decision-making processes on a national level. With this articulation of her interests, Ruffin directed her leadership toward both racial uplift and toward making the world a better place for African Americans to thrive.

By default, Ruffin positioned herself to lead NACW in striking a good balance with both goals, with *Woman's Era* becoming a primary mechanism for implementation. She articulated a four-pronged agenda: communication, community-building, race and gender uplift (as inner-directed priorities) and strategic social reform (as a more outer-directed priority). In reflection, we can confirm that during the formative years of NACW (from 1894 to 1897) Ruffin succeeded quite well in implementing the first three goals. The effectiveness of her organizational work in collaboration with hundreds of other African American women across the nation is evident (see figures 8.2–8.7).

Through this work, club members were successful in shifting the documentary landscape with regard to their visibility and audibility as participants and leaders in several public discourses. Currently, the recovery of this documentary base is growing via the work of contemporary researchers and scholars who are confirming three fundamental measures of effectiveness in the establishment during these early days of a firm foundation for the women's organizational success: (1) the vibrancy and viability of the model of collaboration that Ruffin set in motion; (2) the long list of achievements accrued by individual NACW members across several arenas of engagement, for example, education, community development, the arts, business, medicine, science, technology, law, policy, and more; and (3) the long-standing existence of NACW itself, now well into its second century.

In forwarding strategic goals for social justice and social change, however, Ruffin was less successful. Ideally, primary markers of effectiveness with this priority would have offered evidence that her leadership was a key factor in knitting together within the organization itself a dynamic and sustainable balance for all four operational interests (communication, community-building, race and gender uplift, and social reform) with a clearer mandate for social reform as a top priority. During these formative years, however, there was considerable contention around whether the balancing of priorities should tip toward a more aggressive or a more conservative approach for social reform, or perhaps toward a dual commitment designed to equalize the balancing for both simultaneously. In actual negotiations, some club members were leery of an aggressive approach, especially given the deteriorating environment of post-Reconstruction and the rise of Jim Crow systems. The results for the ongoing development of NACW were that the selection of a pathway for action and engagement was not simple but logistically complicated.

In essence, the decision-making process to determine an official national agenda across four critical concerns centered on the selection of the first president of the new organization. The membership chose Mary Church Terrell, based in Washington, DC, who was identified more clearly in this network with the conservative ideology of Booker T. Washington (since her husband was a political colleague of Washington's), and who was also identified politically (as was Booker T. Washington) with the Republican Party. By the clubwomen's endorsement of Terrell, the membership confirmed that they preferred a more measured process for progress and change. Following patterns of respectability and dissemblance, this approach was designed to be from the inside out with a central focus on racial uplift with the goal of producing an increased level of respectability that they anticipated would engender a clearer application of social justice and social change. This strategic approach constituted a sort of masking of ultimate goals, as it were (in explication of the "dissemblance" approach). African American women's own progress and improvement was positioned more directly in the action spotlight, and changes that might be wrought in society were cast more in shadow away from direct critical attention.

In contrast, Ruffin preferred a bolder approach, one that offered a simultaneous balancing of women's improvement and assertive sociopolitical activism with bolder declarations of desires for social justice and social change as the primary driver for strategic engagement. She envisioned social reform as being front and center, focusing on inequities and injustice, challenges and opportunities, and the urgent need to think innovatively about working in the external environment to bring about progress and change—all while making sure that the women of the race were ready to act when opportunities for action appeared. Emphasis was on both focal points working together to enhance potential and to maximize its effects.

With the clubwomen preferring Terrell, whom they perceived to be more willing and able to provide appropriate leadership for a less aggressive plan, the official national agenda was set. The emphasis was on building the strengths of African American women in order to shift perceptions of their capacity for participation in society and their worthiness as women who deserved respect and regard. The presumption was that a higher regard for the women of the race would mean less resistance in the larger society for necessary social changes that would make the world easier to negotiate for African Americans, and African American women in particular. This approach was deemed less abrasive, more grounded in Booker T. Washington's image of pulling oneself up by one's own bootstraps; less threatening in an environment that was increasingly inhospitable to the ongoing survival and progress of the community; and, in some ways, with their presence and leadership less visible in national public discourses (for example, with regard to their constant activism in support of both woman's suffrage and voter registration in the African American community in general).

At the point of critical choice, Ruffin's four-pronged approach did not prevail in the national organization. Terrell won the election, coining the now well-known NACW motto "Lifting As We Climb," clearly signaling her specific commitment to internal change as the leverage ultimately for external change. The club members preferred what they perceived to be the more gracious touch of Terrell with her articulation of progress through race and gender uplift. In addition in 1897 NACW leadership chose to shift their mechanism for official communication from *Woman's Era* (and Ruffin's influence) to the paper *National Notes*. This publication was organized and edited by Margaret Murray Washington (Booker T. Washington's spouse and helpmate) in Tuskegee, Alabama.

Born in Macon, Mississippi, in 1865, Washington was educated in the Quaker community and at Fisk University. In 1889 she began teaching at Tuskegee Institute, serving as a classroom teacher and dean of women. In 1893 she became the third wife of the renowned conservative leader Booker T. Washington, the president of Tuskegee Institute. Washington organized the Tuskegee Women's Club in support of her community service work, and she functioned throughout her lifetime as its president. Her leadership in club work led also to her being elected president of the Alabama State Federation of Colored Women and to this organization's establishment of a reform school for African American boys and a school for girls. It led also to her being elected president of the Federation of Southern Colored Women's Clubs, to her organizing the International Council of Women of the Darker Races of the World, to her being named a member of the Interracial Commission, and to her attendance at and participation in the 1895 Boston meeting and the founding of NACW, and more.

Initially, *Notes* "was a small sheet of information gathered by Mrs. Booker T. Washington and published at Tuskegee Institute . . . a recording of facts about the Association and also a manifestation of the determination of the Association to give itself a more permanent foundation" (Wesley 1984, 50). When this information sheet was adopted by NACW as its official organ, it was renamed *National Notes*. Thus, the competition between Ruffin's approach and Terrell's approach to strategic action ended with Terrell at the helm. The formation process of NACW serves as an occasion for understanding what, on the surface, may seem like quite subtle differences in African American women's decision-making processes but which in reality constitute a path deliberately chosen with particular effects and consequences.

The imperative here is to draw more direct attention to a handful of critical observations. First, even though within the scope of American sociopolitical practices NACW was an unorthodox design, in point of fact it was very much an organization of elite African American women. Their patterns of leadership and action are intelligible through the lenses not only of race and gender but also of class, status, and ideology. The group was indeed a group of African American leaders. They were women. Overwhelmingly, they were professional women who were highly educated. Often, they were the daughters, sisters, and wives of elite men. They were highly regarded in their communities and networks. They had remarkable histories of success. They were highly respected and garnered significant influence in their communities. Clearly, then, with regard to contemporary efforts to formulate a more robust view of African American women's sociopolitical leadership and action, the pathways for the formation of NACW were linked to elite women. They did not capture pathways for African American women who were more working class and not elite.

One exemplary case from a different positionality than NACW members was Lucy Parsons who was not a member of NACW. In contrast, she was an active and quite radical leader in the labor movement (see chapter 5). Another exemplary case has been documented by Tera W. Hunter in *To 'Joy My Freedom: Southern Black Women's Lives and Labors after the Civil War* (1997). Hunter draws attention to the sociopolitical leadership of working-class women in Atlanta, Georgia. She documents that, during the summer of 1881, twenty women who were working as washerwomen (and a few men) met to organize a trade organization, the Washing Society. The group's intention was to develop a formal mechanism for protesting oppressive working conditions, but particularly to gain higher fees and a uniform rate for their work. The group elected officers, established committees, and set up subsidiary societies in each of the five wards of the city. Membership in the trade union quickly grew from a small group of organizers into the thousands and garnered broad support throughout their communities. In a unique display of interracial cooperation, the society included also the participation of white washerwomen who, like their African American counterparts, wanted better conditions for themselves too, even though their racial group constituted a much smaller percentage of this sector of workers.

On July 19, 1881, understanding their work as essential to the functioning of the city, the washerwomen planned and called a strike. This bold act of resistance was successful. The labor of African American women was acknowledged as essential to the city's economy. Wages were raised and stabilized. Perhaps more importantly, the success of the protest served as an inspiration to others and contributed, arguably, to the culture of activism that in the twentieth century would evolve in the city of Atlanta into its recognition as the cradle of the modern Civil Rights Movement.

Needless to say, unlike the work of NACW members, the activism of the members of the Washing Society is generally unfamiliar to most people, and the names of the society's leaders are unacknowledged, including, for example, Matilda Crawford, Sallie Bell, Carrie Jones, Dora Jones, Orphelia Turner, Sarah A. Collier. This lack of public presence and corporeality confirms that a fuller range of motion for African American women's intellectual strength, their sociopolitical advocacy and activism, and their accomplishments as leaders is yet to be thoroughly articulated. Recognizing the need for more research and scholarship in this area draws attention to the intensity of African American women's work across sociopolitical identities, with regard to class, status, educational access and accomplishment, intellectual frameworks, ideological grounding, participation in social networks, and so forth. It underscores at the same time that their richly deployed array of concerns suggests the multidimensionality of this work both within local communities and in larger scope—whether nationally or internationally. The bottom line, however, is that these stories of activism and leadership remain under-researched and under-told.

Another critical observation is that, from the late nineteenth century onward, African American women advocates, activists, and leaders across a range of locations and ideological perspectives understood the power of collective action. Regardless of the diversity of their standpoints, various cohorts of African American women have been consistent in resisting passivity and finding ways to act in their own interests and in support of others. In doing so, they have been inventive and innovative, exhibiting patterns of unorthodox behaviors of various kinds. Among popularized images for this unorthodoxy the familiar stereotype often referred to as "sassiness" is embedded. With this term, the focus is on African American women as women with vision and purpose who convey a sense of agency and authority to act even when they are not officially sanctioned in the environments in which they live and work to do so (see Trudier Harris 2001). As confirmed by the slate of women showcased in this volume, the presumption, historically, is that African American women, diversely defined, have demonstrated a strong sense of self and an equally strong resolve in support of just getting things done, with persistent tendencies to speak, even when no one is listening; to stand, even when no one is watching; to do what needs to be done by whatever means available. In light of this viewpoint, the call in knowledge-making, history-telling, and storytelling is for the use of more kaleidoscopic analytical and interpretive methodologies to understand their lives and work in broader scope and to incorporate their stories into our narratives of nation.

African American Women's Work as Transformative Action

In returning focus to the formative years of NACW, the success of their efforts to establish a vibrant nationwide organization so quickly—within just two years (1894–1896)—confirmed that they not only had an existing infrastructure of relationships and networks upon which they were building, they also had a sense of urgency in getting NACW up and running well. Their dedication to this transformative action suggests that they were less distracted by the nuances of the various social hierarchies that might be evident among their group, less distracted by the general disregard of them in mainstream society, and more focused on establishing priorities that they thought might work for their new organization in getting things that mattered to them done. To reiterate their organizational choices, while NACW members generally agreed in principle on all four of the goals that Ruffin had articulated through her visionary leadership during the early days of NACW's planning and development (communication, community-building, race and gender uplift, and social reform), they selected Terrell as the organization's first president. Quite likely, they were influenced by Terrell's well-known charismatic presence, style, record of leadership, and status.

With their new leader in place, NACW had made an ideological choice in the sense that Terrell brought to bolder relief the first three organizational goals as the priorities that NACW would take forward. To be sure, in frontloading these three focal points for official national action, the group did not ignore the fourth goal. In broad scope, it was obviously part of the ultimate desires of both Terrell and the membership. Basically however, with regard to the ways in which NACW articulated organizational identity and used collective time and resources, they shifted this fourth set of interests and concerns to a more secondary conceptual space. With this road taken, NACW built its integrity and proved to be both substantive and sustainable, as documented by the fact that in the twenty-first century NACW still exists as the longest-standing African American secular organization in the nation.

In 1896 *Woman's Era* published the announcement of the formation of the National Association of Colored Women as a new organization for progress and change. It was written by Terrell as the president of the organization:

> We, the Colored Women of America, stand before the country today a united sisterhood, pledged to promote the welfare of our race, along all the lines that tend to its development and advancement. . . . As individuals, our women have already accomplished much for the education and cultivation of the race. . . . In accepting the position of honor and trust which my sisters have seen fit to confer

> upon me, I am keenly, almost painfully alive to the great responsibility assumed. . . . The magnitude of the work to which we seem divinely called and are solemnly pledged, far from affrighting and depressing us, inspires to greater effort. (*Woman's Era* 3.3)

Over the next few years, the scope and pace of the organization's work was set, with its motto "Lifting As We Climb" indicating the ideological approach of progress from the inside out.

The formation and development of the NACW and the rise of the Black Clubwomen's Movement were transformative acts. The transformation, however, was not simply in their "finding voice" at the end of the nineteenth century in the dominant public sphere around issues of race and gender. Evidence suggests that they did not need to "find" their voices. They already had them and they had as well dynamic visions for a better world, as evidenced by the steady stream of African American women's sociopolitical work since the founding of the nation. What they did not have, and struggle still to access and sustain, is a listening ear in critical public domains where laws, policies, and practices are created, implemented, monitored, managed, and maintained in support of long-term success.

From this perspective, the founding of NACW and the launching of the Black Clubwomen's Movement constituted dramatic transformative actions. Through this more politically oriented collective effort (beyond church organizations, or literary organizations, or different varieties of community care organizations), African American women stepped forward with confidence and commitment. They created a community for their own voices. They were innovative in designing a nation-wide system to support their explicit desires. They were strategic in developing a woman-led public platform to participate more overtly in an ongoing nation-building agenda—whether others were listening to them or not. The core transformative act, however, was that they created for themselves a "hospitable" place for doing the work that they wanted, needed, and were prepared to do, as educated, professionally engaged, well-connected, highly experienced activists and apprentices.

With *Woman's Era* as a tool during the formative years, this cohort of women leaders was able to generate sharper images and resolution for their viewpoints and visions. They created a space from which to project and amplify their voices—reporting on what they were doing across the nation, proclaiming their ideas for progress and change, and celebrating various types of accomplishments.

They recognized the power of presenting organized collective voices and spreading the word with truth and credibility. With *Woman's Era*, these ambitious women had their own platform and controlled their own possibilities. As in the case of Florida Ruffin Ridley, for example (who was mentored by her mother Josephine St. Pierre Ruffin and her mother's friend Maria Baldwin), the Black Clubwomen's Movement offered a mechanism for advanced training—in honing their rhetorical talents and abilities; in developing their expertise in problem-solving, strategic planning, and implementation processes; in enhancing their experiences as leaders; and in designing socially and ethically responsible solutions for addressing issues and challenges, whether local, national, or international.

In effect, the NACW was not just the name of a lively organization. It constituted a nationwide, diversely defined set of organizations that articulated their sociopolitical intentions. They joined hands in a collaboratively designed movement to facilitate the efforts of African American women leaders to form community around common concerns for collective action. The movement offered evidence of an operational framework that had grown out of their individual and collective intellectual capacities to bring astute critiques to their lived experiences. Their imperatives were anchored by strategies that they believed were capable of leveraging progress and change for themselves and for the whole community. From this perspective, many were inspired by Anna Julia Cooper and Frances E. W. Harper to see the turn of the century as a woman's era—that is, as a compelling kairotic moment for the concerted collective action of African American women. With this ideological framing, the clubwomen were able to be innovative in finding and making opportunities for advocacy, activism, and leadership.

In building strength over the course of the nineteenth century to launch both a movement and an organization, the women of this era chose to define (and sometimes to strike an assertive defense of) themselves by the work they were doing and wanted to do (as human beings with talents and abilities, as women of a downtrodden race, as citizens of the nation but with limited authority, access, and resources, and so forth). Understanding the constraints that surrounded them, they evidenced, nevertheless, a spirit of sassiness in their efforts to speak for themselves rather than through, at the pace of, or by the permission of others. Interestingly, they chose not to focus so quintessentially on the binaries of race and gender as singular concerns but, rather, to focus on the complexities and intersections of these issues and their connections to the persistent problems and challenges that plagued them and the whole race.

Their organizational efforts gained momentum quickly (Wesley 1984).[6] The first national conference of African American women was held in Boston, Massachusetts, from July 29 to 31, 1895, and was a collaboration between the Woman's Era Club and the Colored Woman's League of Washington, DC, the older of the two clubs. The core outcome was the decision to join efforts in forming a national organization, the National Federation of Afro-American Women. The following women were elected officers: Josephine St. Pierre Ruffin, president, from Boston, Massachusetts; Helen A. Cook, vice president, from Washington, DC; Margaret Murray Washington, vice president, from Tuskegee, Alabama; Eliza Carter, secretary, from Boston, Massachusetts. A second national conference, the Atlanta Congress of Colored Women, was held in Atlanta, Georgia, during the same time period as the Cotton States and International Exposition (made infamous by its Jim Crow policies and by a speech in support of an ideology of separate but equal given by Booker T. Washington). The women's conference was assembled under the leadership of Josephine B. Bruce, the wife of Senator Blanche Kelso Bruce of Mississippi. She was the first African American teacher in the Cleveland public schools and a founding member of the Colored Woman's League of Washington, DC.

In July 1896, two groups met in Washington DC—the National Federation of Afro-American women at the Nineteenth Street Baptist Church, led by Josephine Ruffin of Boston, Massachusetts, and the Colored Women's League at the Fifteenth Street Presbyterian Church, led by Helen A. Cook of Washington, DC. Between the two organizations, there were seventy-three delegates representing five thousand members in twenty-three states. Each group sent a committee of seven to attend a joint meeting. They elected Mary Church Terrell as chair, and the group of fourteen worked together to merge their organizational efforts. They created a new organization, recommended the name the National Association of Colored Women, and set up the process for actually establishing the organization: Terrell was elected the first president, an executive board was formed, a constitution written, and an agreement was made to convene the first annual NACW Convention in Nashville, Tennessee, in 1897.

On September 15–17, 1897, the first biennial meeting of NACW was held in Nashville, Tennessee, at the Howard Congregational Church. There were sixty-three delegates representing twenty-six clubs. Several sessions were devoted to a discussion of the organization's constitution and refinements for the organizational structure. Simultaneously, they set an ambitious action agenda to address several problems affecting African Americans, ranging from segregated railroad travel to educational opportunities for children, to homes for the infirm and the aged, to anti-lynching campaigns, and more. This group also elected the first NACW officers:

Mary Church Terrell, president, from Washington, DC
Francis J. Coppin, first vice president, from Philadelphia, Pennsylvania
Josephine St. Pierre Ruffin, second vice president, from Boston, Massachusetts
Frances Ellen Watkins Harper, third vice president, from Philadelphia, Pennsylvania
Josephine Silone Yates, fourth vice president, from Kansas City, Missouri
Sylvania Williams, fifth vice president, from New Orleans, Louisiana
Jennie Chase Williams, sixth vice president, from Abbeyville, South Carolina
Lucy Thurman, seventh vice president, from Jackson City, Mississippi
Anna V. Thompkins, corresponding secretary, from Washington, DC
Alice Ruth Moore, recording secretary, from Medford, Massachusetts
Mary Trisbee Handy, treasurer, from Baltimore, Maryland
Victoria Earle Matthews, national organizer, from New York
Margaret Murray Washington, chairman of the executive board, from Tuskegee, Alabama
J. Napier Kemp, chairman of ways and means, from Minneapolis, Minnesota

Mary Church Terrell served two terms under the NACW banner (1897–1901). The second biennial convention was held in Chicago, Illinois, from August 14 to 16, 1899, at Quinn Chapel AME Church. In 1899 there were 144 delegates representing 46 clubs in 16 states. By the end of her second term in 1901, there were 99 clubs in 28 states and the District of Columbia. The infrastructure for national organization was firmly laid; Josephine Silone Yates of Missouri was elected the second president; *Woman's Era* was replaced as the communicative organ of NACW by *National Notes*, edited by Josephine B. Bruce and published by the Tuskegee-Notasulga Woman's Club, led by Margaret Murray Washington.

In 1896 the NACW was launched by women who understood from generations of experience that they were stronger and more effective agents of change, not as individuals working alone or in small groups, but as women organized in support of a coherent agenda. By 1901, when Terrell stepped down as president, this cohort of advocates, activists, and leaders had grown into an army of people who were securely in place to engage in the work they wanted to do. As Wesley stated: "The establishment of a firm foundation in the first biennial session of the National Association of Colored Women and the selection of a core of officers from several sections of the nation enhanced the character of the national organization which took on an air of permanence" (1984, 55). The success achieved by this generation of African American women in leading and enabling change was remarkable, setting the pace for generations of women's work since that era to define the contours of African American women's intellectualism and action.

Their legacies, beyond the ongoing existence of the organization itself, include three general touchstones, even as the women's range of motion in leadership and action has continued to diversify and expand over the next century and beyond. The first touchstone is a commitment to unorthodox thinking and sassy behavior—speaking truth and exercising a habit of calling a thing by its "true" name. A twenty-first-century example of this pattern is political leader Kamala Harris. As a candidate for president of the United States in 2020, Harris called out fellow presidential candidate Joe Biden in the Democratic debate on June 27, 2019. She questioned his position on the federal government's role in using school busing to integrate schools. Over the course of the campaign, she convinced Biden that she was a good choice for his vice-presidential partner. In 2020, Biden was elected president, and Harris became the first woman, and the first woman of African and South Asian descent, to be elected vice president of the United States.

Another example is Stacey Abrams, Democratic candidate for governor of the state of Georgia in 2018. She was defeated in a questionable loss by Brian Kemp. She called out the problem of a sitting secretary of state being responsible for the administration of his own election. She named the issue election mismanagement and voter suppression. In response to her loss, Abrams continued her commitments to sociopolitical leadership by founding Fair Fight Action, a political action committee, to "encourage voter participation in elections, and educate voters about their voting rights."[7] In 2021 Abrams announced her candidacy for a second run against Kemp as a sitting governor who was perceived by that time in a politically conservative state to have a good record of leadership. Abrams was again unsuccessful, but her leadership and activism continue.

The second touchstone is a habit of seeing issues as complex, rather than simple; of crafting common ground in problem solving to achieve a sustainable balance among competing values; and of finding or making ways to forward progress and change—all of which are practices that are particularly evident in the operations of various important advocacy organizations. One example is the African American Political Forum (AAPF). In 1996, a century after NACW's founding, AAPF was cofounded by Kimberlé Crenshaw (professor at UCLA and Columbia Law Schools) who serves as executive director and Luke Charles Harris (former chair of political science at Vassar College) who serves as assistant director. AAPF is "an innovative think tank that connects academics, activists, and policy-makers to promote efforts to dismantle structural inequality." Another example is Black Lives Matter (BLM), which was cofounded by Alicia Garza, Patrisse Cullors, and Opal Tometi in response to the murder of Trayvon Martin, an African American teenager, in 2013. It is "a global organization in the United States, the United Kingdom, and Canada, whose mission is to eradicate white supremacy and build local power to intervene in violence inflicted on Black communities by the state and vigilantes."[8]

A third touchstone is an emphasis on action, driven in this case by social and ethical responsibility and sociocultural awareness. African American women persistently demonstrate a curiosity about the challenge of seeing the nuances and connections of issues and problems in complex rather than simple terms and then finding innovative ways to identify and sustain solutions that work. They operationalize the view that action requires commitment, compassion, and courage, with the understanding that acting with courage does not always mean moving past fear but, rather, knowing the importance of being inspired by vision, love, compassion, and empathy so that there is a compelling rationale for doing what must be ethically and rationally done to make a better world—even when danger is evident. The evidence of this touchstone is in the women's long history of sociopolitical labor. After many decades of various activities by individuals and multiple efforts by women in collaborations with others, the Black Clubwomen's Movement arose from a network of elite African American women who dreamed of a better world.

These three touchstones are fundamental for clarifying the salience and power of the rise of the Black Clubwomen's Movement as a transformative act that evolved over the full scope of the long nineteenth century. Using this perspective makes more evident that, as the daughters of women of African descent who brought habits and practices with them to the Americas, African American women passed these habits and practices along to subsequent generations (Royster 2000). By the end of the century, African American women leaders had taken advantage of an array of available opportunities, having used their talents and abilities to good effect in their long-standing quest for social justice and social change. They had positioned themselves on forward-facing pathways and demonstrated by their work a determination to push their vision for progress and change forward. They were warrior women fighting for causes that mattered to them. Their legacies of action stand as testaments to their vision, intellectualism, and resilience. Their records of achievements, individually and collectively, confirm, as Anna Julia Cooper suggested in 1892, that the world had entered a new era. Cooper proclaimed that everyone would be wise to look, listen, and believe in the worthiness of African American women and to appreciate the values they consistently add in making the world a better place—a commitment, as they have demonstrated, that for them has been and continues to be philosophical, theoretical, experiential, and quintessentially practical.

Last Words

Envisioning the Last Mile of a Worthy Quest

In his essay "Definition of Man," Kenneth Burke offers a multilayered definition of humanity that is anchored by the concept of our being "symbol-making, symbol-using animals" (1966, 3). He connects this view of symbolic action specifically to language as a distinctive kind of human-made symbolic system affected in its uses and misuses by our tendencies toward the creation of hierarchies and our ideological notions of perfection. With this framing, he highlights the view that language uniquely supports the ability of humans to express themselves in speaking their own viewpoints, lives, and experiences; to interact and communicate with others; to engage in purposeful action in addressing their needs and interests; and to bring substance and texture to the encoding of their beliefs. He draws attention, thereby, to language use as a vital dimension of the decision-making processes by which humans engage with and negotiate their surroundings and create meaning amid the chaos of an abundance of sensory information. Burke's perspectives of the nature, ways, and means of language made dramatic as an operational tool in decision-making processes are instructive in the effort to gain a well-grounded understanding of human behavior from the point of view of particular users and uses—in this case, to analyze, interpret more generatively, and appreciate the sociopolitical work of African American women via a robust examination of the patterns of their rhetorical behavior in context.

Using Burke's theoretical framing, we can assess how nineteenth-century African American women, like others before and after them, used their rhetorical knowledge and expertise as critical assets. They engaged with their world(s) and enhanced their sense of self within these environments. They fashioned a sense of agency and authority, and found ways to express their visions and experiences. They used their rhetorical talents and abilities to negotiate the complexities of their relationships, to participate actively in addressing their own needs and interests, and to advocate for the needs and interests of others, demonstrating by such actions their abilities to understand and speak their own lives. The array of their rhetorical practices offer us much to contemplate regarding the quality of both their words and deeds—as well as the spirit and sensibilities that they embodied in using these strengths despite oppressive constraints.

The Meaning of Work

The question in directing energy toward this type of analysis is why the sociopolitical work of African American women as agents of progress and change with rhetorical expertise has value. The responses to this question get at the heart of the ways that we define citizenship in the United States of America. We proclaim ourselves to be a democratic nation. We declare that, regardless of race, creed, color, gender, or place of origin, every citizen (and by extension all peoples globally since we are a nation of immigrants) has both human rights and civil rights. We assert that these rights are anchored in truth, freedom, justice, equality, and empowerment for all—not just for some. Unfortunately, however, this presumption of values and rights has not been automatically assigned to African Americans, including African American women as the specific focal point for this analysis. From the beginning of the nation in 1776, we have been grounded operationally in incoherence. We proclaimed ourselves to be a democratic nation at the same time that we institutionalized the enslavement of people of African descent and intertwined this societal institution intricately into the nation's cultural core. This incoherence has meant that—in order for African American women as a specific group to experience inclusion as citizens of the nation and to exercise their human and civil rights amid the culturally systemic denial of such rights—more than just the simple declaration of rights for all has been required.

In this analysis, a fundamental goal has been to use the analytical trifecta proposed here (visibility, audibility, intelligibility) as leverage for perceiving and acknowledging critical conceptual gaps on our national landscape and in our narratives of nation. The specific task has been to bring more texture and vibrancy to our perceptions of the lives and work of African American women as a precursor for addressing more explicitly the perennial incoherence of our national values and actions. I have designed the analysis to underscore the ways in which this group, with only occasional exceptions, has been systemically disregarded and disrespected throughout the history of the nation. In effect, this approach casts attention on the group's functioning symbolically as the canaries in the coal mine in helping us to see the critical need for transformative change to deepen the integrity and credibility of the nation. Most directly, the use of these three sight lines brings to bolder relief the foundation from which to declare African American women, specifically, as humans with rights, as actually present in this geographic space, as politically aware of their operational positions as citizens of the nation, and as demonstrably engaged in the work of making room for their own visions, agency, authority, and voices in building, or in their case rebuilding, their communities, the nation, and the world.

The need for analytical and interpretive leverage is palpable. At the core of the challenge is the inescapable problem that the United States was a slaveholding culture for well over 150 years before its founding as an independent nation and, then, for another nine decades until the official ending of this societal practice at the end of the Civil War. Moreover, for yet another century after that, just as inescapable is the evidence of the vibrant operations of white supremacy, Jim Crow practices, and legalized segregation. A specific consequence of this material reality is a clear and present need, at this point in US history, for the nation to think again with critical consciousness and caring about our commitments to bedrock democratic values—as well as about the implementation of these values in law, policy, practice, and systems of accountability for absolutely all citizens.

From this perspective, enhancing the visibility, audibility, and intelligibility of African American women enables a clearer understanding of how the experiences and achievements of this group function as a guidepost for measuring progress and fomenting positive change. With more clarity concerning the disregard and disrespect directed toward this group, researchers, scholars, and indeed citizens in general are far better positioned—despite a long-standing history of profoundly oppressive constraints and conditions—to appreciate African American women and their work. Moreover, they are also better positioned to understand the advantages entailed in having this group included with more corporeality as critical proof of the larger story of American excellence. In other words, the importance of this analytical and interpretive model is definable by its capacity to clarify the ways in which African American women's sociopolitical labor functions in both material and metaphorical terms to speak meaningfully and provocatively for the integrity and credibility of a nation that declares itself to be democratic. Simply put, material realities are key to understanding circumstances and conditions, but metaphors can also be instructive for a more visceral understanding, an actual felt sensibility, of the particular situation in context.

By this convergence of viewpoints, not only do African American women function as the canaries in the coal mine of our national ecosystem, their treatment within this ecosystem can also be magnified by another metaphor in that this group becomes the proof of the American pudding. In essence, we might envision the women collectively as a category of citizens who are milestone markers for our democratic strength as a nation. Their experiences confirm them to be among the most vulnerable members of society. Because of the precarity of this status, they become also a critical metric of accountability for determining the extent to which the nation is living up to its bedrock values and promises. From this perspective, this group offers the nation a signal opportunity to reflect on and assess our viability as the nation we proclaim ourselves to be.

In 2022, however, we have yet another cautionary tale. As explained in "Democracy as a Noble Experiment: Where Do We Go from Here?" (Royster 2022), the work of confirming national values, commitments, and accountabilities is not yet done. The milestone marker, once again, is the experience of African American women. On January 27, 2022, Supreme Court Justice Stephen

Breyer announced his retirement from the Court. In fulfillment of a campaign promise, President Joseph Biden announced that he would be nominating a highly qualified African American woman as the next Supreme Court Justice—a first for the nation after more than 230 years. Immediately, several African American women with remarkable credentials were brought forward for the president's consideration. Just as immediately, stunning insults to the distinguished list of possible nominees emerged—wonders to behold—from sitting members of the US Senate, the group of political leaders charged directly with upholding the Constitution of the nation.

Further, when President Biden nominated Judge Ketanji Brown Jackson the insults only escalated. Judge Brown Jackson's record confirmed that she is a person with a long list of stellar accomplishments from her receiving her law degree from Harvard University to the breadth of her experience as a lawyer, to her many years of service as a judge, to her service on the US Court of Appeals, to her endorsement by a diverse list of key stakeholder organizations of various kinds. During the Senate confirmation hearings, several Republican senators on the Judiciary Committee were willing to accuse Judge Brown Jackson, without any reasonable evidence, of supporting Nazi beliefs and behaviors, of having an inappropriate "judicial philosophy," of being a traitor, a terrorist, a pedophile, soft on crime, a leftist extremist, and more.

The unfettered attempts by this cohort of naysayers was to malign her character and to suggest that she lacked both legal knowledge and an appropriate judicial decision-making framework. As is frequently the case in the treatment of professionals from minority groups, this cohort of detractors tried to discredit Judge Brown Jackson's achievements and to ignore solid evidence of the exact opposite. Their efforts disregarded the fact that her accomplishments had been thoroughly vetted and documented during the review process before the hearings, with the specific verification that her record was, not only appropriate for the role of Supreme Court Justice, but well beyond typical requirements for this leadership and service. Fortunately, despite the insults and unfounded accusations, the full Senate voted to confirm Judge Brown Jackson's nomination, with fifty-three in favor and forty-seven against. By quite ordinary measures, this margin of victory illustrates both the nation's progress toward truth, justice, and equality (in that she was confirmed), as well as the ongoing challenge of upholding these bedrock values for all (in the sense that, despite a distinctive record, a considerable number of these policy elites did not find her to be worthy of confirmation, although there were not enough of them to defeat her candidacy).

Unfortunately, the confirmation process as a whole signaled quite dramatically that, even in the twenty-first century, African American women are still unable to count on being treated with regard or graciousness. In contrast to a process of respectful, fair, and robust critical questioning of a qualified candidate for a top leadership position, the actual confirmation process provided considerable evidenced of relentless, virulent, and unfounded accusations by some members of the Judiciary Committee and ultimately by some senators who spoke from the floor during the voting process. What occurred instead of a persistent application of truth, justice, and equality was that a thoroughly qualified African American woman was subjected, once again, to profoundly insulting, unfair, and oppressive treatment. In a fundamental way, with African American women serving as a case in point for American democracy over time, the call here in envisioning the last mile of a long journey is for all of us to get beyond simply saying who we are as a nation to actually doing the work that makes who we are evident, not only in law and policy but also in practice, accountability systems, and in the cultural contexts in which all occur.

The Leverage of Focus and Perspective

Despite lingering challenges, as evidenced by the hearings for Judge Brown Jackson as a twenty-first century example, efforts to raise the nation's trajectory toward progress and change have been occurring. A transformative point of leverage was the fighting of a bloody and devastating war in the mid-nineteenth century. With a Union victory instead of a Confederate one, we were able to make key adjustments to a credibility gap in our operational identity. By constitutional amendments, we officially clarified the fact that African Americans are human beings, not chattel, and that they have both human and civil rights, as is the case for all citizens of the nation. The operational status for this group shifted from a categorizing of them as rightfully enslaved to their being citizens—with innate rights to truth, freedom, justice, equality under the law, and the pursuit of happiness. From an ethically and socially responsible view, these adjustments enhanced the capacity of the nation to gain integrity and strength from the lives and contributions of African Americans, not as unpaid laborers with precious little sociopolitical mobility but as fully-fledged citizens.

Additional leverage for recalibration came also from the escalating energy that could be officially and legally deployed after the Civil War by African Americans themselves, not simply as individuals fighting for their humanity and for justice and equality but as rightful citizens claiming the benefits of their citizenship. With all members of the community being categorized by constitutional law as citizens of the nation, African Americans, including the women, were inspired by this affirmation of their status, knowing that intrinsically they held fundamental civil rights and that they also held the right to articulate their own visions of reality, to tell their own stories, and to include their own perspectives and experiences, as legal citizens, within our narratives of nation. With critical adjustments in constitutional law on their side, African Americans were officially able to envision themselves beyond just the privilege of residency in the United States of America. By the law of the land, they were explicitly able to proclaim the nation as their nation.

To summarize a pertinent set of conclusions based on this analysis, the analytical and interpretive design proposed here pushes us to go beyond a simple recognition that African American women's lives and work matter because they are human beings with potential, citizens with rights, and individuals with a record of actions in various public arenas. These points, quite simply, are demonstrably true. Simultaneously, what is also true on a quintessential level for knowledge making, history telling, and storytelling is that, in recognizing African American women as a group whom we have barely noticed before (despite their physical presence), researchers and scholars face a challenge. The challenge is to place this group with more intelligibility on the scene. The opportunity is to take more seriously into account that their presence and participation in various arenas have yielded meaningful contributions and they were not passively just the witnesses to action but were themselves actively engaged. In addition, in understanding the historic ecosystems in which they have functioned in civic environments, the opportunity also is to take more seriously the extent to which interrogations of this group's experiences and achievements constitute a useful metric in determining the viability of the nation itself as a democratic nation. On one hand, we might well expect that, as a historically peripheralized group, these women signal progress and change regarding the nation's ability to enact and sustain its bedrock values for all citizens. On the other hand, by this same touchstone of marginalization, we might also expect that the inventiveness of this group in exercising a dedication to sociopolitical work would offer insights regarding the nature, ways, and means of excellence in civic engagement, especially when the actors are unorthodox in their approaches and unauthorized and unentitled in circles of power. The value added is understanding advocacy, activism, and leadership more broadly and more deeply.

Essentially, using the tripartite paradigm of visibility, audibility, and intelligibility permits a more richly endowed embodiment for women who have been present in all sorts of spaces but who generally have not been noticed, acknowledged, or appreciated. The ongoing task, however, is to go beyond naming the problem to be more assertive and consistent in addressing it: (1) to keep shifting the sight lines with viewpoints that are deliberately multifocal, rather than unifocal, where standard practices are anchored by a conscious regard for multiple points of view and by the directing of specific attention toward forging a more inclusive, more fully rendered operational vision; (2) to keep listening for multivocality, rather than univocality, where the many voices of a nation composed of multiple cultures are not suppressed but encouraged to speak up and out with the expectation that they will be listened to respectfully by others; (3) to be persistent in incorporating into knowledge-making, history-telling, and storytelling processes a broader range of lived experiences.

The identification of these types of operational strategies confirm that the process of engagement exhibited here is designed to be multilectical in the sense that the language used is deliberately and persistently deployed from a kaleidoscopic perspective.[1] This type of perspective calls for multiple ways of seeing, listening to, and talking about ideas, experiences, and insights with the goal of resisting tendencies to simplify and flatten sensibilities. Using a multilectical approach counters the habit of flattening by embracing the goal of complicating and enriching the breadth and depth of our understanding. The anticipated outcome is twofold: (1) to enhance our capacities to resist a drifting toward incoherence (for example, via dramatic divisions constructed because of race, gender, class, geographical location, generation, or other sociocultural identities or ideologies); and (2) to create operational spaces to enable cooperation and consensus-building among stakeholders who exhibit—in a nation with multiple cultures—an often sparkling array of differences. This way of thinking underscores the idea that feeding societal incoherence generates tension and gives rise to a calcification of sociopolitical binaries and hierarchies. Such tensions regularly function as a driving force in casting power, entitlements, and coercive oppressions on one end of a continuum and protest, revolution, and perhaps even chaos on the other. Without a commitment to resist imbalances via multilectical engagement, the risk in operational practices is a disruption of the capacity of the nation to sustain core national values (freedom, truth, justice, equality, empowerment for all)—and peace.

The rationality of this analysis and reinterpretation is not only about recasting our viewpoints of a specific group of citizens who have been persistently oppressed and harmed (which, given the nation's bedrock values, is important enough) but also about assisting the nation in seeing the roles that this group perform in the nation being what it claims to be—free and just with equality under the law for all. In focusing on the category of "citizen" in the context of national commitments, we have a signal opportunity to begin retelling the story. In a recalibrated narration, African American women are repositioned—not as backdrop for the narratives of others or as pawns or artifacts in some larger schema but as the subjects of lives that matter. As citizens who have done both ordinary and extraordinary things, despite sociopolitical hierarchies and conditions deliberately designed to disregard, disempower, and defeat them, African American women have resisted oppression and discrimination and have, to the extent possible within their circumstances, claimed and exercised their rights. These rights include the right to live in freedom with an evidence-based accounting of their lives, experiences, conditions, and achievements; to tell their own stories without the debilitating effects of having those stories cast in dark shadows by others who are not held accountable for their (mis)interpretations; to have their insights and contributions, both large and small, honored, respected, accredited, and valued in recognition of the possibility of positive impact; and to have their presence included as meaningful and consequential in our narratives of nation and beyond. In other words, we benefit from focusing on the rights of these women to visibility (the right to be seen as fully fledged citizens of the nation and fully fledged members of humankind), audibility (the right to be heard as people with hearts, minds, and sensibilities), and intelligibility (the right to have their talents and abilities taken seriously as meaningful, valuable, and consequential).

When we presume the presence and corporeality of African American women as citizens in civic environments, we gain a better sight line for understanding them and their work from their own points of view. We enhance our capacity to see that they have persistently demonstrated their desires for and pursuit of core national values, regardless of their status. Often, as unorthodox, unauthorized, unanointed participants in civic processes, their sociopolitical work has offered considerable evidence that they hold fast to and generate strength from a vision of what the last mile of a worthy quest should be like, look like, and feel like. Within this interstitial space they have worked steadfastly and endured. In other words, African American women have exhibited the imagination, in proverbial terms, to dream a better world, and they have simultaneously offered evidence of their steadfast will to resist domination and oppression and to work assiduously to create the world of their desires—if not always for their own benefit, at least for the benefit of others in their communities. As advocates, activists, and leaders, they have shown a faithfulness to finding or making ways to create progress and transformative change, and by such operational habits, they have demonstrated, as well, a resilience in seeing their labor to be worth the effort.

In this study, the imperative has been to show what it has meant for African American women to sustain a long view for fomenting progress and change. In focusing on the time period between the founding of the nation and the turn of the twentieth century, we open up a new vista for understanding the patterns, ways, and means of their sociopolitical engagement as a long-term commitment. We have an opportunity to see more clearly how these women have negotiated conceptual gaps between the nation's words and its deeds. In operational terms, we can employ interrogations of their lives and work that suggest their positioning of democracy as an idea in motion, and we can shed more light, thereby, on the ways that their activities link to bedrock national values.

In this regard, African American women's rhetorical productivity has functioned as an analytical and interpretive asset that has marked in the boldest of terms their civic engagement as persistently holding the nation accountable to its declared values. Their work poignantly underscores how consistent they have had to be in order to bring whatever resources were available to the table in order to create—in a democratic nation—their own hospitable spaces for action and to craft their own participation and sense of possibility. This labor constitutes, in fact, a commitment to accountability. They see the importance of doing what they can do, but they raise for critical interrogation the question of whether and how the nation has enacted its core values truthfully, respectfully, fairly, inclusively (or not). When we listen to their words over time, we can see that they have been quite clear about how systemically barriers and constraints have been placed before them and clear also about the ways in which misalignments between the nation's words and deeds have significantly compromised their ability to participate more fully as citizens of this democratic society. In respecting their points of view, we enhance our capacity to understand that their viewpoints have emerged from their lives, as these lives have been caught in the web of our grand democratic experiment. With this sort of magnification, we are better positioned to understand that their lives and work deserve to be considered and incorporated into decision-making processes, and their achievements deserve to be appreciated as stories that are quintessentially American.

Creating Space for Agency and Action

In their introduction to *Identity and Story: Creating Self in Narrative*, the coeditors Dan P. McAdams, Ruthellen Josselson, and Amia Lieblitch offer an instructive perspective for using narrative to support progress and change. They state: "We are all storytellers, and we are the stories we tell" (2006, 3). They suggest that the stories we tell (and that are told about us) become the stories of who we are. Acknowledging this interconnection underscores the importance of making sure that our narratives are fully, rather than only partially, rendered. Emphasis is on the notion that to enhance the credibility of the nation via its storytelling processes, narrative subjects need to speak their own truths as agents and actors in their own lives, resisting the authority of others to usurp these rights, and resisting the sense of entitlement that others may hold, or wish to hold, and exercise. The imperative is to highlight the notion that point of view matters and that it is the collective of points of view (multifocality, multivocality, and multilecticality) that helps to create and present a better story at the national level.

From this perspective the quotation above, "We are the stories that we tell," permits a specific extrapolation for this analysis. It suggests that the "we" in the statement might be defined as "citizens in the United States as a free and just nation dedicated to assuring equality under the law for all." With such a conceptual infrastructure as guide, African American women claimed the United States as their nation and defined themselves as "humans" and as "citizens." In doing so, they claimed simultaneously their rights to identity, agency, authority, and action. With the incoherence of the operational context in which they found themselves, however, for them a critical strategy has necessarily been to strengthen their claims by fashioning a clear, inclusive, and honorable place within a hostile sociocultural context for them to tell their own stories of their lives, experiences, and achievements, rather than to leave that right in the hands of others.

African American women have taken the authority to write themselves into the narrative, to embrace their own notions of a future that is possible and worth fighting for, and to tell more complex and well-textured stories of various kinds to whomever was willing to listen. Through these efforts, they have taken the authority ultimately to create a more hospitable space for themselves in community-building and nation-building processes. In effect their sociopolitical labor has included their need to shift operational and interpretive paradigms away from restrictive frameworks, to broaden their range of motion, and resist the systems around them that were systemically designed to discount their presence and impact—all with the result of their defying the presumptions of national narratives as a singular story rather than as a complex multidimensional one.

In this instance, cautions continue for conceptual and operational paradigms. Historically, African American women have embodied the consequences to the nation of not permitting the stories that could be told about them and their work to be fully and fairly rendered in national narratives. Their stories have been disregarded. The consequences of nontelling is provocatively explained in the TED Talk presented by novelist Chimamanda Ngozi Adichie on October 10, 2009, "The Danger of a Single Story." Without being given a full and fair presentation and representation, the subjects of untold narratives have considerable difficulty in establishing that the world is more expansive than single stories suggest, or that as subjects they actually exist not as a stereotype but as multidimensional beings, or that their conditions and experiences count—either positively or negatively—in the schema of anything, or that they should be part of our narratives of nation and deemed believable and valuable to the society.

Likewise, as Burke's theories suggest, stories are both material and symbolic. By our narratives, national and otherwise, we render ourselves as sentient beings who belong on the earth in time and space. We declare our materiality and intelligibility in the past, the present, and the future, and we make sense through the analytical and interpretive screens that we create for ourselves. More specific to this analysis is the storytelling processes that are part and parcel of this creation of materiality and intelligibility. As Adichie suggests, stories casts both light and shadow. It becomes all the more important, therefore, to acknowledge and respect that truths function at the intersections of our multiple narratives. In honoring the intersectionalities of our lives, in effect, we strengthen the view that narratives are both material and symbolic, that from our insights and experiences we create the screens through which we articulate and interpret our realities, and that these points of view matter. Honoring this perspective also highlights the importance of acknowledging that shifting points of view (telling more than a single story) also matters. Through vibrant multidimensional storytelling, we are able to construct clearer, more richly endowed, more vibrant accountings in national scope of who we really are as a nation, how, why, and to what sort of effects. Given this type of conceptual framing, then, the history of African American women, with emphasis in this case on their sociopolitical work, is not yet a tale that has been well told.

So, what happens when we do not tell a full enough or a good enough story? What happens when we deliberately leave out people and pieces of the narratives of who and how they are, and of who and how we are together? Then what? Quite essentially, of course, we simply have a limited and narrow notion of who people are, in this case of who African American women are, what their intentions have been, what they have done, how, under what conditions, and with what consequence. In sociopolitical terms, however, consider Anna Julia Cooper's assertion in *A Voice from the South* regarding space for women (and especially African American women): "The world has had to limp along with the wobbling gait and one-sided hesitancy of a man with one eye. Suddenly the bandage is removed from the other eye and the whole body is filled with light. It sees a circle where before it saw a segment. The darkened eye restored, every member rejoices with it" (1988, 122–23). Cooper strikes a resounding and resonant chord. African American women have been steadfast in working to restore the darkened eye, casting light toward deliberately darkened spaces that have often been designated for the marginalized. Their processes of engagement have been passionately linked to the task of presenting a more fully and vibrantly rendered set of truths about their lives and work, and their potential as human beings with desires, talents, abilities, and expertise. As Cooper suggests, African American women have been clear that a critical part of facing the dilemma of their perceived absence, silence, and unintelligibility in narratives of nation is for them to take the authority to envision a better world, to work to make it real, and to be more assertive in telling better stories, in telling their own stories.

As Cooper also states, "I constantly felt (as I suppose many an ambitious girl has felt) a thumping from within unanswered by any beckoning from without" (1988, 76). Embedded in her message is the point that, in 1892, she felt that it was far past time for African American women not to be deterred—at all—by disabling conditions or the lack of advocacy. They just needed to step up and do themselves what needed to be done, what could be done in the interests of generating a many splendored tale—a better world for others and for themselves. What she suggests is that, with the vision, voices, and work of African American women, we (the citizens of a free and just nation) enhance our capacity to know better than we have ever known before—in the full circle of our vision—who we really are as a nation, and who we are not, but perhaps also who we could actually be.

In capturing the benefits of transparency and clarity in narrative space, Homi K. Bhabha states in the introduction to his edited collection *Nation and Narration*: "Traditional histories do not take the nation at its own word, but, for the most part, they do assume that the problem lies with the interpretation of 'events' that have a certain transparency or privileged visibility" (1990, 3). In other words, power elites in our sociopolitical ecosystems have the privilege of setting and controlling the terms for what constitutes the dominant truths of the nation—the stories that we tell and are told about what and who matter. When we apply this viewpoint to the sociopolitical work of African American women as nonprivileged stakeholders, we gain another sight line for understanding the impact of their presence in public arenas as unauthorized and unorthodox participants. By the very existence of their efforts to bring corporeality to their own experiences, needs, and strategies for change, the women disrupt authority and defy the primacy of privileged visibility when there is little or no expectation for them to be visible or audible in public space at all. In effect, they make room for their own agency and authority and, in doing so, underscore the importance of their need for intelligibility—the importance of knowing what it means to be seen, heard, recognized as worthy of regard, and appreciated as present and consequential in trying to make a better world for themselves and others. In other words, including a wider range of narratives in circles of power beyond local levels changes the vista and helps us to see with greater clarity more dynamic possibilities for a stronger democratic nation.

A reminder for this point is that the *word* of the United States symbolically defines the nation as dedicated to truth, freedom, justice, equality, and empowerment. As a prime example of Bhabha's analytical perspective, however, power brokers in the United States have had the privilege historically of ignoring the facts and implications of slavery and have felt entitled by this privilege to present narratives that similarly ignore conceptual gaps between what we say as a nation and what we do. Both literally and symbolically, this privileged visibility cloaked in darkness the reality that some residents of the nation were not free, which pushed African American women into even darker spaces at the intersection of race, gender, and class. It also set aside the observation that in a brighter light the nation was not what it said it was. Rather, it was substantially unjust and unequal with regard to human and civil rights for all, having established laws, policies, and practices that actively nurtured a slate of inequalities, systemically enforced. In effect, the United States as a nation proclaimed truth, freedom, justice, equality, and empowerment while it boldly ignored the day-to-day realities of its deeply ingrained commitments to the idea that for African Americans (and by degree other marginalized citizens) the nation was free but not free, just but not just, equal but not equal—for all.

In effect, obvious conceptual discontinuities between day-to-day realities and the narrative privilege of the power brokers to ignore those realities have made acknowledging gaps and living up to the *word* of the nation problematic. Details of lives and experiences that did not fit the privileged narrative line were cloaked in dark shadows, such that the anointed story lines functioned symbolically as acts of power and privilege. Historically, African American women, as citizens who were not empowered or privileged, were also not entitled to expect this privilege for themselves. The battle for their corporeality in national discourses and narratives, therefore, has not been simply a battle for room in a story but also an intense battle through the stories that we tell for the power and privilege of making and shaping the nation in support of social justice and social change.

Bhabha then continues: "It is when the western nation comes to be seen in Conrad's famous phrases, as one of the dark corners of the earth, that we can begin to explore new places from which to write histories of peoples and construct theories of narration" (6).[2] If, in effect, the United States has been symbolically a dark corner of the earth where the stories of many communities have been cast in deep shadows by the stories of privileged visibility (with African American communities relegated to one of the darkest of those corners), then a challenge for researchers and scholars, and for the nation is to face unprivileged realities as boldly as we have promoted privileged ones. This step constitutes a strategic move toward creating a more inclusive society. As Bhabha's theoretical framing suggests, clarifying the linkages between the narratives that hold privilege of visibility and those that do not creates new opportunities for different, and perhaps better, narratives of nation.

African American Women's Sociopolitical Action as Exhortation

Declaring the importance of the interconnections of narrative and nation offers researchers and scholars a signal opportunity to think again about the nature, ways, and means of African American women's sociopolitical labor. The prime directive in focusing on the nineteenth century in this project was to offer sociohistorical documentation over time of the premise that, through their robust civic engagement African American women advocates, activists, and leaders have been agents of progress and change within their communities and beyond, a premise that serves as a springboard for an exhortation. The appeal is for researchers and scholars to demonstrate that they appreciate these women's accomplishments by being more aggressive in building research agenda of various kinds that help to render the work and the impacts and consequences of it more visible, audible, and intelligible.

The argument for a more robust commitment is twofold. On one hand, despite debilitating circumstances and conditions, these women were successful in creating more hospitable spaces for themselves in terms of leadership and action in support of progress and change. We need to know who they were, what they did, and the differences that their work made across a fuller range of their arenas of action (for example, in science, technology, religion, business and industry, education, and so forth). On the other hand, while the fact of this success across multiple arenas is indeed remarkable and deserving of documentation, a second imperative emerges simultaneously from the first, There is an ongoing need to understand that what is perhaps even more stunning is not just their achievements but the processes by which they made this success possible. Positioned outside of circles of expectation for agency, authority, and consequential action, African American women were called upon, regardless of their various arenas of action, to be master strategists in constructing their own pathways for doing the work that they wanted to do and for making the differences they wished to make. These processes deserve documentation and analysis.

A critical dimension of the argument presented here was to address both imperatives via the example of a specific cohort of women. To summarize the effort, a central goal has been to clarify that focusing not only on the leaders but also on the processes of leadership and action offer leverage in tandem that is particularly useful in drawing forth instructive insights. As the case in point, I directed specific attention toward formative processes in the organization of the Black Clubwomen's Movement as one striking example of what we gain analytically and interpretively by taking African American women and their work more seriously. As an opportune occasion, I identified the nineteenth century as indicative of African American women's long-term commitment to sociopolitical action. I marked this time period to be from the 1770s, during the formative years of the nation, when Phillis Wheatley was participating in the discourses of her day and the 1890s when Josephine St. Pierre Ruffin (and others) were determined to bring leading African American women together to get some important work done with a nationwide scope. The twelve decades in between these two kairotic moments constituted an extended runway along which a broad and diverse group of high-performing African American women dedicated themselves to taking advantage of every opportunity available to them in preparing themselves and those who would follow to be values added in facing the challenge of assuring the survival, prosperity, and sustainability of their people. Their goal by the turn of the nineteenth century was to create their own self-directed platform for action—that is, a national organization to support the work. They accomplished this goal and created a coherent and sustainable organizational design to forward a robust agenda. The goal of this project was to acknowledge and to confirm the worthiness of African American women advocates, activists, and leaders to have their work documented, appreciated, included in national narratives, and celebrated as valuable in making the world a better place.

In retrospect and prospect, then, a shifting in analytical and interpretive paradigms suggests that there are indeed dark corners within our national narratives. The critical opportunity is to see these gaps in knowledge, acknowledgment, and national credibility as incentives to go a step beyond simply recognizing a perennially complicated issue. Instead, we can actually commit to improving sight lines and constructing more inclusive landscapes. The exhortation is to act by declaring in thoughtful ways that there really are discontinuities between national words and deeds, between the stories that we tell and those that we do not. With African American women's sociopolitical leadership and action as leverage, the expectation is not just to see that there is more to the lives, experiences, and accomplishments of this particular cohort (and other groups as well) and to admit that, historically, their stories have not been permitted to meet the mainstream eye, but also to accept the call to action—as Bhabha puts it, "to explore new places from which to write histories of peoples and construct theories of narration" and nation.

In being multifocal, multivocal, and multilectical in the narratives that we write, we are more clearly positioned to render better, more inclusive stories—not simply about who the previously unacknowledged others actually are (again as important as that task might be) but also, just as importantly, who, as a nation, we actually are, have always been, and could be going forward. With a shifting of paradigms, we have a stellar opportunity as the work continues to build communities whose stories we should and can know, respect, and appreciate and simultaneously to build a nation that lives up to its claims to being a democratic nation that believes in and is accountable to its bedrock values: truth, freedom, justice, equality, and empowerment—for all.

Appendix

A Sampling of Nineteenth-Century Women's Autobiographies, Biographies, Diaries, Journals, Memoirs, and Letters

Anderson, John Q., ed. 1972. *Brokenburn: The Journal of Kate Stone, 1861–1868*. Baton Rouge: Louisiana State University Press.

Andrews, Eliza Frances. 2019. *The War-Time Journal of a Georgia Girl, 1864–1865*. First published 1908. Columbia, SC: Digital History Books.

Andrews, William L. n.d. "Harriet A. Jacobs (Harriet Ann), 1813–1897." Documenting the American South. Accessed January 25, 2023. https://docsouth.unc.edu/fpn/jacobs/bio.html.

Bolden, Tonya. 2005. *Maritcha: A Nineteenth-Century American Girl*. New York: Abrams Books.

Boyd, Belle. 1998. *Belle Boyd: In Camp and Prison*. Foreword by Drew Gilpin Faust and introduction by Sharon Kennedy-Nolle. Baton Rouge: Louisiana State University Press.

Burgess, Lauren Cook, ed. 1994. *An Uncommon Soldier: The Civil War Letters of Sarah Rosetta Wakeman*. New York: Oxford University Press, 1994.

Carretta, Vincent. 2011. *Phillis Wheatley: Biography of a Genius in Bondage*. Athens: University of Georgia Press.

Clayton, Sarah Conley. 1999. *Requiem for a Lost City: A Memoir of Civil War Atlanta and the Old South*. Edited by Robert Scott Davis Jr. Macon, GA: Mercer University Press.

Cooper, Anna Julia. 1988. *A Voice from the South*. First published 1892. Schomburg Library of Nineteenth-Century Black Women Writers. New York: Oxford University Press.

Coppin, Fanny Jackson. 2018. *Reminiscences of School Life, and Hints on Teaching*. First published 1913. Emeryville, CA: Franklin Classics.

Cumming, Kate. 1998. *The Journal of a Confederate Nurse*. Edited by Richard Barksdale Harwell. Baton Rouge: Louisiana State University Press.

East, Charles, ed. 1991. *Sarah Morgan: The Civil War Diary of a Southern Woman*. New York: Touchstone/Simon and Schuster, 1991.

Edmonds, Sarah Emma. 1999. *Memoirs of a Soldier, Nurse and Spy: A Woman's Adventures in the Union Army*. Introduction by Elizabeth D. Leonard. DeKalb: Northern Illinois University Press.

Fletcher, Louisa Warren. 1995. *Journal of a Landlady: The Fletcher/Kennesaw House Diary*. Edited by Henry Higgins, Connie Cox, and Jean Cole Anderson. Randallstown, MD: Professional Press.

Griffin, Farah Jasmine, ed. 1999. *Beloved Sisters and Loving Friends: Letters from Rebecca Primus of Royal Oak, Maryland, and Addie Brown of Hartford, Connecticut, 1854–1868*. New York: Alfred A. Knopf.

Gwin, Minrose C., ed. 1992. *A Woman's Civil War: Cornelia Peake McDonald*. Madison: University of Wisconsin Press.

Hicks, Hannah Worcester. 1992. "The Diary of Hannah Hicks." *American Scene* 13:2–24.

Jackson, Fannie Oslin. 1989. *On Both Sides of the Line*. Baltimore, MD: Gateway.

Jacobs, Harriet. 1988. *Incidents in the Life of a Slave Girl*. First published 1861. Edited by Maria Child. Schomburg Library of Nineteenth-Century Black Women Writers. New York: Oxford University Press.

Jeffrey, Katherine Bentley. 2016. *Two Civil Wars: The Curious Journal of a Baton Rouge Schoolgirl and a Union Sailor*. Baton Rouge: Louisiana State University Press.

Keckley, Elizabeth. 2011. *Behind the Scenes, Or, Thirty Years a Slave, and Four Years in the White House*. First published 1868. Scotts Valley, CA: CreateSpace Independent Publishing Platform.

Lee, Mrs. Jarena. 1988. *Religious Experience and Journal of Mrs. Jarena Lee*. First published 1849. Schomburg Library of Nineteenth-Century Black Women Writers. New York: Oxford University Press.

Lunt, Dolly Sumner. 1997. *The Diary of Dolly Lunt Burge, 1848–1879.* Edited by Christine Jacobson Carter. Athens: University of Georgia Press.

Myerson, Joel, and Daniel Shealy, eds. 1989. *The Journals of Louisa May Alcott.* Boston: Little, Brown.

Pember, Phoebe Yates. 2002. *A Southern Woman's Story.* Introduction by George C. Rable. Columbia: University of South Carolina Press.

Smith, John David, and William Cooper Jr., eds. 2000. *A Union Woman in Civil War Kentucky: The Diary of Frances Peter.* Lexington: University Press of Kentucky.

Stevenson, Brenda, ed. 1988. *The Journals of Charlotte Forten Grimké.* New York: Oxford University Press.

Stone, Cyrena Bailey. "Miss Abby's Diary." Hargrett Rare Book and Manuscript Library, The University of Georgia Libraries. http://dlg.galileo.usg.edu/harg/turningpoint/id:harg1000-001-001.

Sumler-Edmond, Janice L. 2008. *The Secret Trust of Aspasia Cruvellier Mirault: The Life and Trials of a Free Woman of Color in Antebellum Georgia.* Fayetteville: University of Arkansas Press.

Taylor, Susie King. 1988. *Reminiscences of My Life: A Black Woman's Civil War Memoirs.* First published 1902. Edited by Patricia W. Romero and Willie Lee Rose. Princeton, NJ: Markus Wiener.

Thomas, Ella Gertrude Clanton. 1990. *The Secret Eye: The Journal of Ella Gertrude Clanton Thomas, 1848–1889.* Edited by Virginia Ingraham Burr. Chapel Hill: University of North Carolina Press.

Thompson, L. S. 2012. *The Story of Mattie J. Jackson.* London: SicPress.

Towne, Laura M. 1993. *Letters and Diaries of Laura M. Towne.* Edited by Rupert Sargent Holland. First published 1912. Southern Historical College. Penn School Papers. Chapel Hill: University of North Carolina.

Velazquez, Loreta Janeta. 1876. *The Woman in Battle: A Narrative of the Exploits, Adventures, and Travels of Madame Loreta Janeta Velazquez, Otherwise Known as Lieutenant Harry T. Buford, Confederate States Army.* Introduction by Jesse Alemán. Richmond, VA: Dustin, Gilman.

Whitehead, Karsonya Wise. 2014. *Notes from a Colored Girl: The Civil War Pocket Diaries of Emilie Frances Davis.* Columbia: University of South Carolina Press.

Woodward, C. Vann, ed. 1981a. *Mary Chestnut's Civil War.* New Haven, CT: Yale University Press.

Notes

Overview

1. Sojourner Truth was born enslaved in New York as Isabella Baumfree in 1797. She walked away from this estate in 1827, freeing herself from slavery in a state that had established an anti-slavery law. She became an itinerant preacher and renamed herself Sojourner Truth in 1843. During the decades before and after the Civil War, she became a staunch abolitionist and a fiery advocate for women's rights. Truth died in Battle Creek, Michigan, in 1883.

Chapter 1: A Pentadic View of African American Women during the American Civil War

1. Current trends in research and scholarship—especially in history, women's studies, and rhetorical studies, and other related fields—are laying excellent ground for countering such presumptions. One measure of the growing oeuvre is that a search of Amazon.com for US Civil War women's history indicates that there are well over six hundred resources available in this category.

2. See, for example, Abbott 2014; Bellafaire 2011; Dunbar 2008; Fore-

man 2010; Freehling 2008; Giesberg 2009; Kantrowitz 2012; Mountjoy 2009; Roberts 2016; Schultz 2007; Silber 2009; Silvery 2008; Stowe 2018; Sumler-Edmond 2008; Varon 2010; Venet 2014; Wagner 2011; Ward 2008; Wells 2011; West 2014; and Ziparo 2017.

3. According to Franklin (1980), in 1865 the Confederate Senate provided for the enlistment of two hundred thousand African Americans and their emancipation if they remained loyal throughout the war. This bill was signed into law on March 13, 1865, by President Davis authorizing General Robert E. Lee to call on each state for additional troops without regard to color. Recruitment of African Americans was slow, however, and came too late to make a difference in the outcome of the war.

4. For more details about Native American participation in the Civil War, see "We Are All Americans—Native Americans in the Civil War" 2021; Wagner 2011; Cunningham 1998; and Katz 1986.

5. For a more detailed explanation of Alcott's life and productivity during this time period, see Myerson and Shealy 1989; Reisen 2009; and Alcott 2003.

6. Louisa May Alcott died on March 6, 1888, the successful author of several volumes. She was best known for *Little Women*. The war functions as the narrative backdrop. Clearly, there is still much work to be done to connect the accomplishments of women writers, in the North and the South, more explicitly and vibrantly to a trajectory of literary and rhetorical productivity, not just before and after the Civil War but also during it. The challenge is to take seriously and to document the existence and nature of "wartime" literature, including poetry, novels, journalism, and other genres, and to document the participation of women in that productivity. One example of recent scholarship in this area is Wells (2011) who sheds light on the participation of southern women.

7. Mitchell was again hit by a car while crossing the street near her home on August 11, 1949. She died from her injuries on August 16, 1949. For more biographical details about Margaret Mitchell, see Brown and Wiley (2011) and Pyron (2005).

8. Bellafaire identifies, to the date of her publication in 2011, twenty-six scholarly monographs, thirty-seven memoirs and biographies, seven articles, and one national website, all focused on the active participation of women in the Civil War.

9. For more details of women away from home and on or near the battlefront, see Massey 1994; Clinton and Silber 1992; Forbes 1998; Royster 2000; Hall 2006; and Bellafaire 2011.

10. For further discussion of African American women spies, see Forbes (1998) and Hall (2006).

11. For a more thorough explanation of women's volunteerism in medical care and the creation and operation of the US Sanitation Commission, see Ross 1999; Garrison 1999; and Giesberg 2000, 2009.

12. Access to public transportation, and public spaces generally, remained a persistent challenge for African Americans' freedom and justice across the United States well into the latter half of the twentieth century, as evidenced by a series of battles that came to a head with the bus boycott in 1955 and 1956 in Montgomery, Alabama, and the rise of Martin Luther King Jr. as a national and international leader in the modern Civil Rights Movement.

13. Alexander also raises the question of the number of free African Americans who did not register because of a range of fears related to exposure from living outside of bondage. These fears included the need to show proof of freedom and to pay a substantial "head tax" for the status.

14. For more details of Mirault's life, accomplishments, and legacies and a discussion of the experiences of her son in the Civil War, see Sumler-Edmond 2008.

15. For more details about the Hunt family and other free African Americans in Middle Georgia, see Alexander 1991.

16. Thomas survived the war. Afterward, she became a leader and activist in her community.

17. A fuller explanation of nineteenth-century southern writers during this time period is available in Wells 2011.

18. For a fuller discussion of the causes and rationales for the Civil War, see Freehling 2008; Huston 2003; McPherson 2003; Potter 2011; Stampp 1992; and Varon 2010.

19. For a full view of both constitutions, see "The Constitution of the United States: A Transcription," National Archives, https://www.archives.gov/founding-docs/constitution-transcript, for the Constitution of the United States, and "Constitution of the Confederate States; March 11, 1861," Lillian Goldman Law Library, Yale Law School, https://avalon.law.yale.edu/19th_century/csa_csa.asp, for the Constitution of the Confederate States. Note the bolded terms; for example, *Person* in the US document and *slaves/slavery* in the CSA document.

Chapter 2: Negotiating Ways Forward

1. I extend this argument in Royster (2021), where I add to the discussion of the founding documents an analysis of the Gettysburg Address, the Pledge of Allegiance, and the Lazarus poem inscribed on the Statue of Liberty, considering them as iconic instruments in national identity

formation. In addition, I trace the ways in which founding principles and values, as encoded in these documents, have been misaligned in practice and have provided a framework for the activist agenda of African Americans and their long-standing quest for freedom, equality, social justice, and human rights.

2. See Sharon Crowley and Debra Hawhee (2004) for a more detailed explanation of intrinsic and extrinsic appeals and of the use of logos, ethos, and pathos in establishing argumentative strength. Specifically, Crowley and Hawhee refer to three criteria articulated by Aristotle for understanding the use of emotion and passion in persuasion: "First, they must understand the state of mind of people who are angry, joyful, or indignant; second, they must know who can excite these emotions in people; third, they must understand the reasons for which people become emotional" (2004, 209).

3. The commitment of federal support for dismantling slavery, ameliorating its devastating impacts on African Americans, and monitoring progress was ending by 1877. More attention was directed toward reconciliation and reincorporating the South into the nation. White supremacist values and power structures reemerged and shifted social, political, and economic hierarchies in the South into a period that we characterize now as the Jim Crow Era. This era would stand steadfast and robust until the modern Civil Rights Movement in the 1950s and 1960s. For a fuller discussion see Du Bois 1998; Franklin 1980; Woodward 1981b, 2002.

4. Alfred A. Knopf first published this volume in 1966 as *Bonnet Brigades*. Jean V. Berlin explains (in Massey 1994, introduction) that Mary Elizabeth Massey, a social historian, was a pioneer in women's history, having published one of the first studies of the Civil War focused on women from both the North and the South. Note that, although many of Massey's factual conclusions about women during the Civil War have resonated through the decades since 1966, her language (e.g., the use of "colored" to refer to African Americans) and her basic analytical frameworks (e.g., the privileging of the experiences of elite white women) were structures that were functioning within the time period in which she was working. Such language and frameworks mark her views and interpretations as more narrowly constructed than the feminist analyses of women's lives, conditions, and contributions that have emerged since that time.

5. Note that *Maritcha: A Nineteenth-Century American Girl* is a biography written for children by Tonya Bolden based on this memoir (2005). Lyons's original memoir is housed in the Harry A. Williamson Papers at

the Schomburg Center for Research in Black Culture of the New York Public Library.

6. For a more comprehensive list of major milestones in higher education for African Americans, see "Chronology of Major Landmarks in the Progress of African Americans in Higher Education," *Journal of Blacks in Higher Education*, https://www.jbhe.com/chronology.

7. See Part III for a fuller explanation of the African American periodical press, as well as a fuller explanation of the civic participation of African American women through their activities associated with the periodical press.

8. I am grateful to Michael Vogel, who was at the time of this research a graduate research assistant in the School of Literature, Media, and Communication at the Georgia Institute of Technology, for his invaluable help in producing the maps related to the African American periodical press included in this volume. Note that these visuals are based on a small data set and are not intended to suggest that the information is comprehensive or complete. Note also that the current versions of the maps are an adaptation of the original maps designed to accommodate the constraints of publishing in black and white.

9. I presented the concept of "traces of a stream" in a volume of the same name, *Traces of a Stream: Literacy and Social Change among African American Women* (2000). Despite there being increasing scholarly attention since this publication on the lives, conditions, and achievements of African American women across many arenas of work, the concept of "traces" of participation and value—rather than more fully and respectfully included accounts of African American women's presence—remains instructive in the ongoing historicizing of African American women's visibility in various and sundry sites of engagement.

Chapter 3: Before the Civil War

1. This writer is Maria Miller Stewart. She married James W. Stewart. According to Marilyn Richardson (1987, 3), she adopted her husband's middle initial at his request after they were married. So she was known as Maria W. Stewart and published her essays as Mrs. Maria W. Stewart. There is no verifiable image of Stewart that I have been able to locate. The images that are typically presented as her are likely not.

2. Note that I have selected Marilyn Richardson's version of Stewart's first essay. As a pace-setting piece, I have included the full essay as presented by Richardson, including her parenthetical clarifications. I have not included, however, her footnotes—a practice I use with the other ex-

emplars as well. Also, for subsequent exemplars, two more points. First, depending on the length of the piece, I have taken the liberty occasionally of excerpting sections from the original texts in order to be mindful of space limitations. Second, I have resisted using footnotes or endnotes. When explanations seem necessary in parts of the text, I have used short parenthetical explanations within the text.

3. Note that Marilyn Richardson cited this poem in the following way: Watts, Hymn 326. In James M. Winchell, A.M., *An Arrangement of the Psalms, Hymns, and Spiritual Songs of the Rev. Isaac Watts*, D.D. (Boston: Lincoln & Edmands, 1821).

Chapter 6: At the Turn of the Century

1. All quotations from *Woman's Era* are from Emory Women Writers Resource Project, https://womenwriters.digitalscholarship.emory.edu.

Chapter 7: Recasting Frameworks for Engagement and Regard

1. The story of African American women as "the hidden figures of NASA" illustrates this point. See Cochrane and Ramirez 2021.

2. The analysis presented in this section builds on earlier research and scholarship that I presented in Royster 2000 (176–238) and Royster 2021. In both publications I focused on ways in which African American women developed professional ethos, formed identities, and came to share their voices in public space.

3. In focusing on the periodicals that were owned and controlled by African Americans, I agree with the approach of Shirley Wilson Logan in *Liberating Language* (2008). Her commitment is not to discount broader journalistic participation but, rather, to underscore the agency and rhetorical decision-making processes from a more direct culturally controlled perspective.

4. Several projects have documented the rising number of newspapers that emerged from 1827 forward. I found several websites to be particularly useful in corralling these details, among them: the Library of Congress (http://chroniclingamerica.loc.gov) and Wisconsin Historical Society (http://wisconsinhistory.org). Also very useful was Penelope Bullock (1981).

5. For a more comprehensive list of known African American periodicals, see Danky and Hady, 1999.

6. The database from which the graphic in figure 7.1 is drawn is not comprehensive or complete. It is a list of 212 newspapers and magazines

published between 1827 and 1900 that were recoverable from multiple sources. It serves, however, to underscore a significant pattern in the steadily increasing numbers of publications that emerged during these decades.

7. Note, for example, the research and scholarship of Evelyn Brooks Higginbotham (1994); Cheryl Townsend Gilkes (2001); and Bettye Collier-Thomas (2013).

8. See Aleta Feinsod Cane and Susan Alves 2001. The quotation in the title of the Cane and Alves volume was drawn from a statement by Margaret Fuller, a writer, journalist, editor, and leader in the New England Transcendentalism Movement, in her essay "American Literature: Its Position in the Present Time, and Prospects for the Future" (1846). Fuller identifies the periodical press as an instrument of choice for educating audiences. Cane and Alves highlight several nineteenth-century writers who made distinctive accomplishments in this arena, including references to African American women.

9. Note that the *A.M.E. Church Review* was published under the auspices of the African Methodist Episcopal Church, with many of the scholars drawn from their elite circle of ministers.

Chapter 8: Shifting Interpretive Paradigms

1. "African American Women in Defense of Ourselves," Sisters Testify, accessed January 2023. https://www.sisterstestify.com.

2. The resolution from the conference "Black Women in the Academy: Defending Our Name, 1894–1994," is archived at the Massachusetts Institute of Technology, Institute Archives and Special Collections, Cambridge, MA.

3. I presented an early version of this argument in Royster 1990.

4. I am grateful to Emily Kim (a graduate student in the Ivan Allen College of Liberal Arts at the Georgia Institute of Technology at the time of this research) for generating the visualizations from data sets we created based on *Woman's Era*.

5. For more information about the Neighborhood Union in Atlanta, see Rouse 2004; Hancock 2015; and the Neighborhood Union Collection at Atlanta University Center Robert W. Woodruff Collection.

6. The information in the next few paragraphs is summarized from data compiled by Charles W. Wesley in his narration of the formative years of NACW (1984, 24–54).

7. The quotation is from Fair Fight, https://fairfight.com.

8. More information about these organizations is available at their

websites: African American Political Forum, https://aapf.org, and Black Lives Matter, https://blacklivesmatter.com.

Last Words

1. For more on multilecticality, the interested reader can see Fellner 2015.

2. The allusion is to Joseph Conrad's *Heart of Darkness* (1899).

Bibliography

Archives and Websites

African American History. https://www.blackpast.org/african-american-history/.

African American Newspapers. Accessible Archives. https://www.accessible-archives.com/collections/african-american-newspapers/.

African American Newspapers. Library of Congress. https://chroniclingamerica.loc.gov/newspapers/.

African American Newspapers and Periodicals. https://www.library.illinois.edu/.

African American Political Forum. https://www.aapf.org/.

Bennett College. https://www.bennett.edu/about/history/.

Black Abolitionist Archive. University of Detroit Mercy. https://www.udmercy.edu/academics/special/black-abolitionist.php.

Black Lives Matter. https://blacklivesmatter.com.

Bolden, Dorothy. Dorothy Lee Bolden Thompson Collection. Auburn Avenue Research Library on African American Culture and History. https://aafa.galileo.usg.edu/repositories/2/resources/36/collection_organization.

Cheyney University. https://cheyney.edu.

"Chronology of Major Landmarks in the Progress of African Americans in Higher Education." *Journal of Blacks in Higher Education*. https://www.jbhe.com/chronology.

Clark Atlanta University. https://www.cau.edu.

Cooper, Anna Julia. https://plato.stanford.edu/entries/anna-julia-cooper.

Cornish, Samuel E. https://www.nyhistory.org/web/africanfreeschool/bios/samuel-cornish.html.

Fair Fight. https://fairfight.com.

Fisk University. https://www.fisk.edu/.

Freedom's Journal, the First U.S. African-American Owned Newspaper. https://www.wisconsinhistory.org/Records/Article/CS4415.

Heslip-Ruffin Family Papers, Amistad Research Center at Tulane University, New Orleans, LA. https://amistad-finding-aids.tulane.edu/repositories/2/resources/167.

Lemoyne-Owen College. https://www.loc.edu/.

Lincoln University of Missouri. https://www.lincolnu.edu/.

Lincoln University of Pennsylvania. https://www.lincoln.edu/.

Lucy Parsons Center. http://lucyparsons.org/.

Morehouse College. https://morehouse.edu/.

National Association of Colored Women's Clubs. https://www.nacwc.com/.

Neighborhood Union. Archives Research Center, Atlanta University Center Robert W. Woodruff Collection. https://findingaids.auctr.edu/repositories/2/resources/8.

John Brown Russwurm Collection, George J. Mitchell Department of Special Collections & Archives, Bowdoin College Library, Brunswick, Maine. https://library.bowdoin.edu/arch/mss/jbrg.

Spelman College. https://www.spelman.edu/.

Wilberforce University. https://wilberforce.edu/.

The Woman's Era. Emory Writers Resource Project. https://womansera.digitalscholarship.emory.edu/.

Articles, Books, and Films

Abbott, Karen. 2014. *Liar, Temptress, Soldier, Spy: Four Women Undercover in the Civil War.* New York: Harper.

Adichie, Chimamanda Ngozi. 2009. "The Danger of a Single Story." https://ted.com/talks/chimamanda_ngozi_adichie_the_danger_of_a_single_story.

"African American Women in Defense of Ourselves." n.d. Sisters Testify. Accessed January 2023. https://www.sisterstestify.com.

Ahrens, Gale, ed. 2004. *Lucy Parsons: Freedom, Equality, and Solidarity, Writings and Speeches, 1878–1937.* Chicago: Charles H. Kerr.

Alcott, Louisa May. 2003. *Little Women.* Edited by Anne K. Phillips and Gregory Eiselein. New York: W. W. Norton.

Alexander, Adele Logan. 1991. *Ambiguous Lives: Free Women of Color in Rural Georgia, 1789–1879.* Fayetteville: University of Arkansas Press.

Anderson, John Q., ed. 1972. *Brokenburn: The Journal of Kate Stone, 1861–1868.* Baton Rouge: Louisiana State University Press.

Andrews, Eliza Frances. 2019. *The War-Time Journal of a Georgia Girl, 1864–1865.* First published 1908. Columbia, SC: Digital History Books.

Andrews, William L. n.d. "Harriet A. Jacobs (Harriet Ann), 1813–1897." Documenting the American South. Accessed January 25, 2023. https://docsouth.unc.edu/fpn/jacobs/bio.html.

Aptheker, Bettina. 1982. *Woman's Legacy: Essays on Race, Sex, and Class in American History.* Amherst: University of Massachusetts Press.

Ashbaugh, Carolyn. 1976. *Lucy Parsons: An American Revolutionary.* Chicago: Haymarket Books.

Axelsen, Diana E. 1985. "Women as Victims of Medical Experimentation: J. Marion Sims's Surgery on Slave Women, 1845–1850." *SAGE: A Scholarly Journal on Black Women* 2, no. 2 (Fall): 10–13.

Barkley Brown, Elsa. 1994. "Negotiating and Transforming the Public Sphere: African American Political Life in the Transition from Slavery to Freedom." *Public Culture* 7, no. 1 (Fall 1994): 107–46.

Bay, Mia. 2015. "The Battle for Womanhood Is the Battle for Race: Black Women and Nineteenth-Century Racial Thought." In *Toward an Intellectual History of Black Women*, edited by Mia Bay, Farah J. Griffin, and Barbara D. Savage, 75–92. Chapel Hill: University of North Carolina Press.

Bellafaire, Judith. 2011. *Women in the United States Military: An Annotated Bibliography.* New York: Routledge.

Beringer, Richard E. 1986. *Why the South Lost the Civil War.* Athens: University of Georgia Press.

Berkin, Carol. 2009. *Civil War Wives: The Lives and Times of Angelina Grimké Weld, Varina Howell Davis, and Julia Dent Grant.* New York: Vintage Books.

Bhabha, Homi K., ed. 1990. *Nation and Narration.* New York: Routledge.

Blackmon, Douglas A. 2009. *Slavery by Another Name: The Reenslavement of Black Americans from the Civil War to World War II.* Reprint ed. New York: Anchor Books.

"Black Women in the Academy: Defending Our Name, 1894–1994." n.d. Massachusetts Institute of Technology. Institute Archives and Special Collections. https://archivesspace.mit.edu/agents/corporate_entities/1275.

Blanton, DeAnne, and Lauren M. Cook. 2002. *They Fought like Demons: Women Soldiers in the Civil War.* New York: Vintage Civil War Library/Vintage Books.

Bolden, Tonya. 2005. *Maritcha: A Nineteenth-Century American Girl.* New York: Abrams Books.

Boyd, Belle. 1998. *Belle Boyd: In Camp and Prison.* Foreword by Drew Gilpin Faust and introduction by Sharon Kennedy-Nolle. Baton Rouge: Louisiana State University Press.

Braxton, Joanne M., and Andrée Nicola McLaughlin, eds. 1990. *Wild Women in the Whirlwind: Afra-American Culture and the Contemporary Literary Renaissance.* New Brunswick, NJ: Rutgers University Press.

Brown, Ellen F., and John Wiley Jr. 2011. *Margaret Mitchell's* Gone with the Wind*: A Bestseller's Odyssey from Atlanta to Hollywood.* New York: Taylor.

Brown, Hallie Quinn. 1988. *Homespun Heroines and Other Women of Distinction.* Schomburg Library of Nineteenth-Century Back Women Writers. New York: Oxford University Press.

Brown, Jeannette E. 2012. *African American Women Chemists.* New York: Oxford University Press.

Buchart, Ronald E. "Susie King Taylor (1848–1912)." 2020. New Georgia Encyclopedia. Last modified July 17, 2020. https://www.georgiaencyclopedia.org/articles/history-archaeology/susie-king-taylor-1848-1912.

Bullock, Penelope. 1981. *The Afro-American Periodical Press, 1838–1909.* Baton Rouge: Louisiana State University Press.

Burgess, Lauren Cook, ed. 1994. *An Uncommon Soldier: The Civil War Letters of Sarah Rosetta Wakeman.* New York: Oxford University Press, 1994.

Burke, Kenneth. 1966. *Language as Symbolic Action.* Berkeley: University of California Press.

Burke, Kenneth. 1969a. *A Grammar of Motives.* First published 1945. Los Angeles: University of California Press.

Burke, Kenneth. 1969b. *A Rhetoric of Motives.* First published 1950. Los Angeles: University of California Press.

Cane, Aleta Feinsod, and Susan Alves, eds. 2001. *The Only Efficient Instrument: American Women Writers and the Periodical.* Iowa City: University of Iowa Press.

Carretta, Vincent. 2011. *Phillis Wheatley: Biography of a Genius in Bondage*. Athens: University of Georgia Press.

Cash, Floris Barnett. 2001. *African American Women and Social Action: The Clubwomen and Volunteerism from Jim Crow to the New Deal, 1896–1936*. Westport, CT: Greenwood Press.

Chang, Ina. 1991. *A Separate Battle: Women and the Civil War*. New York: Puffin Books.

Clayton, Sarah Conley. 1999. *Requiem for a Lost City: A Memoir of Civil War Atlanta and the Old South*. Edited by Robert Scott Davis Jr. Macon, GA: Mercer University Press.

Clinton, Catherine, and Nina Silber, eds. 1992. *Divided Houses: Gender and the Civil War*. New York: Oxford University Press.

Cochrane, Dorothy, and P. Ramirez. 2021. "Hidden No More: Black Women Groundbreakers at NASA." Smithsonian National Air and Space Museum. November 2, 2021. https://airandspace.si.edu/stories/editorial/hidden-no-more-black-women-groundbreakers-nasa.

Collier-Thomas, Bettye. 2013. *Jesus, Jobs, and Justice: African American Women and Religion*. Philadelphia: Temple University Press.

Cooper, Anna Julia. 1988. *A Voice from the South*. First published 1892. Schomburg Library of Nineteenth-Century Black Women Writers. New York: Oxford University Press.

Cooper, Brittney C. 2017. *Beyond Respectability: The Intellectual Thought of Race Women*. Urbana: University of Illinois Press.

Coppin, Fanny Jackson. 2018. *Reminiscences of School Life, and Hints on Teaching*. First published 1913. Emeryville, CA: Franklin Classics.

Creighton, Margaret. 2005. *Colors of Courage: Gettysburg's Forgotten History: Immigrant Women and African Americans in the Civil War*. New York: Basic Books.

Crenshaw, Kimberlé, Neil Gotanda, Gary Peller, and Kendall Thomas, eds. 1996. *Critical Race Theory: The Key Writings That Formed the Movement*. New York: New Press.

Crowley, Sharon, and Debra Hawhee. 2004. *Ancient Rhetorics for Contemporary Students*. New York: Pearson/Longman.

Crumpler, Rebecca. 2016. *A Book of Medical Discourses, In Two Parts*. First published 1883. Dehli: Facsimile.

Culpepper, Marilyn Mayer. 1991. *Trials and Triumphs: The Women of the American Civil War*. East Lansing: Michigan State University Press.

Cumming, Kate. 1998. *The Journal of a Confederate Nurse*. Edited by Richard Barksdale Harwell. Baton Rouge: Louisiana State University Press.

Cunningham, Frank. 1998. *General Stand Watie's Confederate Indians*. First published 1959. Norman: University of Oklahoma Press.

Danky, James P., and Maureen E. Hady, eds. 1999. *African-American Newspapers and Periodicals: A National Bibliography.* Cambridge, MA: Harvard University Press.

Davis, Elizabeth Lindsay. 1933. *Lifting As They Climb.* Chicago: National Association of Colored Women.

Deutsch, Sarah. 2000. *Women and the City: Gender, Space and Power in Boston, 1870–1940.* New York: Oxford University Press.

Du Bois, W. E. B. 1994. *The Souls of Black Folk.* 1903. New York: Gramercy Books.

Du Bois, W. E. B. 1998. *Black Reconstruction in America, 1860–1880.* New York: Free Press.

Dunbar, Erica Armstrong. 2008. *A Fragile Freedom: African American Women and Emancipation in the Antebellum City.* New Haven, CT: Yale University Press.

Dyer, Thomas G. 1999. *Secret Yankees: The Union Circle in Confederate Atlanta.* Baltimore, MD: Johns Hopkins University Press.

East, Charles, ed. 1991. *Sarah Morgan: The Civil War Diary of a Southern Woman.* New York: Touchstone/Simon and Schuster, 1991.

Edmonds, Sarah Emma. 1999. *Memoirs of a Soldier, Nurse and Spy: A Woman's Adventures in the Union Army.* Introduction by Elizabeth D. Leonard. DeKalb: Northern Illinois University Press.

"Elizabeth Proctor Thomas." 2021. National Park Service. Last modified October 15, 2021. https://nps.gov/articles/featured_stories_thomas.htm.

"Elizabeth Proctor Thomas." n.d. American Battlefield Trust. Accessed January 25, 2023. https://battlefields.org/learn/biographies/elizabeth-proctor-thomas.

Emerson, Dorothy May, June Edwards, and Helene Knox, eds. 2000. *Standing before Us: Unitarian Universalist Women and Social Reform, 1776–1936.* Boston: Skinner House.

Faust, Drew Gilpin. 2004. *Mothers of Invention: Women of the Slaveholding South in the American Civil War.* Chapel Hill: University of North Carolina Press.

Fellner, Gene. 2015. "Multilectics and Its Methods." In *Sociocultural Studies and Implications for Science Education: The Experiential and the Virtual,* edited by Catherine Milne, Kenneth Tobin, and Donna DeGennaro, 33–58. New York: Springer.

Fleischner, Jennifer. 2003. *Mrs. Lincoln and Mrs. Keckly: The Remarkable Story of the Friendship between a First Lady and a Former Slave.* New York: Broadway Books.

Fletcher, Louisa Warren. 1995. *Journal of a Landlady: The Fletcher/Ken-*

nesaw House Diary. Edited by Henry Higgins, Connie Cox, and Jean Cole Anderson. Randallstown, MD: Professional Press.

Forbes, Ella. 1998. *African American Women during the Civil War.* New York: Garland.

Foreman, Amanda. 2010. *A World on Fire: Britain's Crucial Role in the American Civil War.* New York: Random House.

Forten Grimké, Charlotte. 1864. "Life on the Sea Islands (Part I)." *Atlantic* (May): 587–96. https://theatlantic.com/magazine/archive/1864/05/life-on-the-sea-islands/308758.

Forten Grimké, Charlotte. 1864. "Life on the Sea Islands (Part II)." *Atlantic* (June): 666–76. https://www.theatlantic.com/magazine/archive/1864/06/life-on-the-sea-islands-continued/308759.

Franklin, John Hope. 1980. *From Slavery to Freedom: A History of Negro Americans.* 5th ed. New York: Alfred A. Knopf.

Franklin, John Hope. 1995. *The Free Negro in North Carolina, 1790–1860.* First published 1943. Chapel Hill: University of North Carolina Press.

Freehling, William W. 2008. *The Road to Disunion: Secessionists Triumphant, 1854–1961.* New York: Oxford University Press.

Freeman, Elsie, Shamel, Wynell Burroughs, and Jean West. 1992. "The Fight for Equal Rights: A Recruiting Poster for Black Soldiers in the Civil War." *Social Education* 56, no. 2 (February): 118–20. Revised and updated in 1999 by Budge Weidman. https://www.archives.gov/education/lessons/blacks-civil-war.

Frelund, Katherine. 2016. "Forget the Master's Tools, We Will Build Our Own House: The *Woman's Era* as a Rhetorical Forum for the Invention of African American Womanhood." *Peitho Journal* 18 (2): 67–98.

Frierson, Jennie C. 2019. "Lugenia Burns Hope." *Journal of Health Care for the Poor and Underserved.* 3, no. 2 (May): xii–xvi.

Gardner, Sarah E. 2004. *Blood and Irony: Southern White Women's Narratives of the Civil War, 1861–1937.* Chapel Hill: University of North Carolina Press.

Garner, Carla. "Sadie T. M. Alexander (1898–1989)." 2010. Blackpast. October 29, 2010. https://www.blackpast.org/african-american-history/alexander-sadie-tanner-mossell-1898-1989.

Garrison, Nancy Scripture. 2003. *With Courage and Delicacy: Civil War on the Peninsula—Women and the U.S. Sanitary Commission.* Cambridge, MA: Da Capo.

Garrison, Webb. 1999. *Amazing Women of the Civil War.* Nashville, TN: Rutledge Hill.

Gates, Henry Louis, Jr. 1988. "Foreword." In *The Collected Works of Phillis Wheatley,* edited by John C. Shields. Schomburg Library of

Nineteenth-Century Black Women Writers. New York: Oxford University Press.

Geertz, Clifford. 1973. *Interpretation of Cultures*. New York: Basic Books.

Giddings, Paula J. 2007. *In Search of Sisterhood: Delta Sigma Theta and the Challenge of the Black Sorority Movement*. New York: Morrow.

Giesberg, Judith. 2000. *Civil War Sisterhood: The U.S. Sanitary Commission and Women's Politics in Transition*. Boston: Northeastern University Press.

Giesberg, Judith. 2009. *Army at Home: Women and the Civil War on the Northern Home Front*. Chapel Hill: University of North Carolina Press.

Gilkes, Cheryl Townsend. 2001. *If It Wasn't for the Women: Black Women's Experience and Womanist Culture in Church and Community*. New York: Orbis.

Glass-Hill, Hermina. 2016. "Susie King Taylor: Civil War Nurse and Early Social Justice Activist." SaportaReport. March 21, 2016. https://saportareport.com/susie-king-taylor-civil-war-nurse-early-social-justice-activist/.

Glory. 1989. Directed by Edward Zwick. Performed by Matthew Broderick, Denzel Washington, Morgan Freeman, and Cary Elwes. TriStar Pictures, 1989. Film.

Graff, Harvey. 1991. *The Literacy Myth: Cultural Integration and Social Structure in the Nineteenth Century*. New Brunswick, NJ: Transaction.

Graham, Maryemma, ed. 1988. *Complete Poems of Frances E. W. Harper*. Schomburg Library of Nineteenth-Century Black Women Writers. New York: Oxford University Press.

Griffin, Farah Jasmine, ed. 1999. *Beloved Sisters and Loving Friends: Letters from Rebecca Primus of Royal Oak, Maryland, and Addie Brown of Hartford, Connecticut, 1854–1868*. New York: Alfred A. Knopf.

Gwin, Minrose C., ed. 1992. *A Woman's Civil War: Cornelia Peake McDonald*. Madison: University of Wisconsin Press.

Hahn, Steven. 2021. "Land of Capital." Review of *Ages of American Capitalism: A History of the United States*, by Jonathan Levy. *Nation*, November 1, 2021. https://www.thenation.com/article/society/jonathan-levy-ages-of-capitalism/.

Hall, Richard H. 2006. *Women on the Civil War Battlefront*. Lawrence: University Press of Kansas.

Hancock, Brittany Leigh. 2015. "The Neighborhood Union and the Transformation of the West Side of Atlanta." PhD diss., University of Houston. https://uh-ir.tdl.org/handle/10657/1240.

Harper, Frances Ellen Watkins. n.d. "Bury Me in a Free Land." Poets.org. https://poets.org/poem/bury-me-free-land.

Harper, Frances Ellen Watkins. 1866. "We Are All Bound Up Together." Archives of Women's Political Communication, Iowa State University. Reproduced from *Proceedings of the Eleventh National Woman's Rights Convention* (May 10, 1866) (New York, NY: Robert J. Johnston), 46-48. https://awpc.cattcenter.iastate.edu/2017/03/21/we-are-all-bound-up-together-may-1866/.

Harper, Frances Ellen Watkins. 1988. *Complete Poems of Frances E. W. Harper*. Edited by Maryemma Graham. Schomburg Library of Nineteenth-Century Black Women Writers. New York: Oxford University Press.

Harper, Frances Ellen Watkins. 1995. "Woman's Political Future." First published 1893. In *With Pen and Voice: A Critical Anthology of Nineteenth-Century African-American Women*, edited by Shirley Wilson Logan, 43–46. Carbondale: Southern Illinois University Press.

Harper, Frances Ellen Watkins. 2018. *Iola Leroy, or Shadows Uplifted*. First published 1893. Edited by Koritha Mitchell. Petersborough, CA: Broadview Press.

Harrell, Willie J., Jr. 2012. "'I Am an Anarchist': The Social Anarchism of Lucy E. Parsons." *Journal of International Women's Studies* 13 (1): 1–18. https://vc.bridgew.edu/jiws/vol13/iss1/1.

Harris, Trudier. 2001. *Saints, Sinners, Saviors: Strong Black Women in African American Literature*. New York: Palgrave Macmillan.

Hicks, Hannah Worcester. 1992. "The Diary of Hannah Hicks." *American Scene* 13:2–24.

Higginbotham, Evelyn Brooks. 1994. *Righteous Discontent: The Women's Movement in the Black Baptist Church, 1880–1920*. Cambridge, MA: Harvard University Press.

"History of the 33rd United States Colored Troops." 2011. Lowcountry Africana: African American Genealogy in SC, GA and FL. January 17, 2011. https://lowcountryafricana.com/project/history-of-the-33rd-united-states-colored-troops-usct/.

Holden, Teresa Blue. 2005. "'Earnest Women Can Do Anything': The Public Career of Josephine St. Pierre Ruffin, 1842–1904." PhD diss., Saint Louis University, Missouri.

hooks, bell. 1984. *Feminist Theory: From Margin to Center.* Cambridge, MA: South End.

Houchins, Sue E. 1988. *Spiritual Narratives*. Schomburg Library of Nineteenth-Century Black Women Writers. New York: Oxford University Press.

Hull, Akasha (Gloria T.), Patricia Bell Scott, and Barbara Smith, eds. 1982. *All the Women Are White, All the Blacks Are Men, but Some of Us Are Brave: Black Women's Studies*. New York: Feminist Press.

Hunter, Tera W. 1997. *To 'Joy My Freedom: Southern Black Women's Lives and Labors after the Civil War.* Cambridge, MA: Harvard University Press.

Hurston, Zora Neale. 2006. *Their Eyes Were Watching God*. New York: Amistad.

Huston, James L. 2003. *Calculating the Value of the Union: Slavery, Property Rights, and the Economic Origins of the Civil War.* Chapel Hill: University of North Carolina Press.

Hutchinson, Louise Daniel. 1981. *Anna J. Cooper: A Voice from the South*. Washington, DC: Smithsonian Institution Press.

Jackson, Errin. "Josephine Silone Yates (1852–1912)." 2007. Blackpast. April 19, 2007. https://www.blackpast.org/african-american-history/yates-josephine-silone-1852-1912/.

Jackson, Fannie Oslin. 1989. *On Both Sides of the Line*. Baltimore, MD: Gateway.

Jacobs, Harriet. 1988. *Incidents in the Life of a Slave Girl*. First published 1861. Edited by Maria Child. Schomburg Library of Nineteenth-Century Black Women Writers. New York: Oxford University Press.

James, Joy. 1997. *Transcending the Talented Tenth: Black Leaders and American Intellectuals*. New York: Routledge.

Jeffrey, Katherine Bentley. 2016. *Two Civil Wars: The Curious Journal of a Baton Rouge Schoolgirl and a Union Sailor.* Baton Rouge: Louisiana State University Press.

Jenkins, Maude. 2000. "Biographical Sketch: Florida Yates Ruffin Ridley." In *Standing before Us: Unitarian Universalist Women and Social Reform, 1776–1936*, edited by Dorothy May Emerson, June Edwards, and Helene Knox, 402–4. Boston: Skinner House.

Johnson, Nancy. 1991. *Nineteenth-Century Rhetoric in North America*. Carbondale: Southern Illinois University Press.

Johnson, Val Marie. 2017. "'The Half Has Never Been Told': Maritcha Lyons' Community, Black Women Educators, the Woman's Loyal Union, and 'the Color Line' in Progressive Era Brooklyn and New York." *Journal of Urban History* 44, no. 5 (February): 835–61.

Johnston, Carolyn. 2003. *Cherokee Women in Crisis: Trail of Tears, Civil War, and Allotment, 1838–1907.* Tuscaloosa: University of Alabama Press.

Jones, Beverly Washington. 1990. *Quest for Equality: The Life and Writings of Mary Eliza Church Terrell, 1863–1954*. Black Women in United States History. Brooklyn: Carlson.

Jones, Jacqueline. 2017. *Goddess of Anarchy: The Life and Times of Lucy Parsons, American Radical.* New York: Basic Books.

Jones, Martha S. 2007. *All Bound Up Together: The Woman Question in African American Culture, 1830–1900.* New York: Columbia University Press.

Kantrowitz, Stephen. 2012. *More than Freedom: Fighting for Black Citizenship in a White Republic, 1829–1889.* New York: Penguin.

Katz, William Loren. 1986. *Black Indians: A Hidden Heritage.* New York: Atheneum.

Keckley, Elizabeth. 2011. *Behind the Scenes, Or, Thirty Years a Slave, and Four Years in the White House.* First published 1868. Scotts Valley, CA: CreateSpace Independent Publishing Platform.

King, Wilma. 2006. *The Essence of Liberty: Free Black Women during the Slave Era.* Columbia: University of Missouri Press.

Knight, Frederick. 2017. "The Many Names for Jarena Lee." *Pennsylvania Magazine of History and Biography* 141, no. 1 (January): 59–68.

Kremer, Gary R., and Cindy M. Mackey. 1996. "'Yours for the Race': The Life and Work of Josephine Silone Yates." *Missouri Historical Review* 90 (2): 199–215.

Lawson, Ellen Nickenzie. 1984. *The Three Sarahs: Documents of Antebellum Black College Women.* Studies in Women and Religion 13. New York: Mellen.

Lee, Mrs. Jarena. 1988. *Religious Experience and Journal of Mrs. Jarena Lee.* First published 1849. Schomburg Library of Nineteenth-Century Black Women Writers. New York: Oxford University Press.

Levy, Jonathan. 2021. *Ages of American Capitalism: A History of the United States.* New York: Random House.

Lincoln, Abraham. 1991. *Great Speeches: Abraham Lincoln.* Notes by John Grafton. Mineola, NY: Dover.

Lincoln, C. Eric, and Lawrence H. Mamiya. 1990. *The Black Church in the African American Experience.* Durham, NC: Duke University Press.

Logan, Shirley Wilson. 2008. *Liberating Language: Sites of Rhetorical Education in Nineteenth-Century Black America.* Carbondale: Southern Illinois University Press.

Lorde, Audre. 1984. "The Transformation of Silence into Language and Action." In *Sister Outsider: Essays and Speeches by Audre Lorde,* 40–44. Freedom, CA: Crossing Press Feminist Series.

Lunt, Dolly Sumner. 1997. *The Diary of Dolly Lunt Burge, 1848–1879.* Edited by Christine Jacobson Carter. Athens: University of Georgia Press.

Majors, Monroe A. 1986. *Noted Negro Women: Their Triumphs and Activities*. First published 1893. The Black Heritage Library Collection. Salem, NH: Ayer Company Press.

Markel, Howard. 2016. "Celebrating Rebecca Lee Crumpler, First African-American Woman Physician." *PBS News Hour*. March 9, 2016. https://pbs.org/newshour/health/celebrating-rebecca-lee-crumpler-first-african-american-physician.

"Mary Ann Shadd Cary." 2019. National Park Service. Last modified July 8, 2019. https://nps.gov/people/mary-ann-shadd-cary.htm.

Massey, Mary Elizabeth. 1994. *Women in the Civil War*. First published 1966. Lincoln: University of Nebraska Press.

Mattingly, Carol. 1998. *Well-Tempered Women: Nineteenth-Century Temperance Rhetoric*. Carbondale: Southern Illinois University Press.

May, Vivian M. 2012. *Anna Julia Cooper: Visionary Black Feminist*. New York: Routledge.

McAdams, Dan P., Ruthellen Josselson, and Amia Lieblich, eds. 2006. *Identity and Story: Creating Self in Narrative*. Washington, DC: American Psychological Association.

McHenry, Elizabeth. 2002. *Forgotten Readers: Recovering the Lost History of African American Literary Societies*. Durham, NC: Duke University Press.

McPherson, James M. 2003. *Battle Cry of Freedom: The Civil War Era*. First published 1988. New York: Oxford University Press.

Mitchell, Margaret. 2008. *Gone with the Wind*. First published 1936. New York: Pocket Books/Simon and Schuster.

Moss, Alfred A., Jr. 1981. *The American Negro Academy: Voice of the Talented Tenth*. Baton Rouge: Louisiana State University Press.

Mossell, Mrs. N. F. (Gertrude Bustill Mossell). 1988. *The Work of the Afro-American Woman*. 1908. Schomburg Library of Nineteenth-Century Black Women Writers. New York: Oxford University Press.

Mountjoy, Shane. 2009. *Technology and the Civil War*. New York: Chelsea House.

Myerson, Joel, and Daniel Shealy, eds. 1989. *The Journals of Louisa May Alcott*. Boston: Little, Brown.

National Park Service. 2011a. *The Civil War Remembered*. Virginia Beach: Donning.

National Park Service. 2011b. *Hispanics and the Civil War: From Battlefield to Homefront*. Washington, DC: National Park Service/US Department of the Interior.

"Nursing through the Years." 2016. American Sentinel College of Nursing and Health Sciences at Post University. September 9, 2016. https://

web.archive.org/web/20211104215909/https://www.americansentinel.edu/blog/2016/09/06/a-timeline-of-nursing-education/. Site discontinued.

"The Only Woman Who Called President Lincoln a Fool." 1952. *The Afro American*, Afro Magazine Section 5. August 30, 1952. https://news.google.com/newspapers.

Parsons, Lucy. 1886. "I AM AN ANARCHIST." https://www.blackpast.org/african-american-history/1886-lucy-parsons-i-am-anarchist/.

Parsons, Lucy. 2004. *Freedom, Equality, and Solidarity: Writings and Speeches, 1878–1937.* Edited by Gale Ahrens. Chicago: Charles H. Kerr.

Pease, Jane H., and William H. Pease. 1999. *A Family of Women: The Carolina Petigrus in Peace and War.* Chapel Hill: University of North Carolina Press.

Pember, Phoebe Yates. 2002. *A Southern Woman's Story.* Introduction by George C. Rable. Columbia: University of South Carolina Press.

Penn, I. Garland. 1891. *The Afro-American Press.* Springfield, MA: Willey and Company.

Pfatteicher, Sarah K. A. 2000. "Crumpler, Rebecca Davis Lee." American National Biography. https://doi.org/10.1093/anb/9780198606697.article.1201058.

Potter, David M. 2011. *The Impending Crisis.* New York: Harper Perennial.

Pyron, Darden Asbury. 2005. *Southern Daughter: The Life of Margaret Mitchell and the Making of* Gone with the Wind. First published 1991. Athens, GA: Hill Street.

Ratcliffe, Krista. 2005. *Rhetorical Listening: Identification, Gender, Whiteness.* Carbondale: Southern Illinois University Press.

Reisen, Harriet. 2009. *Louisa May Alcott: The Woman behind* Little Women. New York: Henry Holt.

Richardson, Marilyn, ed. 1987. *Maria W. Stewart: America's First Black Woman Political Writer.* Bloomington: Indiana University Press.

Roberts, Cokie. 2016. *Capital Dames: The Civil War and the Women of Washington, 1848–1868.* New York: Harper Perennial.

Rooks, Noliwe M. 2004. *Ladies' Pages: African American Women's Magazines and the Culture that Made Them.* New Brunswick, NJ: Rutgers University Press.

Ross, Charles D. 1999. *Trial by Fire: Science, Technology and the Civil War.* Shippensburg, PA: White Mane Books.

Rouse, Jacqueline Anne. 2004. *Lugenia Burns Hope, Black Southern Reformer.* Brown Thrasher Book Series. Athens: University of Georgia Press.

Royster, Jacqueline Jones. 1990. "Perspectives on the Intellectual Tradition of Black Women Writers." In *The Right to Literacy*, edited by Andrea A. Lunsford, Helene Moglen, and James Slevin, 103–12. New York: Modern Language Association.

Royster, Jacqueline Jones. 2000. *Traces of a Stream: Literacy and Social Change among African American Women*. Pittsburgh: University of Pittsburgh Press.

Royster, Jacqueline Jones. 2003. *Profiles of Ohio Women, 1803–2003*. Athens: Ohio University Press.

Royster, Jacqueline Jones. 2016. *Southern Horrors and Other Writings: The Anti-lynching Campaign of Ida B. Wells, 1892–1900*. 2nd ed. Bedford Series in History and Culture. Boston: Bedford/St. Martin's.

Royster, Jacqueline Jones. 2021. "The Long Nineteenth Century and the Bend toward Justice." In *Nineteenth-Century American Activist Rhetorics*, edited by Patricia Bizzell and Lisa Zimmerelli, 318–31. New York: Modern Language Association.

Royster, Jacqueline Jones. 2022. "Democracy as a Noble Experiment: Where Do We Go from Here?" *College Composition and Communication* 74, no. 2 (December): 444–64.

Royster, Jacqueline Jones, and Evelynn Hammonds. 1995. "A Century of Struggle in Defense of Ourselves." *SAGE: A Scholarly Journal on Black Women* 9, no. 2 (Summer): 7–8.

Ruffin, Josephine St. Pierre. 1894. "Greeting." *Woman's Era* 1, no. 1 (March): 8. Emory Women Writers Resource Project. https://womansera.digitalscholarship.emory.edu/volume-1-number-1/.

Ruffin, Josephine St. Pierre. 1895a. "Let Us Confer Together." *Woman's Era* 2, no. 3 (June): 8. Emory Women Writers Resource Project. https://womansera.digitalscholarship.emory.edu/volume-2-number-3/.

Ruffin, Josephine St. Pierre. 1895b. "Address of Josephine St. P Ruffin, President of Conference." *Woman's Era* 2, no. 5 (August): 13–15. Emory Women Writers Resource Project. https://womansera.digitalscholarship.emory.edu/volume-2-number-5/.

Salem, Dorothy. 1990. *To Better Our World: Black Women in Organized Reform, 1890–1920*. In *Black Women in United States History*, edited by Darlene Clark Hine, vol. 14. Brooklyn: Carlson.

"Sarah Jane Woodson Early." n.d. *History of American Women* (blog). Accessed January 25, 2023. http://womenhistoryblog.com/2015/03/sarah-jane-woodson-early.html.

Schultz, Jane C. 2007. *Women at the Front: Hospital Workers in Civil War America*. Chapel Hill: University of North Carolina Press.

Sernett, Milton C. 2007. *Harriet Tubman: Myth, Memory, and History.* Durham, NC: Duke University Press.

Shadd, Mary A. 1998. *Plea for Emigration.* Edited by Richard Almonte. Toronto: Mercury.

Shaw, Stephanie J. 2013. *W.E. B. Du Bois and* The Souls of Black Folks. John Hope Franklin Series in African American History and Culture. Chapel Hill: University of North Carolina Press.

Shields, John C., ed. 1988. *The Collected Works of Phillis Wheatley.* Schomburg Library of Nineteenth-Century Black Women Writers. New York: Oxford University Press.

Silber, Nina. 2009. *Gender and the Sectional Conflict.* Chapel Hill: University of North Carolina Press.

Silvery, Anita. 2008. *I'll Pass for Your Comrade: Women Soldiers in the Civil War.* New York: Clarion.

Sizer, Lyde Cullen. 2000. *The Political Work of Northern Women Writers and the Civil War, 1850–1872.* Chapel Hill: University of North Carolina Press.

Smith, Jessie Carney, ed. 2006. *Notable Black American Women.* 2nd ed. Book II. Detroit, MI: Gale Research.

Smith, John David, and William Cooper Jr., eds. 2000. *A Union Woman in Civil War Kentucky: The Diary of Frances Peter.* Lexington: University Press of Kentucky.

Smith, Mark M. 2002. "Of Bells, Booms, Sounds, and Silences: Listening to the Civil War South." In *The War Was You and Me: Civilians in the American Civil War,* edited by Joan E. Cashin, 9–34. Princeton, NJ: Princeton University Press.

"Sojourner Truth: Ain't I a Woman?" 2017. National Park Service. Last modified November 17, 2017. https://nps.gov/articles/sojourner-truth.htm.

Stampp, Kenneth, ed. 1992. *The Causes of the Civil War.* 3rd ed. New York: Touchstone.

Sterling, Dorothy, ed. 1984. *We Are Your Sisters: Black Women in the Nineteenth Century.* New York: W. W. Norton.

Stevenson, Brenda, ed. 1988. *The Journals of Charlotte Forten Grimké.* New York: Oxford University Press.

Stillé, Charles U. 1866. *History of the United States Sanitary Commission.* Philadelphia: J. B. Lippincott.

Stone, Cyrena Bailey. "Miss Abby's Diary." Hargrett Rare Book and Manuscript Library, The University of Georgia Libraries. http://dlg.galileo.usg.edu/harg/turningpoint/id:harg1000-001-001.

Stowe, Stephen M. 2018. *Keep the Days: Reading the Civil War Diaries of Southern Women*. Chapel Hill: University of North Carolina Press.

Sumler-Edmond, Janice L. 2008. *The Secret Trust of Aspasia Cruvellier Mirault: The Life and Trials of a Free Woman of Color in Antebellum Georgia*. Fayetteville: University of Arkansas Press.

Taylor, Susie King. 1988. *Reminiscences of My Life: A Black Woman's Civil War Memoirs*. First published 1902. Edited by Patricia W. Romero and Willie Lee Rose. Princeton, NJ: Markus Wiener.

Terborg-Penn, Rosalyn. 1998. *African-American Women in the Struggle for the Vote, 1850–1920*. Bloomington: Indiana University Press.

Terrell, Mary Church. 1986. *A Colored Woman in a White World*. First published 1940. Salem, NH: Ayer.

Terrell, Mary Church. 1990. "The Duty of the National Association of Colored Women to the Race." First published 1900. In *Quest for Equality: The Life and Writings of Mary Aliza Church Terrell, 1863–1954*, edited by Beverly Washington Jones, 139–50. Brooklyn: Carlson.

Thomas, Ella Gertrude Clanton. 1990. *The Secret Eye: The Journal of Ella Gertrude Clanton Thomas, 1848–1889*. Edited by Virginia Ingraham Burr. Chapel Hill: University of North Carolina Press.

Thomas, Emory M. 1993. *The Confederate Nation, 1861–1865*. New York: Monticello Editions/History Book Club.

Thompson, L. S. 2012. *The Story of Mattie J. Jackson*. London: SicPress.

Thompson, Mildred I., ed. 1990. *Ida B. Wells-Barnett: An Exploratory Study of an American Black Woman, 1893–1930*. Brooklyn: Carlson.

Towne, Laura M. 1993. *Letters and Diaries of Laura M. Towne*. Edited by Rupert Sargent Holland. First published 1912. Southern Historical College. Penn School Papers. Chapel Hill: University of North Carolina.

Tsui, Bonnie. 2006. *She Went to the Field: Women Soldiers of the Civil War*. Guilford, CT: Globe Pequot.

Tuuri, Rebecca. 2018. *Strategic Sisterhood: The National Council of Negro Women in the Black Freedom Struggle*. Chapel Hill: University of North Carolina.

Varon, Elizabeth R. 2010. *Disunion: The Coming of the American Civil War, 1789–1859*. Chapel Hill: University of North Carolina Press.

Velazquez, Loreta Janeta. 1876. *The Woman in Battle: A Narrative of the Exploits, Adventures, and Travels of Madame Loreta Janeta Velazquez, Otherwise Known as Lieutenant Harry T. Buford, Confederate States Army*. Introduction by Jesse Alemán. Richmond, VA: Dustin, Gilman.

Venet, Wendy Hamand. 2014. *A Changing Wind: Commerce and Conflict in Civil War Atlanta*. New Haven, CT: Yale University Press.

Wagner, Margaret E. 2011. *The Library of Congress Illustrated Timeline of the Civil War.* New York: Little, Brown.

Walker, Alice. 1983. "In Search of Our Mothers' Gardens." In *In Search of Our Mothers' Gardens*, 231–43. New York: Harcourt.

Walker, David. 1993. *David Walker's Appeal, in Four Articles: Together with a Preamble, to the Coloured Citizens of the World, but in Particular, and Very Expressly, to Those of the United States of America.* 1830. Introduction by James Turner. Baltimore, MC: Black Classic.

Ward, Andrew. 2008. *The Slaves' War: The Civil War in the Words of Former Slaves*. Boston: Mariner Books.

"We Are All Americans—Native Americans in the Civil War." 2021. City of Alexandria, Virginia. Last modified December 27, 2021. https://alexandriava.gov/historic-alexandria/basic-page/we-are-all-americans-native-americans-in-the-civil-war.

Wells, Jonathan Daniel. 2011. *Women Writers and Journalists in the Nineteenth-Century South*. New York: Cambridge University Press.

Wells-Barnett, Ida B. 1995. "Lynch Law in All Its Phases (1893)." In *With Pen and Voice: A Critical Anthology of Nineteenth-Century African-American Women*, edited by Shirley Wilson Logan, 80–99. Carbondale: Southern Illinois University Press.

Wesley, Charles Harris. 1984. *The History of the National Association of Colored Women's Clubs: A Legacy of Service*. Washington, DC: National Association of Colored Women's Clubs.

West, Emily. 2014. *Enslaved Women in America: From Colonial Times to Emancipation*. Lanham, MD: Rowman and Littlefield.

Wheatley, Phillis. 1988. *The Collected Works of Phillis Wheatley.* Edited by John C. Shields. Schomburg Library of Nineteenth-Century Black Women Writers. New York: Oxford University Press.

White, Deborah Gray. 1999. *Too Heavy a Load: Black Women in Defense of Themselves, 1894–1994*. New York: W. W. Norton.

Whitehead, Karsonya Wise. 2014. *Notes from a Colored Girl: The Civil War Pocket Diaries of Emilie Frances Davis*. Columbia: University of South Carolina Press.

Winkler, H. Donald. 2010. *Stealing Secrets: How a Few Daring Women Deceived Generals, Impacted Battles, and Altered the Course of the Civil War.* Naperville, IL: Cumberland House.

Wolfe, George C. 1986. *The Colored Museum*. Directed by L. Kenneth Richardson.

Woodward, C. Vann, ed. 1981a. *Mary Chestnut's Civil War.* New Haven, CT: Yale University Press.

Woodward, C. Vann. 1981b. *Origins of the New South, 1877–1913.* Rev. ed. Baton Rouge: Louisiana State University Press.

Woodward, C. Vann. 2002. *The Strange Career of Jim Crow.* Commemorative ed. New York: Oxford University Press.

Yacovone, Donald. 2004. *Freedom's Journey: African American Voices of the Civil War.* Chicago: Chicago Review Press.

Yarhi, Eli. 2022 "Mary Shadd Cary." Britannica.com. Last modified October 5, 2022. https://britannica.com/biography/Mary-Ann-Shadd-Cary.

Zeinert, Karen. 1998. *Those Courageous Women of the Civil War.* Minneapolis: Lerner.

Ziparo, Jessica. 2017. *The Grand Experiment: When Women Entered the Federal Workforce in Civil War Era Washington, D.C.* Chapel Hill: University of North Carolina Press.

Index

Note: References in *italics* refer to figures and tables.